Media and Power

James Curran

Routledge
Taylor & Francis Group

LONDON AND NEW YORK

First published 2002 by Routledge
2 Park Square, Milton Park, Abingdon, Oxon OX14 4RN

Simultaneously published in the USA and Canada
by Routledge
270 Madison Ave, New York, NY 10016

Reprinted 2005

Routledge is an imprint of the Taylor & Francis Group

Typeset in Galliard by RefineCatch Limited, Bungay, Suffolk
Printed and bound in Great Britain by
St Edmundsbury Press Ltd, Bury St Edmunds, Suffolk

British Library Cataloguing in Publication Data
A catalogue record for this book is available from the British Library

Library of Congress Cataloging in Publication Data
A catalog record for this book has been requested

ISBN 0–415–07739–7 (hbk)
ISBN 0–415–07740–0 (pbk)

Media and Power

Media and Power addresses three key questions about the relationship between media and society. How much power do the media have? Who really controls the media? What is the relationship between media and power in society? In this major new book, James Curran reviews the different answers which have been given, before advancing original interpretations in a series of ground-breaking essays.

The book also provides a guided tour of major debates in media studies. What part did the media play in the making of modern society? How did 'new media' change society in the past? Will radical media research recover from its mid-life crisis? What are the limitations of the US-based model of 'communications research'? Is globalization disempowering national electorates or bringing into being a new, progressive global politics? Is public service television the dying product of the nation in an age of globalization? What can be learned from the 'third way' tradition of European media policy?

Curran's response to these questions provides both a clear introduction to media research and an innovative analysis of media power, and is written by one of the field's leading scholars.

James Curran is Professor of Communications at Goldsmiths College, University of London. He is the editor or author of fourteen books about media, including *Power Without Responsibility: The Press and Broadcasting in Britain* (with Jean Seaton, 6th edition, 2002), and *Mass Media and Society* (edited with Michael Gurevitch, 3rd edition, 2000).

COMMUNICATION AND SOCIETY
Series Editor: James Curran

To Margaret

Contents

Introduction

Chapter 1 has been published, in a shorter version, in Dutch; Chapter 2 in Chinese and Swedish; Chapter 3 in Spanish (and in a longer version in Arabic, Chinese, Korean and Portuguese); Chapter 4 in French, Korean, Swedish and Spanish; Chapter 5 in Swedish and Spanish; Chapter 6 in Japanese and Korean; and Chapter 8 in Czech, Chinese, Greek, Korean, Japanese and Roumanian. Chapter 7 is untranslated, uncited and virtually unread.[1]

If it was not for these selective indications of interests, I doubt whether I would have had the temerity to microwave these essays and serve them reheated as a book. In fact I temporized for some time, but in the end went ahead for two main reasons.

The essays that have been selected for republication all focus on some aspect of media and power. They examine, through the lens of different methodologies, traditions and disciplines, three recurring themes: the relationship of the mass media to power in society; how control is exercised over the media; and the nature of the power exerted by the media. Not all essays are consistent in what they argue (though they mostly are), but they offer an underlying coherence and consistency in terms of their focus.

The essays in this book have a further thing in common. They are all critical reappraisals of large bodies of literature. Covering a wide area, they offer a guided tour of major debates in media research. They add up, I hope, to being a maverick kind of textbook.[2]

Since many people will only look at parts of the book rather than read it from beginning to end, it may be helpful to offer a short guide.

Part I is devoted to media history. It begins with a survey that charts for the first time the main rival interpretations of British media history, concluding with an outline synthesis. The second chapter examines the impact of new 'media' – broadly defined as new institutions and channels of communication – over more than a millennium of history. The third chapter examines how changes in the economic structure of the press transformed its place in society. All three chapters attempt in different ways to understand the part played by the media in the making of modern society.

Part II focuses on media sociology, and related areas of work. Chapter 4 describes the mid-life crisis of radical media studies. Chapter 5 takes a look at a more conservative tradition of 'communications' research centred in the United States, and advances a critical alternative. Chapter 6 marvels at how differently two self-referencing traditions – cultural studies and political economy – interpret globalization, and examines initial attempts to reconcile them. All three chapters offer 'historical' accounts of a new field of research and seek to convey the intellectual excitement that has fuelled its development. Taken together, they offer an outline of the field's main traditions of thought; where the main battle lines have been drawn; where the main advances and retreats have taken place; when and why once-conquering ideas and themes have lost impetus, been rejected or revised.

Part III is concerned with the politics of the media. Chapter 7 considers how globalization, new technology and social change are affecting the organization and performance of television, while Chapter 8 reassesses theories of media and democracy. Both chapters are partly expository in that they outline different debates, and partly prescriptive in that they advocate a range of reforms. Chapter 7 argues that public service broadcasting should break free from its one-nation legacy, while Chapter 8 claims that the democratic role of the media can be strengthened through the 'third way' policies of western Europe.

In short, this book lends itself to different uses. It can be read as a textbook offering summaries of academic debates. It can be viewed as a single commentary on media power that attempts to look at media control and influence in the context of wider power relationships in society. And it can be looked at as one person's attempt to make sense of the intellectual arguments that are transforming media studies.

The essays in this book have been edited in different ways. Two early essays (Chapters 2 and 3) have been included relatively unaltered because they are in areas of media history where the currents of change are slow-moving. However, they are preceded by a long, up-to-date survey of media history (Chapter 1) especially written for this book.

By contrast, most of the chapters in the remainder of the book have been revised and updated. New references and data have been added, avoidable duplications removed and the fungus growth of jargon kept in check. However, they have not been reconstituted. Essays are not like houses where lofts can be converted and extensions added with relative ease. Architectonic chaos ensues if an essay is first written, and then subsequently reworked, within different frameworks of reference.

Grateful acknowledgements are made at the beginnings of chapters. However, I would like to thank in particular two people – Rebecca Barden and Chris Cudmore, both at Routledge – who encouraged the conception and delivery of this book.

Acknowledgements

The chapters in this book have been derived from the following publications:

Chapter 2: 'Communications, power and social order' in M. Gurevitch, T. Bennett, J. Curran and J. Woollacott (eds) (1982) *Culture, Society and the Media*, London: Methuen.

Chapter 3: 'Capitalism and control of the press, 1800–1975' in J. Curran, M. Gurevitch and J. Woollacott (eds) (1977) *Mass Communication and Society*, London: Edward Arnold.

Chapter 4: 'New revisionism in mass communication research: a reappraisal' in the *European Journal of Communication*, 5 (2–3), 1990.

Chapter 5: 'Rethinking mass communications' in J. Curran, D. Morley and V. Walkerdine (eds) (1996) *Cultural Studies and Communications*, London: Edward Arnold.

Chapter 6: 'Beyond globalization theory' (with Myung-Jin Park) in J. Curran and M-J. Park (eds) (2000) *De-Westernizing Media Studies*, London: Routledge.

Chapter 7: 'Crisis of public communication: a reappraisal' in T. Liebes and J. Curran (eds) (1998) *Media, Ritual and Identity*, London: Routledge.

Chapter 8: 'Rethinking media and democracy' in J. Curran and M. Gurevitch (eds) (2000) *Mass Media and Society*, London: Edward Arnold.

My thanks go to Arnold, Routledge/Methuen and Sage (publisher of the *European Journal of Communications*) and Myung-Jin Park, for permission to republish these essays. My appreciation is also expressed to the University of Amsterdam Press for clearance to develop and re-present in Chapter 1 the arguments of J. Curran (2002) 'Mediageschiedenis en ideologie' in J. Bardoel, C. Vros, F. Van Vree and H. Wijfjes (eds) *Journalistieke Cultuur in Nederland*, Amsterdam: University of Amsterdam Press.

Part 1

Media history

Rival narratives of media history

INTRODUCTION

In the nineteenth century, pioneer historians of the press laid the foundations of modern media research. They were the first people to take seriously, and study in depth, the organization, content and influence of the emergent media system in Britain.[1] Yet, despite this auspicious beginning, media history has since become marginalized. It is now the neglected grandparent of media studies: isolated, ignored, rarely visited by her offspring.

This neglect is exemplified by a recent, intelligent textbook (Grossberg, Wartella and Whitney 1998). It has a chapter called 'Narratives of media history', which makes no reference – even in passing – to any conventional historical study of the media. Instead, it focuses on technological determinist accounts of media development offered by cultural gurus like Marshall McLuhan, and a related account of the transition from modernity to postmodernity heavily indebted to cultural commentators like Jean Baudrillard.

Yet if media historians labour in the shadows, they are themselves partly to blame. In general, press historians stick rigidly to the press; television historians stay rooted in television; and film historians remain wedded to film. Within each of these specialisms, research is often narrow. Press and broadcasting historians tend to focus on institutional development, while film historians concentrate generally on the content of films – mostly within very limited periods of time. Visits to the neglected grandparent are infrequent because they can seem unrewarding.

However, this body of widely overlooked research does have something important to offer. It sheds light on the central role of mass communications in the making of modern society. It provides insights into the influences that shape the media, both past and present. It also offers alternative ways of thinking about the media's relationship to society. An historical perspective provides a critical distance which can make apparent and clarify things that seem blurred when only viewed in a contemporary context.[2]

This chapter will present media history as a series of competing narratives. Its writing has involved more active reinterpretation than is usual in literature surveys. The histories of each individual medium have been linked or merged to offer general accounts of media development. These have been contextualized in relation to wider trends in society, and the implications of specialist media research have been actively interpreted. Without this degree of intervention, many of the core themes of media history would have remained buried or obscured.

To make this survey manageable, we have confined ourselves to the last 300-odd years of British media history. While its British focus may seem restrictive, this review has wider implications. Many of the narratives which are identified here have counterparts in the histories of the media in other economically developed liberal democracies.[3]

MEDIA FREEDOM AND EMPOWERMENT: THE LIBERAL NARRATIVE

The liberal narrative is the oldest and best established of the competing interpretations of British media history. It comes out of an historical tradition which celebrates the evolution of 'constitutional government' by recording the rise of parliament, the establishment of the rule of law, the erosion of monarchical power, the development of modern political parties and – in the final culmination of this teleological history – the introduction of mass democracy. The right to vote was cautiously extended through five enlargements of the franchise: in 1832, 1867, 1884, 1918 and 1928. This was accompanied by constitutional reforms – secret voting in 1872, a limit on constituency election expenditure in 1883, a curb on the veto power of the House of Lords in 1911 and the culling of hereditary peers with voting rights in 1999 – which helped to democratize the political process.

The central thesis of liberal media history is that this process of democratization was enormously strengthened by the development of modern mass media. This thesis is organized around two key arguments, the first of which is that the media struggled successfully to become free of government.

The first medium to be liberated was allegedly the press.[4] In the seventeenth century, the press ceased to be licensed by government. In the eighteenth century, it acquired greater economic independence and became less subject to legal restriction. However, the key breakthrough is said to have occurred in the mid-nineteenth century when press taxes, intended to price newspapers beyond the means of ordinary people, were finally abolished.

The British cinema is also portrayed as breaking free from state political control.[5] The British Board of Film Censors (BBFC) was set up by the film industry in 1912 as a way of dealing with the unpredictable nature of local council censorship. This 'voluntary' system of self-regulation developed into a tyrannical system of ideological control, linked to the state. During the inter-war period, the BBFC banned films criticizing the monarchy, government, church, police, judiciary and friendly foreign countries. It also proscribed the depiction of current controversial issues, including in 1939 a proposed film featuring the Nazi persecution of Pastor

Niemoller. However, a thaw set in during the Second World War. This was carried over into peacetime Britain, when political (as distinct from moral) censorship was effectively abandoned.

Broadcasting, according to liberal historians,[6] also escaped from the shadow of the state to become independent. The BBC's initial subordination was symbolized by its craven conduct in the 1926 General Strike when it excluded from the microphone both the leader of the Labour Party and the archbishop of Canterbury because they had departed from the government's hymnsheet. However, the BBC subsequently inched its way to freedom, with occasional tactical reverses and pauses. This slow journey was marked by a number of landmarks: the lifting of the ban on radio discussion of controversial issues in 1928; the development of an in-house newsgathering team in the 1930s; the growth of the BBC's prestige and autonomy in the Second World War; and the removal in 1956 of the new 'fourteen day rule' restricting broadcast coverage of issues due to be debated in parliament during the next fortnight. The liberal historical consensus is that broadcasting became effectively free of government by the 1950s, assisted by the arrival of commercial television in 1955. This independence was forcibly demonstrated in 1956 when the BBC refused to suppress, at the behest of government, the Labour leader's broadcast against the Suez War even though it was transmitted to troops as they prepared for battle. Broadcasters were leaned on by government on subsequent occasions, even prompting the BBC's staff to mount a one-day strike against political censorship in 1985. However, liberal accounts are agreed that radio and television continued to be free of government control, not least because broadcasters generally enjoyed strong public support when they came under concerted government attack.

When liberal histories of individual media are woven together, they thus provide a coherent narrative in which the core media system became free over a period of three centuries. The second theme of this narrative is that free media empowered the people. This is worth presenting in some detail since it is the crux of the liberal case.

The emergence of a more independent press in the eighteenth century beamed rays of light into the private, aristocratic world of politics. After licensing lapsed in 1695, newspapers grew in number, increased in circulation and extended their coverage of public affairs. Some papers publicized grassroots campaigns to 'instruct' MPs in the first half of the eighteenth century, and contributed to the rise of the mass petition as a key instrument of politics in the second half. After 1771, newspapers were able to report the debates of parliament (previously a jailable offence). The press, concludes Bob Harris, 'was a major force behind the increasingly public nature of much politics' in the eighteenth century (Harris 1996: 47; cf. Brewer 1989: 243). This, in turn, made the system of government more open and accountable.

The growth of the press also contributed to the expansion of the political community. As newspapers became established in more places, and increased their circulation and political coverage, so they extended the boundaries of the political nation, both horizontally to include peripheral areas distant from London and vertically to include people lower down the social scale. In effect, the rivalries and disagreements of the landed elite who dominated contemporary politics were played out through the press in front of a widening audience. The reactions of this audience began to matter, as is testified by increasing references to public opinion in the later eighteenth century (Barker 1998).

At this point the threads of liberal press history become entangled in a knot and need to be untied. In effect, there are three-and-a-half rival, though overlapping, liberal interpretations. The 'Whig' version argues that an increasingly independent press subjected authority to critical scrutiny, and represented the views of the public to parliament and government. It became the 'fourth estate', the voice of the people in the corridors of power.[7] This transformation is said to have occurred in the early to mid-nineteenth century, although another view[8] – the 'half' interpretation mentioned above – holds that it really took place a century later after an unfortunate interlude when the press was little more than an extension of the party system.

A second interpretation argues that the leading section of the press represented primarily the expanding groups of the 'new' commercial and industrial society. It gave their reform organizations the oxygen of publicity, sustained an independent political agenda, exerted strong pressure for further democratization and helped to alert the landed elite to the need to make major concessions in order to preserve public order.[9]

The third version appears more descriptive than the other two but in fact adds up to a coherent alternative interpretation. It argues that the *ancien régime* (before democratic reform) was well entrenched; that the landed elite enjoyed a long period of political dominance after 1832; and that the real structure of power in nineteenth-century Britain was only slowly modified by the extension of the franchise and economic change.[10] In this stable context, the press contributed to the judicious maturing of the democratic system by relaying the concerns of pressure groups to government and enabling society to commune freely with itself.[11]

Common to all three interpretations is a positive view of the press as an institution that furthered – albeit in different ways – the democratic project. This theme trails off, however, around the 1880s and 1890s when two new themes become prominent in liberal histories of the press – falling editorial standards and the rise of the press barons.[12] However, if the centrepiece of the liberal narrative is lost from sight in studies of the press, it resurfaces in liberal histories of broadcasting where radio and television are portrayed as broadening and deepening democracy during the course of the twentieth century.

Public service broadcasting diminished the knowledge gap between the political elite and the general public because it made informing the public an institutional priority. It consciously sought to offset the 'two nation' division of the country (supported by a polarized, elite and popular press) by scheduling flagship news and current affairs programmes in prime time, and developing a distinctive style of journalism that was both popular and informative. This strategy succeeded in the sense that television became the principal source of news for the majority of the population.[13]

A second, more implicit theme is that broadcasting extended the political nation in a new way. The BBC cultivated from the 1930s onwards an intimate, conversational style of 'talk' about current affairs which conveyed the important democratic message that politics is about everyday things and within the competence of all (Cardiff 1980). A more aggressive style of television interviewing was introduced in the 1950s, which symbolically asserted politicians' accountability to the public (Cockerell 1984). The launch of television political satire in the 1960s, and its subsequent development in a more irreverent (though not neccessarily more radical) form, also promoted a more sceptical orientation to the world of power (Wagg 1992; Seymour-Ure 1996). Rather belatedly, in the 1990s, broadcasting began to develop a less diffident relationship to the royal family (Pimlott 1998). Thus, in different and evolving ways, broadcasting helped to roll back the cultural legacy of the pre-democratic past.

The third claim, again more often implied than explicit, is that radio and television served democracy by enabling different groups – including the disadvantaged and unorganized – to speak to each other, and shape the collective conversation of society. For example, unemployed workers caused a political sensation in the 1930s when they described on BBC radio their personal experiences of the arbitrary and heartless means-testing system, regulating their access to welfare (Scannell 1980). The forgotten poor of the swinging sixties gained public attention through celebrated television plays like *Cathy Come Home*. The marginalized victims of 1980s de-industrialization had their predicament highlighted with angry humour in the television series *Boys from the Blackstuff* (Millington 1993). From the 1970s onwards, the development of phone-in programmes, access programmes, studio audience participation and the new documentary movement gave increased opportunities for members of the general public to contribute to collective dialogue about the direction of society (Livingstone and Lunt 1994: Corner 1995). More generally, it is argued, public service broadcasting promoted not only socially inclusive debate but a reasoning, evidence-based, policy-oriented style of public discourse (Scannell 1992).

In short, the liberal narrative offers a coherent view of the different ways in which increasingly free media strengthened the democratic process. The media extended the political nation by making information about public affairs more widely available and promoting a culture of democracy. The media also empowered the people by subjecting authority to critical scrutiny and representing public opinion to government. Finally, the media – and in particular public service broadcasting – enhanced the functioning of democracy by encouraging constructive and reciprocal communication between different groups in society.

This liberal tradition thus tells media history as a story of progress in which the media became free, switched their allegiance from government to the people, and served democracy. While this remains still a powerful account it has a number of weaknesses, among them that it is a history mainly featuring men. This is redressed by another narrative which tells media history as *her*story. This simple shift of perspective produces a remarkably different account.

ADVANCE OF WOMEN: THE FEMINIST NARRATIVE

It was a truth universally acknowledged in the seventeenth and eighteenth centuries that women were inferior to men. Women were thought to be less rational and less emotionally stable. They were expected to be submissive, modest and obedient. Their subservience was reflected in their inferior legal status. When women married, they lost effective control of their property and could be lawfully confined to their homes by their husbands. As Lawrence Stone (1990: 13) comments, 'a married woman was the nearest approximation in a free society to a slave'.

Yet at the beginning of the twenty-first century, only an ageing minority thinks that women are innately inferior to men. Women's legal rights were transformed through a series of landmark reforms, from the 1853 Aggravated Assaults Act (against wife-beating) through to the Sex Discrimination and Equal Pay Acts of the 1970s. Women also acquired a much greater degree of economic independence, and made significant advances in public life (including the election of the first female prime minister in 1979).

How the media connected to this cumulative social revolution is the central concern of the feminist narrative. This will receive a fuller, more direct exposition than the liberal one since it is less familiar. Indeed, it is usually ignored entirely in conventional media history.

In the early eighteenth century, patriarchal values were strongly embedded in popular culture, and reinforced the subordination of women. Deviants from the gender order – such as weak, hen-pecked husbands – were regularly satirized in the popular ballads of the period. Traditional gender norms were also extolled in contemporary 'conduct books', and found support in a new cultural form, the novel.

Yet, within this patriarchal culture there were also elements of ambiguity, even of veiled protest.[14] Diane Dugaw (1989) identifies over a hundred popular ballads in the seventeenth and eighteenth centuries in which women dressed up and passed themselves off as men, often displaying traditional 'male' virtues such as courage, resourcefulness and self-reliance. These ballads implicitly directed attention to the arbitrary and mutable nature of the gender order. Similarly, in some late eighteenth-century novels, heroines transformed deficient men through their love and sweet nature, or bested them through feminine wiles. This fiction seemingly invited a subversive pleasure in the exercise of female power, and could be read as criticism of conventional masculinity, even if its heroines remained steadfastly 'feminine' (Todd 1989; Shoemaker 1998).

One cause of this ambivalence was that many women were employed in the pre-industrial economy, and for this reason were not wholly dependent on men. The eighteenth century was also a period of transition in which more middle- and upper-class women became educated, exercised economic power in the developing market for goods, and found self-expression through the virtual world of the novel and subscription library. Some women also became active in public roles, most notably in dissenting religion.

These tentative steps towards female liberation provoked a traditionalist backlash that gathered momentum from the later eighteenth century onwards. Women's proper place, it was argued, lay in the home. Women were naturally pure, gentle, self-sacrificing and emotional, whereas men were more worldly, assertive, rational and self-controlled. Woman's virtue made her best suited to the domestic sphere where her moral strength could be harnessed to raising children and exerting a civilizing influence within the home. By contrast man's physical strength, and greater capacity for action, reason and self-command made him better fitted for the rigours of the external world (Hall 1992; Gorham 1982).

This 'two spheres' ideology drew upon traditional ideas that can be found in medieval theology, literature and song.[15] It also gained additional support from new philosophical and medical thought which maintained that men and women had different dispositions as a consequence of their distinctive physiological and reproductive systems. This biologically determinist approach portrayed women as naturally passionless, unlike men. Determinist arguments were also mobilized against women in paid work who were 'excoriated for competing with men for jobs, pitied for their plight, or condemned for degrading themselves and their families by taking up employment' (Kent 1999: 73).

This patriarchal offensive received support from a wide range of male-dominated institutions and social movements. It was also aided by being promoted by women. Publication of women's periodicals began in the 1690s. Although some pioneer titles had broad cultural concerns (Shevelow 1989), women's magazines evolved in an increasingly confining way, offering 'by 1825 . . . a much narrower view of the role and status proper to women' (White 1970: 38; cf. Ballaster *et al.* 1991). The belief that men and women were destined by God and nature to occupy different social roles came to be widely accepted in the women's magazine press. As the *Ladies' Cabinet*, a leading women's journal, apostrophized in 1847:

> [Woman is] given to man as his better angel, to dissuade him from vice, to stimulate him to virtue, to make home delightful and life joyous . . . in the exercise of these gentle and holy charities, she fulfils her high vocation. But great as is the influence of the maiden and wife, it seems to fade away when placed by that of the mother. It is the mother who is to make the citizens for earth . . . and happy are they who thus fulfil the sacred and dignified vocation allotted to them by providence.
>
> (cited in White 1970: 42)

A new generation of periodicals appeared in the 1850s aimed at middle-class women. These sought to professionalise home-making by offering a flow of advice about domestic management, supplemented later by tips about how to be beautiful. In their wake followed working-class women's magazines, and 'tuppenny bloods' for girls, oriented towards romance in which women were defined largely by their relationships to men. In the first two decades of the twentieth century, national newspapers also introduced women's features of a highly traditional kind. Thus, between the eighteenth century and 1918, popular women's journalism gained a significant audience, and defined the central concerns of women as winning and keeping a man, home-making, motherhood and looking good.

The ideal of domestic femininity was also rendered more compelling by being articulated to other ideologies. It became part of the discourse of class, in which femininity was associated with refinement, delicacy and elegant domesticity, while lack of feminity was identified with work-calloused hands, roughness, coarseness, lewdness, the 'male' world of paid work. Patriarchal ideology was also dressed up as social morality. Women were told that the stay-at-home mother promoted a happy home, cared-for children and social improvement, whereas the 'working' mother gave rise to neglected families, badly brought-up children, drunkenness and crime. A further, powerful conjunction was that of female domesticity and male pride. A real man, worthy of respect, could afford to keep his wife at home: an inadequate man forced his wife to work for others in order to make ends meet.

The model of the stay-at-home wife and male breadwinner became an ideal – though a largely unattainable one – for many people in the early nineteenth century. It was not until the period 1850–1914 that female participation in the paid workforce declined significantly. Two spheres ideology also exerted a restrictive influence in other ways. It encouraged the repression of female sexuality through its stress on women's natural 'purity'. It helped to determine wider life opportunities on the basis of biology. It became the principal justification for continuing male control over political and economic life.

But while two spheres ideology was profoundly influential in restructuring gender relations, it did not in fact lead to the increased domestic *confinement* of women. Indeed, in one sense, it backfired because its portrayal of women as angels in the home implied, in Olwen Hufton's ironic phrase, a 'redistribution of virtue' (Hufton 1995: 501). By conferring increased moral authority on women, it justified their entry into the public sphere. Women became increasingly active from the 1780s onwards in 'moral' politics: the campaign against slavery, support for Queen Caroline, the temperance movement, reform of prostitution, the struggle to regulate female and child labour. A gendered pattern of political involvement developed in which it became acceptable for women to take up certain public issues as an extension of their family and charitable roles. By the 1840s, women were speaking at public meetings and were co-ordinating campaigning organizations. This was part of a more general trend in which women became more visible in public places, print, religion, and the new industrial economy (Shoemaker 1998).

Women's growing public activity nurtured the skills, solidarities and connexions that were deployed in organized feminism. The first female suffrage society was established in Sheffield in 1851, followed by the creation of the first British nationally organized women's movement in the 1860s. This was supported by the development of a feminist press, which boosted the morale of the women's movement, promoted its internal cohesion and assisted the spread of its ideas (Harrison 1982). The intellectual case against female subordination was refined and deployed to secure major reforms including, crucially, legal protection of married women's earnings and property, and easier divorce. The women's cause was also greatly strengthened by the growth of female middle-class employment. Even so, the campaign for female suffrage did not fully take off until 1903, and required the special circumstances of the First World War to succeed.

The winning of votes for women (over the age of thirty) in 1918 marked the culminating triumph of the first wave of organized feminism. However, this breakthrough was followed by a period of relative containment in which advances were slow and uneven.[16] Some male-dominated professions were breached in the 1920s. The growth of light industry and office work meant that, after 1939, domestic service ceased to be the main paid occupation for women. The Second World War was an emancipatory period, enabling many women to experience greater economic and cultural freedom. The proportion of *married* women going out to work rose significantly in the 1950s. Women also established an increasing presence in the public sphere, though mostly in relation to female and family-centred issues. Yet, as Ross McKibbin (1998) convincingly shows, through the skilful deployment of early sociology, even in the late 1940s and early 1950s most married women had home-centred, restricted and dependent lives in contrast to the more work-place-oriented, sociable and autonomous world of men. While women could enjoy considerable authority within the home, they still tended to occupy separate spheres from men in a relationship that was fundamentally unequal.

One key explanation for this continuing inequality was that suffragettes had been more successful on the political front than on the cultural one. While women became in 1918 equal *citizens*, many were still socialized through peer group pressure, schools, family tradition and the mass media into acceptance of domestic and subordinate roles.

This pattern of socialization was slow to change. The women's press, for example, long continued to be socially conservative, even when it seemed to be moving with the times. Thus, middle-market women's magazines went through a professionalizing phase in the 1930s (when housewives were briefed about the latest domestic technology and childcare wisdom), a 'make do and mend' phase in the 1940s, and the 'shop and spend' euphoria of the 1950s and 1960s (Greenfield and Reid 1998; White 1970). Yet, despite these changes, they continued to assume that the life of a woman centred on getting and keeping a man, and sustaining a happy home. Mass circulation women's magazines were still telling their readers as late as the 1950s that a 'half-time' mother was 'half-a-mother' to her deprived children (Ferguson 1983). Even the increased stress on consumption in women's magazines in the 1960s was generally presented in terms of expressing individuality within the prescribed categories of conventional femininity (Winship 1987).

Traditional gender norms were also upheld by girls' magazines (Murphy 1987), romantic fiction (McAleer 1992) and popular films (Thumim 1992). Men and women were projected as being different, with distinctive characteristics, performing different roles in ways that were generally fulfilling. Women who deviated from this gender order tended to be portrayed in popular media as incomplete or dissatisfied. In films, they were frequently punished symbolically: they died, their past sins caught up with them, or they lost their man to a nicer, more feminine woman. 'Our exploration of popular films,' concludes Janet Thumim, 'shows that screen representations in the period 1945–65, performed a consistently repressive function in respect of women. There are, simply, no depictions of autonomous, independent women either inside or outside the structure of the family, who survive unscathed at the narrative's close' (Thumim 1992: 210; cf. Harper 1996).

Yet this seeming continuity concealed subtle shifts, one of which was in understandings of masculinity. In the popular, middle-class literature of inter-war Britain, there emerged a home-centred, domesticated, suburban definition of manhood far removed from the mythical patriarchal figure of the Victorian era (Light 1991). The male ideal in girls' magazine fiction also changed from being masterful and stern in the 1920s to being boyish and gentle but still strong in the 1950s (Murphy 1987). Some men found this new demand – to be both sensitive and manly – a difficult double act to pull off. Male anxiety was a notable feature (for a variety of reasons) of numerous 1950s films (Geraghty 2000; Street 1997).

Another gradual change was a discernible increase in the social prestige of women. In First World War popular fiction, women who did 'remarkable' things – like driving a van, flying a plane, or being a bank cashier – were viewed with astonished admiration (Rowbotham 1997). By contrast, there were relatively unfazed responses to women doing 'men's jobs' with calm efficiency in Second World War films and magazines (Murphy 1992; Waller and Vaughan-Rees 1987). The expectations of women also increased. This was reflected, for example, in 1960s films featuring young women in search of self-realization and emotional integrity (Geraghty 1997), a theme that was echoed in new magazines directed at 'independent women' during the 1960s and 1970s (Winship 1987; Ferguson 1983).

Above all, there are indications of an undertow of female resentment. In an important book, Marcia Landy argues that a number of films between 1930 and 1960 'call[ed] into question women's anomalous position', even when they seemed to subscribe to traditional gender values (Landy 1991: 485). For example, a succession of Gainsborough film melodramas in the 1940s portrayed women in acts of rebellion against gendered understandings of 'duty' and morality. While all these women came to a bad end, their escapades allowed vicarious pleasure in their acts of transgression and dramatized the 'tension between the conventional positioning of women and the entertainment of alternatives' (Landy 1991: 17; cf. Aspinall 1983). More recently, Christine Geraghty (2000) shows how a number of realist films in the 1940s and 1950s implicitly raised questions about women's 'proper place' in society through their depiction of isolated and unfulfilled wives, who were locked into miserable marriages. The implication of these, and similar studies, is that the traditional gender order never enjoyed full consent during the post-suffrage period of containment. This helps to explain, in turn, why change was so rapid in the subsequent period.

The last quarter of the twentieth century was the second decisive turning point in the fortunes of women. This was bound up, like the rise of the suffragette movement, with changes in economy. The shift from manufacturing to service industries in the period after 1970 caused a contraction of traditional 'male' jobs and an expansion of 'female' work in a way that significantly altered the distribution of economic opportunities in British society (Thane 1991). A rising proportion of women gained paid work and unprecedented economic independence. Traditional barriers to women's advance were also lowered. In 1999–2000, more women graduated with degrees than men, in sharp contrast to the mainly male intake of universities in the 1950s. The glass ceiling preventing women from rising to the top began to crack, with shards of glass falling, in particular, in the media industries and public administration. Women's rights also gained increased legal protection, and more women played a formative role in politics. This should not obscure the fact that gender inequalities persisted at multiple levels: in terms of power, income, social status, the distribution of work within the home. Even so, the position of women was in general very much better in 2000 than it had been in 1900.

This improvement was supported by a cultural assault on traditional gender norms. Feminism revived from the late 1960s onwards (symbolized by the start of the London Women's Liberation Workshop in 1968). While one strand of feminist thought subverted chauvinist arguments by proclaiming the superiority of women, another strand placed greater emphasis on differences between women. This led ultimately to a rejection of biological essentialism – the assumption that men and women have different natures because they have different anatomies – which had shaped gender relations for over two centuries.[17]

Changes in media representations supported wider changes in society. Feminist research suggests that the media in the 1970s were still dominated by patriarchal values,[18] but that by the 1980s and 1990s they offered more varied and less stereotypical depictions of women.[19] For example, some young women's magazines offered more liberated definitions of femininity than their predecessors (McRobbie 1996). Some American films and programmes, popular in Britain, were strongly influenced by the women's movement (Shattuc 1997; D'Acci

1994). Even the once traditionalist women's sections of national newspapers bore the imprint of feminist debates.[20]

While there were continuities, there were also significant breaks with the past. In 1955, the first ever woman television newscaster, ITV's Barbara Mondell, delivered the midday news in what was judged to be a suitable setting: a crowded kitchen with plates piled up on the sink sideboard behind her. In marked contrast, all female newsreaders now read the news in gender-free contexts. A similar advance took place, though more unevenly, in advertising. Some 1960s advertisements featured women in bikinis reclining on car bonnets. Thirty years later, some car commercials depicted assured women sitting in the driving seat. These changes of representation symbolized the most important social change of the late twentieth century – the advance of women.

The feminist narrative thus views the development of the media in terms of a chequered, incomplete but nonetheless ground-breaking movement towards the liberation of women. It is a powerful and illuminating account which was mostly researched and written during the last two decades. The accelerated advance of women during this period provided a new vantage point from which to survey the past. It also changed the gender composition of social historians, and perhaps as a consequence contributed to a shift in what they researched.

Yet if the feminist narrative is relatively new, there is a still more recent arrival which has yet to attract a label. We will call it the populist narrative.

CULTURAL DEMOCRACY: THE POPULIST NARRATIVE

This narrative only began to take shape during the last fifteen years. It exists even now in fragments, as a series of discrete specialist studies. These fragments are pieced together here for the first time. If the presentation that follows is more extensive than for other narratives, this is only because detailed exposition is needed in order to introduce a newcomer. It is not intended to imply uncritical agreement with its conclusions.

The populist narrative has a villain and a hero. The 'villain' is the Victorian intelligentsia, and their heirs, who sought to foist their cultural tastes on the people. The 'hero' is the market which made the media more responsive to popular demand. This was aided by the decline of social deference, which turned people into more confident and assertive consumers.

The popularization of the media is portrayed as a democratic triumph in which popular preferences were acknowledged to have validity. It is also viewed as being part of the 'revolt of the masses' in which an increase of social egalitarianism eroded the values of hierarchy. Above all, it is represented as marking a real breakthrough in which the media were converted into becoming major sources of popular pleasure.

This narrative has obvious parallels with populist cultural studies.[21] It can also be viewed as an extension of the history of consumerism, pioneered by Cambridge historians in the 1980s. This is worth summarizing briefly because it both contextualizes the populist history of the media, and introduces some of its key ideas.

An advancing network of shops gave rise to 'the new bubbling of excitement in the eighteententh century . . . for the new world of goods' (Brewer and Porter 1993: 7). For example, the shops on London's Regent Street, with their large windows, dazzling mounted displays and brilliant oil lamp lighting, were the object of wonderment and awe in the 1780s (McKendrick 1983a: 79). Consumption, according to this tradition, was not simply a 'material' phenomenon, but also a 'cultural' one in that it could be a way of expressing a sense of individuality, social connection or community (Bermingham and Brewer 1995). The ownership of objects, in this view, could also give rise to pleasures that were profound rather than shallow. For example, a study of a Lancashire woman in the eighteenth century reveals the emotional significance, to do with the creation of a home and family, that she invested in her possessions. These were also her way of endowing future generations, and transmitting 'her personal history' (Vickery 1993).

The retail 'revolution' of the seventeenth and eighteenth centuries gave birth to the consumer society of the nineteenth and twentieth centuries. The train, car and plane extended social horizons. A new world of glamour became accessible to all, symbolized by those once powerful signifiers of allure and excitement – nylons and lipstick. Conveniences such as running water, central heating and the fridge became commonplace. Mass consumption made modern life varied, pleasurable and comfortable.[22]

A central theme of this celebratory history is that the rise of the market was a democratizing force. In the eighteenth century, it enabled the middle class to gain access to new cultural experiences, some of which had been previously the preserve of the upper class (Plumb 1983a). Marketization resulted in control of the performing arts being transfered from court, church and aristocratic patrons to the paying public (Brewer 1997). More generally, the market is portrayed as egalitarian because it did not distinguish between customers on the basis of birth and rank. It encouraged for example social 'cross-dressing', the buying and wearing of clothes that did not accord with people's inherited estate (Klein 1995). Its subversive democracy provoked a reaction in the form of elitist aesthetic theories which sought to stem the rising tide of popular influence over the arts (Bermingham 1995), just as in an earlier age attempts were made to restrict the wearing of elite clothes through sumptuary laws (McKendrick 1983b). More generally, the market is reverenced in this account for extending the pleasures and possessions of the few to the many. This stabilized, it is argued, Britain's social system in contrast to communist regimes which were fatally undermined by their inability 'in the literal sense, to "deliver the goods"' (Brewer and Porter 1993: 1).

The populist narrative can also be viewed as a continuation of the social history of 'de-subordination'. Numerous studies describe a cumulative cultural revolution in which reverence for God, deference to the monarch, respect for the aristocracy, military and professions, and regard for the supposed wisdom of old age, all declined, though in an uneven and discontinuous way.[23] The populist history of the media makes an original contribution to this general account by recording a popular 'revolt' against the leadership of the cultural elite.

This elite is portrayed in populist history as self-serving, self-satisfied and disdainful. Opening the prosecution with forensic skill, John Carey (1992) reveals the patrician public and private thoughts of celebrated novelists, poets and literary critics during the period 1880–1939. He shows how they displayed growing contempt for 'mass culture', associating it with vulgarity, sentimentality, emotional corruption, and a remorseless cultural descent to the lowest common denominator – what is now called 'dumbing down'. Often underlying this contempt was a visceral snobbery (mainly directed in a socially acceptable way against the lower middle class) reflected in scornful dismissals of 'suburban democracy', 'villadom' and 'clerk culture'. This elitism was sometimes overtly anti-democratic, as well as misogynistic in the way it identified the corruption of mass culture with its feminization. Its view of mass taste could have racist overtones, as in Wyndham Lewis's objection to jazz music as an 'idiot mass sound' with 'gross proletarian nigger bumps' (Carey 1992: 194–5). Hostility towards the 'masses' was legitimated by fashionable research filled with foreboding about insupportable population growth, the eugenic degeneration of the human stock, and the irrationality and destructiveness of crowd behaviour. It was also influenced, according to Carey, by intellectuals' growing resentment that their taste and leadership had been rejected by the people. However, this was expressed as a seemingly impersonal aesthetic in which, it was argued, timeless cultural values are embodied by art and literature of transcendant quality. It was the duty of a natural aristocracy, constituted by its taste and discernment, to uphold these values against the rising tide of commercial philistinism.

Carey argues that intellectuals' principal response to 'the revolt of the masses' was ultimately to take refuge in obscurity and the *avant garde*. 'The early twentieth century', he writes, 'saw a determined effort, on the part of the European intelligentsia, to exclude the masses from culture. In England this movement has become known as modernism' (Carey 1992: 16). Its aim was allegedly to disavow the power and significance of the people through the cultivation of modernist experiment accessible only to the elect few.

Carey's brilliantly written attack on scholarship seeks to delegitimate this modernist version of 'high culture', and its rejection of popular culture. However, he offers a very selective portrait of the intelligentsia by concentrating on those who disdainfully turned their backs on the people. There also existed throughout the period 1860–1939 another influential group of intellectuals – typified by Henry Brougham, Matthew Arnold, G.M. Trevelyan and John Reith – who sought to democratize access to knowledge and high culture. Their principal way of doing this was to press for the establishment of free or cheap cultural institutions supported by the state: schools, museums, art galleries, libraries and public service radio.

This latter group is the rather unfocused target of LeMahieu's influential cultural history of inter-war Britain. 'Cultivated elites', he argues, feared the egalitarian nature of the market, and sought to frustrate its operation through state intervention. They engineered the establishment of the BBC as a state broadcasting monopoly, and later secured state sponsorship of the arts and documentary film movement. If they sought to widen access to the culture of the privileged, this was merely in order to facilitate 'the reassertion of cultural hierarchy' (LeMahieu 1988: 138).

The response of the cultural elite to the rise of mass culture is thus portrayed as either taking refuge in obscure intellectualism or enlisting the power of the state to impose elite preferences on the people. Much of populist history is devoted to revealing gleefully how this latter strategy came unstuck.

We will start this 'narrative' in 1850 when municipal public libraries were first introduced on a piecemeal basis. The main purpose behind their establishment was to promote moral improvement, cultural enlightenment and social harmony (Black 1996). Consistent with this high-mindedness, some moralists argued that novels should have no place in public libraries or, alternatively, that they should incur a borrowing charge unlike works of instruction. This opposition to fiction on the rates, inspired by a combination of puritanism and parsimony, was effectively defeated by the 1880s (Snape 1995).

Thereafter, a key issue in public libraries became what sort of balance should be struck between education, edification and 'recreation' in the selection of library books. Municipal libraries followed different policies between 1880 and 1914, reflecting the different cultural politics of their local communities (Snape 1995). In Liberal, Congregationalist Darwen, priority was given to stocking works of literary and moral merit, culminating in the decision in 1901 to discontinue the buying of *all* light fiction. This was the logical extension of the 'civic gospel' mission of Darwen's community leaders, who also organized Bands of Hope, sewing groups, reading circles and sponsored picnics in an attempt to build a New Jerusalem. However, this veto on new library entertainment provoked a storm of protest in a politicized community, and had to be quickly reversed. A similar policy of running down the stock of light fiction was pursued in Conservative Wigan. In this case, it was because resources were diverted to building the reference library into a temple of education and scholarship – the pet project of the local Tory grandee, the twenty-sixth earl of Crawford. In this more deferential community there was no protest, merely a sharp decline in the number of books borrowed from the library. In Conservative Blackburn, by contrast, the purchase of library books was linked closely to popular demand. The local businessmen, controlling the council, wanted to foster a contented, trouble-free workforce and community. However, their flexibile pragmatism had limits: the municipal library was not allowed to subscribe to socialist newspapers.

A proselytizing approach persisted within the public library system well into the twentieth century.[24] Some libraries put fiction and non-fiction on alternate shelves in order to tempt people into reading non-fiction; others allowed users to borrow a larger number of meritorious than ordinary books; others still developed lecture programmes and reading groups to guide their users' reading habits. It was also standard library policy, for a long time, to give low priority to 'lowbrow', popular books like Mills and Boon romances. Yet, public libraries did undergo a general process of popularization in a form that has yet to be adequately investigated.

If the initial breakthrough was the free loan of fiction in public libraries, this was followed by another landmark: the rise of 'new journalism' in the 1880s and 1890s. The lay-out of the popular press became more accessible; its tone more assertive; and more space was given to human interest stories, crime and sport at the expense of political coverage. This is portrayed by Joel Wiener as marking the beginnings of 'a democracy of print' largely inspired by the 'egalitarian' example of the American press, and imported with the help of expatriate American journalists (Wiener 1996: 62).

Thus, a change in the press traditionally associated with editorial decline is reinterpreted by Wiener as an advance. Similarly, D.L. LeMahieu maintains that the continued growth of human interest stories in the inter-war press shifted attention from the elite world of high politics to everyday life, and symbolically asserted that the lives of ordinary people mattered. The language of the press also became more egalitarian, 'analagous to a conversation between friends' (LeMahieu 1988: 55). In addition, the press drew readers into a pleasurable world of fantasy about youth, sex, beauty, wealth and fame by providing extensive coverage of film stars.

The popularization of the press was followed by that of radio, though only after an initial period of stiff-necked paternalism. In a ground-breaking study, Scannell and Cardiff argue that the BBC was transformed during its 'era of uplift' (1922–34) from a national network of local stations, some with local popular roots, into a cultural missionary organization led from the top. Its cultural evangelism resulted in some regular programmes being scheduled at different times in order to keep listeners on their toes and prevent 'lazy' listening. A period of silence was also imposed between appropiate programmes in order to give listeners the time to recompose themselves in readiness for the next aural treat. Programme schedules were weighted in favour of the serious and improving, culminating in the BBC's Sunday moral tonic – a morning religious service followed by serious music, talks and an evening religious programme (Scannell and Cardiff 1991: 232). The mind-set of the BBC during this period is perhaps best illustrated by the experience of R.S. Lambert, the editor of the *Listener*, the BBC's cultural weekly magazine. In his first five years as editor (1929–34), he was not allowed to see his magazine's circulation figures in case this distorted his editorial judgement (Chaney 1987: 266).

However this seclusion came to an end. Between 1931 and 1938, the BBC's licence-paying audience soared from 27 per cent to 71 per cent of British households (Pegg 1983: 16, table 1.2). Overseas commercial radio stations (in particular, Radio Luxembourg and Normandie) with improved transmission facilities also became significant rivals. The combined force of the 1930s radio craze and foreign competition caused the BBC to tack to the wind of popular demand. In 1936, the corporation established the Listener Research Unit under the direction of a top advertising agency market researcher (Silvey 1974). More money and airtime were allocated in the late 1930s to quizzes, parlour games, undemanding drama serials and also innovative variety and comedy shows that exploited the creative and comic potential of radio.

During the Second World War (1939–45) the BBC came under renewed pressure, this time from the armed forces and the Ministry of Information, to give greater priority to entertainment in order to boost morale (Cardiff and Scannell 1986). This pressure was reinforced by the increasingly assertive demands of the public during a period of declining deference (Cardiff and Scannell 1981). The BBC responded by rethinking its programme strategy and cultural approach. Before the war, its two channels had a diverse mix of programmes intended to extend listeners' cultural horizons. However, in 1940 the BBC introduced the Forces Programme devoted mainly to entertainment. This included programmes aimed primarily at a working-class audience (with paternalistic titles like *Workers Playtime* and *Music While You Work*), presenters with regional accents, more topical and mildly subversive comedy, imported American programmes and a substantial increase of popular dance music and 'crooning' (the latter being something which the BBC had even thought of banning in the 1930s (Scannell and Cardiff 1991: 189)).

The Forces Programme was an instant success. It was followed by the introduction of 'cultural streaming' in 1945-6, in the form of three channels (Light, Home and Third) concentrating on different types of programme. This represented a significant watershed in the history of broadcasting. The Reithian conception of radio as a cultural rope-ladder, and of broadcasters as mountain guides assisting listeners' ascent to the summit of cultural achievement, was modified. It came to be accepted reluctantly that different groups of people liked different kinds of programmes.

If BBC radio forged a closer relationship to its public, so also did the British cinema during the 1930s. This was manifested, according to Jeffrey Richards (1989), by the rise of three home-grown film stars each of whom embodied different aspects of British popular culture: Gracie Fields, a homely, high-spirited and shrewd 'Lancashire lass', with whom many working-class women could identify; George Formby, 'the working-class Everyman' (Richards 1989: 206), who triumphed over adversity in comedies that drew upon the humour of the music hall and seaside picture postcard; and Jessie Mathews, who sparkled in films about the madcap, enviable world of Bright Young Things, appealing to a more middle-class and aspirational audience.

The British cinema struck still more of a popular chord during the war years by providing entertainment at a time of crisis, responding to the rise of social democratic values and connecting to the interior lives of its audience.[25] During the same period, the *Daily Mirror* and *Sunday Pictorial* ventriloquized the language and idiom of working-class readers, and their 'us and them' view of the world, to be rewarded with soaring circulation.[26]

While populist historians agree that the British media became more audience oriented during the 1930s and 1940s, they disagree about the extent and significance of this shift. LeMahieu (1988) argues that the growth of consumption of more commercialized media gave rise in the 1930s to the formation of an egalitarian, common culture. Other populist historians maintain that Britain was still so rooted in social hierarchy that whole sections of its population became cultural asylum-seekers. Writing about the 1930s, Scannell and Cardiff declare that 'working people in Britain massively enjoyed and consumed American entertainment because it did not treat them as second-class citizens' but 'bespoke a more equal, open society than Britain' (Scannell and Cardiff 1991: 298–9). Similarly, George Perry argues that the British cinema failed in the inter-war period because it was 'a middle class institution' that drove cinemagoers to opt 'for the classless accents of America' (Perry 1975: 65).

The most elaborated presentation of this 'critical' view is provided by Paul Swann's study of the British cinema in the late 1940s. In 1947, the Labour government introduced an import duty which led Hollywood to ban the export of new films to Britain. This provoked a furious outcry from the British public, and led to a humiliating government reversal of policy. Paul Swann argues that this episode revealed the continuing popular hegemony of American films, based on their superior cultural as well as aesthetic appeal. Hollywood had 'a fundamentally egalitarian element in most of its films which the British films simply lacked' (Swann 1987: 64). American films revolved around the individual and offered aspirational hope to people in a collectivist culture where 'the desires of the individual were very rarely fulfilled by British films, or indeed in real life' (Swann 1987: 64). American films also offered glamour, optimism, vitality and consumer luxury in contrast to the austerity and rationing of post-war Britain. Thus, the global market allegedly enabled British cinema-goers to break free from the cultural limitations of their own society, and connect to the values and experiences of a more egalitarian, successful alternative.

Populist historians argue that while the British media had made some adjustments to popular demand by the early post-war period, they still had a long way to go. For example, Robert Chapman complains that BBC radio's continued commitment to quality resulted in a concealed class bias in its allocation of resources. In 1952, the upscale Third Programme, with less than 1 per cent of listeners, accounted for 46 per cent of the BBC's music spending, whereas the Light Programme, with 70 per cent of the audience, had only a 15 per cent share of music expenditure (Chapman 1992: 20).

Similarly, Peter Black characterizes BBC television in this period as paternalistic and lacking a popular touch, even when it tried. He describes a telling occasion in November 1953 when the BBC presented the entire evening's television as the

Tudor Elizabethans might have seen it, in honour of the recently crowned Queen Elizabeth II. The announcer appeared in doublet and hose; the television cook expert prepared 'a conceit of coneys'; a fashion historian presented the latest fashions 'newly out of France'; a play was performed in a round theatre; an actor impersonating Sir Walter Raleigh featured in a press conference. What seemed to BBC executives a jolly jape went down like a lead balloon, and revealed BBC television's remoteness from its audience.

However, commercial television was launched in 1955–6 and won the lion's share of the audience. 'Once they had a choice', writes Peter Black (1973: 109), 'the working class audience left the BBC at a pace that suggested that ill will was more deeply entrenched than good.' Commercial television pioneered in Britain new types of television programme, notably giveaway shows like *Double Your Money* which drew upon a fairground tradition of fun, entertainment programmes like *People are Funny* (which was constructed around elaborate practical jokes played on friends) and soap opera built around the drama of everyday life. Its success forced BBC television to fight back with the popular Billy Cotton Bandshow, followed, under a new director general, Sir Hugh Greene (1960–9), by a succession of innovative entertainment programmes ranging from situation comedy to satire. Commercial competition made the corporation 'compromise between a commitment to the best and desire to please. . . . ' (Tracey 1998: 97). The result was a transformation of BBC television 'from an elitist channel to one which was closer to the people', leading to 'the democratization of popular choice' (Tracey 1998: 92 and 96).

Commercial competition was also the spur for a renewed shake-up of BBC radio after it failed to respond adequately to the rise of rock and youth-oriented pop music. In the early 1960s, the BBC's Light Programme floundered by trying to please a mass audience with offerings ranging from the Animals to Mantovani and even Gilbert and Sullivan. The corporation was also encumbered by an agreement, designed to promote live music, which restricted the playing of records. The result was a strict rationing of pop music hits, to the mounting fury of young listeners.

'Pirate' radio stations filled the gap created by the BBC's middle-aged response to the rise of a youth culture.[27] Over twenty new offshore commercial radio stations were set up in the late 1950s and early 1960s. By 1965, two of these (Caroline North/South and Radio London) had captured a major share of the youth audience. This led the BBC to set up belatedly in 1967 its own imitation pirate station – Radio 1 – mainly staffed by former pirate radio DJs. This was part of a wider reorganization of BBC radio into generic channels, offering differentiated programme schedules for different publics. This marked the final break with cultural evangelism – ambushing listeners with programmes they 'ought' to hear through mixed scheduling – which had been modified but not abandoned fully in the 1940s (Lewis and Booth 1989).

The British cinema industry also enjoyed an Indian summer during the 1960s. Its output included innovative social realist movies (Woodfall films); blockbusters for the international market (Bond films); and low budget popular films for the domestic market (*Carry On* films). It is these last which attract most attention from populist historians, usually in the form of text-based studies that seek to understand the basis of their popularity. Thus, Marion Jordan attributes the long-running success of the *Carry On* films to their 'lower-class, masculine resistance to refinement', their humorous release from sexual repression, and their defiant stess on the need for 'shiftiness in an impossibly demanding industrial society' (Jordan 1983: 327).

The populist narrative is not adequately developed for the last three decades of the twentieth century. However, its central arguments can be recapitulated in a way which covers this period. One key theme of populist history is that broadcasting was rescued from elite cultural control, and forged a closer connexion with its audience in a series of incremental steps. Key landmarks in this process included the first BBC radio serial featuring a working-class family (the Plums) in 1937; the establishment of an entertainment-oriented radio channel (Forces Programme) in 1940; the projection of ordinary domestic life as an adventure story in 1950s commercial television soap opera; BBC radio's full conversion to pop music in the 1960s; the introduction of commercial local radio in 1973 (and subsequent development into generic channels); the rise of television alternative comedy and transmission of pub-based sports in the 1980s; the advent of national commercial radio in 1992, and the growth of new television sport and film channels in the 1990s.

More generally, the media are portrayed as evolving from paternalism to consumerism. A communication system in which some libraries were crammed with improving books, leading newspapers published columns of parliamentary speeches and, later, enriching silence filled gaps between radio programmes, gave way to a reconstituted system in which libraries stocked pop videos, newspapers published pin-ups, and television entertained with giveaway programmes like *Who Wants to Be a Millionaire?* This shift is hailed unequivocally as an advance in which the media were weaned from worthiness, gave people what they wanted and promoted a culture of democracy.

Above all, this tradition offers a rather compelling account of how each new medium – film, radio, gramophone and television – was the object of widespread wonder and excitement, became absorbed into the rituals of family and social life, and was the staple of everyday conversation.[28] The mass media also conveyed, it is stressed, richly textured meanings which connected with the imaginative lives of their audiences and elicited active responses.[29] The media became a source of mass pleasure that was meaningful.

Contributors to this narrative come from ideological homes as divergent as neo-liberalism and neo-Marxism. They range from Americans who love their country's culture with possessive pride (LeMahieu, Swann and Wiener) to British radical patriots (Richards and Smith). They number among their ranks eloquent critics of elite culture (Carey and Hebdige) but also writers who betray residual traces of the elite paternalism they denigrate (Scannell and Tracey). The only thing that most members of this extraordinarily heterogeneous group have in common is that they distrust professional and state power, stress the importance of social respect ('culture of democracy') and view the media primarily as a source of consumer pleasure. What binds this group together, and overides its differences, are the hegemonic values of the 1980s and 1990s. The populist narrative echoes the ideological script of the Reagan–Thatcher era and the post-communist aftermath.

If the populist narrative is new, there is another narrative which exists only in embryo. We will try to bring this embryo to life for the more recent period.

CULTURE WARS: THE LIBERTARIAN NARRATIVE

From the last quarter of the nineteenth century onwards, there was a cumulative process of de-Christianization. Britain changed from being a country where religion was a central force in shaping public attitudes to becoming one of the most godless societies in the world. During the same period, the further embedding of the market system, and the decline of the factory, trade union, church, local neighbourhood and extended family, contributed to the strengthening of individualism. These two historic shifts – the erosion of religion and the rise of individualism – encouraged greater moral pluralism and acceptance of different life styles. The key period of change was the 1960s when laws regulating the private sphere (divorce, homosexuality and abortion) were liberalized, and attitudes towards what had been previously considered 'sins' (such as pre-marital sex) were modified.

This liberal trend encountered strong resistance from moral traditionalists, which is not so much explained as delegitimated in the libertarian narrative.[30] This resistance is portrayed as the product of primitive religious belief, resentments aroused by social change and phobic responses to female sexuality, new technology and the working class.[31]

The best-known study in this debunking tradition is Geoffrey Pearson's (1983) cultural history of hooliganism. He shows that, for over a century, each new generation tended to lament contemporary lawlessness and contrast it with a former era of social discipline and relative freedom from crime, usually located in that generation's childhood. From the outcry against 'street arabs' in the 1840s and 'garotters' in the 1860s right through to the denunciations of 'Teddy Boys' in the 1950s and 'muggers' in the 1970s, these cyclical outbursts bore little relationship to the changing rate of crime. Yet, time and again, they identified the same sinister processes at work: moral deterioration among the young, malign foreign influence and the ill-effects of the media (whether this be the Victorian music hall, the Edwardian comic, 1920s film, or television). The implication of this iconoclastic study is that law and order attitudes and morally censorious responses to the media are often rooted in nostalgia, prejudice and social myth.

This is complemented by two celebrated studies of Thatcherism and its antecedents,[32] which argue that moral authoritarianism drew upon displaced discontents and fears arising from black and Asian immigration, the 1960s youth revolution and national decline. It harked back to the moral values and certainties of the Victorian era, and sought to secure their return as a solution to contemporary ills. This traditionalist strand of conservatism was entwined with other strands to produce a powerful ideological discourse that changed the politics of the 1970s and 1980s.

Moral traditionalism is thus presented as an irrational, repressive, backward-looking but potent force. It is opposed, in the libertarian narrative, by the 'modern' tradition of tolerance and moral pluralism. The development of the media is described in terms of the Manichean struggle between these two traditions.

This struggle erupted into periodic 'culture wars', often contested in relation to symbolic 'out' groups: members of youth cultures, from 1920s flapppers to 1970s punk and moral 'deviants', from sexual minorities to unmarried mothers. These battles marked out where the outer perimeter of the 'acceptable' lay. For traditionalists, these out groups often symbolized a deeper moral malaise that required an appropriate level of societal response – whether this be setting a 'better example', greater moral regulation of the young through education, tougher sanctions or new punitive laws. To liberals, these out groups were often victims of prejudice and a pretext for the extension of unacceptable authoritarianism.

This normative contest can be illustrated by a brief historical account of the media and sexual minorities. During the Victorian era, growing traditionalist pressure led to the passage of the Criminal Law Amendment Act of 1885 which made sex between men – whether in public or private – a criminal activity. It was under this act that the playwright, Oscar Wilde, was charged in a second trial in 1895, and sentenced to two years' hard labour. This was a key moment in the mobilization of popular animosity against gay men. Wilde was widely denounced in the press as an evil corrupter of youth, encouraging what one London newspaper gleefully called at the time a 'dash of wholesome bigotry' (cited in Ellmann 1988: 450). In an increasingly homophobic climate of opinion, the word 'effeminate' changed its meaning, from characterizing men who spent too much time with women and were unduly influenced by the sensualizing effects of female company, to denoting men who liked other men and were disposed to have sex with them (Kent 1999: 248). This change of language was part of an increased public sensitization to the 'problem' of homosexuality, which led to demands for further public protection. A new, repressive anti-gay law was passed in 1898 (Weeks 1991).

Lesbians were not in the firing line in the same way as gay men, partly because less was known about lesbianism and also because two spheres ideology decreed that women were 'passionless'. However, public knowledge was raised by another act of moral entrepreneurship, again involving a well-publicized trial. In 1928, Radclyffe Hall's lesbian novel, *Well of Loneliness*, was prosecuted and found to be obscene. It was better, according to the *Sunday Express*, to 'give a healthy girl a phial of prussic acid than this novel' since 'poison kills the body, but moral poison kills the soul' (cited in McKibbin 1998: 324). This outburst was part of a press-backed crusade against lesbianism which influenced contemporary women's fashion. Prejudice against homosexuality in general was further stoked in the inter-war era by films which portrayed gay men as weak and silly or evil and corrupting (Gross 1998 and 1989).

In the 1960s, liberals fought back partly through films which depicted gay men in a sympathetic light as victims or loyal friends, though rarely as 'ordinary' people (Street 1997), as well as through books and plays which became less subject to censorship. The gay community became better organized, and found a collective voice through the successful launch of *Gay News* in 1962. Adult homosexuality was decriminalized in 1967, following the recommendation of the Wolfenden report published ten years before.

However, the development of a more liberal climate was interrupted by the AIDS moral panic of 1983–7. The popular press revived homophobic attitudes by portraying gay men as carriers of the 'killer plague' which threatened the 'innocent' community.[33] Some newspapers further fuelled animosity towards gay men by greatly exaggerating the risk of acquiring HIV through coming into casual, non-sexual contact with carriers. This phase of tabloid coverage culminated in Britain's best-selling daily, the *Sun*, offering gays a permanent, one-way ticket to Norway, under the headline 'Fly away Gays – And We Will Pay' (cited in Watney 1987: 147). Legislation ('section 28') was passed in 1988 which made it illegal for any local authority to 'promote the teaching in any maintained school of the acceptance of homosexuality as a pretended family relationship', among other anti-gay proscriptions (cited in Kent 1999: 352).

However the AIDS moral panic had subsided by the late 1980s. In the subsequent period, film and television depictions of gays and lesbians became more varied and accepting (Dyer 1990: Gross 1998). The tabloid press turned its back on routine 'anti-queer' features like the 1963 *Sunday Pictorial*'s 'How to spot the homo' (cited in Weeks 1977: 163), and became in relative terms less prejudiced. These shifts of media representation, and of underlying attitudes, paved the way for law reform. In 2001, the age of consent for gay and straight sex was equalized at sixteen.

The second way in which liberals and traditionalists clashed was over moral regulation of the media.[34] We will pick up this theme from the 1950s onwards when liberals gained the upper hand. In 1951, the 'X' certificate for adult-only films was introduced, which opened the door to celluloid sex, within strict limits and preferably in foreign, subtitled films. In an attempt to arrest the growing trend towards liberalization, the authorities in 1960 prosecuted as 'obscene' D.H. Lawrence's *Lady Chatterley's Lover*. 'Is it a book you would wish your wife or servants to read?', the prosecuting barrister, Mervyn Griffith-Jones, asked startled members of the jury (cited in Morgan 1999: 186). They found in favour of the publisher, Penguin Books, which opened the floodgates. The word 'bloody' was allowed in films in 1963; 'bugger' in 1967; and 'fuck' in 1970. The discreet displays of flesh in wholesome 1950s naturist films evolved into full-frontal nudity in adult-only movies by 1968–9. The 'public morality' convention that criminals *must* fail or come to a sticky end by the last reel also died during the 1960s. While film censorship persisted, the role of the Lord Chamberlain as official theatre censor was phased out in 1968. Shortly before his departure, he defiantly imposed cuts on the Edward Bond play, *Early Morning*, depicting Queen Victoria as a lesbian.

A concerted attempt was made in the 1980s and early 1990s to turn back this 'permissive' tide, with the explicit backing of the prime minister, Margaret Thatcher (1979–90). Stricter censorship of videos was introduced in 1984, and the Broadcasting Standards Council (later Commission) was established in 1988 in the hope that it would 'clean up' programmes through moral injunction. However this attempt to remoralize failed, mainly because deregulatory measures made television more subject to commercial pressures. There was more television sex and violence in the 1990s than ever before. The drive to promote traditional moral values was undermined by the desire to foster market freedom.

The libertarian narrative thus describes how traditionalists and liberals fought each other both through the media and over its control. The studies which make up this narrative are largely written by academics (like Aldgate, Barker, Murdock, Pearson and Petley) who were profoundly influenced by the cultural revolution of the mid-twentieth century. If the populist narrative is the product of the 1980s and 1990s, the libertarian narrative is the signature tune of the 1960s.

However the growth of individualism that contributed to greater social tolerance also gave rise to a less cohesive society. This directs attention to a fifth narrative concerned with the part played by the media in forging social bonds between people, and sustaining a sense of national community.

BUILDING A NATION: THE ANTHROPOLOGICAL NARRATIVE

The anthropologist, Benedict Anderson, argues that the nation is an 'imagined political community'. 'It is imagined', he continues, 'because the members of even the smallest nations will never know most of their fellow-members, meet them, or even hear of them, yet in the minds of each lives the image of their communion' (Anderson 1983: 15). The rise of the novel and newspaper were especially important, he suggests, in making the nation a focus of identity. Anderson thus offers two insights: the nation is a cultural construct and the media have played a part in its construction. These arguments have influenced both social and media history. When this work is pulled together, a new and compelling narrative of media history is born.

Britain (or, as it is officially known, the 'United Kingdom of Great Britain and Northern Ireland') is a relatively new country. England and Wales only merged politically with Scotland in 1707, following an earlier dynastic union. Ireland did not become *constitutionally* part of Britain until 1800, and became (apart from the six northern counties) independent in 1921.

At its formation, Britain was also made up of 'nations' with different languages, religions, histories, traditions and identities. In addition, Britain was in 1707 a parochial society where the lives of most people were defined by local customs, ties and loyalties. How, then, did this decentralized, conglomerate state manage to forge a sense of national unity and persuade its inhabitants to identify with each other?

The great unifying force that helped to cement Britain as a nation in its first half century, after 1707, was a Protestant sense of destiny.[35] Print-based media promoted the view that Britain was a freedom-loving, constitutional, Protestant country in contrast to the tyrannical, Catholic nations of Europe. This drew upon an historical conspiracy theory in which Britain was menaced by its papist foes abroad, notably 'Catholic' Spain and France, and by its papist traitors at home, from Guy Fawkes to the Jacobite rebels. This theory was sustained by popular anti-Catholicism fomented by state, pulpit and print from the sixteenth century.[36]

However, unification did not only take place in the mind. It was also advanced by the extension of the national state, increased economic integration within the national free trade area and growing intermarriage between English, Welsh, Scots and Irish elites. But in so far as Britain was an imagined community, Protestant bigotry provided its initial inspiration.

From the 1760s onwards, this national-religious identity was overlaid by the new identity of imperialism, which became central to how many British people thought about themselves for the next two centuries. The appeal of imperialism to all parts of Britain was rooted in self-interest: the Scots, Welsh and Irish – not just the English – took part in developing and managing the empire, and derived economic benefit from its expansion. However, the unifying power of imperialism also operated through the imagination. From the outset, the empire generated stirring images of intrepid explorers, sailors, merchants, missionaries and administrators. These images came to be organized around two themes: one centred on honour, manhood, adventure and bravery, and the other on progress, moral leadership and saving souls. These generated two competing understandings of empire – as an adventure story and as a moral project. These were increasingly woven together in the later Victorian period into a seductive synthesis in which imperial success was attributed to the strength of national character. It came to be widely assumed that Britain controlled the largest formal empire the world had ever known not because of its military technology and economic power but because of the superiority of the British people. Just to be British, and have British characteristics, was to be part of Britain's imperial greatness.

This vainglory reached its peak during the last quarter of the nineteenth century, after which it gradually receded. Imperialism received support from schools, the armed forces, churches and above all the emergent mass media. The late Victorian music hall was strongly imperialistic (Bailey 1986 and 1978). Numerous popular books in Victorian and Edwardian Britain, such as those by

G.A. Henty, celebrated the superiority of the British people in relation to other races (Mackenzie 1984). The British cinema made a succession of imperial epics in which, as Richards (1997b: 57) puts it, 'the gods of Empire were British archetypes, embodying the values and virtues of Britishness'. Most of the British national newspaper press beat the drum for empire throughout the period 1850–1939. The BBC played a key role in popularizing the imperial monarchy and projecting the idea that, in the words of its 1935 Empire Day programme, 'the British Empire . . . is made up of one big family' (cited in Cardiff and Scannell 1987: 163). A sense of being at the hub of a great empire sometimes had racial and zenophobic overtones, expressed most overtly in boy's comics. This was typified by the popular comic villain, Chao-Feng, who was fond of warning that 'the white race will learn one day the power of the Yellow Peril' (cited in McKibbin 1998: 498).

Imperialism came under increasing attack from the early twentieth century onwards. Perhaps for this reason, Britishness was projected during the 1930s and 1940s primarily through a soft-focused, insular communalism symbolized by an arcadian image of rural Britain. This was a profoundly misleading image of a heavily industrialized and urbanized country. However, rural arcadian myths had a long literary history as a perennially unreal source of representation (Williams 1973). They had flourished significantly in the eighteenth century, when new farming methods and increased social conflict were destroying the settled rural life they commemorated (Brewer 1997). In the 1930s and 1940s, the rural idyll served as a powerful unifying symbol because it signified different things to different people. For the right it evoked a vanishing world of hierarchy, harmony and order, while for the left it conjured up the dream of free yeomen leading the simple, good life before the ravages of industrial capitalism. Britishness thus came to be embodied by ambiguous make-believe about the past.

Even if unifying images of Britain were sometimes fragile, the country's national identity was strengthened by cumulative changes in the structure of the media. These changes will be described, for the sake of expository clarity, first in relation to the period 1800–1960 – before Britain's sense of itself underwent a significant change. A 'national' newspaper press appeared in the early nineteenth century, but only overtook the combined circulation of the local and regional daily press in the 1930s (Kaldor and Silverman 1948: 84, table 5). National music hall networks first emerged in the 1880s (Bailey 1978), and were followed by the creation of great national cinema chains in the late 1920s (Street 1997). Radio was transformed into a centralized national system in the 1920s, as was in effect television in the 1940s and 1950s. Of course, there had long been local, regional, Scottish, Welsh and Northern Irish newspapers, and these were supplemented in due course by their radio and television counterparts. However, the more important point is that national media became dominant within the British media system during the 1920s and 1930s, and were already well established by the Victorian period.

The content of the emergent media system in the nineteenth century was also largely British. This changed with the arrival of the cinema and gramophone, which increased Britain's exposure to global and, in particular, American cultural influence. From 1910 onwards, American films dominated the British market, causing protectionist legislation – already mentioned in relation to 1947/8 – to be initiated in 1927 and strengthened in 1938 (Street 1997). Afro-American music (to employ a simplifying category) was restricted by visa controls on the employment of American musicians, but was popularized with the help of the gramophone boom of the 1920s and 1930s. By the 1940s, it was the dominant influence on popular music in Britain.

However, countervailing trends restabilized the British media system. Radio was organized as a national monopoly in 1922, and subsequently withstood foreign competition. Television was heavily protected as a national medium when in 1955 it ceased to be a public monopoly. Non-Commonwealth ownership of television franchises was forbidden and strict limits on the import of programmes were imposed. Media autarchy was further strengthened when British-controlled television grew at the expense of American-dominated film. In effect, Britain's cultural drawbridge was lowered during the early twentieth century and then partly raised.

However, the growth of a protected national media system did not give rise in a simple sense to a national 'common culture' since British society was stratified by powerful class, gender, Celtic and other sub-cultures. Thus, when large numbers of working-class families bought for the first time a regular daily paper in the 1930s, many chose different papers from those read primarily in middle-class households.[37] If they lived in Scotland, some chose a Scottish daily paper rather than a Scottish edition of a national paper.[38] During the same period, women tended to read different magazines from men, different books from men, and even to some extent different articles in the newspapers they shared with men.[39] But these sectional cultures and identities were nevertheless strongly challenged by the brute force of oligopoly. Most towns had only a small number of single-screen cinemas, and what these showed was severely restricted during the period 1930–60 by the decline of independent cinemas and the growth of giant cinema chains serviced by dominant distributors and film majors.[40] Television evolved during the same period from a one-channel monopoly to a two-channel duopoly, each with a programme schedule directed at a mass, national audience. Only radio adapted in the 1940s to distinct, class-based publics, but it had operated a one-nation scheduling policy before that. In short, the majority came to consume some of the same media, regardless of where they lived and what social grouping they belonged to.

The increase of national media consumption created a framework of shared national experience and common talking points. It also strengthened a sense of national identity. In particular, the British cinema during its golden age (roughly 1930–70) enabled people to *visualize* Britain. It portrayed the nation in terms of geographically defined archetypes – canny Scots, lyrical Welsh, plain-spoken northerners, dodgy but loveable cockneys, simple West Country people – that made the nation seem both knowable as a community and also a familiar object of affection. It also constructed the nation as a repertory company of class stereotypes, from the cloth-capped worker to the bowler-hatted civil servant. While these could potentially symbolize class conflict, British films in the 1930s tended to emphasize the interdependence of social groups, their shared humanity and their mutual bonding through consensual social relations.[41] This idealization was followed in the Second World War by films and documentaries depicting people from different social backgrounds pulling together unselfishly for the common good, and in the 1950s by numerous war films recapturing the mythologised social solidarity of the war years.[42] Indeed, the communitarian ethos of 1930s and 1940s British films was so strong that it gave rise to a distinctive national film aesthetic. This took the form of episodic plots with multiple characters and a wide-angled framing of social space in contrast to Hollywood's more individual-centred perspective and evocation of a more interior, private space (Higson 1997).

If film and later television[43] made it easier to visualize British society, radio helped people to feel part of it. Radio, in its ascendancy (1930–55), brought together the diverse elements of national life, and presented them in a single, unified context.[44] Whether it was major religious festivals, days of shared memory like Armistice Day, occasions of national pride like Empire Day, key sporting events like the Football Assocation Cup Final, or seasonal rituals like the spring-time song of the nightingale from Surrey woods, the different components of national life were edited together by BBC radio to evoke a sense of national unity. Members of the audience were encouraged to feel that, through listening, they were present at national events, and were participants in the collective life of the nation. The natural rhythms of the BBC calendar, the predictable way in which radio events unfolded through the year, also conveyed, according to Scannell and Cardiff (1991), a reassuring sense of the stability and continuity of national life.

Although the press addressed a fragmented audience, it encouraged a national 'we-feeling' through its shared news values. The allocation of space in the popular press assumed that readers were eight times more interested in home news than than in foreign news in 1947.[45] A national frame of reference also influenced what overseas news was reported (so that, for example, a major accident taking place abroad was more newsworthy if it involved British people). The national press during this period also encouraged its readers to feel a sense of pride in British success and also chagrin at national failure (especially in Test cricket and the Olympic games).

During the early 1960s, there was a reaction against this strong sense of national identity and belonging. Young people increasingly refused to stand to attention when the national anthem was played in cinemas at the end of the evening performance. The imperial romance was then largely over, not least because most of the empire had been dismantled by the 1960s (Mackenzie 1984). A nostalgic view of Britain as an unchanging Constable painting lost its appeal in an era celebrating newness and modernity. The communal conception of Britishness was also attacked as suffocating and conformist, not least in a succession of influential 1960s films.[46]

The weakening of national identity was reinforced by Britain's entry into the European Union (then, the European Economic Community, EEC) in 1973. This led to a cumulative strengthening of links with mainland Europe in terms of shared political sovereignty, cultural and sporting ties, and a realignment of trade. Some people began to think of themselves as 'Europeans'. However, European consciousness was only weakly supported by the development of the media. An attempt to launch a pan-European, public service satellite television service in 1985 ended in inglorious failure (Collins 1992). More generally, the European Commission's attempts to overcome the national fragmentation of Europe's television industry only succeeded in increasing American programme imports (Levy 1999). Very few programmes originated in continental Europe were viewed in Britain. Eventually, an embryonic Euro-media system developed in response to the rise of the European state, but by the late 1990s it reached only a tiny elite audience (Schlesinger 1999). It was offset by Britain's mass circulation press which became increasingly hostile to European institutions (Anderson and Weymouth 1999).

British nationalism was also challenged by resurgent Celtic nationalism. The Scottish and Welsh nationalist parties gained increased political support from the 1970s onwards. Their advance paved the way for the establishment of the Scottish Parliament and Welsh Assembly in 1999. This was preceded by an anticipatory reorientation of the Scottish media towards the new national parliamentary centre (Schlesinger 1998). A 'return' to a pre-1707 arrangement, in the context of the European Union, no longer seemed inconceivable.

British national identity was also eroded by increased globalization. The ability of the British state to generate employment, collect taxes from business and manage the economy declined as a consequence of the deregulation of the global economy and increased mobility of transnational business. Less able to protect the interests of its people, the British state commanded less allegiance. Globalization also loosened the link between the media system and the nation, although not as strongly as it is sometimes claimed. The British film industry fell into deep crisis from the early 1970s onwards. What little of it that survived outside the umbrella of public service broadcasting relied heavily on American finance, and tended to be international in orientation. The limit on the import of non-European programmes – previously fixed at a draconian 14 per cent of transmission time – was in effect raised to 35 per cent in 1993 in the case of ITV, and 40 per cent and 45 per cent in 1998 in the case of Channel 4 and 5 respectively, with much lower or no fixed limits for cable and satellite television channels.[47]

But if British national identity became weaker, it also became more inclusive. After a period of uncertainty and contention, there emerged in the 1980s and 1990s what might be called a new 'draft' national identity. It was based on a view of Britain which belatedly acknowledged a significant intake of immigrants and the effect of social change in creating a more diverse society. While this revised understanding was actively resisted by a section of the press, it received support from other parts of the media system. Afro-Caribbean and Asian British people became more visible in television and film fiction, and were presented in more positive and multifarious ways.[48] More generally, the rise of minority media – Channel 4, gay and lesbian cinema, Bollywood, feminist publishing, ethnic community radio, specialist magazines and independent music labels – both reflected, but also publicly affirmed, a more plural and hybrid definition of 'Britishness'.[49]

In short, Britain has gone through a number of transformations as an 'imagined community' during the last three centuries. Conceived in Protestant bigotry, it evolved to include people of other denominations and religions, as well as those of none. Defined initially by a sense of imperial and racial superiority, it came to include non-white British people – though still in contested way.

This narrative thus emphasizes the constructed and changing nature of British national identity. However, it should not be inferred from this that rival Celtic national identities were any more authentic, or that the nations they reified were any more 'natural' and 'organic' than Britain. In fact, Wales lacked a national government, and an agreed capital city, before it was absorbed into England during the Tudor period, and its uneven industrialization in the nineteenth century reinforced divisions that persist to this day. Scotland was divided between Gaelic-speaking highlanders and Scots-speaking lowlanders, when it merged with England and Wales. Ireland was multiply divided between its rulers in London and the Pale, its colonists concentrated in the north, and the remainder which, as revisionist historians now point out, was not one oppressed mass but riven and self-exploiting.[50]

As in Britain, ideological 'work' was needed to forge national unity out of diversity. Thus, the romantic Celtic revival of the late eighteenth century in Scotland spawned a number of myths: among them, the invention of the supposedly ancient Scottish poet, Ossian, and the reinvention of kilts and tartans as quintessential symbols of Scottishness. Tartans were originally a mark of status rather than of clan. Their transformation into carefully differentiated emblems of clan membership was largely the work of the late eighteenth-century British army, nineteenth-century textile manufacturers and the Sobieski Stuarts, two fantasists whose discovery of ancient tartans was as spurious as their claim to royal blood. The contemporary version of the kilt – as a shortish skirt separated from the plaid, with pleats already sewn in – was 'first designed, and first worn', by an English Quaker industrialist, Thomas Rawlinson in the eighteenth century (Trevor-Roper 1983: 22).

Hollywood was the great manufacturer of Celtic nationalist dreams in the twentieth century (Richards 1997b). Films like *Braveheart* (1995), *The Quiet Man* (1952), *How Green Was My Valley* (1941) and *The Informer* (1935) celebrated the natural warmth and spontaneity of the Scottish/Irish/Welsh people, often contrasted with the coldness and insincerity of the English and their allies. Some of these films also offered a mythic view of the past. For example, the Scottish freedom fighters in *Braveheart* wore 'woad a thousand years too late and clan tartans five hundred years too early' (Richards 1997b: 185). The elements that helped to bind Britain as a nation – Protestant conspiracy theory, imperial fantasy and arcadian make-believe – thus have a counterpart in the mythologies that defined Ireland, Wales and Scotland as 'nations'.

This account of media history unmasks the ideologies of nationalism. It has emerged at a time when the 'given' nature of nation states – as part of the unchanging, fixed order of things – has come to be questioned as a consequence of increased globalization. This has opened up a new avenue of enquiry and a new narrative of media history.

AFFIRMATIVE NARRATIVES

There is a clear affinity between the five narratives which have been considered. They are all about things getting better.

In liberal history, the winning of media freedom empowered the people. In populist history, the people demanded and obtained the media entertainment they wanted. In feminist history, the media responded to the increased liberation of women. In libertarian and anthropological accounts, the media came to promote greater social tolerance and to represent the nation in a more socially inclusive way.

It is tempting therefore to weave together all these narratives into a single meta-narrative of progress. In a sense, three distinguished media historians – Cardiff, Scannell and Richards – have initiated this process. Their work straddles a number of affirmative narratives, though not the same ones, and not in relation to the same media. It would be possible to continue where they have left off.

However, standing in the way of this inviting synthesis is a sixth narrative – radical media history. This tells a different story in which the development of the media introduced more darkness than light.

ELITE CONTROL: THE RADICAL NARRATIVE

Much the best known work, in this tradition, is Jurgen Habermas's account of the rise and fall of public reason (1989 [1962]). He argues that in the eighteenth century a public sphere of rational debate came into being. It was guided, at least in principle, by concern for the public good, and gave rise to a consensus which influenced government. This public sphere functioned primarily through face-to-face interaction in coffee-houses and salons, and through an independent press, which both staged reasoned debate and represented public opinion to government. But while this public sphere was ostensibly open to all, in practice it tended to be restricted to the privileged.

During the nineteenth and twentieth centuries, according to Habermas, this public sphere underwent a structural transformation. Instead of being constituted by private individuals gathered together as a public, it was largely taken over by organized private interests and an expanded state. The reason-based functioning of public life was corrupted in a process that he refers to as 'refeudalization'. Modern media fell under the sway of public relations, advertising and big business. Whereas the early press had facilitated participation in reasoned public debate, the new mass media encouraged consumer apathy, presented politics as a spectacle and provided pre-packaged, convenience thought. The media, in short, managed the public rather than expressed the public will.

This account thus tells a story of qualified advance – the creation of a reason-based 'public sphere' with a restricted membership – followed by a descent into manipulation and control. However, this widely cited radical narrative is not the only one on offer. An interesting alternative was advanced at about the same time by Raymond Williams (1965 [1961]). He argued that the rise of the mass media was inextricably linked to three revolutions: the democratic revolution which gave rise to popular self-government; the cultural revolution which extended literacy and education; and the industrial revolution which brought prosperity. Together these constituted a 'long revolution' of social advance in which new potentialities were realized by 'breaking through the processes of older forms of society' (Williams 1965: 375). While this advance was subject to periodic checks, it also registered 'spectacular' successes – a point which Williams was at pains to emphasize in opposition to 'mass society' pessimists (of which 'early' Habermas, cited above, was one).

Yet, this narrative was left tantalisingly vague. Williams later described with engaging candour his sense of 'approaching panic' as he realized that he was developing an argument for a 'general account of the whole social process' unfolding over centuries, which he felt unqualified, as a non-historian, to write. 'I . . . knew', confided Williams, 'that I could not do anything at all if I had to undertake anything beyond my own field' (Williams 1979: 152). So his brilliant, pioneering book, *The Long Revolution* (Williams 1965), took the form of linked essays, loosely bound together by a suggestive but undeveloped narrative framework.

Williams never developed this narrative more fully, partly perhaps because his thinking changed. He modified his earlier radical social democratic view of the last two centuries as a process of chequered improvement in favour of a much more pessimistic and explicitly Marxist perspective of a long-term defeat of popular forces (though with the implication that this could change).[51] While this revised perspective of the past was never presented as a formal history, it surfaced subsequently in historical fragments, most notably in his account of the incorporation of radical journalism by the commercial press (Williams 1970), his passing references to elite subversion of public service broadcasting (Williams 1966 and 1974), and his portrayal of a failed Labour movement leadership squandering the inheritence of the popular radical tradition (Williams 1984).

Stuart Hall's underrated historical writing can be viewed as continuing where the later, Marxist, Raymond Williams left off.[52] Hall asks why the introduction of mass democracy, with its promise of sharing and 'equalizing' political power, did not lead to a more equal society (Hall 1986c). After all, as he points out in different publications,[53] there were recurring manifestations of grassroots radicalism – from the moral economy of the eighteenth century crowd to the potentially 'ruptural' sub-cultures of the 1960s and 1970s – even if these did not take necessarily a conventional 'political' form. Why, then, did these not lead to a transformation of society? Part of his explanation lies in the shortcomings of the organized centre-left – the contradictions of social liberalism (Hall and Schwarz 1985), the limitations of corporatist social democracy (Hall *et al.* 1978) and the inadequate ideological leadership of 'Labourism' (Hall 1983 and 1984). But his main explanation for the 'containment of democracy' (Hall 1986c: 38) is the exercise of cultural power by leading groups in society. This led him to a sophisticated theorization of the ways in which dominant forces cohered, adapted, reconstituted themselves and sought to renew their authority in the face of challenges from below, in which he drew on the work of the Italian Marxist, Antonio Gramsci.[54]

The radical counter-narrative thus recalls an era of progress followed by an extended period when the forward march of the people was halted or reversed. It offers a thought-provoking alternative to the Whiggish drift of most media history, with its reassuring accounts of greater freedom, popular power and pleasure. However, this alternative view of the media's development is painted in gouache. Its mixture of watercolour paint and gum conveys the contours of something interesting, but nonetheless vague.

SPECIALIST SUPPORT

Some of this vagueness is brought into sharper focus by specialist historical and pioneer media sociological research, which offers an explanatory account of why 'free' media became subject to elite control.

One part of this explanation is that the free market was itself a system of control rather than an engine of freedom. Thus, James Curran argues that the shift from craft to industrial production of newspapers, the development of advertising dependence and the growth of oligopoly led to a systemic distortion of journalism.[55] This argument is presented in Chapter 3 and need not be repeated here. Peter Bailey (1978) advances a similar thesis in relation to the history of the music hall. In its radical phase during the first half of the nineteenth century, according to Bailey, the music hall was typically a small-scale venture, often little more than the singing saloon of a pub in which amateurs as well as professionals took part. However, the take-off of music halls as mass entertainment in the 1850s led to rising levels of capital outlay. Large, purpose-built music hall theatres were constructed; national chains were developed; and a high-salary, star system came into being. By 1900, the Moss Empires music hall syndicate had a capitalization approaching £2 million. The rise of theatrical capitalists, Bailey argues, led to the de-radicalization of music halls, in the context of an increasingly defensive working-class culture.

This argument in effect maintains that market failure led to the privileging of right-wing views because it gave rise to unrepresentative control of the media. Another related position, advanced by some radical historians, is that the market was constituted in a way that made it inherently opposed to radical change. Profit-seeking entrepreneurs were better adapted to the needs of the market than radical organizations seeking political objectives. They pursued sales-maximizing strategies that led to the partial incorporation, and cumulative attrition, of radical popular culture. Thus, it is argued that the template of modern popular journalism was first established in the 1840s and 1850s by popular Sunday newspapers which combined the moralistic entertainment tradition of gallowsheets and other street literature with the rhetoric, stripped of real substance, of the radical movement press.[56] In this way a superficially radical tone of voice rather than a dissenting world view was reproduced in a form that was designed to appeal to both radical and non-radical reader alike. A similarly deradicalizing synthesis was achieved, it is argued, in the development of mass sporting entertainment through the merging of a class-based, solidary tradition with money and star values (Williams 1970).

This second argument usually concludes with the claim that the market kept working people ignorant but amused. As Jean Chalaby puts it, the commercial press offered a mystifying 'magic-mirror' of society that entertained and diverted the popular classes, but denied 'them knowledge about the world and knowledge about their position in the world' (Chalaby 1998: 5). Similarly, Raymond Williams concludes that popular, commercial culture offered compensatory 'ways of adapting, from disadvantage, to a dominant social order, finding relief and satisfaction or diversion inside it' (Williams 1970: 25).

Some radical historians also argue that the media were tamed by the state before, during and after the introduction of mass democracy. The coercive approach of the eighteenth century, based on repressive laws and secret service subsidies to pro-government newspapers, gave way during the course of the nineteenth century to a more subtle approach. The lobby system (regular unattributed government briefings of accredited journalists) was established in 1855 as a way of cultivating friendly relations with the press by satisfying its commercial need for information. In addition, ties between government ministers and press controllers were strengthened through growing party and social connexions.[57]

However, the modern apparatus of public relations only came into being in the twentieth century. The Foreign Office led the way in 1919 by establishing the first peacetime government press office (Taylor 1981). In the 1930s, the government's publicity machine was restructured in a way that made the prime minister's office the fount of news management, and restricted journalists' access to other departments of state. Frequent, high-level contacts also took place between media controllers and the prime minister, Neville Chamberlain and his immediate coterie. According to Richard Cockett, a virtual alliance between the government and controllers of the press developed in support of a foreign policy of appeasing Hitler during the later 1930s. 'Newspaper policy', he concludes (1989: 64), 'was thus being directed by a small body of men at the top imposing their directions, taken from the Chamberlites' in a way that, by 1938, deviated both from the views of most journalists and also from public opinion. The BBC also largely excluded dissenting, Conservative critics of appeasement, while newsreels (apart from Paramount) were also strongly pro-appeasement (Pronay 1987).

The state's publicity machine grew rapidly in the subsequent period, particularly in the 1980s and 1990s.[58] This involved a huge expansion not only in the number of press officers, but also those concerned with polling, focus groups and advertising designed to promote effective state communication. Politicians also reskilled themselves from the 1950s onwards by learning the techniques of electronic communication (Cockerell 1988). News management was thus transformed from *ad hoc* patronage into a modern, technicized system employing large numbers of people with different skills.

Thus, this tradition argues that the market and government news management served as a dual system of control. However, this still leaves unanswered a number of troublesome questions. How does the market-as-control argument apply to public service broadcasting, whether in the form of the BBC or regulated commercial broadcasting like ITV? These organizations cannot be accused of depoliticizing the public through non-stop entertainment because they were required to offer significant amounts of news and current affairs programmes as a condition of their charter or licence. Nor can they be said to have been right-wing in the manner of the predominantly Conservative press because they were required by law to display due impartiality in relation to controversial issues. Similarly, the influence sometimes attributed to the refinement of public relations seems disproportionate. Even if news management became more sophisticated, surely the growth of professional consciousness among journalists encouraged some degree of autonomy from government propagandists?

These questions are implicitly addressed and answered by pioneer radical media sociology, to which we now turn. Its central argument is that the political elite's control over broadcast media was exercised at one remove, through their influence on the political organization and ideas of society. This elite included senior public officials and the leaderships of the major political parties. Their shared views and assumptions helped to frame, it is argued, broadcast coverage.

Thus, a celebrated study conducted in the 1970s argues that broadcasters' strategy for presenting themselves as neutral, and for coping with the pressures of time, was to use the formal debates conducted through the institutions of the state – parliament, government, judiciary, civil service and the political parties – as the principal framework for organizing broadcasting debate. 'For being impartial in terms broadly pre-defined by the state', writes Philip Schlesinger (1978: 178), 'it [the BBC] is rewarded with the gift of independence.'

This state-oriented framing of debate was policed within the BBC through retrospective reviews, the authority of the news editor, rewards and punishments (including, crucially, the allocation of work assignments), and more generally through the socialization of journalists into the norms of the corporation. 'The power of the state', Schlesinger concludes, 'to circumscribe the broadcast media's coverage of events, issues and points of view . . . has been handled not through overt censorship, but rather through a *mediated* intervention' in which the boundaries of the permissable were fixed 'preeminently through a tightening of editorial controls within the broadcasting organizations' (Schlesinger 1978: 205).

This institutional self-censorship resulted, according to Schlesinger (1978: 168), in television 'depreciation' of the 'new politics' of the 1960s and after – student protests, demonstrations, squatting, rent strikes, ethnic protests, unofficial strikes and factory occupations. It also led to the closure of debate around issues on which the political elite were agreed. For example, television in the 1970s did not debate whether British rule in Northern Ireland should continue since this was not a contentious issue in Westminster, unlike in Belfast and Dublin. Instead broadcasters followed, according to Schlesinger, the Westminster consensus in viewing the conflict in Northern Ireland as being primarily between the rule of law and terrorists. This conclusion was qualified in a subsequent, collaborative examination of a wider range of television programmes including drama, which conceded that there was 'some scope for certain kinds of dissent, much hedged about with restrictions and conditions' (Schlesinger, Murdock and Elliott 1983: 110). However, this second study's overall judgement was still that 'the state has largely succeeded in imposing its terms of reference' on television coverage of Northern Ireland (Schlesinger *et al.* 1983: 137).

A broadly comparable argument is marshalled by the Glasgow University Media Group (GUMG) (1980) in relation to television reporting of the economic management of Britain during the mid-1970s. Television's terms of reference were mainly derived from 'the views of the dominant political group' (GUMG 1980: 111), and took for granted that Britain's main economic problem was inflation, and its main solution was wage restraint. Alternative understandings were generally either excluded or expressed as subordinate elements within this dominant framework. In general, television coverage tacitly accepted the workings of the economic system and 'the assumptions of the powerful about what is important, necessary and possible within it' (GUMG 1980: 115).[59]

In short, the claim of liberal historians that broadcasting became independent of government is countered by the argument of radical media sociologists that broadcasting remained subject to a political elite dominating the state. What this tradition of media sociology seeks to do is to explain how influence in one sphere – the formal terrain of politics – was translated into influence in another sphere, broadcasting, without the exertion of direct controls.

A similar argument is to be found in other accounts of the past, which are concerned not only with politics but more broadly with the culture of society. Their claim is that dominant groups shaped the ideas that media workers absorbed involuntarily from their surroundings. This hegemonic influence is sometimes conceived as a dominant ideology (Mackenzie 1984); as a pervasive image of society (Higson 1997); as a loose network of discourses in which there were interlocking themes (Hall 1985). While these approaches can differ in quite significant ways, they are at one in arguing that the media were influenced by the dominant thought of the time.

This radical tradition thus argues that the media came broadly to support the social order as a consequence of controls exerted through the market, state and elite cultural power. The high-water mark of this tradition was the 1970s, when new left influence in universities was at its height and when it was claimed that a gap had opened up between the world of formal politics and the experiences and views of a significant number of people. This prompted an old question – when did the media become free of government? – to be reformulated as a new question: did the media become independent of the underlying structure of power? In the more conservative climate of the 1980s and 1990s, this second question increasingly ceased to be addressed.[60]

CRITICAL STOCK-TAKING

This chapter was conceived after seeing an engaging play, *Copenhagen*, which offered different accounts of the same history (Frayn 1998). But whereas this left unresolved which version of the past was 'correct', this review needs to go further.

We are presented with six different versions of media history. These subdivide into five affirmative accounts of things getting better and a sixth, pessimistic account of the people's advance being reversed or halted. These different narratives are summarized for convenience in Table 1.1.

One way of responding to these differences is to conclude, with a relativistic shrug, that each historical interpretation is a product of its time and 'discourse position', with the implication that each has an equal claim to validity. This is inadequate on two counts. It evades the critical issue of which narratives are best supported by evidence and logical inference. It also fails to consider how these different narratives might best be combined to offer a fuller and more complete account.

It is necessary, in other words, to critically evaluate each narrative in turn. The brief stock-taking that follows will concentrate – for the sake of brevity – on some of the weaknesses of each tradition rather than their strengths.

Liberal media history

The central theme of liberal history is that the media became free, and empowered the people. The principal challenge to this interpretation comes from radical history and sociology. To recapitulate, this argues that the media never

Table 1.1 Rival narratives of media history

	Liberal	Feminist	Populist
Context	Introduction of mass democracy	Advance of women	Rise of consumer market
Media narrative	Freedom from government	From gender control to contest	Defeat of cultural elite
Key moment	Lapse of print licensing (1695)	Suffragette triumph (1918)	1940s and 1950s
Outcome	Popular empowerment	Weakening of patriarchy	Consumer pleasure
	Libertarian	Anthropological	Radical
Context	Decline of religion	Forging of new nation	Containment of democracy
Media narrative	Battle between traditionalism and liberalism	Britain as imagined community	New system of media management
Key moment	1960s	Early 18th century	Second half of 19th century
Outcome	Greater freedom and tolerance	Greater social inclusion	Elite control

became truly free of the power structure of society and never functioned fully as an agency of popular empowerment. While this argument is not without defects, it mounts a sufficiently strong, evidence-based case to warrant a reassessment of the liberal interpretation of media history.

To this must be added the challenge of feminist history. This cuts across liberal history by subdividing the 'people' – supposedly championed by free media – into men and women. The former, feminist historians argue, were empowered by the media at the expense of the latter, although this was modified over time. Again, the evidence assembled by this alternative view calls for liberal media history to be rethought.

Yet, there is clearly also a kernel of truth in the liberal thesis. State coercion – in the form of the mutilation or execution of dissenting writers in the sixteenth century, and the licensing of newspapers in a climate of intolerance and legal coercion in the seventeenth century – represents a different order of control from that operating in the nineteenth and twentieth centuries highlighted in critical accounts. Even if liberal history is inclined to paint too rosy a picture of free media acting as the 'voice of the people', there were occasions when genuinely heroic journalists acted for society by exposing the abuse of power – from girl prostitution in the Victorian era to the imprisonment of innocent people, wrongly convicted of bombing, in Thatcher's Britain.

The way forward would seem to lie in some kind of recasting of liberal media history, rather than its abandonment. Yet, even effecting running repairs – still less the major work of reconstruction that is needed – is something that liberal historians seem disinclined to do. Their interpretation is the longest established and most widely accepted one in media history. Secure in their status as the guardians of the leading orthodoxy, they have tended to ignore or dismiss arguments originating outside their intellectual orbit.

This can be illustrated by countless examples. We will cite just one, picked because it is an especially illuminating essay written by one of the most distinguished liberal historians of broadcasting. Paddy Scannell (1992) argues that the development of radio and television extended people's 'communicative entitlements': by which he means the right to know, to understand, to speak, to hold to account, to listen and be heard. This claim is advanced with numerous telling examples, and with some circumspection. Yet, the body of critical media sociology that contradicts this thesis by arguing that broadcasting sustained elite power and influence gets short shrift. Only the work of Stuart Hall and his Birmingham colleagues is considered and then summarily dispatched as 'one-dimensional' (Scannell 1992: 339). All other critical accounts – including, incidentally, *all* the studies of 1970s television which were summarized in the radical narrative above – were ignored. This is typical of the way in which liberal media history routinely ignores or marginalizes evidence that challenges hallowed liberal themes.

Populist history

One central theme of populist history is that the media broke free from elite cultural control and offered people what they wanted. This theme is advanced through the mobilisation of two binary distinctions: paternalism *versus* respect, uplift *versus* pleasure. Framed in this way, this account seemingly carries all before it. Who could possibly be in favour of condescending worthiness, and not rejoice in its defeat?

However, a fundamental flaw of this approach is its refusal to make judgements of value other than those of the market. This gives rise to a double astigmatism: an unwillingness to contemplate the idea that some unpopular media had merit, and secondly a refusal to discriminate between the good and bad in popular media output. The limitations of this approach are illuminated by a now forgotten but extremely good book (Hall and Whannel 1964). While its authors adopt in general a positive view of mass media entertainment, they do not just cheer. They make critical assessments based, in the current jargon of literary studies, on multiple regimes of value. This results in a fine-grained and informative account.

A good way of illustrating this alternative approach is to summarize Hall and

Whannel's case for viewing *Z Cars* (a popular police television series started by the BBC in 1962, which continued into the 1970s) as a major advance in television drama. According to Hall and Whannel, it broke new ground by portraying the police from a critical distance (in marked contrast to other television series which uncritically celebrated the professionalism or fair-minded authority of the police). *Z Cars* also evoked a powerful sense of place and community, and featured a group of closely observed and well delineated characters who developed over time. It offered penetrating insights into the often casual nature of violence and its consequences. The series was also superior to most contemporary television drama in terms of its acting, editing and camera work.

An undoubted omission of this analysis is that it does not explicitly analyse why the series was popular. However, it offers an evaluation on the basis of multiple criteria – ideological ('critical'), aesthetic ('original'), moral (insight into violence), literary (evocation of place and character) and technical (quality of editing etc). It is this kind of carefully argued, textually supported examination that is the absent centre of most populist media history.

The second main theme of this tradition is that the popularization of the media promoted values of equality opposed to those of social hierarchy. Spearheading this change is supposedly the marketization of the media, and the rise of Hollywood which made available the cultural products of a 'more equal, open society' than Britain.

This general argument needs to be critically assessed in relation to the available evidence. In what way, for example, did the popularization of the press make it 'egalitarian'? Throughout the twentieth century, most national newspapers viewed inequality as a necessary and desirable feature of the market system, and argued that certain qualities – usually enterprise and hard work – needed to be rewarded if the economy was to prosper. Indeed, during the last quarter of the twentieth century, this theme was given increased prominence. Numerous editorials published, for example in the mid- and later 1980s, supported the view that increased rewards for the very rich generated additional wealth that 'trickled down', and were therefore in everyone's interest.

The explanation offered by LeMahieu as to why the press became more egalitarian in the inter-war period is that it gave more attention to the doings of ordinary people, was more responsive to what they wanted, and adopted a more intimate, familiar mode of address. The *Daily Mail* is examined at length as an exemplary illustration of this egalitarian trend (LeMahieu 1988: 27–43). However, LeMahieu omits to mention that the *Daily Mail* was throughout this period a racist, snobbish paper with political views so right-wing that it initially welcomed the rise of Hitler. Nazi anti-Semitism was even justified by the paper on the grounds that 'Israelites of international attachments were insinuating themselves into key positions' in Germany (*Daily Mail*, 10 July 1933). In this distorted view, what establishes a paper's egalitarian credentials is its use of language and interest in the lives of film stars and ordinary people – but not its explicit ideology.

The Hollywood film industry is a more complex case than the British press. Some Hollywood films were explicitly anti-egalitarian. In the inter-war era, for example, Hollywood produced films, such as *Gunga Din* (1939), which hymned the British empire and belittled Asian or black people. It also produced a still larger number of 'westerns' which justified the American holocaust – the near-extermination of native Americans. Yet, Hollywood also went through a radical-democratic phase in the late 1930s and early 1940s, and again in the late 1960s and early 1970s, followed in both cases by strongly conservative reactions. To this variability over time can be added the internal contradictions of some celebrated American films which contained both progresive and conservative elements. To condense this oscillation and complexity into a single generalisation is not easy, and perhaps not even sensible. But if one was to do so, McKibbin's verdict that American films 'made inequality acceptable by making it glamorous' (McKibbin 1998: 524), seems closer to the truth than the opposing claim mounted by populist history.

The populist thesis about equality and class culture, described earlier, is also over-simplified. It rightly argues that media commercialization, and the market values it fostered, weakened social stratification based on birth and ascribed status. But what it omits to mention is that the strengthening of market values also eroded working-class culture and the principal organizations in Britain committed to greater social equality – trade unions and ('old') Labour. Their decline facilitated the increase of economic inequality that occurred in the 1980s and 1990s.

The simplifications of populist history derive from its failure to distinguish between the politics of *recognition* and of *distribution*. Populist understanding of egalitarianism is essentially about recognition. It is about equality of esteem, as reflected in respect for mass audiences, 'ordinary' people and popular taste. It has little to do with other dimensions of equality: about the distribution of wealth, income, power, public spending, life opportunities or space. Why, then, does this populist history invoke the concept of egalitarianism so frequently, yet in such a limited and selective way? The answer is that many writers of populist history come out of a capitalist republican tradition which is opposed to the values of aristocracy, but not those of business and the market place. This tradition views the United States as a land of equality since it scores high in terms of the civic respect accorded to its citizens. The fact that the United States also has greater inequalities of wealth and income than any other major Western country is not thought to matter because this aspect of equality is not judged to be important. This also accounts for a puzzling feature of much populist media history (and also populist cultural studies): its lack of interest in the link between democratic social recognition and redistributive politics. Its focus tends to stay limited to 'recognition' because this defines, with exceptions, the extent of its much flaunted radicalism.

However, this tradition documents a significant shift in the media's content and orientation, and draws attention to the increased importance of the media as a source of entertainment and pleasure in a more leisured age. It also sheds light on the loss of influence of a 'cultural elite' rooted in the traditional professions. There are particles of gold in the populist narrative, waiting to be panned and filtered.

Affirmative histories

We will devote less space to assessing the remaining affirmative traditions since they are still in their infancy. The version of the feminist narrative reconstructed in this chapter derives largely from social rather than media history. Feminist media historians are in the slow lane of research. There are enormous gaps in the feminist narrative of the media, save for film and women's magazine history.

Feminist media history also tends to see gender as a separate category from class, rather than as something that is penetrated by class. This accounts for a significant absence in the feminist narrative – its failure to recognize the growing gap that developed between middle- and working-class women during the last twenty years, and to assess the part played by the media in this process.[61]

The anthropological narrative also has major gaps: for example, the role of television in the construction and reconstruction of Britain as an imagined community. This tradition tends also to leave out of focus the wider ideological contests in society over how different sectional interests were signified in relation to the 'national interest', and over who was included and excluded as British. Yet, how the media represented the nation was powerfully influenced by this wider battle for legitimacy and visibility.

In the case of the libertarian narrative, some writers documenting the deep roots, continuity and repressive nature of moral traditionalism, appear not to be aware that it was a tradition in steep decline. In general, this narrative is better at attacking traditionalism than understanding it and is also not fully alert to the problems that increasing individualism in turn has produced.

Yet, all three narratives represent important new developments in media history, which have greatly broadened our understanding. No account of media development can now be complete without them.

Radical media history

Radical media history calls for more detailed critical comment because, in its current form, it contradicts all five affirmative traditions. We will begin with a brief evaluation of Habermas's account of the rise and decline of the public sphere (Habermas 1989 [1962]), summarized earlier, since this has given rise to a small cottage industry of admiring exegesis.[62] The early part of Habermas's history is loved by liberals, while the latter part is relished by radicals. This is because Habermas offers an impeccably liberal history, with an unhappy ending derived from the Frankfurt school.

Habermas's account of the rise of the bourgeois public sphere moves uneasily between a normative analysis of what ought to have happened in principle and a descriptive account of what happened in reality.[63] The result is an equivocal idealization of the role of public reason in the eighteenth century. This gives little indication that public life was structured by the disposal of patronage and lubricated by social connexion. It provides still less inkling that the press contained numerous publications that deviated from Habermas's model of rational-critical exchange. Some London newspapers received secret subsidies in return for political favours; some scandal sheets demanded fees in return for the contradiction or suppression of scurrilous stories; and some local papers were small, marginal businesses fearful of powerful local interests.[64] The first problem with Habermas's account of the rise of the public sphere is thus that it pays too little attention to low politics, clientelist power relations and debased journalism.

The second problem has to do with Habermas's idealization of public reason. The point has been made forcibly that the discursive conventions of the public sphere marginalized women (Fraser 1992). The same was true of the working class in general. Habermas (1989: 168) writes in a self-revealing way that 'the same economic situation that pressured the masses into participating in the public sphere in the political realm denied them the level of education that would have enabled them to participate in the mode and on the level of the bourgeois readers of the journals' (Habermas 1989: 168). In fact, the masses did not fall below the 'mode' and 'level' of their bourgeois superiors but read, in the first half of the nineteenth century, papers which questioned with powerful intelligence the assumptions of bourgeois ideology.[65] What took place was not a battle between reason and sub-reason, but a growing working-class refusal to be put down by the exclusionary norms and self-serving premises of bourgeois, 'rational' debate.[66]

If Habermas's account of the public sphere's golden age is flawed, so too is his requiem for its demise. His portrayal of new electronic media as engines of indoctrination able to 'draw the eyes and ears of the public under their spell but . . . deprive it of the opportunity to say something and disagree' (Habermas 1989: 171) has been refuted by two generations of audience research,[67] and also fails to take account of the informative role of public service broadcasting. More generally, Habermas ignores or discounts the empowering consequences of the introduction of mass democracy, mass education, extensive state welfare, female liberation and the growth of prosperity.[68] What he views as a descent into a new feudal age is better understood as the 'people's century'.

Yet, Habermas's portrayal of the media as managers of opinion at the behest of the powerful contains an element of truth. This theme is in fact developed more fully in specialist research documenting the unobtrusive controls to which the media remained subject. However, this critical literature tends to overstate the effectiveness of these controls and to understate the significance of countervailing influences (not least the rise of organised labour). To this we shall return when we consider what form a new media history might take.

The radical perspective is powerfully supported and developed by pioneer media sociology. However, the main limitation of this work from an historical point of view is that it is sociology. Its conclusions become potentially misleading if they are viewed as generalizations that apply outside their specific setting. Take, for example, sociological research showing that television represented the conflict in Northern Ireland in the 1970s as a struggle between the forces of law and order and terrorism. This might seem to lend support to a fundamentalist view of public service broadcasting as an institution sustaining the *status quo*. However, the available historical evidence about media representations of Northern Ireland[69] documents change rather than continuity. In the 1940s, the BBC tacitly legitimated the Unionist ascendancy in Ulster. In the 1950s and the 1960s, the concerns of the minority community received more media attention. In the 1970s and 1980s, television adopted a law-and-order perspective of the 'troubles', though with increasing reluctance. By the late 1990s, television signified the conflict in Northern Ireland as a struggle between moderates and extremists in *both* communities. Thus, broadcasting shifted over fifty years from underwriting Unionist hegemony to tacitly supporting a power-sharing compromise. While many factors were involved in this change, the most important one was that the Catholic minority ceased to co-operate in its oppression.

The second problem raised by much pioneer media sociology is its simplistic view of parliamentary parties as institutions of the state upholding the social order.[70] This is only half right. Political parties straddle the state and civil society, and have been important agencies of change. For example, in the 1900s, 1980s and, in a more complex way, in the 1940s, a major political party broke with the prior political consensus, transformed the media into a real battleground, and won democratic support for modifying the social system.

More generally, there is a certain fuzziness in characterisations of the 'power structure' in many of the studies that make up the radical narrative. Different formulations – ruling class, elite/elites, dominant group/bloc/alliance, structure of privilege etc. – crop up as seemingly interchangeable synonyms. But in fact these terms do not denote the same thing. A key feature of radical analysis – its conception of the dominant power controlling the media – is in need of greater clarity.

In short, media history is vulnerable to criticism on several counts. Its account of refeudalization or containment is overdrawn, and sometimes vague. It understates the role of the media as an agency of change. Above all, and this perhaps lies at the heart of the radical narrative's weakness, it pays too little attention to the way in which underlying conflict gave rise to pressures for reform that at times gained a media hearing or even endorsement. Yet, if the radical narrative is vulnerable to criticism, it also offers a valuable corrective to the Panglossian drift of much media history.

NEW AGENDA

Where does all this leave us? It would seem that no one narrative is above criticism, yet each has something to offer. The obvious next step is to construct a new media history which judiciously weaves together all six narrative threads.

The first step in achieving this is to recognize the need to synthesize. The excessive over-specialization of British media history is underlined by the fact that it was not until 1981 that a general academic history of *British* media was first published, in the modest form of the opening two hundred-odd pages of a general media book (Curran and Seaton 1981). More than twenty years, and six editions, later it has been joined by only one other general British media history (Williams 1998). This second study broadly supports rather than challenges the conclusions of the first. Both histories also adopt the same strategy for reconciling conflicting interpretation. They argue that the press and broadcasting evolved differently, and had a different relationship to society, because they were organized differently. However, both books omit some of the narratives that have been identified here. They also adhere to the limiting convention of describing the development of each medium separately.

One way of constructing a new synthesis is to fold the history of the British media into a narrative of British society. The advantage of this approach over the more traditional institutional one is that it brings out more clearly the way in which the media shaped – and was shaped by – the development of modern society. What follows is an attempt to outline what this new media history might look like. It also provides an opportunity to recapitulate some key points of this chapter.

TOWARDS A NEW SYNTHESIS

The 'long eighteenth century' started in 1688 and ended in 1832.[71] During this period, Britain was dominated by a landed elite of aristocracy and gentry, which controlled parliament though its influence over a limited and corrupt franchise, exercised economic power as the principal landowners in a predominantly rural economy, and provided the leadership of the armed forces and Anglican church. Under its hegemony (aided rather than challenged by an imported royal family), Britain was increasingly integrated as one country around the unifying ideologies of Protestantism and later imperialism. From around the mid-eighteenth century onwards, there was also a determined attempt to reinforce patriarchal authority by promoting a cult of domestic feminity.

Initially, the emergent media system was integrated into this structure of elite male power. While the press ceased to be licensed in 1695, it was managed in other, evolving ways – through restrictive laws, patronage, rising press taxes, news management and ideological influence. The press, and the expanding culture of print, contributed to the unification of Britain, supported essentialist ideas

about gender, and played a significant part in renewing elite authority in the 1790s.

However, a shift became discernible in the second half of this period, broadly between 1760 and 1832. Britain became the leading trading power and the first country to industrialize. Economic growth multiplied the number of people, with significant economic and cultural resources, who were excluded from the formal political system. They developed spheres of opinion and organizations independent of aristocratic control, supported by new papers and periodicals which they owned or funded. Thus, while there were still Establishment newspapers, there also developed a formidable press opposed to the *ancien régime*.

The 'long nineteenth century' can be viewed as beginning in 1832 and ending in 1918. In 1832, the first Reform Act extended the franchise to the male middle class but still excluded women and the working class. This set in motion the formation of a new alliance of landed, industrial, financial and professional male elites in a protracted process of coalition-building which took a generation to complete, and which culminated in marginalizing working-class radicals. This new alliance was cemented through acceptance of a number of reforms, most notably the repeal of the Corn Laws (agricultural protection), gradual elimination of 'old corruption', and repeal of the 'taxes on knowledge' in 1853–61, which entrenched a capitalist press supportive of the social order but independent of government control.

This new elite coalition consolidated its position of ascendancy between the 1850s and 1918 by establishing a popular political base, extending the franchise and presiding over spectacular economic success, imperial expansion, and social reform. It was also the main driving force behind proselytizing attempts to promote moral and political 'enlightenment' (on its terms) through the churches, mass state education, public libraries, charities, voluntary associations and the family. This encouraged, among other things, more women to withdraw from the labour force and become economically dependent on their husbands. The rise of an imperialistic, patriarchal press and music hall helped to build support for this reconstituted social order.

However this renewal of elite male hegemony was incomplete and increasingly contested in later Victorian and Edwardian Britain. A national women's movement was established for the first time in the 1860s, and became increasingly influential. The rise of 'social liberalism' caused cracks to appear in the ruling elite coalition. The growth of Irish nationalism set Britain and Ireland on a collision course which ended in divorce in 1921. Growing numbers of unskilled and semi-skilled workers were recruited into general trade unions, creating a new critical mass of organized workers. While new social forces were initially under-represented by the media, the growth of a minority socialist and feminist press in the early twentieth century was a portent of things to come.

In 1918, women over the age of thirty and numerous, excluded males became eligible to vote for the first time, and transformed the Labour Party into a major political force. The subsequent growth of influence of organized labour, and the imperatives of fighting a 'total' war (1939–45), led to a reconstruction of the power structure. The old pattern of elite control was replaced by a liberal corporatist system, based on informal, 'tripartite' negotiations between representatives of big business, organized labour and the state which helped to define the prevailing political consensus. Between the 1940s and 1970s, this consensus included cradle-to-the-grave welfare, full employment policies and industrial co-operation in return for a share of increased prosperity.

The social forces that gave rise to this new regime also changed the media. The labour movement became a major publisher of newspapers until the 1960s. The political rise of the Labour Party legitimated left-of-centre ideas as being part of the national debate reproduced by broadcasting. Indeed, radio and television became very closely aligned to the liberal corporatist system of power between the 1940s and 1970s, and helped to sustain it during this period. This was a Janus-faced relationship: progressive in that it supported a modestly redistributive social system, but conservative in that it tended to exclude radical voices outside corporatist networks of influence.

The corporatist system was dismantled in the 1980s by the Conservative government headed by Margaret Thatcher, with cheerleading support from much of the press. Trade unions were emasculated by changes in labour law and public policies favouring the primacy of the market. The resulting shift in the balance of power was sealed by the perpetuation, in a modified form, of these policies by New Labour in the late 1990s. This post-corporatist regime lacked the deep foundations of its predecessor which, in its heyday, rested on two mass political parties anchored to stable class moorings and the 'incorporation' of both business and labour in the maintenance of a stable consensus. Instead, it relied on networking within the political-media complex, populist political initiatives and skilled presentation. Within this less grounded system of power, the media acquired a greater degree of autonomy and independent influence.

If the rise and decline of organized labour was one change shaping the twentieth-century media, another was the belated rise of women. Their advance was largely contained during the fifty-year period after 1918, partly because large numbers of women were socialized into acceptance of a 'two spheres' division of labour and influence. The media reinforced this division by tending to depict women in restricted social roles, and representing gender difference in traditionalist ways.

However, structural changes in the economy after 1970 greatly increased the job opportunities and economic independence of women. The cultural changes this set in motion were strengthened by the revival of feminism and a sustained assault on essentialist ideas about gender. Many women still did not have the same advantages as men, and the gap between rich and poor women widened. Yet, an historic shift occurred in the relations between men and women that began to roll back centuries of gender inequality and social conditioning. The media workforce also became more feminized, and media representations of women became more varied. In effect, the media evolved from being an agency of patriarchy to becoming an arena in which different understandings of gender were contested.

The third key change influencing the media was the rise and decline of the professional class. The creation of the BBC in the 1920s was a monument to the prestige of public bureaucracy, and the idea that the public interest was best secured by disinterested professionals 'serving the nation'. This public interest came to be defined as making a national radio service available to all, providing access to quality programmes and informing the electorate.

During the middle decades of the twentieth century, a new deal was struck between professional and market values. Commercial television was introduced in a regulated form, and forced BBC television to adapt. It inaugurated what the government claimed at the time to be the best of both worlds: market pressures that curtailed unreponsive paternalism, but also a continuing commitment to public interest objectives. This experiment helped to produce in the 1960s the golden age of British television: an explosion of creative talent, innovation and distinguished popular as well as minority programmes.

Underpinning this advance was the increased autonomy allowed to television producers (especially in drama and entertainment). The BBC responded to competition by giving its staff greater freedom, while the television regulatory authority (with increased powers) shielded commercial television producers from the tyranny of market ratings. In the 1960s, Fleet Street journalists also gained in general greater autonomy, and this led to the significant improvement of some papers.

However, during the 1980s and 1990s, the authority of the professions diminished as a consequence of repeated attacks on their competence and disinterestedness. It was also eroded by the expansion of the market and exaltation of market values. The BBC became a more centralized institution, following its market-inspired managerial reorganization under John Birt (1992–2000). Producers in commercial television became more constrained by market pressures, as a consequence of the weakening of the regulatory authority, a new policy of selling franchises and television company mergers. Programmes became in general more formulaic and commercial television news and current affairs programmes were shunted increasingly to the margins of prime time. The autonomy of national print journalists also declined as a consequence of increased centralization and casualization. This led to a decline in editorial standards and a further drop of public trust in the press.

The erosion of professional power, and of the public purpose it embodied, had positive features. It created more space for entertainment in the press, radio, television and public libraries. It also deflated the initial class condescension of the BBC. But the decline of professional power also had negative aspects as well: less creativity, falling editorial standards, diminished public information. A productive tension was institutionalized during the middle of the twentieth century between market and professional values. The triumph of one at the expense of the other towards the end of the century led to a decline in the quality of the British media.

The fourth key change shaping the media was that Britain became a more pluralistic society. The erosion of the Victorian moral consensus, the growth of individualism, the decline of class as a source of social identity, the proliferation of sub-cultures, the revival of Celtic nationalism and an increased intake of immigrants from different cultures were just some of the developments that made Britain less homogeneous.

The media ultimately responded to this increased diversity. In 1900, British people were offered from numerous sources a unifying imperial identity which had racist overtones and encouraged submission to class authority. Those at the bottom of the social structure were encouraged to derive self-esteem from being 'masters of human kind', and to view the national project of which they were a part as well led and successful. By the 1940s, the media increasingly offered an insular, communitarian, pastoral image of Britain. As represented by 1940s propaganda films, this could signify conciliation between the major classes in a way that tacitly acknowledged the power of each (albeit in an unequal way). By the 1960s, imperial and pastoral conceptions of Britishness were increasingly repudiated, leaving the way open to a new understanding. Rival versions were proposed, debated and contested. The one which proved to be the most dynamic, and which ultimately won increasing media support, was a multi-ethnic, multi-cultural, plural version of Britishness. This was more inclusive, and less tied to established authority, than the conception of 'land of hope and glory' which had held sway in the early part of the century.

Another way in which the pluralization of society was manifested was through a growing conflict between traditionalists and liberals over the terms of the moral order. In this battle, the liberals gained the upper hand. Moral censorship of the media declined, and media representations of sexual minorities, and some other 'out' groups, became in general less hostile. However, the same changes that gave rise to greater social tolerance also produced a more privatized and more individual-centred society.

This synthesis thus differs from conventional accounts. Instead of telling a story of things getting better or worse, it offers a more contingent view of ebb and flow, opening and closure, advances in some areas and reverses in others. The contextualization of media history dissolves linear narratives – whether of progress or regress.[72]

EPILOGUE: SEVENTH NARRATIVE

This review has left to the end the one narrative routinely cited in media textbooks – technological determinist accounts of the media's transformative influence. These accounts are flawed and do not fit readily within a national historical framework. Yet, no survey would be adequate without, at least, summarizing this technological determinist tradition. Its sprawling literature can be condensed to four central arguments.

First, each new means of communication influenced the organization of society by altering dimensions of space and time.[73] Thus, according to Innis (1951), communication in the form of hieroglyphics carved in stone fostered the development of static, geographically confined societies because stone carvings were difficult to revise and transport. However, the invention of papyrus (an early forerunner of paper) encouraged the development of far-flung empires, because papyrus provided a light, transportable and flexible means of communication between the centre and periphery. The subsequent development of the printing press extended control over time, and encouraged a sustained cultural advance by providing a cheap, efficient way of preserving and distributing knowledge from the past (Eisenstein 1979). But its potential for spanning space was limited by the entrenchment of national vernacular languages. Consequently, the development of print encouraged the circulation of communications primarily within national frontiers, and fostered nationalism rather than internationalism (Anderson 1983). However, the rise of new forms of communication – in particular, the telegraph and telephone, satellite television and the internet – increased the availability of communications through *both* time and space. Messages could be received almost simultaneously around the world. The consequences of this are viewed in different ways, from the upbeat view that it increased understanding within the 'global village' (McLuhan 1967) to the cautious claim that it led to 'new kinds of interconnectedness and indeterminacy', including a greater sense of responsibility for distant people and events (Thompson 1995: 118).

Second, it is argued that new means of communication changed the nature of human senses and perception. According to McLuhan (1962 and 1967), oral communication promoted an interdependent, face-to-face culture in which visual, aural and tactile senses were all engaged. The introduction of the printing press made sight the dominant sense, and promoted an individualistic, introspective, rational pattern of thought through the isolated, linear process of absorbing meaning through reading (cf. Ong 1982). This was then reversed by the rise of electronic media which reintegrated the senses, and fostered a more inclusive, associative, 'retribalized' culture. In a similarly mystical vein, Baudrillard argues that the rise of electronic media saturated society with mediated images of the world. The virtual merged with the real, to produce what he calls 'hyperreality' (Baudrillard 1980 and 1983).

Third, the evolution of the media is said to have altered the structure of interpersonal relations. The best-known exponent of this position is Joshua Meyrowitz (1985) who argues that print reinforced the separateness of the social spheres occupied by men and women, adults and children, leaders and led, because each group tended to read different publications. By contrast, electronic media lowered social barriers between these groups because they tended to watch the same things (especially during the era of limited channel, free-to-air television). Television demystified men and women for each other, eroding the belief that they were fundamentally different. Public figures were rendered more knowable and accessible, less distant and shrouded in august mystery, because television put them on show and redrew boundaries between public and private life. Similarly, children were introduced through television to a grown-up world in a way that diminished adult authority. More generally, television weakened the link between socialization and physical location, creating opportunities for new forms of social interaction between different groups of people and encouraging, as a consequence, new forms of social identification. This last argument has since been advanced in relation to the internet (Turkle 1995).

The fourth contention of this tradition is that new media disturbed established flows of communication and influence. They 'disintermediated' agencies of authority, and provided a new source of potentially empowering or subversive information. Thus the printing press is said to have diffused knowledge and power to the people (McLuhan 1962). Similarly, cable television is causing 'representative government of de facto elites' to be replaced by 'government of direct participation' (Meyrowitz 1985: 323). The internet is also allegedly inaugurating a new era of 'netizen' cyberdemocracy because it is facilitating 'many-to-many' communication through channels that transcend structures of geo-political power and control.[74]

These sweeping generalizations often beguile by presenting simple ideas in elliptical prose that conveys the impression of profundity. Indeed in the view of some university lecturers, the technological determinist tradition 'takes care' of media history. All that needs to be known about the evolution of the media and their place in human history is contained, it is assumed, in the speculative commentary of writers like Marshal McLuhan. The history of mass communication can be conveniently ticked off without the need to read a single, serious work of history.

Why this tradition should be invested with such intellectual authority is difficult to understand. It has a number of weaknesses, the most important of which is its tendency to overstate the determining influence of communications by discounting other influences. This either takes the form of simplistic mono-causal explanations or, more often, mono-track interpretations which monitor only the effects of communications technology. This latter approach often acknowledges formally that a number of other factors contributed to the change under review. It then tacitly inflates the significance of communications technology by failing to identify these other factors and assess their relative importance.

This tradition also tends to view communications technology as an autonomous cause of change. However, the invention, development and application of new communications technology are usually influenced by the wider context of society, and are not simply the product of some inner technological logic. For example, metal moveable type was invented almost simultaneously in different parts of Europe in the fifteenth century because the development of a market for books, the prior organization of a book trade and advances in the manufacture of paper all made the modern printing press an invention waiting to happen (Febvre and Martin 1976). By contrast the wider environment was less receptive for a variety of reasons to the development of television. It was conceived and patented in the nineteenth century, but not operationalized and diffused until significantly later (Winston 1998).

Yet even though the technological determinist tradition is vulnerable to criticism, it also offers occasional shafts of insight. Take for example its claim that new media disturb established patterns of communication and power. This theme is now being taken up enthusiastically by sociologists. Thus, Manuel Castells maintains that the internet, and also telecommunications and videos, enabled the Zapatistas, rebels from the southern Mexican state of Chiapas, to win national and international support. By being 'the first informational guerilla movement', the Zapatistas were transformed from militarily weak insurgents into a potent, globally backed force with whom the Mexican government had to negotiate (Castells 1997: 79).[75] Similarly, McNair (2000) and Sparks (2000), among others, argue that communist regimes in the Soviet Union and eastern Europe were weakened in the 1980s partly because some of their citizens gained access to alternative ideas and sources of information through satellite and 'overspill' terrestial broadcasting from the West. Likewise, Anabelle Sreberny (2000) argues that patriarchal authority in the Islamic Middle East, and indirectly its political regimes which are inextricably bound up with male power, are now being challenged by Hollywood feminism, transmitted through film videos and satellite television.

All these studies argue, in effect, that new channels of communication subvert structures of authority sustained by censorship. It is an interesting – and suspiciously reassuring – idea that needs to be explored further. This is attempted in the next chapter though a review of over a thousand years of communications history.

Chapter 2

New media and power

Mass communications are generally discussed as if they were exclusively modern phenomena.[1] Indeed, this assumption is embodied in most social scientific definitions of the mass media. According to McQuail (1969: 2), for instance, 'mass communications comprise the institutions and techniques by which specialized groups employ technological devices (press, radio, films, etc.) to disseminate symbolic content to large, heterogeneous, and widely dispersed audiences'. Only modern technology, it is widely assumed, has made possible the transmission of communications to mass audiences; for, as Maisel (1973: 160) among others would have us believe, 'in the pre-industrial period, the communication system was restricted to direct face-to-face communication between individuals'.

In fact, a variety of signifying forms apart from face-to-face interaction – buildings, pictures, statues, coins, banners, stained glass, songs, medallions, rituals of all kinds – were deployed in pre-industrial societies to express sometimes highly complex ideas. At times, these signifying forms reached vast audiences. For instance, the proportion of the adult population in Europe regularly attending mass during the central Middle Ages was almost certainly higher than the proportion of adults in Europe now regularly reading a newspaper.[2] Since the rituals of religious worship were laid down in set liturgies, the papal curia exercised a much more centralized control over the symbolic content mediated through public worship in the central Middle Ages than even the controllers of the highly concentrated and monopolistic press of contemporary Europe.

Centralized control over mass communications is thus scarcely new. An historical comparison with older communication forms – including communications reaching small elites as well as mass audiences – serves, moreover, to throw into sharp relief certain aspects of the impact of communication media that the 'effects' research tradition, relying upon survey and experimental laboratory research techniques, has tended to ignore. In particular, this chapter will examine how the emergence of new channels of communication influenced the power structure of society. It will argue that new media gave rise to new centres of power, which increased tensions within the prevailing structure of authority. It will also argue that new media *sometimes* undermined the hierarchical control of social knowledge by bypassing established mediating agencies and distributing

prohibited or restricted information. At other times, new media were incorporated within the system of power, and their potential for disturbing established
flows of influence was contained.

   This survey will concentrate mainly on the central Middle Ages, early modern
Europe and modern Britain. It will take the form of a schematic analysis in which
we will move backwards and forwards in time in order to elucidate particular
aspects of the impact of the media.[3] Inevitably a survey covering so broad a canvas
will be highly selective and, in places, conjectural. But hopefully it will serve as a
mild antidote to the 'effects' approach, in which the media are tacitly portrayed as
autonomous organizations transmitting messages to aggregates of individuals
with laboriously measured and often inconclusive results.

RISE OF NEW POWER CENTRES

The rise of papal government is one of the most striking and extraordinary features of the Middle Ages. How did the see of Rome, which even in the early
fourth century was merely a local bishopric with no special claim to legal or
constitutional pre-eminence, become the undisputed sovereign head of the western Christian church? Still more remarkable, how did a local church with no large
private army of its own and initially no great material wealth and which for long
periods was controlled by minor Italian aristocrats develop into the most powerful feudal court in Europe, receiving oaths of allegiance from princes and kings,
exacting taxes and interfering in affairs of state throughout Christendom and
even initiating a series of imperialist invasions that changed the face of the Middle
East?

   The see of Rome had, of course, certain initial advantages which provided the
basis of its early influence. It was sited in the capital of the old Roman empire; it
was accorded a special status by the emperors in Constantinople who were anxious to unite their Christian subjects in the west; and it was the only church in
western Europe which was thought to have been founded by St Peter.

   The papacy capitalized on this initial legacy by spearheading the missionary
expansion of the church and by skilfully exploiting the divisions within the deeply
fissured power structure of medieval Europe to its own advantage. Successive
popes played off rival monarchies against each other, exploited the tensions and
conflicts between monarchies and feudatories and even, on rare occasions, backed
popular resistance to aristocratic repression. The papacy also utilized the desire of
some leading ecclesiastics to increase their independence from lay control, as well
as the tensions and rivalries within the church itself, notably between the episcopacy and the monastic orders. The rise of papal government, as a number of
scholars (for example, Brooke 1964; Southern 1970; Richards 1979) have convincingly shown, was thus partly the result of the dexterity with which the papacy
harnessed the interests and influence of competing power groups to build up its
own power. But neither the papacy's imperial and apostolic legacy nor its policy of

divide and rule adequately accounts for the transformation of a local bishop into a papal emperor. In particular, they do not explain why (as opposed to how) the papacy should have profited so greatly from its interventions in the power politics of medieval Europe, nor do they adequately explain why the papacy managed quite rapidly to expand its power over the church far beyond the authority accorded to it by the Roman emperors. The rise of the papacy can only be properly understood in terms of its early dominance over institutional processes of ideological production that created and maintained support for its exercise of power. As St Bernard of Clairvaux wrote perceptively to the pope in 1150: 'Your power is not in possessions, but in the hearts of men' (cited in Morris 1972: 14).

The expansion of the Christian church in early modern Europe provided the institutional basis of papal hegemony. It created a new communications network capable of transmitting a common ideology throughout western Europe. Rome could not exploit this network, however, until it had asserted its authority over the western Church.[4] During the fourth century, the papacy upgraded the status accorded to it by the emperors in the east by claiming leadership of the church on the basis of scriptural authority. Its claim rested upon a passage in St Matthew's gospel in which Jesus hails St Peter as 'this rock (upon) which I will build my church . . . '. As a title-deed, it left much to be desired, not least because it made no reference to the see of Rome. The omission was made good, however, by the production of a spurious letter, the *Epistola Clementis*, whose author was stated to be Clement, the first historic bishop of Rome, informing St James of the last dispositions of St Peter which designated the bishops of Rome as his successors. This was followed by additional forgeries of which the most influential was the *Donation of Constantine*, which purported to document how the Emperor Constantine had formally handed over large, but mostly unspecified, provinces in the western hemisphere to Pope Silvester; and a collection of canon law called *Pseudo-Isidore*, which included fraudulent canons of the early Christian councils and equally spurious decrees of early bishops of Rome, representing the pope as the primate of the early Christian church. Distinguished early popes added to this myth-making by proclaiming as fact obviously false stories about the development of the early Christian church.[5] The papacy and its allies thus set about reinterpreting history – a practice common to all great ideologies, although in this case conducted with unusual thoroughness by the actual fabrication of historical sources.

The ideological strength of the papacy was based, however, not so much on a single biblical text (important though this was), or on a selective view of history, but on what Kantorowicz (1957) calls 'the monopolization of the Bible' – the selective interpretation of the Bible in a way that constituted a compelling way of viewing the world. Papal and ecclesiastical propaganda provided a teleological view of existence in which all actions of Christians were directed towards the attainment of salvation. According to this perspective, the pope as the supreme ruler of the church had the duty to direct all men towards the goal of salvation by means of a divinely authorized system of law. And since every aspect of human life was encompassed within the corporate and indivisible body of the Christian church, the pope as head of the church had a universal sovereignty. There was, according to papal ideology, no inherent right to power or property, because these derived from the grace of God and could be revoked or suspended by God's appointed agents. In short, the papacy constructed an ideological system based on two central premises: (a) that all power derived from God; and (b) that the church was indivisible. These premises provided the foundation for an elaborate superstructure of thought that expanded the bishop of Rome's claim to headship of the church into a divine-right, absolutist authority over humankind (Ullmann 1970).

The hierocratic themes of the papacy were mediated within the church through the established hierarchical channels of communication. The papal curia had the largest collection of records and archives and the most sophisticated team of scholars and polemicists in the western hemisphere during the early and central Middle Ages. It reiterated with relentless insistence the central tenets of papal propaganda in correspondence, official pronouncements and legal judgements.

To some extent the mediation of papal themes within the institution of the church also occurred independently of curial supervision. Ullmann (1969) shows, for instance, that the Frankish episcopacy during the Carolingian period stressed the sovereignty of the papacy, and the assumptions that underlay it, in an attempt to establish their autonomy from royal and feudal control. There was thus a natural affinity of interest between the papacy, in remote Italy, and the ecclesiastical hierarchy in other parts of Christendom that resulted in a partly unco-ordinated assertion of the sovereignty of the papacy and the primacy of the clergy in an impersonal ecclesiastical order. This facilitated, in turn, the extension of papal control over the Christian church in the west. Through increased influence over senior ecclesiastical appointments, insistence upon regular visits to Rome by bishops and the extension of direct papal control over the monastic order, the papacy was able to exercise increasingly centralized power over the Catholic church and to harness its resources to the advancement of its power and authority within western Europe.

The Catholic church translated the sophisticated, hierocratic ideology of the papacy into graphic and readily comprehensible forms in an age when the overwhelming majority of the population – including the nobility – were illiterate. Such has been the preoccupation of medievalists with literary sources, however, that too little attention has been given to the role of non-verbal communication, and in particular to religious magic, in shaping the outlooks and perspectives of the mass population in the Middle Ages.[6] Yet the whole paraphernalia of ecclesiastical sorcery and ritual was of crucial importance in mediating an ecclesiastical construction of reality that underpinned papal hegemony.

The medieval church acted as a repository of magical power which it dispensed to the faithful to help them cope with a wide range of daily activities and secular problems. In this way, it symbolically affirmed the indivisibility of the church, while at the same time asserting the magical potency of God and the special role of the church as the mediator of divine power. Thus the rites of passage (baptism, confirmation, marriage, purification after childbirth, extreme unction and burial) administered by the church invested with religious significance each stage of the life cycle, thereby affirming that every aspect of human existence fell within the compass of the church. Their impact was reinforced by the cluster of superstitions that developed around each rite. Baptism, for instance, did not merely signify the absolution of original sin: many believed that it was essential if the child was not to be condemned to an eternal limbo or, as some churchmen insisted, to the tortures of hell and damnation, if it died before baptism. Similarly, the church both sanctioned and fostered the medieval cult of the saints: the superstitious belief in miracle-working spirits whose aid could be enlisted through pilgrimages to their shrines, through acts of propitiation before their images or by simple invocation. While clergy were mere paramedics in sacred magic, the saints were prestigious specialists whose help could be invoked in situations requiring special skills. St Agatha, for instance, was popularly thought to be best for sore breasts, St Margaret for reducing the pangs of labour and so on. The church also administered a battery of rituals, normally entailing the presence of a priest, holy water and the use of the appropriate incantations, as stipulated in medieval liturgical books, for blessing homes, purifying wells, preventing kilns from breaking, rendering tools safe and efficient, making women or cattle fertile, ensuring a good harvest or a safe journey. Indeed, there were few secular activities for which the church did not issue a form of liturgical insurance policy and few secular problems for which the church did not offer a magical specific.

Religious charms, talismans and amulets were worn as prophylactic agents against bad luck. Such devices were the essential props of medieval superstition, symbolically expressing the potency of religious magic mediated by the church. The church also daily displayed an impressive feat of magic in transubstantiating inanimate objects through the sacrament of the eucharist. Magical power was invoked in relation to the afterlife, not least in the form of indulgences which shortened people's stay in purgatory. In addition to this powerful arsenal of sacred magic, the church expressed, through religious architecture and art, basic tenets of papal ideology (Panovsky 1951; Evans 1948). The construction of churches towering above their pastoral flock symbolized the looming presence of God over all aspects of life. Sculpture, paintings and glass windows that depicted the divinity of Christ and the macabre tortures of hell served a similar purpose: they were a reminder of God's omnipotence in both the earthly world and the afterlife. As Pope Gregory I commented, the illiterate 'could at least read by looking at the walls what they cannot read in books' (cited in Innis 1950: 124).

The bizarre superstitions that encumbered popular medieval devotion were not all imposed from above. In part they derived from participation by a superstitious laity. However they had their origin in the sacred magic proclaimed and administered by the medieval church and were tolerated by the often sophisticated incumbents of the papacy as the expression of simple piety binding God and his children closer together (Thomas 1973). They served the wider purpose of maintaining the ecclesiological conception of the universe that legitimized papal imperialism.

Indeed, the conscious ideological 'work' that sometimes went into the elaboration of religious ritual is clearly revealed, for instance, by successive modifications made in the liturgical orders of the coronation of the Holy Roman Emperors in the west, a ritual of central importance since it was intended to remove the papacy still further from the authority of the emperors in the east by establishing a western emperor. Scrupulous care was taken to ensure that the ritual investment of the western emperor clearly designated his subordinate status to the pope. Following the coronation of the first western emperor, Charlemagne, the papacy introduced a new rite, the anointing of the emperor with holy oil, in order to symbolize the central theme of papal propaganda that imperial power 'descended' from God through the mediation of the papacy. At the next coronation (AD 823) yet another new feature was introduced – the giving of a sword to the emperor by the pope – to stress that the role of the emperor was to defend and protect the pope and carry out, through physical force if necessary, his will as a *filius-defensor*. And finally, to avoid any possible ambiguity and misunderstanding (such as the notion that the emperor was consecrated an autonomous priest-ruler), coronation ceremonies by the eleventh century utilized a liturgically inferior grade of oil, which was used to anoint the emperor, not on the head as before, but on his right arm and between his shoulder-blades. These and other innovations, involving the introduction of new symbols, gestures and prayer-texts, were graphic ways of expressing to an illiterate nobility through one ritual the complex theoretical ideas of papal hierocracy (Ullmann 1970).

In addition to non-verbal techniques of communication, the ecclesiastical authorities actively proselytized their congregation through conventional methods. Priests reached in aggregate a mass audience through sermons delivered in vernacular languages; the legatine system reached all corners of Europe, and papal legates addressed large crowds during their tours. The law administered through the ecclesiastical courts both embodied and mediated papal hierocratic themes. And from the thirteenth century onwards, the growing number of travelling friars, who often combined their evangelical role with reporting 'the news' to curious listeners, became an effective propaganda arm of the papacy.

The ecclesiastical hierarchy also decisively shaped elite culture in ways that supported the exercise of papal authority. Monasteries dominated book production until the development of university scriptoria from the thirteenth century onwards. As a result, texts supporting or expounding papal ideology were generally copied at the expense of texts that explicitly or implicitly challenged an ecclesiastical view of the universe. The clerical and monastic orders also dominated the transmission of knowledge through formal education during the early and central Middle Ages. Until the eleventh century, education was confined largely to the clergy and its content was decisively shaped by the ecclesiastical hierarchy from at least the ninth century (Laistner 1957; Leff 1958). It was only in the twelfth century that there was a substantial increase in lay education and lay centres of learning, and even many of these centres came under direct or indirect ecclesiastical supervision (Cobban 1969).

The nature of this cultural domination is illustrated by the steps taken to contain the threat posed by Aristotle. His teaching challenged the dominant perspective of a single political-religious society, an indivisible church that underpinned papal hegemony. Perhaps for this reason, the principal works of Aristotle were allowed to 'disappear' during the early Middle Ages. When they were rediscovered, their study was banned at Paris University until such time as they had been 'purified'. And when William of Moerbeke finally translated Aristotle from Greek into Latin in the thirteenth century, he was obliged to use words like *politicus* (political) and *politia* (government) with which most of his colleagues were unfamiliar. Even to make a distinction between religious and political matters, between church and state, a distinction that directly challenged a key premise of papal ideology, required the learning of new terms. The principal medium of communication between the cultured elite, the universal language of Christendom, was thus itself shaped and defined by the precepts of papal ideology (Ullmann 1975).

It was thus not simply the power of religious faith that sustained papal authority. The success of the ecclesiastical hierarchy in shaping the dominant culture led, for a long time, to the general (but not total) exclusion of ideas and concepts that might undermine papal ascendancy. Scholars were induced to perceive and, therefore, to 'experience' reality in a way that sustained papal rule regardless of whether they were or were not pious members of the church.

The papacy's cultural domination, even during the meridian of its power in the central Middle Ages, was admittedly far from complete. There is ample evidence of a lay culture expressing 'secular' values in song, dance, story-telling and poetry, existing independently of, but overlapping with, a more church-centred religious culture (Southern 1959). The secular organization of medieval society also often functioned on very different principles from those of the ecclesiastical order projected in papal propaganda (Bloch 1961). And the papacy's direct control over the principal agency of mass communication, the church, was even at the height of its power far from absolute in practice.

But although the papacy's hegemony was never total, its dual domination over the institutions of mental production and mass communication was nevertheless sufficient to enable it to gain increased authority and power at the expense of adversaries with apparently infinitely greater resources at their disposal. This process of aggrandisement can be briefly illustrated by perhaps the best-known confrontation of the Middle Ages. In 1075, Pope Gregory VII brought to a head the papal assault on lay control over ecclesiastical appointments by banning lay investiture (the ritual symbolizing lay conferment of ecclesiastical offices). This was followed by public pronouncements, sermons and pamphlets in a sustained propaganda war. The German monarch, Henry IV, found to his cost that this ideological assault was highly effective, because it drew upon a consensus of opinion that had been built up over the centuries through constant reiteration of ecclesiastical propaganda. When he was excommunicated, temporarily deposed and the oaths of allegiance made to him by his vassals suspended by the pope, his position became increasingly perilous. His itinerant court did not possess the historical records that would have been needed to challenge effectively the papacy's claim to sovereignty over the church, and he had no access to an alternative, literate tradition of thought that would have legitimized his authority as ruler independent of the church. He was king by the grace of God, and this grace had been withdrawn by God's supreme agent. His vassals began to defect with, as Brooke (1964) put it, 'the gates of hell clanging about their ears', though in some cases defections were clearly caused by more opportunistic motives. At the Diet of Tribur, the German princes formally declared that Henry IV would forfeit his throne unless he secured absolution from the pope. The most powerful ruler in the west, who had merely sought to maintain the practice of lay investiture sanctioned by custom for centuries, was forced to go to Italy as a penitent to seek the pope's absolution. Although the papal cause subsequently suffered a number of reverses, the German monarchy finally abandoned lay investiture of the clergy after the Concordat of Worms in 1122 (Davies 1957; Brooke 1964; Ullmann 1970 and 1977).

In short, the rise of papal government in the early and central Middle Ages was based ultimately on the papacy's successful manipulation of elite and mass media to transmit not merely its claims to church leadership but an ideological perspective of the world that legitimized its domination of Christendom. It was only when the papacy's domination of the elite centres of knowledge and mass communications was successfully challenged in the later Middle Ages that the papacy's ideological ascendancy was broken.[7] With the loss of its ideological control, the papacy's power declined. The issuing of excommunications which had brought the most powerful European monarch literally to his knees in 1077 was not sufficient even to insure the payment of papal taxes by the fifteenth century.

Just as the extension of the Christian church throughout Europe in the early Middle Ages laid the foundation of papal power, so the development of new media of communication created new power groups. Perhaps the most notorious of these in British media history were the press barons. Their rise is of interest, however, as much for the contrast as for the comparison it affords with the rise of the papacy.

In the eighteenth century, press proprietors were, for the most part, unimportant and far from respectable tradesmen. The practice of showing advance copy of scurrilous stories to their victims in order to extract a fee for suppressing their publication lowered the reputation of those associated with the press. In 1777, for instance, it was said of William Dodd, a preacher charged with forgery, almost as corroboration of the charge, that he had 'descended so low as to become the editor of a newspaper' (cited in Smith 1978a: 65). Apart from exceptional proprietors like James Perry, the wealthy owner of the biggest-circulation Whig daily in the late eighteenth century, owners of newspapers were not admitted into polite society (Christie 1970). Even writing articles for the press was judged by aristocratic politicians to be, in Lord Brougham's phrase, 'dirty work' (cited in Asquith 1976: 277). The low prestige of press proprietors was also a reflection of their lack of independent political influence. Few papers sold more than 1,000 copies before 1800, and many papers were heavily dependent upon political patronage in the form of subsidies, sinecures, politically tied advertising and information handouts.

During the nineteenth century the prestige and influence of press proprietors increased as a consequence of the growing circulations they commanded and an increased measure of political autonomy. Leading proprietors and editors were assiduously cultivated by government ministers (Anon 1935 and 1939; Hindle 1937) and a growing number of them entered parliament. Their increased political weight was reflected in the substantial legal privileges awarded to the press during the period 1868–88 (Lee 1976). At the same time, the role of the press was widely reinterpreted as that of an independent fourth estate in order, as Boyce (1978) has argued, to establish for newspapers a 'claim for a recognized and respectable place in the British political system'.

But it was only when newspapers acquired mass circulations that the position of proprietors underwent a fundamental change. *Lloyd's Weekly* was the first Sunday paper to gain a 1 million circulation in 1896, and the *Daily Mail* was the first daily to cross this threshold at the turn of the century. By 1920, the national Sunday press had an aggregate circulation of 13.5 million, with a mass working-class as well as middle-class following.

National dailies subsequently gained a mass readership among the working class, their circulation growing from 5.4 million to 10.6 million between 1920 and 1939 (Kaldor and Silverman 1948). The growth of the press as a mass medium was accompanied by increased concentration of ownership, giving leading press magnates ultimate control over vast aggregate circulations. Three men – Rothermere, Beaverbrook and Kemsley – controlled in 1937, for instance, 45 per cent of national daily circulation and 51 per cent of provincial morning circulation, with an aggregate readership (including their evening papers) of over 15 million people.[8]

This domination over the principal agency of political communication transformed the social standing of press proprietors. Men whose occupations would have caused them to have been shunned by aristocratic politicians in an earlier age as mere tradesmen were showered with titles and honours. As Northcliffe's sister Geraldine wrote facetiously in 1918, 'in view of the paper shortage, I think the family ought to issue printed forms like Field Service postcards, viz: Many congratulations on you being made Archbishop of Canterbury/Pope/Duke/ Viscount/Knight, etc.' (cited in Ferris 1971: 215). She was not entirely joking: five of her brothers were given between them two viscountcies, one barony and two baronetcies. Indeed, Viscount Rothermere was singled out for an even greater honour. After campaigning vigorously in his papers for the return of lost territories to Hungary, he was seriously asked by leading Hungarian monarchists whether he would fill the vacant throne of St Stephen as king of Hungary. He contented himself with an address of gratitude signed by a million and a quarter Hungarians.

The tsars of the new media also exercised real power. Northcliffe's campaign against the shortage of shells on the western front in 1915 reinforced mounting opposition to Asquith and contributed to the formation of the coalition government under Lloyd George in 1916. The press barons' fiefdoms helped them to gain political office, as in the case of Rothermere (in charge of the air ministry 1917–18), Northcliffe (director of propaganda in enemy territories, 1918–19) and Beaverbrook (minister of state and production 1941–2, among other posts). They also exercised a more intangible but nonetheless important influence in sustaining the dominant political consensus between the wars and in mobilizing conservative forces in opposition to radical change (Curran and Seaton 1981).

But the direct influence exercised through their papers was none the less severely circumscribed. When pitted against entrenched political power, the major campaigns initiated by the press barons were relative failures. Rothermere's campaign against 'squandermania' after the First World War met with only limited success, and his attempt to force the coalition government's hand by backing Anti-Waste League candidates in parliamentary by-elections ultimately failed, despite three notable successes. The Empire Free Trade campaign promoted by both Beaverbrook and Rothermere also failed through lack of sufficient Tory party support, and their subsequent attempt to force through a change of policy by launching the United Empire Party was largely, though not entirely, unsuccessful (Taylor 1972). These and other failures underlined the fact that the mass audiences reached daily by the press barons had an independent mind of their own. A more realistic appraisal of the power exercised by press magnates reduced their influence on internal politics within the Conservative Party. When Rothermere's demand to be informed of at least eight or ten cabinet ministers in Baldwin's next ministry as a condition of his continued support was repudiated by Baldwin in a famous speech as 'a preposterous and insolent demand' in 1931, the limitations of press power were publicly proclaimed. The point was rammed home a few weeks later when the official Conservative candidate loyal to Baldwin defeated an independent conservative backed by both Rothermere and Beaverbrook in the celebrated St George's Westminster by-election. The press magnates' ability to address a mass public, based on a cash nexus, proved to be no match for a political machine able to call upon party loyalty.

The contrast between the extensive secular power exercised by the papacy in the central Middle Ages and the more limited influence of the press barons reflects a number of important differences. The papacy sought to exercise a universal sovereignty, whereas the ambitions of the press magnates were more modest. The papacy developed a powerful ideological programme that legitimized its claim to divine-right monarchy: the press barons articulated a more defensive 'fourth estate' ideology that sought merely to legitimize their place within the constitution (for example, Northcliffe 1922; Beaverbrook 1925). The papacy successfully dominated for a time all the principal institutions of ideological production and promoted a construction of reality that legitimized its supremacy. In contrast, the press barons merely amplified systems of representation furnished by others (such as politicians, civil servants, judges and leading interest groups) that legitimized a power structure of which they were only a constituent element. Furthermore, press barons were unable to impose a uniform media view of society. Their control over the press itself was incomplete; they did not always share the same political perspective; and they had little influence over other agencies of mass communication – books, films, radio and later television. And by comparison with the papacy, they dealt with a much more unified power bloc, offering fewer opportunities for them to play off rival factions in order to build up their own power.

INCREASED TENSIONS

The emergence of a new power centre, linked to the development of a new channel of communication, tends to increase tensions within the overall structure of power. This will be illustrated by examining the conflicts exacerbated by the papacy in the Middle Ages and by the effect of the modern mass media on the development of the British political system.

The extension of the Catholic church throughout Europe created, in one sense, a new element of instability in medieval society. As we have seen, the papacy and the ecclesiastical hierarchy sought to regulate social knowledge through their control over medieval communications in order to appropriate some of the power and authority exercised by the traditional leaders of feudal society. This process of aggrandisement was made more disruptive by the fact that the papacy possessed the moral authority to undermine its opponents, without possessing the military means to conquer them. Consequently, the papacy was forced to rely upon others to take up arms on its behalf, and this sometimes led to a positive incitement of fissiparous elements opposed to the nation-building, centralizing strategies of medieval monarchies. Thus, the papacy played a leading part in deliberately provoking feudatories to oppose the German monarchy during the long drawn-out conflict over control of ecclesiastical appointments, thereby contributing to the growing instability of Germany and north Italy in the eleventh and twelfth centuries.

The development of communications under religious control had a destabilizing impact in another, more indirect way. The ecclesiastical hierarchy used its control over medieval media to support the building up of monarchical power. While the initiative for this often came from monarchs themselves, they found in the clergy willing and skilled agents in the ideological reconstruction of their authority. This was partly because the traditional feudal conception of kingship, and the ideological tradition from which it derived, posed a direct challenge to the ecclesiological world view that the church sought to promulgate. According to papal ideology, all power *descended* from God and was institutionalized in the form of law-giving by divinely appointed monarchies under the jurisdiction of the papal emperor with absolute authority over the children of God. But according to indigenous feudal tradition, all power *ascended* from below: the monarch was not an absolute ruler, but the first among equals bound by the reciprocal obligations of the feudal contract and constrained by natural law enshrined in custom. The early medieval institution of the monarchy was thus a functioning denial of the impersonal ecclesiastical order which the papacy proclaimed, the embodiment of an older, oral ideological tradition that directly challenged the premises of papal ideology.

The ecclesiastical hierarchy sought to refashion the institution of the monarchy through learned tracts, sermons, official pronouncements, liturgical symbolism and public ritual. Thus, numerous innovations were made in royal coronation ceremonies, for instance, during the period AD 400–1300, in an attempt to suppress the traditional feudal conception of kingship and establish in its place a divine-right monarchy whose power derived through the mediation of the church (Kantorowicz 1957; Ullmann 1969, 1975 and 1978). The person of the monarch was deliberately invested with sacred magic properties, with the result that throughout much of Europe the superstition developed that kings could cure scrofula by touching its victim. Even armed resistance to the king, unless he was deposed by the church, was defined by clergy as an act of sacrilege against the Lord's anointed. In addition to reinterpreting the basis of authority of the monarchy, the clergy also played a central role in developing court administrations as more effective agencies of management.

This concerted attempt to transform the position of medieval monarchs in accordance with the interests and ideology of the ecclesiastical order posed a major threat to established interests within the hierarchy of power since it advanced royal authority at the expense of aristocratic power. It implied, moreover, a fundamental change in the relationship of the monarch to his feudatories, from that of feudal chieftain with limited powers to that of divine-right monarch with absolute powers accountable only to God and his appointed agents. Inevitably this attempt to alter the distribution of power led to fierce resistance, of which the successful baronial revolt against King John of England in the early thirteenth century was merely one of numerous examples (Ullmann 1978).

The rise of professional communicators in modern Britain was, by comparison, less dislocative, largely because professional communicators more readily accepted a subaltern role. Unlike the medieval priesthood, journalists did not seek to transform society by placing themselves at the centre of a new system of power.

However, the rise of journalists introduced new tensions within the political structure. This was partly disguised during the second half of the nineteenth century because much of the press functioned as an extension of the party system. Many leading proprietors and editors were ardent party supporters and committed their papers to promoting a party cause. Indeed, the expansion of the partisan press during this period was a key factor in transforming political parties from aristocratic factions in parliament into mass political movements (Vincent 1972; Lee 1976).

During the course of the twentieth century, the character of the British press changed. An increasing number of newspapers became more loosely connected to the political parties,[9] and offered – relatively speaking – more bipartisan coverage of politics than before (Seymour-Ure 1977). The popular press also became more entertainment oriented, some papers roughly halving their coverage of public affairs as a proportion of editorial space between 1936 and 1976 (Curran, Douglas and Whannel 1980). The traditional connexion between a partisan press and readership weakened. By 1979, over a third of national daily newspaper readers brought papers with political allegiances different from their own. Much of the remainder looked to the press to be briefed and entertained rather than to have their political commitments reinforced.

The media were also transformed as a consequence of the rise of radio and television, both of which were obliged by law to be politically impartial. During the the 1950s and 1960s television greatly increased its political coverage, and built mass audiences for its prime-time news programmes. It became the principal source of information about public affairs, greatly increasing the electorate's exposure to bipartisan communications.

The effect of these changes was compounded by growing occupational rivalry between journalists and politicians. As Gurevitch and Blumler (1977) point out, the two groups developed competing forms of legitimacy. Politicians argued that they were the democratically elected representatives of the people, while journalists claimed the right as members of the 'fourth estate' to oversee politicians on behalf of the public. Fuelling tension between the two groups was the fact that both needed each other, yet wanted different things out of their relationship. In general, politicans wanted to advance their political and personal objectives, while the main concern of journalists was to get 'good copy'.

This fraught relationship could generate media responses that were not so much bipartisan as anti-partisan. This is typified by an excerpt from a *Sunday Times* editorial:

> Mr Callaghan condemns the income tax cuts forced on the government by the Tories and other opposition parties as looking after the rich and striking a blow at the family budget. . . . The Prime Minister is a politician and is therefore no doubt, entitled under the rules of the game to play politics. But a newspaper is equally entitled to remind readers that politics is what he is playing. We must not be tempted by rhetoric to take Ministers' words at face value, and forget what they have said in the past. What the Conservatives have done for the higher tax-payers is precisely what the Government itself would do if it had the political nerve – or if its party would let it.
>
> (*Sunday Times*, 14 May 1978)

This editorial makes unusually explicit some of the assumptions that underpin the rhetoric of media anti-partisanship. Prime ministers 'play politics' whereas the *Sunday Times* is disinterested. Politicians dissemble and lie, while the press fearlessly speaks its mind. Politicians are encumbered by vested interests and party ties, whereas the *Sunday Times* is concerned only with the public interest – even when advocating tax cuts for affluent *Sunday Times* journalists and readers.

However, this media anti-partisanship sometimes went deeper than mere occupational rivalry, and seemed to take on the characterstics of a cultural clash. During much of the twentieth century, the political system was based on a contest between two opposing ideologies, each with a different class-based constituency. Yet the culture of the professions, to which journalism gravitated, was strongly 'anti-ideological'. It stressed knowledge, expertise and rationality – central to the credentials and public legitimation of the professions – in opposition to prejudice and unthinking partisanship. It also took pride in the supposed disinterest of professional people who were able to serve the public interest, because they were independent of both business and labour.

Media anti-partisanship was influenced, in other words, by the cultural traditions and self-regard of the intermediate strata of which professional communicators were a part. As Reith, the founder of the BBC (and former engineer), wrote revealingly in his diary: 'I reflect sometimes on "politics". The whole horrid technique should be abolished. Government of a country is a matter of policy and proper administration, in other words efficiency' (11 October 1932, quoted in Stewart 1975). This distaste became increasingly prominent in media reporting and commentary during the 1960s and early 1970s. It took the form of an implicit vision of what politics should be about – rational problem-solving and the efficient delivery of services – contrasted with the 'reality' of personality clashes, posturing, manipulation, opportunism and shabby compromise. Not merely politicians but in effect the traditional party system got a bad 'press'.

However, the tensions and rivalries between politicans and journalists were contained within a framework that was strongly supportive of the principles and functioning of the electoral system. The media conferred legitimacy on political parties by giving prominence to the parliamentary process. The media publicity given to general elections was also crucially important in enabling parties to mobilise their supporters to the polls, and in renewing the legitimacy of the democratic process. However, the decline of the old party press, the rise of television as a bipartisan medium of communication, and the development of media anti-partisanship, also weakened the political parties. The loyal support they once commanded began to erode from the 1960s onwards, and they lost both members and influence. By thus contributing to the decline of political parties,[10] the media loosened a cornerstone of traditional liberal democracy.

THE DISPLACEMENT OF MEDIATING AGENCIES

The introduction of new techniques of mass communication tended to undermine the prestige and influence of established mediating organizations and groups. New media also posed a threat to the *status quo* since they could potentially bypass existing structures of control, and make available new ideas and information. The best illustration of this process of displacement, and attendant dislocation, is provided by the rise of the book in late medieval and early modern Europe.

From the thirteenth century onwards, paper rapidly displaced parchment as the principal raw material of books, thereby making the preparation of manuscripts cheaper, simpler and faster. This important innovation was accompanied by a massive increase in the number of people (mostly women) engaged in the copying of books, with the development of commercial and university scriptoria, and by the establishment of a fully organized international book trade, in the later Middle Ages. The introduction of printing with moveable metal type for commercial purposes in 1450 was thus the culmination, rather than the beginning, of a major expansion of a book-based culture. Print resulted, however, in an enormous gain in productivity, with output per capita engaged in book production rising by well over a hundred-fold, to judge from estimates provided by Eisenstein (1968). Print also led to a sharp reduction in costs, so that the printed works of Luther, for instance, could be purchased in England for 4d or 6d a copy in 1520 – the equivalent of about a day's wage for a craftsman. This increase in output and fall in costs, combined with rising rates of literacy, resulted in a spectacular increase in book consumption. About 20 million books were produced in Europe between 1450 and 1500, and production increased sharply thereafter (Febvre and Martin 1976).

This expansion of book production resulted in the mass dissemination of religious texts, and in particular Bibles, in vernacular languages. There were, for example, nineteen editions of the Bible in High German before Luther. Luther's own translation of the Bible was published in whole or in part in no less than 430 editions between 1522 and 1546. This diffusion of the Bible undermined the monopolistic position of the clergy as agents of religious communication, and threatened their authority as mediators of religious knowledge by providing direct access to an alternative, more authoritative source of religious teaching – that of God as revealed in the scriptures. As John Hobbes wrote disapprovingly in the seventeenth century: 'every man, nay, every boy and wench that could read English thought they spoke with God Almighty, and understood what He said' (cited in Hill 1974: 154).

It was mainly in order to maintain priestly, hierarchical control over religious knowledge that determined attempts were made to restrict public access to the Bible in the sixteenth century. The Catholic church proscribed Bibles printed in languages that people could understand. The English church under Henry VIII tried a more discriminating approach. It banned Bible-reading among the impressionable in need of special protection – women, apprentices and husbandmen (Bennett 1952).

In a less immediately apparent way, the rise of the book undermined the authority of priests by diminishing their ritual role. Their prestige derived ultimately from their mediation of divine grace – that is, the favour of God resulting in the bestowal of blessings and the salvation of sinners – through the seven sacred rites which they administered. More generally, the expressive iconography and music of religious worship also powerfully evoked a sense of supernatural power and of its mediation through the corporate organization of the church. However, the development of a book-based culture encouraged a different definition of religious experience centred on the word of God mediated through print. This took the form of a more private, individualistic approach which gave precedence to the study of the Bible and private prayer at the expense of collective worship. In its more extreme form, this bibliolatry led to a turning away in disgust from 'pre-literate' forms of religious observance, and even to questioning the meaning and efficacy of established religious ritual. Print thus helped to detract from the mediatory and intercessionary role of the priesthood, and of the church itself, by providing a new channel of communication between Christians and God.

The development of a lay scribal and print culture also undermined the ideological ascendancy of the church. The growth of commercial scriptoria and subsequently commercial printing enterprises made it more difficult for the ecclesiastical authorities, who had previously directly controlled the means of book production, to exercise effective censorship. The failure of the church to maintain its domination over centres of learning in the later Middle Ages also weakened its grip on the content of elite culture. Through the medium of the written and printed word (as well as in a sense through changing styles of representation in Renaissance art), an anthropomorphic view of the world that stressed man's innate capacity to regulate his environment was expressed that directly confronted the more traditional theocentric view of a divinely ordained and ordered universe that underpinned papal imperialism. Developments in political thought – most notably the modern distinction between church and state and a belief in the legitimacy of state power as being derived from people rather than from God – were also mediated through books to a larger elite audience, undermining the premises that sustained papal ascendancy (Wilks 1963; Ullmann 1977).

In a marginal and (sometimes overstated) way, the rise of print also weakened the authority of church leadership by compressing the dimensions of space and time. The book, pamphlet and flysheet contributed to increased knowledge of early church history in which Rome had played a relatively inconspicuous part, and spread information about the greed and corruption of the Renaissance papacy which, though probably no worse than that of the papacy in the tenth and early eleventh centuries, became more widely known. In a more general sense, the rise of the manuscript and subsequently of the printed book also fostered the development of an alternative culture. Although the bulk of scribal and early print output was in Latin and religious in content, the production and dissemination of vernacular texts helped to foster a parallel secular culture based on national languages and dialects, drawing upon indigenous cultural traditions. The ecclesiastical hierarchy in late medieval Europe sought to contain the threat of this 'new learning' through censorship, direct patronage and the creation of what Southern (1970) calls 'a separate university system' through the Franciscan and Dominican orders. However, it was unable initially to neutralize the disruptive influence of the printed word which by-passed the established information order of the Catholic church.

Indeed, the rise of the book not only subverted the authority of the church, but also acted as a directly centrifugal force within it. The close connection between Bible-reading and heresy has often been observed by historians (for example, Dickens 1964 and Thomson 1965). Just why there should have been this connexion is less than clear without reference to modern media research. This shows that people tend to read, understand and recall elements within communications selectively, in ways that accord with their prior dispositions and beliefs (see, for example, Cooper and Jahoda 1947; Hovland, Janis and Kelley 1953; Klapper 1960). Widely divergent responses to the printed Bible can thus be explained partly in terms of the different religious orientations, cultural traditions and social experiences of the people that made up the new Bible public. To see the Bible as 'producing' heresy is misleading; rather, exposure to the Bible caused prior differences between readers to be expressed in the explosive form of textually supported, doctrinal disagreement. Discursive difference was transposed through Bible-reading into theological dissent.

Other contingent factors probably reinforced the schismatic impact of vernacular Bibles. Centuries of exegetical analysis and interpretation had produced Catholic doctrines lacking a clear scriptural basis. The Bible is an inherently polysemic text which is accessible to divergent interpretation. The failure of the ecclesiastical authorities to prepare the ground adequately for the reception of the Bible also limited their ability to defuse its divisive impact. While the research of historians like Heath (1969) and Elton (1975) clearly calls into question traditional conceptions of a 'corrupt' pre-Reformation church, there can be no doubt that inadequate, if improved, clerical training and the continuing ritualistic formalism of the late medieval church prevented effective ecclesiastical supervision of lay responses to the Bible.

The causes of the rise of Protestantism are exceedingly complex and are only partly to do with religion. But, at one level at least, Protestantism can be viewed as a synthesis of the different disruptive tendencies set in motion by a new technique of mass communication. It was a movement that was inspired, in part, by access to an alternative source of religious doctrine, the Bible, mediated through print, that competed with hierarchically mediated orthodoxy; it took the form of a fundamentalist reconstruction of Christian dogma based on a literal interpretation of the scriptures; it was a book-centred definition of religious experience that rejected many of the pre-literate, ritualistic forms of religious communication and the central intermediary role of the Catholic priesthood; it was a revolt against papal sovereignty, which the printed word had helped to foster by contributing to the decline of the papacy's prestige and ideological ascendancy; and Protestantism was also the expression of a growing secularism and nationalism which the growth of a lay scribal and print culture helped to promote.

That Protestantism was, in some respects, the product of print is underlined by the way in which Protestant churches sought quite deliberately to supplant traditional, pre-literate modes of religious communication with a new system of communication based on the printed word. Church murals were whitewashed over, beautiful stained glass was smashed and replaced with pane glass, holy relics were destroyed and the statues of saints were even given to children as toys to play with. Some rites were suppressed, church ritual was simplified and the role of the priest was demystified with the abandonment of celibacy. Instead, the Protestant churches encouraged the mass production of the Bible, trained pastors as biblical experts and promoted a literacy drive aimed at enabling people to understand God's teachings through the printed word.

In contrast, the Catholic church set in motion from the late sixteenth century onwards a more effective programme for minimizing the effects of print. This resulted in the enforcement of the *Index*, the proscription not only of vernacular Bibles but also of many religious best-selling commentaries and the relative neglect of primary education in Catholic countries. The church also encouraged the renewal of Catholic musical, art and architectural traditions, and embedded the intermediary role of the priest at the centre of the religious experience. If Protestanism was print based, Tridentine Catholicism drew enhanced strength from image and ritual.

The Anglican church established by the Elizabethan Settlement hovered uneasily between these two definitions of religion. Its actual form of worship was a negotiation between the iconography of Catholicism and the bibliolatry of Protestanism (Thomas 1973). Its doctrinal evasions were a pragmatic attempt to accommodate differences of belief that had been fanned by a war of words conducted through print (Davies 1976). The Church of England sought neither to entrench nor to exclude print, but merely to defuse the problems it created.[11]

MEDIA AND CLASS CONFLICT

The rise of new media, it has been argued, threatened the authority of established mediating agencies, and subverted their control over knowledge. However, this general argument needs to be qualified. New media did not necessarily challenge established patterns of influence and authority. Their impact was crucially influenced by how effectively they were regulated, and how consensual was the environment in which they emerged. This will be highlighted by contrasting the impact of the rise of the newspaper in the eighteenth and nineteenth centuries with that of modern media in the twentieth century.[12]

During the early eighteenth century, the middle class in Britain was largely excluded from the institutional political process by the limited franchise which gave the great landed families effective control over small and unrepresentative constituencies. The middle class also had restricted access to the spoils of the patronage system, and tended to be marginalized by the anti-democratic consensus of the landed elite. Central to this consensus was the concept of 'virtual representation' by which politicians drawn from the landed elite were said to represent the public by virtue of their independence and tradition of public service, even though they were not directly elected by the people. Great stress was laid also on the independent, deliberative role of the parliamentarian and the complexity of statecraft in a way that discouraged popular participation in the political process. As Burke put it, the parliamentarian is like 'a physician [who] does not take his remedy from the ravings of the patient' (cited in Brewer 1976: 237).

Regulation of the press was one means by which aristocratic political ascendancy was maintained. Newspapers were subject to strict legal controls – the law of seditious libel, which was used to prevent criticism of the political system, general warrants issued at the discretion of the authorities against people suspected of committing a seditious libel, and a legal ban on the reporting of parliament. In addition, taxes on newspapers, advertisements and paper were introduced in 1712 mainly in order to increase the price of newspapers and thereby restrict their circulation. Successive administrations also sought to manage the political press by offering secret service subsidies, official advertising and exclusive information to pro-government newspapers as well as by giving rewards and sinecures to sympathetic journalists. Opposition groups in parliament countered with similar tactics in order to sustain an opposition press. Consequently, the 'political' press (consisting largely of London papers) was initially dominated by the landed elite which controlled both government and parliament.

However, sustained expansion of the economy created a growing middle-class public for newspapers and a rising volume of advertising which aided its development. The number of local provincial newspapers increased from twenty-two to about fifty titles between 1714 and 1782 (Cranfield 1962; Read 1961). The provincial press also increased its coverage of public affairs, assisted by the improvement in local and postal communications and the increase in the number of metropolitan papers from which it shamelessly plagiarized material. This expansion of a more politicized, regional press fostered the development of a middle-class political culture, centred on the clubs, political societies and coffee-houses of provincial England. In promoting a political awareness amongst its readers, the emergent commercial press helped to lay the foundations for the subsequent middle-class assault on the aristocratic order.

The commercial press in the provinces both catered for and was mainly controlled by the commercial middle class. The majority of newspaper proprietors were merchants, tradesmen, printers or booksellers. Journalists came from more varied backgrounds, but would seem to have been drawn primarily from the petite bourgeoisie (Cranfield 1962 and 1978; Rogers 1972). This created a situation in which those outside the political system in effect possessed control over a significant means of communication.

The person who unleashed the subversive potential of the commercial press was John Wilkes, a political outsider married into a rich brewing family (Brewer 1976). He transformed a fairly commonplace occurrence – his imprisonment by general warrant in 1763 for writing an article attacking the government – into a major political issue. His subsequent exclusion from the House of Commons, despite repeated re-elections, became a national scandal; and his calculated act of defiance as a magistrate in freeing printers who had published reports of parliament, brought the mobs out onto the streets of London in a mass action of support that created consternation in parliament (Rude 1962).

The controversies surrounding Wilkes were the first notable occasions in the eighteenth century when a section of the press broke free from aristocratic influence, and defined the political agenda in an independent way. They also demonstrated the power of the press to build up a popular champion, and enable him to appeal over the heads of the elite for wider public support. Press reporting, backed up by flysheets and printed ballads, helped to mobilize demonstrations, marches and petitions in support of 'Wilkes and Liberty' in many parts of the country from Berwick-on-Tweed to Falmouth. Largely as a result of popular pressure, general warrants were declared illegal in 1765 and the ban on the reporting of parliament was effectively abandoned in 1771. The press was increasingly free to subject parliamentary proceedings and government to public scrutiny, and became more responsive to the concerns of middle-class groups. The politics of oligarchy were at an end: Wilkes inaugurated a new era of political participation sustained by the commercial press.

The 1760s were a watershed in another sense. The commercial press began for the first time to challenge the legitimacy of the political system. Its critique was cautious and indirect at first, taking the form of extensive coverage of American criticism of British colonial rule. The argument that there should be 'no taxation without representation' used to mobilize resistance to the stamp duty in America was widely reported in Britain, and contributed to a chain reaction of critical thought. By the 1780s, some commercial reform papers were arguing that the government was oppressive, corrupt and inefficient because it was unrepresentative, and needed to be elected by a broader franchise.

The commercial press expanded steadily during the late Georgian and early Victorian period. Between 1781 and 1851 the number of newspapers increased from about 76 to 563; their aggregate annual sales rose from 14 million in 1780 to 85 million in 1851 (Asquith 1978). This expansion accelerated after the lifting of press taxes in the mid-nineteenth century.

Commercial newspapers also became more independent of authority. The ability of governments to control the press through the law was limited by two important reforms. In 1792, the seditious libel law was weakened by Fox's Libel Act which made juries the judges of libel suits. Libel law was further modified by Lord Campbell's Libel Act of 1843, which made the statement of truth in the public interest a legitimate defence against the charge of criminal libel. No less important, there was a spectacular increase in advertising expenditure on the press (reflected, for instance, in a five-fold increase in the advertising revenue of the principal London dailies between 1780 and 1820) which profoundly influenced the character of the commercial press. Increased advertising largely financed the development of independent news-gathering resources that rendered newspapers less dependent upon official information. It also encouraged a more independent attitude among proprietors by making it more lucrative to maximize advertising through increasing circulation than to appeal to government and opposition for political subsidies. While the effect of the growth of press advertising has been, in general, greatly mythologized, it contributed at this particular conjuncture to the greater editorial independence of the commercial press from aristocratic influence (Aspinall 1973; Christie 1970; Asquith 1975, 1976 and 1978; Cranfield 1978).[13]

A section of this expanding commercial press fostered a positive social identity among its readers by characterizing 'the middle classes' as the economic and moral backbone of England. 'Never in any country beneath the sun', declared the *Leeds Mercury* in 1821, 'was an order of men more estimable and valuable, more praised and praiseworthy than the middle class of society in England' (cited in Read 1961: 119). The *Mercury*'s assessment was modest by comparison with those that appeared in other middle-class publications of the same period. James Mill in the *Westminster Review*, for instance, hailed the middle class in 1826 'as the glory of England; as that which alone has given our eminence among nations; as that portion of our people to whom every thing that is good among us may with certainty be traced' (cited in Perkin 1969: 230). Florid tributes like these, expressed in the new language of class, encouraged a new self-definition and sense of social consequence among readers of the commercial press.

The commercial reform press contributed, moreover, in a very direct way to the advancement of middle-class interests (as well as those of others). Between 1830 and 1874, the reform press was involved in a series of campaigns that resulted in the extension of the franchise, the increasing decontrol of agriculture and trade, and the reform of the civil service, armed forces and universities which opened up new avenues of lucrative and influential employment for the middle class.

Although the landed elite continued to dominate national politics until late into the nineteenth century, it remained responsive to the concerns of the middle-class public. This was partly a consequence of electoral competition within an enlarged franchise, but it also owed something to the effective way in which reform papers and periodicals mobilized public support. A number of key newspapers also helped to maintain a flow of communication and reciprocal influence within the new ruling social coalition of the aristocracy and middle class that took shape after 1832. In addition, the commercial press furnished a moral framework legitimating the market system during a dislocative phase of its development, and contributed to its growing acceptance.

How, then, should we view the overall impact of the commercial press in the eighteenth and nineteenth centuries? It was disruptive in the sense that reform newspapers sometimes became caught up in popular agitation that led to temporary breakdowns of public order, as in the mid-1760s, 1810s and early 1830s. However, over the long term, the commercial press exerted a stabilizing influence. It gave a voice to a disenfranchized but increasingly influential class. It reinforced pressure for an extension of the franchise, the replacement of the patronage system with the party system and the purging of state corruption. Above all, it encouraged the peaceful adaptation of aristocratic rule, and the incorporation of the middle class into a reconstituted structure of power. In short, the rise of the commercial newspaper helped the social system to adjust to changes in the underlying balance of social forces brought about by changes in the economy.

A radical press developed alongside the commercial press in the early nineteenth century. Funded from within the working class, or closely linked to popular radical movements, it posed a more serious challenge to the *ancien régime* than the commercial press. Its politics were more radical and it reached a section of the public with less to lose. Individual radical newspapers also gained a higher circulation than most of their respectable rivals throughout most of the period, 1815–55.

This new press encouraged a positive working-class identity, based on the argument that the wealth of society was created by working people. It thus promoted a way of viewing the world which turned upside-down the established hierarchy of status in society. It also helped to build support for trade unions and the Chartist movement, and to contribute to a new climate of hope by repeatedly arguing that social conditions could be changed through the force of 'combination'. Above all, it provided a forum of debate in which workers were able to make sense of society in new and more radical ways, and explore ideas about how to improve it. This led to the development of a more radical critique in which oppression was viewed not just as a political but also as an economic process. From this was derived a more far-reaching political programme than that proposed by the liberal reform press. Workers, proclaimed the *Poor Man's Guardian* (19 October 1833), should 'be at the top instead of at the bottom of society – or rather [where] there should be no bottom or top at all'.[14]

In the event, the working-class movement was defeated for over a generation when the Chartist movement collapsed in 1850. The radical press also went into decline, and failed to recover its leading position in popular journalism when organized labour revived and became more militant. The reasons for this eclipse are explored in the next chapter, and need not be elaborated here. It is sufficent to say that the press became subject to a new system of economic regulation when it became industrialized.

MEDIA AND SOCIAL CONTROL

The 'new media' of radio and television – introduced in the 1920s and 1930s respectively – also became subject to an effective form of regulation. The legal requirement to be impartial was broadly interpreted by broadcasters to mean 'holding the middle ground' (Kumar 1975). Broadcasters also unconsciously internalized the dominant culture in the ways they represented society (Glasgow University Media Group 1976).

Indeed, the media as a whole became an agency of social integration in ways that had striking parallels with the church in the central Middle Ages. Like the medieval church, the media linked together different groups and provided a shared experience that promoted social solidarity. The media also emphasized collective values which bound people closer together, in a way that was comparable to the influence of the medieval church. The commonality of the Christian faith was replaced by the commonality of consumerism, feted in consumer advertising, and of nationalism affirmed by ritualized national media events. Indeed, the two institutions engaged in very similar ideological 'work', despite the difference of time that separated them. The monarchy was projected by the modern British media as a symbol of collective identity just as it was by the medieval church. The modern media also gave, at different times, massive and disproportionate attention to a series of 'outsiders' – youth gangs, muggers, squatters, drug addicts, student radicals, trade-union militants – who tended to be presented as powerful and irrational threats to society (Young 1971; Cohen 1980; Hall 1974; Morley 1976; Hall *et al.* 1978; Whannel 1979). The stigmatization of these 'outsiders' had effects comparable to the hunting down and parading of witches by the medieval and early modern church. In both cases, moral panics were created that strengthened adherence to dominant social norms and encouraged a sense of beleaguered unity in the face of supposedly dangerous threats.

The modern media assumed the role of the church, in a more secular age, of interpreting and making sense of the world to the mass public. Like their priestly predecessors, professional communicators amplified systems of representation that legitimated the social system. The priesthood told their congregations that the power structure was divinely sanctioned; their successors implied that it was endorsed at regular intervals by the ballot box. Dissidents were frequently delegitimized by churchmen as 'infidels' intent upon resisting God's will; dissidents in modern Britain were similarly stigmatized as anti-democratic 'extremists' (Murdock 1973). The medieval church taught that the only legitimate way of securing redress for injustice was to appeal to the oppressor's conscience and, failing that, to a higher secular authority; the modern mass media also upheld constitutional and lawful processes as the only legitimate methods of protest (Hall 1974). The medieval church masked the sources of inequality by ascribing social injustice to the sin of the individual; modern media entertainment tended also to offer an individual-centred view of the world in which both problems and solutions were portrayed as personal rather than structural. By stressing the randomness of God's unseen hand, the medieval church encouraged passive acceptance of a subordinate status in society: the randomness of fate was a recurrent theme of modern media entertainment (Curran, Douglas and Whannel 1980). The church none the less offered the chiliastic consolation of eternal salvation to 'the meek [who] shall inherit the earth'; the media similarly gave compensatory prominence to showbusiness personalities and football stars who, as 'a powerless elite', provided symbols of hope and vicarious fulfilment (Alberoni 1972).

There was, of course, some differentiation in the output of twentieth-century media just as there was in the teaching of the medieval church. Conflicts also developed between the media and other power centres in modern Britain just as there were conflicts between the papacy, episcopacy and the monarchies of the Middle Ages. But these conflicts were usually confined within a framework supportive of established power. The new priesthood of the modern media supplanted the old in building consent for an inegalitarian social order.

Chapter 3

Capitalism and control of the press

INTRODUCTION

The history of the British press has remained stuck in the same mould for over a century.[1] Acccording to convention, the British press became free partly as a consequence of a heroic struggle against state control. The first major breakthrough is usually said to have occurred during the Interregnum of 1649–60 with the abolition of the Court of the Star Chamber. It was followed by the abandonment of press licensing in 1695 and the introduction of a new and less repressive control system, based primarily on press taxes, in 1712. Further concessions were secured in the reign of George III, notably the relaxation of restrictions on the reporting of parliament in the 1770s and Fox's Libel Act of 1792, which made juries the judges of seditious libel suits. But it was only in the Victorian era, according to the received wisdom, that the forces of progress finally triumphed with the reform of libel law in 1843 and the repeal of 'the taxes on knowledge' in the period 1853–61. An independent press emerged free of the legal and fiscal controls by which governments had sought to control it.[2]

This struggle was accompanied by a development which is generally held to be of even greater significance for the emergence of a free press – the *economic* emancipation of the press from state control. For 'the true censorship', John Roach writes of the late Georgian press, 'lay in the fact that the newspaper had not yet reached financial independence' (Roach 1965: 181). It was only with the growth of newspaper profits, largely from advertising, that newspapers were supposedly able to free themselves from state and party subsidies and develop an independent organization for gathering news. This conventional wisdom, embedded in all the standard academic histories of the press, is succinctly restated by Ivon Asquith in a study of the early nineteenth-century press:

> Since sales were inadequate to cover the costs of producing a paper, it was the growing income from advertising which provided the material base for the change of attitude from subservience to independence. The chief methods by which governments could influence the press – a direct subsidy, official advertisements, and priority of intelligence – were rendered less effective

because proprietors could afford to do without them. . . . The growth of advertising revenue was the most important single factor in enabling the press to emerge as the Fourth Estate of the realm.

(Asquith 1975: 721).[3]

A number of important studies documenting the rise of the early radical press provide evidence which, by implication at least, casts doubt on this conventional wisdom.[4] Unfortunately, in one sense, these studies are primarily concerned with the development of the British working class rather than with the history of British journalism. And, insofar as they are explicitly situated in the context of the historical development of the British press, they broadly accept the Whig framework of a triumphant struggle to establish an independent press (Wickwar 1928: 310; Thompson 1963: 772; Williams 1965: 209; Wiener 1969a: xi; Hollis 1970: 10).[5] In effect, they substitute for traditional Whig heroes new working-class ones. The only two historians in this tradition who pay any serious attention to the middle-class press also subscribe to the legend of advertising as the midwife of press freedom (Williams 1965: 209 *et passim*; Hollis 1970: 27–8).

This historical legend is not merely of academic interest. It is a persuasive interpretation of press history which legitimates the market-based system. It is explicitly invoked, for instance, by popular historians of the press to justify the role of advertising in the press. Thus, Francis Williams writes:

The dangerous dependence of newspapers on advertising has often been the theme of newspaper reformers – usually from outside its ranks. But the daily press would not have come into existence as a force in public and social life if it had not been for the need of men of commerce to advertise. Only through the growth of advertising did the press achieve independence.

(Williams 1957: 50; cf. Herd 1952: 65)

The same historical theme was skilfully deployed by the Advertising Association in its evidence to two successive Royal Commissions on the Press, apparently with remarkable effect (Advertising Association 1949 and 1961). It partly explains the innocent view of the first Royal Commission that the receipt of advertising 'creates a relationship both remote and impersonal', a belief largely endorsed by its successor (1949: 143; 1962: 87).

The portrayal of the mid-nineteenth-century British press which accompanies this historical legend serves a similar mythological purpose. According to the *New Cambridge Modern History*, for instance, financially independent newspapers became 'great organs of the public mind', amplifying the voice of the people rather than that of governments and politicians (Crawley 1965: 26). The rise of an independent press, argues Professor Christie (1970), democratized British political institutions by exposing them to the full blast of public opinion. At the same time, the emergence of an independent press led to an increasingly non-partisan news coverage, enabling people to form balanced political judgements and to participate in a more mature political democracy. 'The period from 1855', writes Raymond Williams, 'is in one sense the development of a new and better journalism, with a much greater emphasis on news than in the faction-ridden first half of the century . . . most newspapers were able to drop their frantic pamphlet-eering' (Williams 1965: 218). In short, historical convention has encouraged a limited understanding of the role of the press as an independent source of news and intermediary between government and governed. This perspective has dominated public inquiries into the press in Britain, and discouraged serious consideration of structural reform.[6]

This chapter is a long overdue attempt to reappraise the standard interpretation of press history during the formative phase of its development. It indicates the need not only to re-examine critically the accepted view of the historical emer-gence of a 'free' press but to stand it on its head. The period around the middle of the nineteenth century, it will be argued, did not inaugurate a new era of press freedom: rather, it introduced a new system of press censorship more effective than anything that had gone before. Market forces succeeded where legal repres-sion had failed in establishing the press as an instrument of social control, with lasting consequences for the development of modern British society.

BREAKDOWN OF THE CONTROL SYSTEM

Direct state censorship of the printed word in Britain was never fully effective. Even during the period of the most systematic repression under the early Stuart monarchy when offending authors could be publicly whipped, their faces branded, their nostrils slit and their ears chopped off (on alternate weeks, allow-ing for recuperation), the absence of modern law enforcement agencies prevented the effective control of print. As a number of specialist studies demonstrate, the state lacked the sophisticated apparatus necessary to control production, monitor output, regulate distribution, stop the import of prohibited printed material and neutralize or destroy dissident elements in society – essential if coercive censor-ship was to be effective (Siebert 1952; Frank 1961; Rostenburg 1971). The celebrated termination of press licensing in 1695, as Hanson (1936) has shown, was prompted not so much by libertarian sentiment as by a realistic recognition that the licensing system was unenforceable. Even the less ambitious control system introduced under Queen Anne was only partly effective (Cranfield 1962; Wiles 1965; Haigh 1968; Harris 1974). By the nineteenth century it had become increasingly inadequate, even when strengthened by the notorious Six Acts of 1819.

The front line in the struggle for an independent press was occupied not by leading respectable publishers and editors, whose famous and much quoted pro-clamations of independence were often belied by their covert attempts to secure subsidies from government in the form of official advertising and by their willing-ness to co-operate in the system of exclusive intelligence by which successive governments managed the flow of news (see, for instance, *History of The Times* [Anon 1935, 1939] and Hindle 1937). Ownership and control of the respectable press continued, in any case, to be inextricably linked to government through partisan involvement in parliamentary politics well into the twentieth century.[7] And while respectable newspapers increasingly voiced criticism of government, independent criticism was kept well within the confines of the ideological framework legitimating the capitalist system.

The principal challenge to hegemonic control came from an increasingly radical press appealing by the 1830s to a predominantly working-class audience. It was confronted not by the subtle systems of management based on exclusive information, official advertising and Treasury subsidies but by the direct force of legal repression. The first legal sanction available for controlling the press was the law of seditious and blasphemous libel, defined in such all-embracing terms that it provided an infinitely flexible instrument of prosecution.[8] Its effectiveness was seriously reduced, however, by Fox's Libel Act of 1792, since successive governments found it increasingly difficult to get juries to convict. It also became increasingly apparent that libel prosecutions, even when upheld, were often counter-productive. The circulation of the *Republican*, for instance, increased by over 50 per cent in 1819 when its editor was prosecuted (Wickwar 1928: 94). Seditious libel prosecutions became a valuable source of promotion for the radical press. 'A libeller', concluded the disillusioned attorney-general in 1832, 'thirsted for nothing more than the valuable advertisement of a public trial in a Court of justice' (cited in Wiener 1969a: 196). For these reasons, the number of libel prosecutions fell sharply. Whereas there were 167 prosecutions for seditious and blasphemous libel in the period 1817–24, there were only 16 subsequently in 1825–34 (Wickwar 1928: appendix B, 315). Libel law was no longer an effective instrument for gagging the press, and was substantially modified by Lord Campbell's Act of 1843.

The government relied increasingly, instead, upon the so called 'taxes on knowledge' – a stamp duty on each copy of a press publication sold to the public, a duty on each advertisement placed in the press and a tax on paper. These had two objectives: to restrict readership of the press to the respectable members of society by forcing up the price of press publications; and to restrict ownership of newspapers to people who, in the words of Cresset Pelham, 'would conduct them in a more respectable manner than was likely to be the result of pauper management' by increasing the costs of publishing (cited in Hollis 1970: vi). The last objective was further served by a state security system (£300 for London papers and £200 for provincial papers) ostensibly designed to provide guarantees for the payment of fines but, in reality, aimed to exclude 'pauper' management of newspapers.

Yet, even press taxes, though sharply increased in the period 1780–1815, proved increasingly ineffectual as an instrument of censorship. Ever since their introduction in 1712, individual publishers had evaded payment. However, the authorities were faced in the early 1830s with an entirely new situation – the concerted non-payment of the stamp duty by a highly organized underground press with well-developed distribution networks, and 'victim funds' to help the families of people imprisoned by the authorities. The government initiated a campaign of suppression, prosecuting publishers and printers, seizing supplies and smashing, wherever possible, networks of distributors. At least 1,130 cases of selling unstamped newspapers were prosecuted in London alone in 1830–36. Yet by the summer of 1836, the government was forced to concede defeat. The Chancellor of the Exchequer informed the Commons on 20 June that the government

> had resorted to all means afforded by the existing law for preventing the publication of unstamped newspapers. The law officers of the Crown at the same time stated that the existing law was altogether ineffectual to the purpose of putting an end to the unstamped papers.
>
> (*Parliamentary Debates*, vol. 34, 20 June 1836, col. 627–8)

By the summer of 1836, the gross readership of the radical unstamped press published in London exceeded 2 million.[9] Its circulation exceeded even that of the respectable newspaper press (Hollis 1970).[10] The Whig government responded to this situation with a well-prepared counter-offensive. New measures were passed which strengthened the search and confiscation powers of the government; increased the penalties of being found in possession of an unstamped newspaper; and reduced the stamp duty by 75 per cent in order to reduce the advantages of 'smuggling'. What has been widely hailed as a liberalizing measure, a landmark of press freedom, was manifestly repressive both in intention and effect. As Spring Rice, the Chancellor of the Exchequer, explained to the Commons, a strategic concession, combined with increased coercive powers, was necessary in order to enforce a system that had broken down (*Parl. Deb.*, vol. 34, 20 June 1836, col. 627–31). The aim of these new measures, he stated candidly, was 'to protect the capitalist' and 'put down the unstamped papers' (*Parl. Deb.*, vol. 37, 13 April 1837, col. 1165).

In the face of this fresh onslaught, the underground press capitulated. 'No unstamped paper can be attempted with success', declared Hetherington, a leading radical publisher, shortly after being released from prison, unless 'some means can be devised either to print the newspaper without types and presses, or render the premises . . . inaccessible to armed force' (*London Dispatch*, 17 September 1836). By 1837, all the principal radical publishers paid the stamp duty.

This forced radical newspapers to increase their prices sharply. Whereas most unstamped papers had sold at 1d in the early 1830s, their successors in the 1840s sold at 4d to 5d – a price that was well beyond the means of individual working-class consumers. Yet, the authorities' attempt to break the radical press failed as a consequence of collective resistance. Some people pooled their resources to buy a shared newspaper each week; others paid a subscription through the branches of their unions, clubs and political associations; and others, still, even pressurized taverns into buying radical papers by threatening to go elsewhere. Despite the stamp duty, new radical papers emerged which attained even larger sales than the leading unstamped papers had achieved. The largest selling unstamped paper, the radical *Weekly Police Gazette*, had a circulation of 40,000.[11] In 1839, the *Northern Star* reached over 50,000 circulation (Read 1961: 101) setting a new record for the radical press, which was in turn surpassed by *Reynolds' News* in the 1850s (Berridge 1975).

These circulations seem very small by modern standards. But then circulation provides a highly anachronistic guide to readership in the first half of the nineteenth century. The modal number of readers per copy of national newspapers in the first half of the 1970s was 2 to 3 (National Readership Surveys, 1970–75): the modal number of readers per copy of cheap unstamped papers in the 1830s was certainly not less than 10 and was probably even higher in the case of their high-priced successors like the *Northern Star*.[12] The *Northern Star* and *Reynolds' News* each reached, at their meridian, at least half a million readers before the repeal of the stamp duty.[13]

Furthermore, radical newspapers were the pace-setters in terms of circulation during the first half of the nineteenth century. *Twopenny Trash*, in 1816–17, gained several times the circulation of most respectable papers.[14] The *Weekly Police Gazette*'s circulation in 1836 was over three times that of *The Times*. The *Northern Star* set yet another record, gaining the largest circulation of any paper published in the provinces (Select Committee on Newspaper Stamps, 1851: 524–57).[15] And the Chartist *Reynolds' News*, only a little behind the radical-liberal *Lloyds Weekly*, the circulation leader of the early 1850s, also had a leading position in contemporary journalism (Berridge 1975). The extent of the dominance of radical newspapers in the first half of the nineteenth century is, moreover, understated by these comparative circulation figures since radical papers had a very much larger number of readers per sale than the respectable press.[16]

The control system administered through the state had failed. Neither libel law nor press taxes had been able to prevent the rise of a radical popular press in the first half of the nineteenth century representing the interests and aspirations of the working class.

THE IMPACT OF THE RADICAL PRESS

One of the most important, and least commented upon, aspects of the development of the radical press in the first half of the nineteenth century was that its leading publications developed a country-wide circulation. Even as early as the second decade, leading radical papers like the *Political Register* and *Republican* were read as far afield as Yorkshire, Lancashire, the Midlands and East Anglia, as well as in the South of England. By the early 1830s, the principal circulation radical newspapers like the *Weekly Police Gazette* and *Poor Man's Guardian* had a distribution network extending from Glasgow to Land's End and from Carmarthen to Norwich. This distribution network was further developed by radical papers, notably the *Northern Star* and *Reynolds' News*, in subsequent decades. Part of the impact of the radical press stemmed from this central fact – the extent of its geographical distribution.

The radical press was important in unifying different groups of workers partly because its leading publications were national media, providing national coverage and reaching a national working-class audience. It helped to extend the often exclusive occupational solidarity of the new trade unionism to other sectors of the labour movement by showing the common predicament of workers in different occupations and in different trades throughout the country. People struggling to establish a trade union in their locality could read in the radical press in 1833–4, for instance, of similar struggles by glove workers in Yeovil, cabinet-makers and joiners in Carlisle and Glasgow, shoemakers and smiths in Northampton, and bricklayers and masons in London (to mention only some) as well as the struggles of workers in Belgium and Germany. The radical press helped to reduce the geographical isolation of local labour communities by revealing that localized agitation – whether against local Poor Law Commissioners, new machinery, long working hours or wage cutting – conformed to a common pattern throughout the country. The radical press carried news that none of the respectable papers carried, and focused attention on the common problems of working people. In this way, it helped to forge a connexion between disparate groups fragmented by localist loyalties, and promote a sense of common identity. It was, in the words of the Chartist leader, Feargus O'Connor, 'the link that binds the industrious classes together' *(Northern Star*, 16 January 1841).

Because of their national circulation, radical newspapers also profoundly influenced the institutional development of the working class. They helped to transform local community action into nationally organized campaigns. The *Poor Man's Guardian*, for instance, provided a vital institutional link between the different branches of the National Union of the Working Classes during the early 1830s just as the *Northern Star* was to perform a similar function for the Chartist movement in the late 1830s and the 1840s. Both papers acted as important mediators between the leadership and the rank and file. They helped to create a common platform on which to unite; to give a national direction to local activities; and to make local activists conscious of their place in a wider national movement. The radical press helped, in short, to sustain powerful agencies for the development of working-class consciousness.

The radical press also contributed to the growth of working-class political and industrial organizations in more concrete ways. It publicized meetings and helped to raise funds. It brought into national prominence the vanguard of the working-class movement. (For example, the publicity given to agricultural workers in the remote village of Tolpuddle, who in 1834 were transported to Australia for joining a trade union, helped to transform them into national working-class martyrs.) Radical press publicity attracted new recruits into the ranks of the activist working-class movement; it stimulated people into spontaneously setting up local branches; and, no less important, it fortified the commitment of working-class activists and sustained through publicity the belief that they were succeeding in the face of seemingly impossible odds. Without the *Northern Star*, declared one speaker at a local Chartist meeting, 'their own sounds might echo through the wilderness' *(Northern Star*, 18 August 1833).

Above all, radical newspapers contributed to a cultural reorientation of the working class. We have become so accustomed to the privatized pattern of newspaper consumption amid a steady flow of information from a variety of institutionally mediated sources that it requires an effort of historical imagination to understand the cultural meaning and importance of the newspaper in early nineteenth-century Britain. The arrival of a newspaper was often an eagerly awaited event. 'On the day', recalls Fielden, 'the newspaper, the *Northern Star*, O'Connor's paper, was due, the people used to line the roadside waiting for its arrival, which was paramount to everything else for the time being' (cited in Epstein 1976: 11). Newspaper reading was a social activity: newspapers were often read in a social setting outside the home or shared between friends. Above all, radical newspapers were frequently read out aloud (and indeed were written to be read aloud), providing a focal point of interaction. The ideas transmitted by the radical press were diffused widely beyond their immediate audience.

The radical press, reflecting in the main the perspectives of the vanguard of the working-class movement,[17] profoundly influenced the attitudes and beliefs of large numbers of working people. It described society not in terms of a series of disconnected events but as a system of exploitation. Early radical papers argued that a corrupt and parasitic 'crew' of placemen and pensioners, royalty and priests, lawyers, monopolists and aristocrats, lived off the productive classes. This became fused with a more sophisticated proto-Marxist analysis in the 1830s, focusing on profits as the means by which the capitalist class appropriated the wealth created by workers. Reality was defined not as given – 'the way things are' – but as a process of oppression which could be replaced by a new social order organized on different principles. The world could be changed, it was repeatedly argued, if workers combined together.

The radical press also helped to undermine normative support for the social order by challenging the legitimacy of the political and economic institutions on which it was based. The sanctity of property ownership was denied on the grounds that all land had been stolen from the people in a former age or was acquired through the labour of workers. The law came to be portrayed as the means by which capitalists legitimated this 'fraud'. The 'property people', declared the *Poor Man's Guardian*, 'having all the law making to themselves, make and maintain fraudulent institutions, by which they continue (under false pretences) to transfer the wealth of producers to themselves' *(Poor Man's Guardian*, 26 July 1834). 'A million of individuals', declared the *Reynolds' News* in a similar vein, 'qualified by the possession of a certain amount of that property which is either produced by the working classes or due to their natural heritage, will be called upon to elect law-makers and tax-imposers for twenty six millions at home and a hundred million abroad' *(Reynolds' News*, 5 January 1851).

The militant press sought to inoculate its readers against the virus of liberal reformism. 'Don't believe those', declared the *Poor Man's Guardian*, 'who tell you that the middle and working classes have one and the same interest . . . their respective interests [are] as directly opposed to each other as two fighting bulls.' The solution to poverty and oppression lay in the fundamental reconstruction of society based, as *Reynolds' News* was arguing in the early 1850s, on winning state power through universal suffrage and the public ownership of land and 'machinery'.

The radical press never achieved a consistently oppositional perspective of society. Even the more radical papers tended to combine a liberal and proto-socialist critique in an uncertain synthesis, and to be rather vague about the economic programme they advocated. However, the rise of the radical press created an influential forum of debate within the working class, enabling its activists to search for new ways of understanding a rapidly changing society, and to grapple with how best to change it. The radical press sustained a radical sub-culture from which emerged the Grand National Consolidated Trades Union, Chartism and the General Strike of 1842. As John Foster (1974) has shown, the latter was not a momentary eruption of frustration but a planned mass action which received extensive support in industrial Lancashire, much of Yorkshire and parts of the Midlands. While it was crushed, and 1,500 labour leaders imprisoned, it was a sign of an increasingly unstable society in which the radical press had become a significant force.

ECONOMIC STRUCTURE OF THE RADICAL PRESS 1815–55

The radical press grew out of the rise of trade unions and popular radical movements. What also made it possible was the prevailing economic structure of publishing. Since this is an important aspect of the central argument that follows, it is worth examining in some detail the finances of the early radical press.

The initial capital required to set up a radical paper in the early part of the nineteenth century was extremely small. Most of the radical unstamped papers were printed not on a steam press but on hand presses, costing anything from £10 to acquire. Metal type was often hired by the hour and print workers paid on a piecework basis.

The leading stamped radical papers after 1836 were printed on more sophisticated machinery. The *London Dispatch*, for instance, was printed on a Napier machine, bought with the help of a wealthy well-wisher and the retained profits from Hetherington's other publications. The *Northern Star* had a press especially constructed for it in London. Even so, launch costs were extremely small by comparison with the subsequent period. The *Northern Star*, for instance, was launched with a total capital of £690 raised mostly by public subscription in northern towns (Glasgow 1954).

The run-in costs of the radical press were also extremely small. Radical unstamped papers paid no tax: they relied heavily upon news reports filed by their readers on a voluntary basis; they recruited street-sellers mainly from the army of unemployed; and they had a small newsprint bill due to their high readership per copy. Hollis estimates, for instance, that the *Poor Man's Guardian*, a leading newspaper of the early 1830s, broke even with a sale as small as 2,500 (Hollis 1970: 132).

Compliance with the law after 1836 meant that a penny stamp duty had to be paid on each copy sold. Even so, running costs were still very small by later standards. The influential *London Dispatch* reported, for instance, that 'the whole expense allowed for editing, reporting, reviewing, literary contributions, etc., in fact, the entire cost of what is technically called "making up" the paper is only six pounds per week' *(London Dispatch*, 17 September 1836). In the same issue, it reported that, at its selling price of 3½d, it could break even with a circulation of 16,000. Similarly, the *Northern Star*, which developed, unlike its predecessors, a substantial network of paid correspondents, claimed to be spending just over £9.10s a week on its reporting establishment in 1841. Selling at 4½d, it was able to break even with a sale of about 6,200 copies a week (Read 1961). The limited money required to cover running costs before it broke even (which it did almost immediately) was probably met by its controller, Feargus O'Connor (Epstein 1976).

The low launch and establishment costs of newspaper publishing in the first half of the nineteenth century fundamentally affected the character of the British popular press. It was still possible for newspapers to be financed from within the working class, and consequently for the ownership and control of newspapers to be in the hands of people committed, in the words of Joshua Hobson, an ex-handloom weaver and publisher of the *Voice of West Riding*, 'to support the rights and interests of the order and class to which it is my pride to belong' (Hollis 1970: 94). Some newspapers like the *Voice of the People*, the *Northern Star*, the *Liberator* and *Trades Newspaper* were owned principally by working men and trade union organizations. Other leading papers were owned by individual proprietors like Cleave, Watson and Hetherington, people mostly of humble origins who had risen to prominence through the working-class movement. While not lacking in ruthlessness or business acumen, the people they entrusted to edit their newspapers were all former manual workers like William Hill and Joshua Hobson or middle-class activists like O'Brien and Lorymer whose experience had been shaped by long involvement in working-class politics. Indeed, full-time correspondents of both the *Northern Star* and the early *Reynolds' News* sometimes acted in a double capacity as political organizers.

These men had very different conceptions of their role as journalists from those of the institutionalized journalists of the popular press in the subsequent period. They viewed themselves as class representatives rather than as neutral professionals; they sought to interpret as well as to report the news; they recruited readers as correspondents and news sources; and some saw themselves as ventriloquists of their public. As the editor wrote in the *Northern Star* on its fifth anniversary, 'I have ever sought to make it [the *Northern Star*] rather a reflex of your minds than a medium through which to exhibit any supposed talent or intelligence of my own. This is precisely my conception of what a people's organ should be' (cited in Epstein 1976: 85).

The second important feature of the economic structure of the radical press in the first half of the nineteenth century was that it was self-sufficient on the proceeds of sales alone. The radical unstamped press carried very little commercial advertising and the stamped radical press fared little better. The *London Dispatch* complained bitterly, for instance, of the 'prosecutions, fines and the like *et ceteras* with which a paper of our principles *is* sure to be more largely honoured than by the lucrative patronage of advertisers' (17 September 1836). The grudge held by the *London Dispatch* and other radical newspapers against advertisers was more than justified. An examination of the official advertisement duty returns reveals a marked difference in the amount of advertising support received by the radical press compared with its more respectable rivals. Set out in Table 3.1, for instance, are the official returns for advertisement duties paid per 1,000 copies by the *Northern Star* and its principal rivals – Liberal and Tory weeklies in Leeds, where the *Northern Star* was published – and London dailies which, like the *Northern Star*, had a countrywide circulation. Advertisement duty per 1,000 copies provides a useful index of comparison since it takes into account differences of circulation. However, it does not take into account the much lower advertising rates (and therefore revenue) of the *Northern Star* compared with its rivals, and underestimates therefore the disadvantage which it suffered. Even so, the official returns reveal a disparity of advertising support of massive proportions. In 1840, for instance, the leading national paper and the two middle-class papers, published in Leeds, each paid an advertisement duty per 1,000 circulation more than fifty times that of the *Northern Star*. Perhaps of even greater significance for the future development of the press, the Liberal reform *Leeds Times*, edited by Samuel Smiles, with a predominantly lower middle-class audience, but including also a working-class readership, paid twenty-three times more advertisement duty per 1,000 circulation in 1840 than the *Northern Star*.

A similar pattern emerges in the case of other leading radical papers for which returns are available. In 1817, for instance, Cobbett's *Political Register* received only three advertisements: its advertisement duty per 1,000 copies was less than a hundredth of rival periodicals like the *Examiner, Age, National Register* and *Duckett's Weekly Dispatch*. The *London Dispatch* in 1837 was only a little better placed: it paid per 1,000 copies less than one twenty-fifth of the advertisement duty paid by daily papers in London, also with a country-wide circulation; and also less than one twenty-fifth of the duty per 1,000 copies paid by leading middle-class weeklies in Manchester, Liverpool, Leeds and York.

This lack of support placed radical stamped newspapers at a serious disadvantage. They were deprived of the patronage which financed increased editorial outlay by their competitors. They were forced to close down with circulations

Table 3.1 Advertisement duties paid by selected newspapers 1838–42

	1838		1840		1842*	
	Advertise-ment Duty £	Advertise-ment Duty per 1,000 circulation £	Advertise-ment Duty £	Advertise-ment Duty per 1,000 circulation £	Advertise-ment Duty £	Advertise-ment Duty per 1,000 circulation £
Leeds Mercury	943	2.05	1,042	2.11	948	1.97
Leeds Times	193	1.46	157	0.93	178	1.55
Leeds Intelli-gence	518	2.99	568	2.66	567	1.97
Northern Star	115	0.20	45	0.04	57	0.08
Times	11,238	2.63	13,887	2.74	15,223	2.41
Morning Post	3,191	3.64	3,468	3.64	3,662	3.08
Morning Chronicle	4,796	2.23	4,415	2.22	4,313	2.25
Morning Advertiser	3,849	2.46	3,822	2.24	3,068	2.17

Source: Stamp and Advertisement Duty Returns, recorded in *House of Commons Accounts and Papers* 1840, vol. xxix and 1842, vol xxvi.
* Estimated from half-yearly returns.

whose equivalent enabled other papers, buoyed up with advertising, to make a profit. This last factor severely inhibited the growth of a radical stamped press at a time when the price of contemporary newspapers, inflated by the stamp duty, was a major deterrent against buying papers among the working class.

Yet, despite these very substantial disadvantages, the absence of advertising did not force closure. While fortunes were not easily made from radical newspaper publishing, radical newspapers – both stamped and unstamped – could be profitable. Without significant advertising patronage in 1837, Hetherington, the publisher of the stamped *London Dispatch*, was reported to be making £1,000 a year from his business (Hollis 1970: 135). Similarly, the stamped *Northern Star* was estimated to have produced a phenomenal profit of £13,000 in 1839 and £6,500 in 1840 (Schoyen 1958: 133) which, as we have seen, was generated from sales rather than advertising revenue.

This absence of dependence on advertising profoundly influenced the development of the radical press. It did not need to pander to the political prejudices of advertisers. It was able to attack 'buy cheap and sell dear shopocrats', 'millocrats' and 'capitalists', without fear of the consequences. No less important, radical newspapers could address themselves directly to the working class without the need to appeal to people who constituted a more valuable advertising market. Whereas pioneer radical publications appealed to both middle- and working-class readers, their more radical successors tended to be directed more towards working-class audiences.[18] These papers were able to project a polarized model of conflict because they could afford to alienate potential middle-class readers which advertisers wanted to reach. They depended upon their readers' pennies, not the largesse of advertisers, for their survival.

THE UGLY FACE OF REFORM

The middle-class campaign against 'the taxes on knowledge' was informed by a variety of special interests, not the least the concern of campaigners like Milner Gibson and Cobden in the 1850s to extend the influence of the liberal, free-trade press. The central issue that divided most middle-class supporters and opponents of press taxes, however, was how best to establish the press as an instrument of social control.

Traditionalists argued that press taxes were the last line of defence holding back a flood of radical publications. The reduction of newspaper prices, following repeal, would result in the general dissemination of 'doctrines injurious to the middle and upper classes, and damaging to the real and lasting interests of the public . . . their malignant influence will be immeasurably increased by the Repeal of the Stamp Duty' (Westmacott 1836). It would also facilitate the establishment of many more radical papers by reducing publishing costs. As Mowbray Morris, Manager of *The Times*, told the Select Committee on Newspaper Stamps, it is in 'the interest of the public that any branch of industry such as that of producing newspapers should be limited to a few hands, and be in the hands of parties who are great capitalists' (Anon 1939: 205).

Middle-class opponents of press taxes argued that, on the contrary, press taxes prevented the dissemination of sound principles since it restricted the development of the press. Repeal of the advertisement duty would release and also redirect a flow of advertising patronage for the establishment of new newspapers. The repeal of the stamp and paper duties would increase access to 'sound doctrines' by reducing newspaper prices. It would dispel 'ignorance', argued the *Spectator*, and promote public order (*Spectator*, 1 August 1835). 'Readers are not rioters: readers are not rick-burners', Hickson told the Select Committee on Newspaper Stamps (1851: 479). The diffusion of sound principles, through repeal, would prove a more effective instrument of social control than state coercion. 'Is it not time to consider', declared Bulwer Lytton in a famous speech against the stamp duty, 'whether the printer and his types may not provide better for the peace and honour of a free state than the gaoler and the hangman?' (cited in Wiener 1969b: 68).

The confidence placed by opponents of press taxes in the 'free' market place of opinion was more than justified. In the second half of the nineteenth century, following the repeal of the advertisement duty in 1853 and the stamp duty in 1855, the radical popular press was eclipsed. Why this happened has never been adequately explained.

MARKET FORCES AS A CONTROL SYSTEM 1855–1920

The decline of radicalism in the popular press in the immediate post-stamp era can be attributed partly to the decline of working-class radicalism with the restabilization of the social order. Yet, as we shall see, the decline of the radical press was part of this process of restabilization. And the '*zeitgeist*' theory does not explain why the revival of working-class radicalism did not lead to a similar revival of radical journalism. Indeed, the national press was more radical in 1860, a period of relative tranquillity, than it was fifty years later at a time of militant working-class agitation. There was manifestly no close correlation between the climate of opinion in the country and changes in the ideological perspectives mediated by the press in Victorian and Edwardian Britain.

Virginia Berridge (1965) offers a seemingly plausible explanation for the change in popular journalism in a pioneering study of the popular Victorian press. The decline of radicalism, she argues, was due to the 'commercialization' of the popular press. Newspapers concentrated upon the easy arousal of sensationalism rather than taxing political analysis in order to maximize sales: reports of crime, scandal and sport displaced attacks on capitalism as more saleable commodities.

However, this analysis implies a bigger departure from the tradition of radical journalism of the 1830s and 1840s than is justified. The growth of the radical press in this period was based partly upon the skill with which some radical publishers exploited the street literature tradition of radical sensationalism and scandal. The shift from a periodical quarto to newspaper broadsheet format among unstamped papers in the early 1830s was accompanied by a marked trend towards 'general' and sensational news coverage. Hetherington, publisher of the *Poor Man's Guardian*, *Destructive* and *London Dispatch*, announced the change with characteristic aplomb, promising his readers

> all the gems and treasures, and fun and frolic and news and occurrences of the week . . . Police Intelligence, Murder, Rapes, Suicides, Burnings, Maimings, Theatricals, Races, Pugilism, and all manner of moving accidents by flood and field. In short, it will be stuffed with every sort of devilment that will make it sell . . . Our object is not to make money, but to beat the Government.
>
> (Cited in Hollis 1970: 122)

While the press entrepreneurs of the subsequent period carried this trend a stage further and included a higher proportion of non-political features in their papers, this hardly constitutes an adequate explanation of an extraordinary phenomenon – the complete transformation of the popular press. For not only was the radical press increasingly absorbed into the liberal press or eliminated, a whole new generation of national popular newspapers emerged which were predominantly on the right or the extreme right of the political spectrum.

The commercialization thesis is, in effect, an historical version of the mass culture critique based on the assumption that material processed for a mass audience is inevitably trivialized and sensationalized in order to cater for the common denominator of mass taste (e.g. Wilensky 1964). Not only is this assumption sometimes a dubious one, and the cultural judgements that underlie it open to question, as I have argued elsewhere (Curran 1977), it obscures under the general heading of 'commercialization' the complex system of controls institutionalized by the consolidation of the capitalist press in mid-Victorian Britain.

THE FREEDOM OF CAPITAL

One of the central objectives of press taxes – to exclude pauper management of the press – was attained only by their repeal.

The enormous expansion of demand, following the abandonment of newspaper taxation, resulted in what A.E. Musson calls an 'industrial revolution' in the press (Musson 1954: 214). Hoe printing presses were introduced in the 1860s and 1870s and were gradually replaced by rotary machines of increasing size and sophistication. 'Craft' composing was revolutionized by Hattersley's composing machine in the 1860s, and this in turn was replaced by the linotype machine in the 1880s and 1890s. Numerous innovations were also made in graphic reproduction during the Victorian period. These developments led to a sharp rise in fixed capital costs. Northcliffe estimated £0.5m as 'the initial cost of machinery, buildings, ink factories and the like, and this was altogether apart from the capital required for daily working expenses' in setting up the *Daily Mail*, although this figure almost certainly includes the cost of the establishing the paper in a building which housed other publications (Pound and Harmsworth 1959: 206). The enormous increase in capital needs of publishing conferred considerable scale advantages on entrepreneurs who established multiple newspapers and jobbing companies making maximum use of shared plant and facilities. The vertical integration of publishing – Edward Lloyd led the way in the 1870s and 1880s by establishing paper mills and growing esparto grass on 100,000 acres of plantation for the production of paper – also assisted large-scale enterprises. Even so, the rising capital costs of newspaper publishing did not constitute an insuperable obstacle to the launch of new publications with limited fianancial resources even in the national market. Newspapers, like the *Daily Herald* in 1912, could be launched with little money by being printed on a contract basis by an independent printer.

Much more important was the effect of growing demand, released by the repeal of press taxes, on the running costs and cash flow requirements of newspaper publishing. Circulation levels in the mass market soared: *Lloyd's Weekly* had a circulation in 1896 about 15 times that of leading circulation papers fifty years before (although its audience was not correspondingly larger, due to a sharp reduction in the ratio of readers per copy). The increasing scale of production raised costs. There was also a steady rise of paging levels (and therefore newsprint costs), a substantial increase in expenditure on news-gathering and processing, and an increase in promotion costs (partly in the form of sale-or-return agreements to distributors). This rise in costs led in turn to a increase in the circulations that were needed in order to make a profit. The break-even point was also forced up by the reduction of newspaper prices. New newspapers could be launched with limited funds and derelict newspapers could be bought relatively cheaply. It was the *establishment* of newspapers that required large capital resources.

This important change can be illustrated by the history of individual newspapers in the period. In 1855, it required a capital investment of £4,000 to relaunch the then liberal *Daily Telegraph* and establish it as the circulation leader in the national daily press (Burnham 1955: 2). By the 1870s, Edward Lloyd needed to spend £150,000 to re-establish the *Daily Chronicle* (Herd 1952: 185). During the period 1906-8, Thomasson spent about double that amount attempting to establish the Liberal daily, *Tribune* (Lee 1976: 166). In 1919–22, Beaverbrook invested £200,000 on the development of the *Daily Express* and took nothing out (Taylor 1972: 171); and he invested a further £2 million in the *Sunday Express* (even though it was able to take advantage of the plant facilities established for the *Daily Express*) before it broke even (Taylor 1972: 175). Similarly, Lord Cowdray invested perhaps £750,000 attempting to convert the *Westminster Gazette* into a morning paper (Seymour-Ure 1975: 242).

These statistics illustrate the freedom of capital in the creation of the modern press. Even when the capital costs of launch and establishment were relatively low in the 1850s and 1860s, they still exceeded the resources readily available to the working class. The *Bee-Hive*, for instance, was launched in 1862 with a capital of less than £250 raised by trade-union organizations and a well-to-do sympathizer. Its under-capitalization put it at a serious disadvantage; it sold at a price twice that of its leading competitors; and it lacked the resources necessary to maintain its original commitment to providing general news coverage despite the small amount of additional capital put up by unions and other contributors. In effect, its lack of capital support condemned it to the margins of national publishing as a specialist if influential weekly paper (Coltham 1960).[19]

As the resources of organized labour increased, so did the costs of establishing a national paper. It was not until 1912 that papers controlled by activists in the working-class movement, and financed from within the working class, made their first appearance in national daily journalism, and then their belated appearance occurred long after most national daily papers had become well established. The brief career of the *Daily Citizen*, and the chequered early history of the *Daily Herald*, illustrate the economic obstacles to establishing papers under working-class control. The *Daily Citizen*, launched in 1912 with a capital of only £30,000 subscribed mainly by trade unions, reached a peak circulation of 250,000 within two years and was only 50,000 short of overhauling the *Daily Express*, which had been launched in 1900. Although the *Daily Citizen* almost certainly had more working-class readers than any other daily in the country, subsequent capital support was insufficient to prevent its closure three years after its launch (Holton

1974). The more left-wing *Daily Herald*, launched with a capital of only £300 and sustained by public donations (notably from two wealthy socialists, the Countess de la Warr and R.D. Harben, the son of the chairman of Prudential Insurance), lurched from one crisis to another despite also reaching a circulation of 250,000 at its meridian before 1914. On one occasion, it came out in pages of different sizes and shapes because someone 'found' old discarded paper supplies when the *Daily Herald* could no longer afford to pay for paper. On other occasions, it bought small quantities of paper under fictitious names from suppliers all over the country. The directors of the *Daily Herald* even threatened organized industrial action against paper manufacturers, a stratagem that secured paper supplies without a guarantee (Lansbury 1925). While the *Daily Citizen* closed, the *Daily Herald* survived by switching from being a daily to becoming a weekly during the period 1914 to 1919. From these humble beginnings emerged a paper that became, for a time, the biggest circulation daily paper in the western world.

The rise in publishing costs helps to explain why the genuinely radical press in the late nineteenth century survived only in an emasculated form as low-budget, high-price specialist weeklies like the *Clarion* and *Labour Leader* (both of which attained surprisingly large circulations)[20] and as local community papers, an important but as yet under-researched aspect of the residual survival of the radical press.

But if the rise of market-entry costs helps to explain why the popular press during its formative phase of development was owned largely by wealthy capitalists, it still leaves unanswered why radical newspapers in existence before the repeal of press taxes were mostly absorbed ideologically or closed. Nor does it adequately explain why small circulation radical newspapers did not evolve over time into mass circulation publications and generate capital through retained profits for the launch of new radical publications. For an answer, we need to look elsewhere.

THE NEW LICENSING SYSTEM

The crucial element of the new control system was the role of advertising in the development of the press after the repeal of the advertisement duty. The reduction of the advertisement duty from 3s to 1s 6d in 1833 led to a 35 per cent growth of London press advertising and a 27 per cent growth of provincial press advertising in the space of one year (Aspinall 1950). Between 1836 and 1848, the total volume of press advertising in Britain, as measured by the number of advertisements, increased by a further 36 per cent. Examination of the distribution of this increase shows, however, that a disproportionate amount went to upscale London newspapers.[21]

It was not until the repeal of the duty in 1853 that a radically different situation emerged. The advertisement duty, even in modified form, had influenced the structure of advertising expenditure. As John Cassell, the publisher of 'useful

knowledge' publications complained to the Select Committee on Stamps '*it*
[advertisement duty] entirely prevents a certain class of advertisements from
appearing; it is only such as costly books and property sales by auction that really
afford an opportunity of advertising and for paying the duty' (Select Committee
on Newspaper Stamps 1851: 236). Milner Gibson, chairman of the Select
Committee, succinctly summarized the point: 'the advertisement duty must really
destroy the advertisements that are not worth the duty' (ibid 440).

However, its repeal led to a boom in *popular* newspaper advertising. In the four
years between 1854 and 1858, *Reynolds' News*, for instance, increased its volume
of advertising by over 50 per cent (Berridge 1975). This growth of advertising, in
conjunction with the repeal of the stamp and paper duty, resulted in the modal
price of popular newspapers being halved in the 1850s and halved again in the
early 1860s. This transformed the economic structure of popular publishing. All
national newspapers in the mass market cost more to produce and distribute than
the net price at which they were sold.[22] Advertisers acquired a *de facto* licensing
authority since, without their support, newspapers ceased to be economically
viable. The old licensing system introduced by Henry VIII, and abandoned in
1695 as unenforceable, was restored in a new form.

The falling price of newsprint and increasing scale economies offered no relief
from dependence on advertising. There was a rapid growth of advertising in the
period after 1860 as a result of the growth in domestic consumption and structural changes in the economy. By 1907, Critchley (1974) estimates that total
advertising expenditure in the United Kingdom – most of which was spent on the
press – had reached £20m. This flow of advertising to the press exerted an
upwards pressure on costs: it led to a steady increase in editorial outlay and paging
levels noted earlier. More important, it also contributed to a further halving of
the price of most popular papers to ½d in the late Victorian period. National
newspapers continued to depend upon advertising in order to be profitable.

How advertising patronage was distributed consequently largely determined
the structure of the press. There is some evidence that advertisers withheld their
support from papers on political grounds. Certainly, successive governments
normally boycotted opposition papers when placing official advertisements and
announcements throughout most of the nineteenth century. In the 1850s, a
leading press proprietor like Lord Glenesk of the *Morning Post* expected as a
matter of course to receive official advertising from a Tory Government in preference to Liberal papers (Hindle 1937). Even as late as the 1880s, government
advertisements were usually sent only to pro-government papers and, while the
Liberals were in power, the *Morning Post* was not on the list (Lucas 1910: 113).
Some independent advertisers may also have discriminated against radical publications. Lord Crowther, for instance, urged his friends in 1832 to advertise in the
Tory local press (Aspinall 1973: 367). Charles Mitchell, the head of probably the
largest advertising agency in the country in mid-Victorian Britain, clearly thought
it relevant to document the political orientation of every newspaper in the country. As he explained in the introduction of his *Directory* in 1856 (5th edition), 'till

this *Directory* was published, the advertiser had no means of accurately determining which journal might be best adapted to his views, and most likely to forward his interests'. Even as late as 1925, Norman Hunter in *Advertising Through the Press*, one of Pitman's practical handbooks, advised the advertiser to 'pick out those [publications] which by the *soundness of their policy*, the extent of their circulation and the price of their advertisements, appear most likely to be beneficial for his purpose' (Hunter 1925: 50, my italics). Norman Hunter was the exception rather than the rule; by then it had become common for advertising texts to remonstrate against mixing politics with business. However, the trouble in practice was that it was sometimes difficult to separate politics from commercial judgement. Because there were no reliable readership surveys until the 1930s, the political orientation of newspapers provided a useful indication of their readers' purchasing power and social class. This sometimes led to the simplistic identification of 'socialist' papers with a working-class readership.[23]

While the extent of political discrimination (both conscious and unconscious) by advertisers in the Victorian and Edwardian era can never be clearly established, it is clear that working-class media were consistently discriminated against on the grounds that their audiences did not constitute valuable markets to reach. As Mitchell declared in 1856, 'some of the most widely circulated journals in the Empire are the worst possible to advertise in. Their readers are not purchasers; and any money thrown upon them is so much thrown away' (*Mitchell's* 1856: 7). The thinking underlying such judgements was simple. As the *Guide to Advertisers* put it, 'character is of more importance than number. A journal that circulates a thousand among the upper or middle classes is a better medium than would be one circulating a hundred thousand among the lower classes' (Anon 1851). The explicit preference for middle-class media in advertising texts of the mid-Victorian period was modified in the latter part of the century with the development of mass marketing. But the stress on the disparity of income persisted in guides to media evaluation. This led to a crucial distinction being made between middle-market and down-market media, between papers which appealed to all classes alike and papers which appealed to the poor. Thus, as Cyril Fox, a lecturer in advertising at the Regent Street Polytechnic, wrote in a standard advertising text of the early 1920s, 'for an average proposition, not a Rolls Royce motor car or a three-penny fire-lighter, you cannot afford to place your advertisements in a paper which is read by the down-at-heels who buy it to scan the Situations Vacant column. . . . The paper which appeals to the bulk of the buyers is best for you' (Freer 1921: 203).

The strategic control acquired by advertisers over the press profoundly shaped its development. In the first place, it exerted a powerful pressure on the radical press to move up market as an essential strategy for survival. It forced radical newspapers to redefine their target audience, and this in turn caused them to moderate their radicalism in order to attract readers that advertisers wanted to reach. This process is well illustrated by the career of *Reynolds' News*. It was founded in 1850 by George Reynolds, who was not only a member of the Chartist national executive but also a member of its left-wing faction. Reynolds had urged a 'physical force' strategy in 1848 and consistently opposed middle-class collaboration in the early 1850s. His paper was in the *Northern Star* tradition of class-conscious radicalism, attacking industrial capitalism and the exploitation of labour. Like the *Northern Star*, it had close institutional links with the working-class movement, raising money for working-class causes and publishing reports sent in by readers.

Yet, despite its radical origins, *Reynolds' News* progressively changed under the impact of the new economic imperatives of newspaper publishing. The fact that it never offered, at the outset, a fully developed oppositional perspective doubtless made it vulnerable to ideological incorporation. It inevitably responded to the decline of radicalism in the country during the 1850s and early 1860s. But an important factor in its absorption was the need to attract advertising revenue. The change was symbolized by the inclusion of a regular investment column on friendly societies in the year after the repeal of the advertisement duty as a ploy to attract advertising. A movement that had been regularly attacked in radical newspapers as 'a hoax' to persuade working-class people to identify with capitalism became a valuable and much needed source of revenue for the *Reynolds' News*. While the paper continued for a long time to take a radical stand on most major events of the day, it also expressed increasingly the individualistic middle-class values of the readers it needed to attract. It adopted many of the tenets of political economy that it had so virulently attacked during the 1850s, even to the extent of accepting the palliatives of 'prudent marriage' (i.e. sexual restraint) and emigration as solutions to unemployment. It reverted to those common denominators of radicalism that united the lower middle and working classes – attacks on 'the vices' of the aristocracy, privilege, corruption in high places, the monarchy, placemen and the church. Attacks on industrial capital were scaled down to attacks on monopoly and speculators. *Reynolds' News* became a populist paper catering for a coalition of middle-class and working-class readers necessary for its survival. Under new ownership, it evolved into becoming a Liberal paper in the late nineteenth century. Reynolds was accused of commercial opportunism by his radical contemporaries, yet it is difficult to see what else he could have done if the *Reynolds' News* was to survive the transition to an advertising-based system. Even the radical *People's Paper* stressed in an advertisement placed in *Mitchell's Directory* (1857–8) that it circulated not only among 'the working class generally' but also 'among high paid trades and shopkeepers'. Despite the fact that its circulation far exceeded that of most of its rivals selling at the same price, it was forced to close down.[24]

Radical newspapers could survive in the new economic environment only if they moved up market to attract an audience desired by advertisers or remained in a small working-class ghetto, with manageable losses that could be met from donations. Once they moved out of that ghetto and attracted a growing working-class audience, they courted disaster. Each paper cost more to produce than the net price at which it was sold, so that any increase in circulation meant increased losses unless supported by increased advertising.

This was the problem that confronted the radical *Evening Echo*, a London paper which was taken over by wealthy radicals in 1901 and given a further push to the left under its new editor in 1902. A special number was issued setting out the aims and policy of the paper under new management, firmly committing it to 'the interests of Labour as against the tyranny of organized capital'. In the period 1902–4, its circulation rose by a phenomenal 60 per cent, leading to its abrupt closure in 1905. The growth of advertising had failed to keep pace with the growth of circulation, making the continuance of the paper impossible (Pethick-Lawrence 1943: 65). The same thing nearly happened to the *Daily Herald*, when it was relaunched as a daily in 1919. It spent £10,000 on promotion – a small amount by comparison with its rivals (the *Daily Mail* spent over £1 million alone on free gifts and other forms of below-the-line promotion during the 1920s) but sufficient nevertheless to boost its sales. 'Our success in circulation', recalled George Lansbury, 'was our undoing. The more copies we sold the more money we lost' (Lansbury 1925: 160). The situation became increasingly desperate when, partly aided by the unexpected publicity of attacks on the *Daily Herald* by leading members of the government alleging that it was financed with 'red gold', the *Daily Herald*'s circulation continued to rise in 1920. 'Every copy we sold was sold at a loss,' mourned Lansbury. 'The rise in circulation, following the government's attacks, bought us nearer and nearer to disaster' (Lansbury 1925: 161). The money raised from whist drives, dances, draws and the like was not enough to offset its growing losses. Even the desperate expedient of doubling the paper's price – charging twice as much as its main rivals for a much smaller paper – did not make up the shortfall of advertising. Money from the miners and the railwaymen prevented the paper from closing. But the only way to secure the *Daily Herald*'s future was for it to be taken over by the Trades Union Congress (TUC) in 1922. A paper which had been a free-wheeling vehicle of the left, and an important outlet for syndicalist ideas, became the official mouthpiece of the moderate leadership of the labour movement. Lack of advertising forced it to become subservient to a new form of control.

In short, one of four things happened to national radical papers that failed to meet the requirements of advertisers.[25] They either closed down; accommodated to advertising pressure by moving up-market; stayed in a small audience ghetto with manageable losses; or accepted an alternative source of institutional patronage. The obverse to this is that the section of the press that did prosper and expand consisted of publications which conformed to the requirements of advertisers – professional, trade and technical journals providing a commercially useful specialist segmentation of the market; newspapers reaching the 'quality' market; newspapers that reached 'middle England'; or those that straddled the social classes. The rapid growth of advertising encouraged the launch of these categories of publication; it also subsidized their costs, financed their development and contributed to their profits. Its impact can be observed in the phenomenal growth of magazines in the Victorian era (many of them trade, technical, professional and 'class' publications) from 557 magazines in 1866 to 2,097 in 1896; in the creation of a regional daily press which did not exist in England before the repeal of the advertisement duty but which numbered 196 regional dailies in 1900; in the rapid expansion of middle-class and middle-market community papers (there was a total of 868 newspapers in 1860, compared with 2,355 in 1896) and, above all, in the development of a middle-market popular national press.[26]

THE POST-STAMP PRESS 1855–1920

The development of the post-stamp press helped to divide and fragment the working-class movement and facilitate its incorporation into the Liberal and Tory parties. Most radical papers during the first half of the nineteenth century consistently denounced the parliamentary parties. In contrast, the majority of newspapers that sprang up after the repeal of the press taxes were closely affiliated to a major political party. Thus, ten of the new regional dailies that emerged between 1855 to 1860 were affiliated to the Liberal party; eighteen of the new regional dailies created between 1860 and 1870 were affiliated to the Tory or Liberal parties; and forty-one of the regional dailies created in the following decade were similarly linked to the two great parties (*Mitchell's* 1860–80). They played an important part in transforming what had previously been political groups in parliament, without a popular base, into mass organizations. No less important, the popular press played a significant role, as John Vincent (1972) has shown in his study of the Liberal Party, in invigorating the parliamentary parties themselves, by providing a vitalizing channel of communication with their rank and file.

The new popular national press that developed notably during the period 1880–1920 was also a powerful source of social cohesion. The values and perspectives that it mediated were profoundly different from those of early radical newspapers. A construction of reality as a system of exploitation gave way to a new definition of society in which class conflict was tacitly denied (a position resolutely maintained even in relation to the General Strike of 1926).[27] The portrayal of labour as the source of wealth was replaced by a celebration of the market as the engine of prosperity. The stress on collective action gave way to an emphasis on individual self-improvement and social partnership. The extent of the editorial transformation that took place is perhaps best exemplified by how little support the Labour Party obtained when it became a major political force. In the 1922 general election, for example, it obtained the backing of only 4 per cent of national daily circulation despite obtaining 30 per cent of the vote.[28]

The reconfiguration of the press also gave rise to growing imperialism. Britain's imperial involvements were portrayed as adventure stories, and (in some sectors of the press) as evangelical missions for spreading civilization, Christianity and prosperity. The following excerpt from a report of the 1898 Sudan expedition in the *Westminster Gazette* conveys the ethos of the late Victorian press:

A large number of the Tommies had never been under fire before . . . and there was a curious look of suppressed excitement in some of the faces. . . . Now and then I caught in a man's eye the curious gleam which comes from the joy of shedding blood – that mysterious impulse which, despite all the veneer of civilization, still holds its own in man's nature, whether he is killing rats with a terrier, rejoicing in a prize fight, playing a salmon or potting Dervishes. It was a fine day and we were out to kill something. Call it what you like, the experience is a big factor in the joy of living.

(Cited in Knightley 1975: 41).

The paper which celebrated 'potting Dervishes' was, in terms of the political spectrum represented by the national press, on 'the left' (i.e. Liberal) and one of the few papers not to join in the hysterical campaign of hatred against the Boers one year later (Spender 1927; Price 1972).

THE MODERN PRESS 1920–75

Space does not permit a detailed examination of the press in the post-First World War period. All that will be attempted is a brief outline of the salient developments that took place between 1920 and 1975.

The structure of the British national newspaper industry was determined by the interplay of market forces *before* 1920. The rise of publishing costs became so prohibitive, and the market position of leading publications became so well entrenched, that only two new national papers, both with small circulations, were established in the fifty-year period after 1920. These were the Communist *Sunday Worker*, launched in 1925 and converted into the *Daily Worker* and subsequently *Morning Star*, and the *Sunday Telegraph*, launched in 1961.

The ownership of the press became more concentrated. The leading three publishers controlled before 1890 only a small fraction of the national press. By 1976, the top three controlled 72 per cent of national daily and 86 per cent of national Sunday circulation.[29] Underlying this trend towards concentration was a number of interacting factors of which the effect of economies of scale and consolidation were perhaps the most important.

The advertising licensing system persisted. Without exception, every single national paper in the period 1920–75 made a loss on its sales alone (except during the period of stringent newsprint rationing during and immediately after the Second World War). There were, however, important changes in advertising media planning which affected the character of the British press (Curran 1976). During the inter-war period, the growth of mass consumption enhanced the value of working-class publications; the development of market research encouraged greater awareness of the importance of the mass working-class market; and the establishment of readership research and formalized criteria of media evaluation reduced the subjective element in advertising selection which had tended to operate against the left. All these changes led to a modest redistribution of advertising expenditure in favour of working-class and left publications. In 1936, the middle-class *Daily Mail* had only about twice the display advertising revenue per copy of the working-class *Daily Herald* – a smaller disparity than before.[30] The reallocation of advertising encouraged the relaunch of the *Daily Mirror* in 1934–6 as a populist paper redirected down-market. Its politics became more progressive, and it became more entertainment-centred. In 1937, the *Daily Mirror* devoted 10 per cent of its total *news* space to coverage of political, social and economic issues in Britain, half of what it had done ten years before (Royal Commission on the Press 1949: appendix 7, table 4: 250).

The post-war period witnessed further developments in advertising-media planning, which benefited working-class publications, notably the development of a new classification system, based on product categories, for analysing newspaper readership that emphasized the increasing purchasing power of working-class readerships. However, its effects, as far as the national popular press were concerned, were offset by the impact of television, the growth of classified advertising (which mainly benefited the quality press) and the sharp rise in publishing costs that resulted from the non-price competitive strategies adopted by the leading newspapers. In effect, the advertising licensing system was modified in a form that allowed deradicalized, entertainment-centred, mass circulation papers (whether conservative or social democratic) to prosper. However, the advertising system still withheld significant support from papers with a minority following primarily among the working class. This was underlined when the *Daily Herald* was eventually forced to close in 1964. Myths die hard and it is a recurrent theme of right-wing journalists that, in the words of Sir Denis Hamilton (Chairman of Times Newspaper) 'the *Herald* was beset by the problem which has dogged nearly every newspaper vowed to a political idea: not enough people wanted to read it' (Hamilton 1976). In fact, the *Daily Herald*, on its deathbed, was read by 4.7 million people – nearly twice as many as the readers of *The Times, Financial Times* and *Guardian* combined (National Readership Surveys 1963–4). Survey research also reveals that the *Daily Herald* was more valued, and read more thoroughly, by its readership than was any other popular national daily (Curran 1970). The *Daily Herald*, the lone consistent voice of 'labourism', died because its readers constituted neither a sufficiently mass nor a sufficiently affluent market to be attractive to advertisers.

The effect of the economic structuring of the press is illustrated by the response of the press to the two events in the inter-war period that polarized opinion between left and right – the General Strike of 1926 and the general election of 1931. Only one national daily paper (the *Daily Herald*) out of eleven supported the General Strike (or the 'Strike Evil' as the *Daily Mirror* called it). Only two national daily papers (the *Daily Herald* and the newly created *Daily Worker*) supported the Labour Party in the 1931 general election. Although the centre-left press became more significant in the ensuing period, it was strongly canted towards the centre.

CONCLUSION

The traditional system of control of the press administered through the state broke down in the early nineteenth century in the face of determined opposition from radical journalists sustained by an increasingly politically conscious working class. The stamp duty was reduced in 1836 in a successful bid to restore its effectiveness. However, this did not prevent the continued rise of the radical press, which became an increasingly influential and radicalising force in society.

In the middle of the nineteenth century, the state control system was replaced by a new system based on impersonal economic forces. Unlike the law, these could be neither evaded nor defied. The rise in publishing costs led to a cumulative transfer of ownership and control of the popular press to capitalist entrepreneurs, while the advertising licensing system encouraged the absorption or elimination of the early radical press and effectively stifled its re-emergence. Although the modern press was modified by changes in the operation of market forces that took place after 1920, the press still remained predominantly supportive of established power. Its enduring influence contributed significantly to the remarkable stability and underlying conservatism of British society.[31]

Part II

Media sociology

Chapter 4

New revisionism in media and cultural studies

During the conservative 1980s, a new revisionist movement emerged in media and cultural studies. Coming initially out of the radical tradition, it devoted much of its creative energy to attacking the premises and assumptions of that tradition. Indeed, in its fully fledged form, the new revisionism rejected the models of society, the ways of conceptualizing the role of the media, the explanatory frameworks and problematics of the principal radical paradigms in mass communication research.

This new revisionism presented itself as original and innovative, as an emancipatory movement that was throwing off the shackles of tradition. This was misleading. Part of the new thinking was revivalist rather than revisionist, a reversion to previous received wisdoms rather than a reconnaissance of the new. Another strand can be seen as a continuation of the 'radical' tradition but in a qualified form that owed as much to old as to new ideas.

During the same period, the liberal pluralist tradition of communications research also adapted and changed. Some researchers within this tradition modified their approach in response to attacks from radical critics: in effect, they moved against the flow of traffic coming the other way.

In short, media and cultural studies went through a profound change during the 1980s (and early 1990s). In an attempt to make sense of what happened, I have tried to provide a selective 'reading' of key developments during this formative period, concentrating mainly on media research in the United Kingdom but with an occasional sideways glance at studies in continental Europe, Scandinavia and the United States.[1]

POLARIZATION BETWEEN LIBERAL AND RADICAL RESEARCH TRADITIONS c.1975

Two readers, *Mass Communication and Society* and *Culture, Society and the Media*, published respectively in 1977 and 1982 but both mostly written in 1976, provide a useful starting point, since they crystallized a radical moment in the historical development of communications research (Curran *et al.* 1977;

Gurevitch *et al.* 1982). They were constructed around the antinomy between liberal pluralist and Marxist perspectives on the media, which were characterized in ideal-typical terms:

> The pluralists see society as a complex of competing groups and interests, none of them predominant all of the time. Media organizations are seen as bounded organizational systems, enjoying an important degree of autonomy from the state, political parties and institutionalized pressure groups. Control of the media is said to be in the hands of an autonomous managerial elite who allow a considerable degree of flexibility to media professionals. A basic symmetry is seen to exist between media institutions and their audiences, since in McQuail's words, the 'relationship is generally entered into voluntarily and on apparently equal terms' (McQuail 1977b). Audiences are seen as capable of manipulating the media in an infinite variety of ways according to their prior needs and dispositions and as a consequence of having access to what Halloran (1977) calls 'the plural values of society' enabling them to 'conform, accommodate or reject'.
>
> Marxists view capitalist society as being one of class domination; the media are seen as part of an ideological arena in which various class views are fought out, although within the context of the dominance of certain classes; ultimate control is increasingly concentrated in monopoly capital; media professionals, while enjoying the illusion of autonomy, are socialized into and internalize the norms of the dominant culture. The media, taken as a whole, relay interpretive frameworks consonant with the interests of the dominant classes, and media audiences, while sometimes negotiating and contesting these frameworks, lack ready access to alternative meaning systems that would enable them to reject the definitions offered by the media in favour of oppositional definitions.
>
> (Curran and Gurevitch 1977: 4–5)

The intention of most people involved in the production of these readers was to promote a polarized conflict between the two perspectives. This was partly a pedagogic device, since both books arose out of an Open University course and the aim was to encourage students to think for themselves and decide in favour of one or other tradition or to consider whether there might be a more convincing intermediate position. But the aim was also to assert as central to the debate an intellectual tradition – Marxism – that had been marginalized in British academic life for much of the post-war period. In particular, we wanted to resist the American domination of the field, with what seemed to many of us at the time as its sterile consensus, its endless flow of repetitive and inconclusive 'effects' studies situated in a largely 'taken-for-granted' liberal pluralist model of society, and instead to generate a debate that reflected the diversity of European intellectual thought.

This phase of the field's development has been outlined elsewhere (Curran *et al.* 1982; Hall 1986b) and does not need to be repeated. Arguably, the most original research during this period was in cultural studies and was preoccupied in one form or other with a debate about the determination and implications of the culture of everyday life. However, so far as journalism research was concerned, the most salient development was the Glasgow University Media Group's concerted assault on a liberal conception of public service broadcasting as a disinterested source of information and balanced forum of public debate. They argued on the basis of a series of well-documented studies that much television reporting reflected the assumptions of the powerful (Glasgow University Media Group 1976, 1980, 1982 and 1985). Although provoking angry denunciations from broadcasters, this research was not subjected to detailed, scholarly counter-attack from a liberal perspective with one notable exception (Harrison 1985).[2] The Glasgow Group's broadsides were accompanied by a fusillade of fire from other researchers who also argued that broadcasting coverage was structured by domin-ant discourses (e.g. Hall, Connell and Curti 1976; Morley 1981; Connell 1980; Hartmann 1975). Implicit in some of this research was the assumption – later to be questioned – that television content was relatively unambiguous and that audi-ence understandings of programmes were determined in a general sense by the meanings immanent in texts.

This attack was accompanied by a series of studies of 'moral panics'. Most of these studies argued that stereotypical and misleading portrayals of 'outsider' groups in the media helped to deflect wider social conflict and reinforce dominant social and political norms. This was illustrated by studies of media representation of political protest (Halloran, Elliott and Murdock 1970; Hall 1973a), youth gangs (Cohen 1980), drug addicts (Young 1974), muggers (Hall *et al.* 1978), union militants (Beharrell and Philo 1977), football hooligans (Whannel 1979), 'scroungers' (Golding and Middleton 1982) and homosexuals (Watney 1987) among others (Cohen and Young 1981). Implicit or explicit in most of these studies were two key assumptions that were later to be challenged. The media's construction of reality was assumed to reflect the dominant culture; that is, the media were portrayed as offering a selective definition of reality that was conson-ant with dominant interests or, in a stronger version of this argument, of 'bend-ing reality' in a way that promoted false consciousness. It was also assumed that the media were influential in terms of mapping society and furnishing conceptual categories and frames of reference through which people made sense of society. The media had, as Hall (1977) argued in an influential essay, an 'ideological effect'.

The stress on the 'effectivity' of the media was seemingly echoed by an influen-tial group of film and television analysts associated with the journal, *Screen*, which occupied a separatist and esoteric niche in the emergent radical tradition. They published a number of studies dissecting the textual strategies employed in films and programmes to generate supposedly 'subject' positions for the spectator. Thus, the optical point-of-view shot and the classic shot/reverse shot sequence were portrayed as 'suturing' devices for fostering audience identification and involvement (Heath, 1976 and 1977; cf. Heath and Skirrow 1977). The general thrust of this research was that professional communicators are able to deploy compelling visual and narrative techniques which organize audience responses in certain prescribed ways.

This necessarily abridged account focuses on the common denominator of the critiques of the liberal perspective and pays little attention to the internal debates that took place between the divergent wings of the radical tradition. Nonetheless, reference should be made to one family dispute among 'critical' researchers since this had a direct bearing on what happened later. This centred on explanations of why the media had a subaltern role in relation to dominant groups. One approach, associated with the Leicester Centre for Mass Communication Research and the Polytechnic of Central London (later renamed University of Westminister), emphasized the importance of economic processes – in particular, media ownership, advertising, the structure and logic of the market – as import- ant influences that shaped the media (Murdock and Golding 1977; Murdock 1982; Curran 1980 and 1986; Garnham 1990). An alternative, radical culturalist approach, associated with the Birmingham Centre for Contemporary Cultural Studies, attributed the media's subordination principally to ideological control, in particular to the unconscious internalization of the assumptions of the dominant culture by journalists, and their reliance on powerful groups and institutions as news sources (Chibnall 1977; Hall *et al.* 1978; Connell 1980). But despite their sometimes heavily accentuated differences, both approaches had a lot in com- mon. Both worked within a neo-Marxist model of society; both perceived a con- nexion, whether weak or strong, between economic interests and ideological representations; and both portrayed the media as serving dominant groups.

REVISIONIST MODELS OF POWER AND IDEOLOGICAL REPRESENTATION

Support for this radical tradition was gradually weakened by growing misgivings about the class-conflict model of society that framed much of its research output. One key influence promoting this disenchantment was the writing of Michel Foucault (1978, 1980, 1982). He argued that manifold relationships of power are in play in different situations. These cannot be subsumed, according to Foucault, within a binary and all-encompassing opposition of class interests or traced to the mode of production and social formation. As he put it, with uncharacteristic succinctness:

> Power relations are rooted in the system of social networks. This is not to say, however, that there is a primary and fundamental principle of power which dominates society down to the smallest detail but taking as a point of depart- ure the possibility of action upon the action of others (which is coextensive

with every societal relationship), multiple forms of individual disparity, of objectives, of the given application of power over ourselves or others, of, in varying degrees, partial or universal institutionalization, or more or less deliberate organization, one can define different forms of power.

(Foucault 1982: 224)

The Foucauldian approach was adapted by some researchers to construct studies of the media on a different axis from the Marxist approach but in a form that was recognizably radical. The role of the media was still considered in the wider context of social struggle but primarily against patriarchal rather than class authority.

However, the Foucauldian legacy was ambivalent. Its complex theorization of power became linked to a postmodern approach which rejected all 'foundational theories' and 'master narratives' of society.[3] This 'turn' (to use a favourite word of this tradition) to postmodernism encouraged a decentring of cultural and media research. In some studies, the role of the media was reduced to a succession of reader-text encounters in the context of a society which was analytically disaggregated into a series of discrete instances (e.g. Bondebjerg 1989) or in which power external to discourse was largely excluded (e.g. Grodal 1989). In reality this was not very different from the American liberal tradition in which the media are typically analysed in isolation from power relationships or are situated within a model of society in which, it is assumed, power is fragmented and widely diffused. Indeed, in the influential and prolific writing of John Fiske (1987, 1989a, 1989b and 1989c), the convergence was more or less explicit. His celebration of 'semiotic democracy', in which people drawn from 'a vast shifting range of subcultures and groups' construct their own meanings within an autonomous cultural economy, enthusiastically embraced the central themes of sovereign consumer pluralism.

To complicate matters still further, there was to some extent a shift within the liberal pluralist tradition away from discrete analyses of the media typified by conventional investigations into media effects on violence and voting behaviour. Greater interest was shown by liberal researchers in the wider role of the media: their impact on the structures and functioning of the political system (Seymour-Ure 1989; Blumler 1989a), their influence on socio-cultural integration (Graber 1988; McLeod 1988); the formation of social identity (Reimer and Rosengren 1989); and, more broadly and crucially, the relationship between media and social change (Rosengren 1981; Noelle-Neumann 1981; McQuail 1987). This coincided with the proliferation of narrowly focused, discrete research – most notably, audience reception studies – in what could still be termed loosely the 'radical' camp. Thus, the split between theorized and relatively untheorized research, between a holistic and discrete approach, between concern for macro- and micro-issues, that once characterized the difference between radical and liberal research traditions, became increasingly blurred.

This was partly because the totalizing themes of Marxism came under attack from a powerful revisionist movement within the radical tradition. As Stuart Hall (1988b) proclaimed:

> . . . classical Marxism depended on an assumed correspondence between 'the economic' and 'the political': one could read off our political attitudes, interests and motivations from our class interests and position. This correspondence between 'the political' and 'the economic' is exactly what has now disintegrated – practically and theoretically.
>
> (Hall, 1988b: 25)

Althusser, now often remembered ironically as an exponent of a crude Marxist functionalism, played a significant part in this reappraisal by emphasizing the relative autonomy of social practice (Althusser 1971 and 1976). Many post-Althusserians, following in his wake, rejected the notion of economic determinacy even in a weak, non-reductive form. This trend was reinforced by the claim that we are living in a new era of uncertainty and flux characterized by 'post-Fordist' production regimes, the pluralization of social and cultural life and the rise of individualism and subjectivity in which the primacy of the economic has been dethroned (Baudrillard 1985; Gorz 1983; Lyotard 1984).

Dissatisfaction with traditional Marxist formulations was also influentially expressed in a much-reprinted book by Abercrombie, Hill and Turner (1984). They argued that the concept of a 'dominant ideology' (a key concept which had strongly influenced radical media and cultural studies in the 1970s and early 1980s) was based on an illusion. In most eras, they claimed, the dominant ideology dissolved under close inspection into a miscellany of inconsistent and even contradictory themes, and were rarely dominant in the sense they were uncritically accepted by subordinate classes. Social stability, they also argued, was best explained in terms of resignation and routine rather than ideological incorporation. Their argument was not fully or adequately documented for the modern period, but subsequently received powerful support in a major empirically based study (Marshall et al. 1989).

This attack was in a sense anticipated and pre-emptively answered in a reformulated theory of the media and society influenced by Gramsci (1971 and 1985). This reformulation entailed rethinking an earlier functionalist paradigm of the media. It reconceptualized the dominant power as a shifting and sometimes precarious alliance of different social strata, rather than as a single, unified group. The dominant ideology was redefined as a 'field' of dominant discourses, an unstable constellation of ideas and themes, which could potentially disaggregate into its component elements. The media were portrayed as a site of contest between opposed social forces, in a context where there were both tensions within the power structure and sometimes organized opposition to it. Instead of functioning merely to secure consent for the social order, the media were viewed as agencies caught up in a battle of ideas whose outcome was uncertain and contingent. Underlying this reconception was a rather belated recognition that conflict could generate dissent and disagreement in a way that influenced how the media represented society.

This reformulation was already gaining ground in the mid-1970s but in an uneven and partly assimilated form. For example, Hall's collaborative work, *Policing the Crisis*, was an uneasy synthesis of radical functionalist and Gramscian perspectives, reflected in its interchangeable use of two differently nuanced concepts – 'control culture' and 'dominant field of the ruling ideologies' (Hall *et al*. 1978). His subsequent work (e.g. Hall 1988a) was grounded much more fully in a Gramscian analysis highlighting ideological contest. This reformulation was a persuasive attempt to renew the critical tradition, at a time when it was coming under mounting attack.

REVISIONIST ACCOUNTS OF MEDIA ORGANIZATIONS

The development of 'critical' research into media organizations can also be viewed as a forced retreat from former positions. Radical political economy had been the dominant way of 'explaining' media institutions within the radical tradition. However, its assumption that journalists were to a significant degree controlled through pre-selection, socialization and managerial supervision was openly questioned by Birmingham researchers. They insisted that 'the day-to-day "relative autonomy" of the journalist and news producers' was a reality of most modern media organisations (Hall *et al*. 1978: 57). This led them to look for external rather than internal forms of control.

The radical political economy tradition continued to argue that the media were powerfully shaped by their political and economic organization, in multiple, complex ways. However, it began to pay more attention than before to wider cultural and ideological influences. Thus Peter Golding stressed the importance of ideological management and the individualist values of reporters rather than economic ownership of the press in accounting for the tabloid crusade against 'scrounging' welfare claimants (Golding and Middleton 1982). Similarly, Murdock – another leading British political economist of the media – explained the pattern of media reporting of the 1981 race riots in terms of source availability and the conservative discourses that were widely circulated in society. Again, little reference was made to capitalist economic ownership and managerial pressure in explaining why this reporting took such a reactionary form (Murdock 1984).

Yet, radical culturalist interpretations provided an uncertain refuge. In its classic British formulation advanced by Hall and associates, it was claimed that powerful institutions and groups were 'primary definers' who furnished the organizing frameworks for interpreting news stories, while journalists were 'secondary definers' who converted these frameworks into a popular idiom. This position was sustained by a case study which showed that the police, judiciary and other sources offered a closed loop of interpretation of law and order issues which the press largely reproduced (Hall *et al.* 1978).

However, Philip Schlesinger (1990) fired a devastating Exocet against this 'primary definer' model of the news process. His argument was that it unduly simplified. 'Primary definers', he pointed out, sometimes disagreed and advanced conflicting interpretations of the news; they did not have equal credibility; their composition and authority shifted in response to wider changes in society; and a view of journalists as 'secondary' overstated their passivity. Some aspects of this general argument were exemplified in concrete terms by case studies in Britain and the United States (Curran 1990b; Hallin 1989). In effect, this critique was an extension of the reappraisal noted earlier in which the view of society as 'dominated' was challenged by another conception which drew attention to 'contest'.

This new stress on the media as a battlefield clearly represented a movement towards a classic liberal conception of the media as an open forum of debate. However, two key arguments differentiated these two perspectives. The first was the insistence of radical analysts that groups and classes within society have unequal access to the media and unequal resources with which to generalize their views and interests. Here, interestingly, there was a shift within the liberal tradition of media research. The stress on the individual autonomy of journalists in an organizational setting, exemplified by Tunstall's pioneering and illuminating research (Tunstall 1971), gave way to a greater emphasis on the interconnections between media organizations and power centres (e.g. Hess 1984; Sigal 1987; Ericson, Baranek and Chan 1987 and 1989; Schudson 1989). In effect, some researchers within the liberal tradition came round to the view that the organizational routines and news values of most media institutions were skewed towards powerful interests.

The second argument was the continuing claim that capitalist ownership can shape the norms and values of news organizations principally through control of senior editorial appointments, and more generally that the market operates in a way which advantages privilege. Here again, there were some signs of a shift in liberal research, most notably in a study of the Canadian media, which documented the way in which changes in senior appointments influenced routine reporting (Ericson, Baranek and Chan 1987).

Thus, the classic liberal perspective of the media as an 'open' forum ran into as much flak as the classic Marxist vision of the media as an ideological state apparatus. An intermediate perspective situated between these two positions emerged, with reciprocal shifts on the part of researchers in both liberal and radical camps. This said, continuing differences in the way in which power was conceptualized by these two traditions prevented a full convergence from taking place.

REVISIONIST ASSESSMENTS OF AUDIENCE RECEPTION

However, it was around the issues raised by the production of meaning and audience reception that revisionist writing had most impact. The radical tradition of mass communication research was for the most part grounded in a relatively unproblematic analysis of meaning. But a new tradition of revisionist scholarship emerged that emphasized the inconsistencies, contradictions, gaps and even internal oppositions within texts. The shift was exemplified by a comparison between the pessimistic 'state-of-the-art' collection of essays on women and the media edited by Helen Baehr (1980) and more optimistic, redemptive readings of texts by revisionists like Cook and Johnston (1988)[4] and Modleski (1982) which emphasized internal points of resistance to patriarchal values or crucial ambivalences. This revisionist perspective was expressed in its most extreme form in the claim that television is a medium that often produces relatively open and ambiguous programmes, 'producerly texts' that 'delegate[s] the production of meaning to the viewer-producer' (Fiske 1989c).

The second key shift was a reconceptualization of the audience as an active producer of meaning. This is an area of media research that was extensively mythologized – a theme to which we shall return later. It is sufficient to note here that the assumption that audiences responded in prescribed ways to fixed, preconstituted meanings in texts, to be found in certain forms of formalist analysis, was challenged by the notion that meaning was constructed through the interaction of the text and the social and discourse positions of audiences. This point was well made in a notable study of reactions to two *Nationwide* programmes by David Morley, one of the most distinguished and influential revisionist critics. He showed that divergent groups responded in very different ways to *Nationwide*, and that these differences reflected the different discourses and institutions in which they were situated. It was a particularly acute analysis, not least because of the way it illuminated the importance of different subcultural formations within the same class in generating different audience responses (Morley 1980).

The revisionist stress on audience autonomy encouraged a more cautious assessment of media influence. Typical of this reorientation was a case study of a media 'moral panic' that not only failed but backfired (Curran 1987). Similarly, the failure of trans-European satellite television to secure a mass audience was explained in terms of audience autonomy rooted in linguistic and cultural differences (Collins 1989).

Finally, the implicit conclusion that the media had only limited influence encouraged some researchers to shift their focus of interest. The political aesthetic gave way to the popular aesthetic; the focus of investigation shifted from whether media representations advanced or retarded political and cultural struggle to the question of why the mass media were popular. This encouraged 'readings' of media content that sought to infer the nature of people's pleasure in them (e.g.

Drotner 1989), and ethnographic studies of the audience that sought to probe the roots of their pleasure (e.g. Kippax 1988).

REDISCOVERING THE WHEEL?

This revisionism was often presented in assertive terms as an example of intellectual progress in which those hitherto mired in error had been confounded and enlightened. Thus, Morley (1989: 16–17) recounts how 'the whole tradition of effects studies' was dominated by 'a hypodermic model of influence' until the uses and gratifications approach advanced the concept of the active audience. This was an improvement, we are told, because 'from this perspective one can no longer talk about the "effects" of a message on a homogeneous mass audience who are expected to be affected in the same way'. However, even this improvement was 'severely limited', because it ultimately explained differential responses to the media in terms of 'individual differences of personality or psychology'. Only the new revisionism, we are informed, introduced a more satisfactory and rounded account.

This was a breath-taking, though often repeated,[5] caricature of the history of communications research that erased a whole generation of researchers. It presented as innovation what was in reality a process of rediscovery. This mythologizing also had the effect of obscuring the multiple lines of intersection between past media research in the liberal tradition and the new revisionism emerging out of the radical tradition. Effects research cannot be said in any meaningful sense to have been 'dominated' by the hypodermic model. On the contrary, its main thrust ever since the 1940s was to assert the independence and autonomy of media audiences and dispel the widespread notion that people were easily influenced by the media. It did this by developing many of the same insights that were proclaimed afresh in 1980s 'reception' studies, even if this earlier tradition used a different technical language and deployed a more simple understanding of meaning.

Thus, effects researchers argued long ago that the predispositions that people bring to texts crucially influence their understanding of these texts, and that different predispositions generate different understandings. To cite one now forgotten study almost at random, Hastorf and Cantril (1954) showed a film of a particularly dirty football match between Dartmouth and Princeton to two groups of students, one from each institution and asked them among other things to log the number of infractions of the rules committed by each side. The Princeton students concluded that the Dartmouth team committed more than twice as many fouls as their side, whereas the majority of the Dartmouth group concluded that both sides were about equally at fault. This prompted the authors to advance a 'transactional' perspective, in which 'it is inaccurate or misleading to say that different people have different attitudes to the same thing. For the thing is *not* the same for different people, whether the thing is a football game, a presidential candidate, communism, or spinach.' Their conclusion was that the cliché, 'seeing is believing', should be recast as 'believing is seeing' since prior attitudes influence perception.

This study was not unusual for this period in attributing differences of audience response to differences of shared disposition rather than, as Morley dismissively puts it, to 'individual differences of personality or psychology'. But it was also characteristic in offering a relatively simple, one-dimensional account of audience adaptation of meaning.

However, some effects researchers developed a much more complex model of audience interactions which anticipated revisionists' subsequent discovery of 'the interdiscursive processes of text-reader encounters'. An early example of this more sophisticated approach is provided by Patricia Kendall and Katherine Wolff's (1949) analysis of reactions to anti-racist cartoons among white American men. The cartoons featured Mr Biggott, an unattractive and cantankerous middle-aged man whose absurdity (highlighted by cobwebs coming out of his pin-point head) and extreme views were intended to discredit racist ideas. The study showed that 31 percent failed to recognize either that Mr Biggott was racially prejudiced or that the cartoons were intended to satirize racism, and that in general there was a considerable diversity in the way in which audience members understood the cartoons. Some resisted their propagandistic intention by resorting to various means of disidentification; they viewed Mr Biggott negatively not because of his views (which they shared) but because he was judged to be intellectually or socially inferior. A few even found in the cartoons confirmation of their prejudices, completely subverting the cartoons' intention.[6]

But perhaps the most illuminating part of this study was its explanation of why respondents negotiated the cartoons' meanings in the way that they did, based on lengthy individual interviews. One group of respondents who were secure in their racist beliefs felt no need to distance themselves from Mr Biggott's racism and remained unaware that the cartoon was attacking their opinions. A second group of prejudiced respondents had a momentary understanding of the satirical purpose of the cartoon, experienced it as punishing, did a double-take by disidentifying with Mr Biggott (in one case identifying him as a Jew) and thus succeeded in obscuring from themselves the proselytizing intention of the cartoon. The key to understanding their complex reaction was their own feelings of guilt, uncertainty or embarrassment about their racist views. A third group of young prejudiced men imposed a different frame of reference that cut across the intended framework of meaning in the cartoon. Instead of seeing the cartoons as an attack on their own views, they viewed them as a satirical attack on the older generation in which Mr Biggott symbolized the weakness, powerlessness and absurdity of flawed authority figures (with one respondent making explicit reference to his father). In some of the interviews with this group, one had a glimpse of the cartoons 'working' in the sense that they encouraged a reappraisal of prejudiced views within a discourse of modernity directed against the parental generation.

That audiences respond to mass-communicated meanings differently has been a central finding of media effects research for nearly half a century. Another aspect of the relative autonomy of the audience, documented by Lazarsfeld, Berelson and Gaudet as early as 1944, is the tendency of people to seek out media content that reinforces what they think and to avoid content that challenges their beliefs. However, researchers argued that that the rise of television during the 1950s reduced deliberate avoidance of incongruent communications, although defensive avoidance of dissonant messages was found to persist to some degree in the form of inattention as well as non-selection. [7]

During the 1940s researchers also showed that group-supported perspectives influenced the evaluation of mediated communications (e.g. Hyman and Sheatsley 1947). This became a recurrent finding of 'effects' research, as can be briefly illustrated by a clutch of studies about *All in the Family*, a successful American television series, which featured a bigoted, chauvinist, politically reactionary but 'lovable' working-class protagonist, Archie Bunker, who had regular arguments with his liberal-minded son-in-law, Mike. Racially prejudiced adolescents in Canada and the United States were much more inclined to think that bigoted Archie made sense and won in the end than young viewers with less prejudiced views (Vidmar and Rokeach 1974; cf. Brigham and Giesbrecht 1976). A comparable study in Holland revealed a more complex picture in which groups with different clusters of attitudes – whether ethnocentric, authoritarian or traditionalist – responded to the series in partially different ways (Wilhoit and de Bock 1976). Another study of the series, based on responses of six- to ten-year-olds to a single programme, stressed that selective audience responses were embedded in the wider social processes of society. Its conclusion was that 'different types of children, bringing different beliefs, attitudes, and values to the viewing of the show as a result of different socialization processes, are affected in distinctly different ways' (Meyer 1976).

Brief reference should be made to two other strands of the 'effects' tradition, both of which are underdeveloped in 'reception' studies. The first is the stress on the dynamic processes of peer group mediation in blocking, reinforcing or modifying mass communicated messages, following Katz and Lazarsfeld's landmark research (1955). [8] The other is the emphasis given in some studies to the selective retention of information. Levine and Murphy (1943) found that pro- and anti-communist groups tended to remember information which accorded with what they already believed, and to forget information which did not fit their world view; and that this selective forgetfulness increased over time. Subsequent research on retention has since substantially revised and refined understanding of the variables affecting selective memory.

The 'effects' tradition thus prefigures revisionist arguments by documenting the multiple meanings generated by texts, the active and creative role of audiences and the ways in which different socially embedded values and beliefs influenced audience responses. In short, the research of the new revisionists is only startling and innovative from a foreshortened perspective of communications research in which the year AD begins with textual analyses of films and television programmes in the journal *Screen*, and everything before that is shrouded in the eddying mists of time.

This said, the revisionist approach taken as a whole represented at one level an advance. It focused more attention on textual meaning, understood not as 'messages' through the lens of early social psychology but in more sophisticated ways illuminated by studies of semiology and ideology. It offered a much richer and fuller understanding of interdiscursive processes in audience reception. At best, it also located audience research in a more adequate sociological context. Much of this advance can be attributed to the pioneering work of David Morley, and what followed in its wake. But reception analysis also represented at another level a backward step in its reluctance to quantify; its over-reliance on group discussions and consequent failure to probe adequately intra-group and individual differences;[9] and its over-reliance on the loose concept of 'decoding', which some researchers in the effects tradition more usefully differentiated analytically in a terms of attention, comprehension, evaluation and retention.

This is also an appropriate point to consider parallels between revisionist, ethnographic studies of the audience and the 'uses and gratifications' approach. It became commonplace among revisionists to point to the shortcomings of uses and gratifications research as a preliminary to proclaiming the superiority of their own research. Thus, Ang (1985) argues that the revisionist approach is an improvement on the old because it pays more attention to the mechanisms by which pleasure is aroused. It also breaks new ground, she claims, because it avoids an essentialist conception of need.

While there is some truth in these arguments, there are also points of affinity between revisionist, ethnographic research and the earlier tradition that she attacks. This can be illustrated by comparing her own clever and illuminating study of Dutch reception of *Dallas* with a uses and gratifications study of radio serial listening in the United States conducted by Herzog (1944) some four decades earlier. Both enquiries pointed to the way in which soap opera can relativize the problems of audience members and make them more bearable or indeed pleasurable. Both also indicated the way in which soap opera provides scope for idealized but playful identification. But while Herzog paid little attention to the actual content of soap operas, she did not resort to an essentialist definition of need and gratification. Indeed, she provided in some ways a more socially situated account of women's pleasure in soap opera than Ang because she drew upon interview material rather than, as in Ang's case, letters. This enabled Herzog to illustrate what Ang calls 'the tragic structure of feeling' in terms of the particular predicaments that women found themselves in, even if she did not generalize a feminist perspective.

Quite simply, uses and gratifications research did not always resemble the way in which it was represented by those asserting the novelty of the revisionist approach. There were similarities between some work in the two traditions. Moreover, the inferences derived from reception analysis *as a whole* did not always lead to new horizons of thought. In some cases, they resulted in old liberal dishes being reheated and presented as new cuisine.

REVISIONIST MODELS OF MEDIA INFLUENCE

The empirical demonstration of relative audience autonomy was a key building block in liberal perspectives of the media. The 'findings' of empirical research were deployed to considerable effect to refute a model of the media as an agency of class or elite control. This refutation came to be anchored to a conception of society as a honeycomb of small groups in which power is widely diffused, and in which public opinion is shaped by personal influence and everyday social interaction (e.g. Katz and Lazarsfeld 1955).

A somewhat similar argument was formulated by some revisionist critics within a different framework. Liberal pluralism gave way to postmodern pluralism. Reception studies documenting audience selectivity were invoked to challenge the view that the media were the principal means by which consent for the social order was engineered. This new revisionism sometimes became linked to a view of society as a fluid complex of social groups with mobile identities and creative sub-cultures. By implication, the autonomous power to make sense of society in diverse ways was widely diffused in society. There are no dominant discourses, merely a semiotic democracy of pluralist voices. However, this new version of the pluralist argument overstated its case not least because it exaggerated the impermeability of audiences to media influence.

In the first place, media texts are rarely wholly open but take the form of what Morley (1980) usefully calls 'structured polysemy'. That is to say, denotative symbols in texts cue, to a lesser or greater degree, audience understandings in certain preferred ways, even if these can be and sometimes are rejected. A simple illustration of this occurs in an account of a group discussion in which a respond-ent pointed to a television still and challenged the interpretation that was being put on it by another member of the group, by saying simply and with visible effect 'they don't look like a mob' (Philo 1989). In effect, the respondent invoked a widely shared understanding of denotative signs as 'evidence' to persuade others of the validity of her 'reading'. Second, audiences do not have an infinite reper-toire of discourses to draw upon in adapting television meanings. Indeed, the evidence suggests that the location of audience members in the social structure influences which discourses are available to them.

The combination of these two limitations on audience autonomy – signifying mechanisms in texts, and a variable degree of social access to ideas and meanings which facilitate contrary 'readings' of the media – has certain consequences. This is well brought out in Philo's study of audience reception of British television news reporting of the miners' strike in 1984–5 (Philo 1990). This shows that there was a clear correspondence between certain recurrent themes in television reporting of the strike and what was understood, believed and remembered by many people after a considerable lapse of time, perhaps because the miners' strike was long drawn-out and very prominently reported. Thus, the images and explanatory themes of television reporting of the dispute were not drowned out by the diverse discourses that audiences brought to their viewing.

Indeed, the most revealing part of this important study is the double insight it provides into the dialogue that takes place between viewers and television news. On the one hand, it highlights the variety of resources that audience subjects drew upon in resisting or negotiating television meanings – first-hand knowledge (and, even more important, word-of-mouth relaying of first-hand knowledge), class experiences, political cultures, other media accounts, sceptical dispositions towards the news media and internal processes of logic. Conversely, it also shows the way in which some people adjusted their opinions in the light of the information they received from television, including, crucially, people who strongly identified with the striking National Union of Mineworkers (NUM) but who reluctantly came to accept certain recurrent, anti-NUM themes in television news reports (Philo 1990).

This study is consistent with a shift in mainstream effects research. The minimal effects model that dominated empirical American research for a generation came under mounting attack from liberal researchers from the 1970s onwards. They increasingly argued that the media exert considerable influence, in certain circumstances, on audience beliefs, cognitions and opinions (McLeod and McDonald 1985; Iyengar and Kinder 1987; Kosicki and McLeod 1990). In doing so, they were qualifying a central tenet of the pluralist canon. Thus, by a curious irony, revisionist celebrants of semiotic democracy moved towards a position that liberal pluralists were abandoning. They engaged not so much in revisionism, as an act of revivalism; they reverted to the discredited received wisdom of the past.

CONTINUITY AND DISCONTINUITY

However, revisionist reception studies were not homogeneous. There were two distinctive tendencies: one, a continuation of the radical tradition; and another which in effect crosses over into liberalism.

The radical tendency continued to situate cultural consumption in the broader context of social struggle. Janice Radway's celebrated study of American addicts of romantic novels exemplified this approach. Her subjects were engaged, she argued, in a compensatory, symbolic reconstruction of masculinity. They were drawn to formulaic books in which hard, insensitive or unfeeling men were humanized by the love of a woman and were transformed into sensitive, nurturant and caring people (Radway 1987). There was a recognizable affinity between her report from the patriarchal front and Birmingham researchers' earlier reports from the class front, such as Hebdige's sympathetic portrayal of English 'teddy boys', 'mods' and 'rockers' (Hebdige 1979) and insightful account of racist 'skinheads' (Hebdige 1981). Both researchers sought to relate pleasure in cultural consumption to the social experience of their subjects, conceived in terms of their unwilling submission to inequality. Their pleasure in media consumption was interpreted as a form of resistance in which they sought an imaginary way out of their subordination.

Another strand of reception analysis developed which was grounded in a less radical conception of society, and which framed cultural consumption in different terms. This approach was exemplified at its best by Fornas, Lindberg and Sernhede's (1988) ethnographic study of amateur teenage rock groups in Sweden.[10] The underlying assumption of this and similar research was that popular culture provided the raw material for the creative exploration of social identities in the context of a postmodern society where the walls of tradition that supported and confined people were crumbling. In this case, rock music was viewed as an experimental resource for the production of identity by adolescents seeking to define an independent self. The study was notable for the meticulous and close-grained observation that it brought to bear in a way that did not always have a counterpart in radical research. Thus, even Radway's (1987) *tour de force* offered an account of romance addicts' relationship to patriarchy but not to their flesh-and-blood husbands. However, Fornas *et al.*'s study, and others like it, were engaged in analysing cultural consumption and identity formation almost as an end in itself. It belonged more to the liberal literature on socialization than to the radical tradition of cultural studies concerned with 'rituals of resistance'.

REVISIONIST ASSESSMENTS OF CULTURAL VALUE

The other notable contribution of revisionist thinking was that it rejected the elitist pessimism about mass culture that had been a significant strand within the radical tradition, represented by the Frankfurt school. A key formative influence in this shift was Pierre Bourdieu. He showed that there was a close correspondence in France between socio-economic position and patterns of taste in art and music. Cultural and aesthetic judgements, he concluded, had no absolute, universal validity but were merely ways of defining, fixing and legitimating social differences (Bourdieu 1986a and b). This insight was also developed by cultural historians who revealed that the boundary lines between high and low culture shifted over time in response to strategies of exclusion pursued by elites seeking to maintain their social leadership (Dimaggio 1986) and in response to struggles over material rewards and prestige within the artistic community (Fyffe 1985).

A relativistic orientation was further reinforced by growing recognition that meaning is created in the context of media consumption. This led logically to the conclusion that audiences can *create* quality in popular culture. For example, Hobson (1982) argued that the insights and understandings that audiences brought to their viewing of the widely despised British soap opera, *Crossroads*, reconstituted its cultural value. Similarly, Schroder (1989) argued that Shakespeare's plays and *Dynasty* have a comparable cultural validity since they generated comparable audience experiences. Underlying this study, and many comparable works, is a key assumption succinctly stated by the American sociologist, Michael Schudson (1987: 59): 'the quality of art lies in how it is received, or how it is created within the context of reception, rather than in some quality intrinsic to the art object itself'. By implication, judgements about so-called popular or high culture are judgements about their audiences and their cultural competences. But these competences take different forms and are distributed in ways that do not correspond to a conventional hierarchy of taste. Thus, as Brunsdon (1981) argued, soap opera requires a certain amount of cultural capital on the part of the audience, just as a Godard film does. These and similar arguments led increasingly to the abandonment of literary norms in making judgements about the quality of popular culture and encouraged instead a tacit system of valorization based on audience pleasure. Indeed, Ericson (1989) argues approvingly that this became almost the defining characteristic of revisionist Scandinavian cultural studies.

However, this reorientation within the radical tradition did not in fact break entirely new ground. Within the liberal tradition, there had also been an anti-elitist reaction which took a similar, though less pronounced, form. It was directed against critics of mass culture such as the poet, T.S. Eliot (1948), and Dwight Macdonald (1957). This initially took the form of the defensive claim, advanced by liberal sociologists like Shils (1961) and Gans (1974), that the mass media made available some cultural products of high quality when judged in relation to what most people ordinarily consumed. This championing of popular culture took on a more aggressive form, however, when the revival of uses and gratifications research in the 1970s drew attention to the diversity and richness of people's pleasure in the media. This prompted researchers like McQuail, Blumler and Brown (1972) to attack the elitist assumption that mass consumption of 'common denominator' programmes is homogeneous, shallow and superficial. For example, they showed in an admirable study that, although television quiz shows were viewed by some as relaxing entertainment, they were experienced by others, particularly those with limited schooling, as an educative experience.

Liberal writers like Blumler later drew back from the implicit populism of uses and gratifications research to advance highly traditional arguments about the need for preserving television 'quality', 'standards' and worthwhile categories of programme like 'original drama'. He also argued that broadcasting policy should take account of humanist and communitarian concerns. Television, in his view, should 'deepen the expression of experience about the human and social condition' and assist 'society in all its parts to bind, reconnect and commune with itself' (Blumler 1989b: 87–8).

There was a parallel pulling back from cultural relativism in at least part of the radical revisionist camp. For example, Seiter et al. (1989) argued that the move towards a popular aesthetic contained dangers:

> The popularity of US television programmes on export around the world should not make us forget that other forms of television might also please

(and, possibly, please better). In our concern for audiences' pleasures in such programmes, we run the risk of continually validating Hollywood's domination of the worldwide television market.

(Seiter *et al.* 1989: 5)

Underlying this argument was recognition that audience subversion of Hollywood was an imperfect substitute for programmes that actively promoted emancipated sensibilities. 'Soap operas allow women viewers to take pleasure in the character of the villainess, but they do not provide characters that radically challenge the ideology of femininity' (Seiter *et al.* 1989: 5).

One cause of this shared re-thinking, perhaps, was concern that uncritical celebration of the popular might provide unintended support for the extension of corporate media control. The deregulation of broadcasting was advocated by the right on the grounds that it would end elitist control of television, and generate programmes that people wanted to watch (Adam Smith Institute 1984; Gallagher 1989). Cultural relativism was also challenged by a return of more politicized concerns across the field of media studies, prompted in part by the policy choices thrown into sharp relief by the new right. This may have been be merely a local, British phenomenon. But the possibility that broadcasting could be remodelled along the free market lines of the capitalist press in Britain prompted fresh thought to be given to how this would affect relationships of power. The result was a headlong movement towards revalorizing public service broadcasting by qualifying earlier radical accounts (e.g. Hood 1980 and Curtis 1984) of British television as an agency of the dominant order. Thus, McNair (1988) argued that minority news and documentary programmes were more open to critical perspectives than mainstream programmes; Schlesinger, Murdock and Elliott (1983) argued that drama was less ideologically closed than current affairs; and a case study of municipal socialism claimed that public service broadcasting was more receptive to the arguments of the left than than the more 'closed' organizations of the popular press (Curran 1987 and 1990b). A somewhat similar shift of evaluation took place in the literature on the British welfare state, perhaps partly for the same reason. Both the welfare state and public service broadcasting came under attack from the new right, causing liberal and radical researchers to find more common ground with each other.

CONCLUSION

This account deliberately focuses attention on the changes that took place in the 1980s. However, this stress on discontinuity needs to be qualifed in two ways. Some media researchers, particularly historians and social psychologists, remained unaffected by the intellectual ferment around them, and carried on doing the same kind of research as before. There was also an underlying continuity of thought, an evolutionary pace to some of the seemingly abrupt shifts of direction that occurred. For example, the rise of audience reception studies in the 1980s owed a large debt to the theoretical formulations of Barthes (1975), Eco (1972) and Hall (1973b) in the early 1970s, and had, as we have seen, points of affinity with early audience research before the 1970s.

Nonetheless, the 1980s were a watershed period. Within the radical tradition, there was a general shift away from the totalizing, explanatory frameworks of Marxism; a reconceptualisation of the media audience as creative and active; a spate of 'redemptive' studies of popular media; and a new emphasis on the media as a source of pleasure. Because much of this revisionist movement was inspired by an internal debate within the radical tradition, the extent to which it moved towards liberal positions was partly obscured. But a sea-change occurred in the 1980s, which reshaped – for better *and* worse – the development of media and cultural studies.

EPILOGUE

For nearly a decade, I have been reading at regular intervals new publications written by my friend, David Morley which denounce – always courteously – this essay. They deploy broadly the same arguments and recycle even some of the same phrases (Morley 1992a and b, 1993, 1996, 1997 and 1999). David Morley clearly hopes to extirpate any remaining traces of heresy through the force of repetition. He is joined by two spirited allies (Moores 1993 and Ang 1996).[11]

In David Morley's view, this chapter offers a misleading history of audience research based on the citation of untypical work interpreted with the benefit of hindsight.

> Curran's own principal tactic is to bolster his argument by quoting the work of hitherto neglected figures within mainstream traditions of audience research who argue against any simple hypodermic theory of 'effects', or who stress issues such as the social setting of media reception, thus demonstrating that recent emphasis on such issues is no more than old wine in new bottles.
>
> (Morley 1992b: 22)

My account, he continues, is based on a selective discovery of 'unrecognised or neglected' work whose significance is only now apparent in the light of revisionist achievement.

This is not true. Much of the pioneer, pre-1975 audience work that I cite was thought important at the time, and was given prominence in early overviews of the field (e.g. Klapper 1960; McQuail 1969; Wright 1975). Indeed, most academic commentary on this essay endorses its conclusion that there is an underlying continuity in the development of audience research (Rosengren 1993 and

1996; Kavoori and Gurevitch 1993; Silverstone 1994; Swanson 1996; Nowak 1997; Garnham 2000; Blackman and Walkerdine 2001, among others). As Nicholas Garnham (2000: 120) puts it, 'it is better to read recent developments in audience research as a revisionist return to pre-existing problems and models of research rather than a revolutionary dawn'.

However, in revising this chapter I have accentuated slightly more differences between new and old audience research.[12] David Morley's latest contribution (1999) stresses more than he did ten years earlier (1989) continuities between first- and second-generation audience research. Perhaps on this note of near agreement, we can lay this debate to rest.

Indeed, it is possible to conclude on a still more positive point of accord. David Morley (1996) is right to insist, in an engaging autobiographical account, that reception studies profoundly changed radical media and cultural studies in *Britain*. But this is only because much of the British radical tradition was then so locked into its debates and paradigms that it paid scant attention to past liberal audience research, conducted mostly but not exclusively in the United States.[13]

A very similar process of coterie exclusion is again taking place. Only this time, it is mainly revisionist writers who seem reluctant to stray outside the canon of fashionable work. The centre of revisionist research attention shifted during the 1990s from audiences to globalization. This led to a fresh outburst of scorn for what was seen as the fundamentalist left, and provided a new basis for infectious optimism. It also resulted, in some cases, in a complacent view of globalization sustained by a deep reluctance to engage with points of view and evidence other than those marked out by revisionist argument. This will be the subject of Chapter 6.

But before tracking this latest phase of revisionism, and placing it in context, it is worth taking a second, wide-angled look at media organizations and their place in society. This takes more fully into account the US-based tradition of 'communications' research.

Chapter 5

Renewing the radical tradition

INTRODUCTION

The route taken in this chapter will be different from that in the last in that we will stop off mostly at different places, and reach a different destination. If certain arguments are re-encountered, this is only because they have to be included in a general survey of media sociology.

LIBERAL REFLECTION THEORIES

The liberal approach is the dominant way of thinking about the media in the United States and increasingly around the world.[1] This liberal approach tends to see the media as reflecting rather than shaping society, though what precisely is reflected in the 'mirror' that the media hold up to society is the subject of dispute.

One view still popular among liberal journalists is to see the media as a faithful reflection of reality. It is a view eloquently expressed in Neil Simon's *The Odd Couple* by the lifting of an eyebrow:

> *Cecily:* What field of endeavour are you engaged in?
> *Felix:* I write the news for CBS.
> *Cecily:* Oh. Fascinating.
> *Gwendolyn:* Where do you get your ideas from?
> *Felix:* *(He looks at her as though she is a Martian):* From the news.
> *Gwendolyn:* Oh yes, of course. Silly me . . .
>
> (cited in Golding 1981: 64)

For Felix, and other like-minded journalists, the media are merely messengers: the message is reality. Good journalists have a 'nose' for news, an instinct partly innate and partly trained for distinguishing what is important from what is unimportant. This ensures allegedly that the news is a record of everything that is fit to be published. 'True professionals' check the accuracy of what is reported and are painstakingly neutral in the way in which they balance contending opinion.

They have standards and procedures that are a guarantee of good faith in reporting the world 'as it is'.

This celebration of the craft of journalism is not entirely fanciful. The conventions of professionalism do constrain the way in which personal biases and subjective experiences shape news output. This is why the view that news reporting is *merely* the expression of the personal views and backgrounds of journalists[2] – whether they be conceived as being biased as a consequence of being mainly left-wing or right-wing, men or middle class – is partly misleading. People with different views and experiences can in fact produce surprisingly similar news reports, providing they work within the same news conventions (Epstein 1973 and 1975).

This said, the canons of professionalism are not sufficient to sustain the claim that the media reflect objective reality. The news we receive, as numerous critics point out, is the product of organizational processes and human interaction. It is shaped by public relations management, the methods and sources used by journalists in gathering the news, and the organizational requirements, resources and policies of the institutions they work for (Kaniss 1991; Tiffen 1989). To take but one example, the need of news organizations to secure regular, predictable and usable copy results in some journalists being assigned to particular 'beats' – such as the town hall, law courts or legislature. This encourages activity in these areas to be reported more fully (Tuchman 1978a; Hess 1984). It also locks journalists into a complex pattern of interaction with key sources in which information is traded for publicity (Gandy 1982; Ericson et al. 1989). And it encourages group conformity in which journalists on the same beat tend to form collective news judgements (Tunstall 1971). In short, a prior decision about the allocation of personnel within a news organization can influence what news is reported and how it is reported.

Some liberal critics also point out that information is selected and presented as news within socially constructed frameworks of meaning (Hallin and Mancini 1984; Schudson 1991a). The news is signified through the 'symbolic system' of society. It draws upon the ideas, images and assumptions that are embedded in cultural tradition. The news is also structured by the formats and genre conventions of news reporting, which vary in different societies and evolve over time (Schudson 1982 and 1994). News in this view is thus the product of the culture of society in which it is processed.

This kind of cautious reasoning has prompted some people to see the output of the media not as a reflection of raw, unmediated reality but rather as a social index of attitudes and feelings. As the novelist, Virginia Woolf, elegantly put it, 'newspapers are thin sheets of gelatine pressed nightly on the brain and heart of the world' (Woolf 1965: 93). An eloquent presentation of this view is provided by Kjell Nowak (1984), who shows that there was a marked decrease in prestige appeals and overt class coding in advertisements in the Swedish press between the mid-1960s and mid-1970s. This was accompanied by a decline in the formal pronoun of address, and an increase in positive references to equality in press editorials. All these changes in the press, carefully quantified, were a reflection, he argues, of the growth of egalitarianism in Swedish society, which was also manifested in a more equal distribution of incomes during approximately the same period.

A somewhat similar argument, though from a different perspective, is advanced by Leo Lowenthal (1961), who showed that there was a shift of attention from business leaders to sports and entertainment stars in selected American publications in the first half of the twentieth century. This reflected, in his view, a shift in the 'dream world' of American society from the 'idols of production' to 'idols of consumption'. Likewise, analysts regularly attribute changes in programme content to wider social and political change. For example, the growth of socially relevant television drama in early 1970s American television is widely attributed to a change in the *zeitgeist* of American society (D'Acci 1994; Gitlin 1994).

These accounts usually see the media as responding to generalized changes in society, conceived as a single entity. This approach is implicitly problematized by other accounts which portray the media as a variegated system relating to different groups in society. For example, some programmes, films, magazines and books are directed primarily towards women, and relate specifically to their experiences and concerns as distinct from those of men. However, some women's media address different subgroups within the general female population, ranging from traditionalist magazines celebrating conventional definitions of femininity to campaigning feminist publications (Ferguson 1983; Winship 1987). Some of these media also relate to different (and sometimes contradictory) identities and structures of feeling within the same individual (Winship 1987; Ang and Hermes 1991). The media are thus portrayed as reflecting not a common culture and unified society but a plurality of social groups and the hybridity of individual personalities.

A further complication is introduced by those analysts who distinguish between values and normative attitudes (Alexander 1981), or between consensus and controversy (Blumler and Gurevitch 1986). Here, the argument is that the media both express the values and beliefs that most people hold in common, and also give voice to those differences of opinion and orientation that characterize a pluralist democracy. One way in which television reflects change, it is argued, is that its different modes of reporting record shifts between areas of consensus and legitimated dissent (Hallin 1994).

INDEPENDENT MEDIA

While there are different opinions about what aspect of society the media reflect, there is broad agreement within the liberal tradition that the media have a high degree of autonomy in advanced liberal democracies. This is the cornerstone, almost the sacred oath of allegiance, of the liberal approach. In its most thoroughbred version, in Parsonian sociology, the media in the United States are portrayed as independent both of the state and also of social 'subsystems' comprised by political, economic or solidary groups. This confers on the media the essential freedom they need to respond to the *totality* of society. As the Parsonian sociologist, Jeffery Alexander (1981: 35) claims of the American news media, 'its peculiar social position [as an independent institution] means that it "reflects" the conditions around it'.

However, changes in the ownership and structure of the media pose problems for the liberal tradition. Many media are now owned by large business corporations. This seems to fly in the face of the much vaunted claim that the media are neutral instituitions which have severed links with sectional interests. There has also been a long-term, though discontinuous, trend towards media concentration, and in some sectors (most notably the press) towards monopoly, which weakens the assumption of public control through market competition.

Liberal theorists usually respond to these difficulties in two ways. First, their traditional claim is that staff, with a commitment to professional goals, have achieved a high degree of autonomy within media organizations. This is viewed as the culmination of a historical process in which media staff acquired a stronger sense of their own worth, gained increasing personal decision-making power as a consequence of the growing division of labour and specialization within media organizations, and developed a commitment to a professional set of values transcending the demands of their employers. The building-up of this professional power and consciousness has ensured that the media continue to be independent even if most media are now owned by big business (Gans 1980; Alexander 1981; Hetherington 1985).

Second, liberal analysts suggest that there has been a growing trend towards the 'dissolution' of ownership. The dispersal of shareholdings in large media conglomerates and the increase in the scale of their operation have weakened and diluted 'proprietorial' control. More power has been ceded to professional managers concerned with market performance rather than the pursuit of ideological goals. In contrast to previous epochs characterized by a party-controlled press, or media moguls in the mould of Hearst who sought to exercise personal and unaccountable power, the new generation of media managers are more inclined to be market-oriented pragmatists (Emery 1972; Hoyer *et al.* 1975; Whale 1977; Koss 1984).

Certain inferences are derived from this conception of a market-oriented but professionally staffed media system. One is that media staff are integrated into the consensus of society, and articulate unconsciously its collective aims and values, albeit sometimes in an inflected form (Gans 1980). Another claim is that good journalists develop an instinctive rapport with their audiences by identifying with them and subjectively experiencing life from their viewpoint (King 1967; Smith 1975). A third argument is that the professional rules of balance ensure, or should ensure, that all important points of view are represented in the media (O'Neill 1990). There are thus assumed to be unobtrusive but important ways in which the media are connected to society, and reflect its concerns.

However, the argument most often stressed in liberal accounts is that competition within a market system compels the media to respond to the wants, needs and views of the public. In this view, the ratings antennae of commercial television pick up the first perceptible indication of a change in public preferences. Much of the effort, energy and creativity of television corporations and other commercial media enterprises are directed towards pleasing the audience. Media corporations have developed strategies for doing this: researching and pre-testing products; building creative teams; repeating or recombining formulae that have been successful in the past; scanning the boundaries of the market for new talent and ideas; developing stars who resonate with the public, and command a faithful following; oversupplying new products, but backing pre-selected 'winners' with extra resources, as a way of adapting to market uncertainty; integrating businesses horizontally (i.e. across media) or vertically (from production to sales outlets) in order to gain economies of consolidation and increased market control; and developing ways of selling the same or spin-off product in different media packages or 'windows' (Hirsch 1972; Turow 1991; Cantor and Cantor 1992; Gitlin 1994). Yet, despite their best efforts, goes the argument, media corporations even in market-dominant positions are constantly wrongfooted by rivals, back losers, get it wrong (Collins 1990). The vagaries of the market keep the media alert and submissive, always subject to the whim of the wayward consumer.

This necessarily simplified and condensed summary edits out a number of important debates within the liberal tradition, which need to be mentioned briefly. One area of discussion is concerned with the degree to which the public interest claims of media professionalism are justified. Some are sceptical, echoing Bernard Shaw's (1979: 496) charge that 'all professions are conspiracies against the laity' (Tuchman 1972; Schudson 1978). Others are relatively uncritical, arguing that professionalism should be reinforced through professional leadership and the benign influence of university-based, media education (Peterson 1956; Stepp 1990).

Another line of criticism within the liberal tradition challenges the notion that journalists, and media staff more generally, are ventriloquists of their audience's thoughts. Some participant observation studies or surveys portray media workers as unrepresentative, out of touch or even downright hostile towards their publics (Tunstall 1971; Elliott 1977; Gans 1980). Media staff are also featured as belonging to a self-enclosed world in which colleagues and friends – or, in the case of independent Hollywood television producers, network executives – become surrogates for the real audience (Cantor 1971; Burns 1977; Gans 1980). But while all these studies cast doubt on the assumption that media staff have a natural rapport with their audience, they are balanced in a sense by portrayals of media managers as the people who provide the driving force behind the media's commitment to pleasing the public (D'Acci 1994; Gitlin 1994).

A third line of criticism is concerned with what it sees as the erosion of professional power within media organizations as a consequence of increased shareholder pressure, leading to the increasing blurring of the distinction between news and entertainment (McManus 1994). This produces a split liberal response.

One position argues that the professional commitments of media staff should be strengthened in order to build a fire-wall against excessive marketization (Hallin 1994). Another reaction applauds increased commercialization on the grounds that it is leading to greater public control, and accuses critics of being part of an elite who disdain the preferences of the general public (Murdoch 1989).

The study of media processes is an area where radical and liberal traditions overlap, and where some of the most interesting analysts have one foot inside and one foot outside the liberal tradition. There are critical debates about the implications of professionalization, the representative character of journalists, and the ethics and performance of the media. But this should not obscure the central credo of the liberal tradition: its belief that the media in free societies serve the public as a consequence of being independent from government, accountable to the public through the market and influenced by the professional concerns of media staff.

LIMITED MEDIA INFLUENCE

Whereas liberal orthodoxy portrays the media as reflecting and serving society, its radical counterpart maintains that the media are implicated in the management of society. This latter position was attacked with seeming finesse by pioneer, liberal audience researchers. Their central contention was that audiences selectively attend to, understand, evaluate and retain information from the media.[3] This is because the public is not an empty vessel waiting to be filled by media propaganda. On the contrary, most people possess values, opinions and understandings, formed by early socialization, membership of social networks and personal experience, which structure their responses to the media. Even when people are exposed to communications from the media on a topic they know nothing about, they have core beliefs and general orientations – 'interpretive schema' – which results in selective assimilation of information.[4]

A good example of this debunking approach is a landmark study by Katz and Lazarsfeld (1955) which attacks 'popular' overestimation of media power and the assumption of 'vertical control' which often underpins it. Where this approach goes wrong, in their view, is that it fails to take account of 'horizontal opinion leadership, that is, leadership which emerges on each rung of the socio-economic ladder, and all through the community' (Katz and Lazarsfeld 1955: 325, original emphasis). Personal networks, they argue, filter media influence. These networks also act as a check on elite flows of influence since 'some individuals of high social status apparently wield little independent influence, and some of low status have considerable personal influence', and 'each arena . . . has a corps of leaders of its own' (Katz and Lazarsfeld 1955: 334). In short, the simplistic image of top-down control, and of the media as instruments of this control, should be abandoned in favour of a conception of a complex delta of influences flowing in different directions throughout society. This is because interaction between families, friends and work colleagues create self-regulating spaces in which people frame their ideas and preferences in ways that are significantly independent.

Katz and Lazarsfeld went on to argue that the media exert some influence primarily through peer group opinion leaders. However, the majority of pioneer audience researchers emphasized audience autonomy and social mediation in ways that portrayed media power as minimal. 'Mass communications', concluded Joseph Klapper in an influential survey of this early work, 'ordinarily do not serve as a necessary and sufficient cause of audience effects' (Klapper 1960: 8).

This minimal effects consensus was challenged within the liberal camp by a new generation of effects researchers from the early 1970s onwards. One part of their argument was that the media had become more important as a consequence of changes in the media and society. When television eclipsed the press, it established a bipartisan medium as the main source of news. This had the effect of reducing selective avoidance of dissonant communications as a filter limiting media influence (Blumler and Gurevitch 1982). The erosion of party allegiances made voting behaviour more accessible to media influence (Miller 1991). The number of people seeking guidance and orientation from the media also increased in response to the greater flux and uncertainty of the contemporary world (De Fleur and Ball-Rokeach 1989).

The second part of their argument took the form of a series of small-print qualifications and refinements. These added up to saying that the media can influence small numbers of people, in certain circumstances. Audience members with certain characteristics – such as those who are non-partisan, with a low interest in politics, with no tacit theory of the topic under review, or who are uncertain – are, in specific contexts, more prone to political influence by the media than others (Blumler and McQuail 1968; McLeod et al. 1974; Blumler and McLeod 1983; Iyengar and Kinder 1987; McCombs 1994). Media influence also increases, it is argued, if the mediated communication accords with audience members' prior disposition, resonates with personal experience, is supported by interpersonal influences or is consistent with social norms and accepted behaviour (Rogers and Shoemaker 1971; Gerbner et al. 1986; Perloff 1993).

Third, some researchers made a distinction between attitudes and cognitions, arguing that the latter are more subject to media influence. The media can have a pronounced short-term effect on what issues people think are important (Iyengar and Kinder 1987; Rogers and Dearing 1988; McCombs 1994).[5] They can also affect how people make evaluations – for example, the issues on which the performance of political leaders are judged (Iyengar and Kinder 1987). More interestingly, television news can influence perceptions of contemporary problems (of which more later) (Iyengar 1991). However, audience research which argues that the media provide a symbolic environment which fundamentally structures heavy television viewers' understanding of the world (Buerkel-Rothfuss and Mayes 1981; Morgan 1982; Gerbner et al. 1986, 1994) is more open to question, since its conclusions are explicable in terms of other factors.[6]

Thus, a new generation of liberal audience researchers revised 'upwards' estimations of media influence. Yet, their work failed to undermine the central conclusion of pioneer audience work: namely, that most people have independent minds of their own, and are not easily persuaded by the media.

LIBERAL FUNCTIONALISM

The conclusions of effects research gave rise to considerable agitation within the liberal tradition. Most pioneer, liberal researchers were first drawn to the study of the media by the belief that the media are important. They spent most of their working lives seemingly discovering the opposite. This prompted the obvious question: why carry on studying the media?

Communications research eventually provided a coherent answer to this question – liberal functionalism. Even if the media do not greatly change people's thinking and behaviour, it is argued, the media are still important. The media's true significance, their real claim on our attention, is best understood in terms of their contribution to the functioning of society rather than their effects on audiences.

However, before outlining the central arguments of this evolving position, brief reference should be made to two other lines of thought in the liberal tradition which emphasize the central importance of the media. A mainly historical tradition argues that the mass media have changed society by modifying dimensions of time and place (see Chapter one). There is also a political studies tradition which argues that even if the media do not change the minds of most voters, they have changed the political process. Modern media have transformed the conduct of elections, influenced the selection of political leaders (who have now to be good on television), encouraged centralization within political parties, diminished the symbolic role of national legislative assemblies and, more contentiously,[7] encouraged manipulative soundbites and photo opportunities, and the media-friendly evocation of images and values, at the expense of rational policy debate (Ranney 1983; Cockerell 1988; Seymour-Ure 1989; Allen 1993; Hallin 1994; McQuail 1994; Newman 1994; McManus 1994).

However, the main way in which the media are said to 'matter' in liberal analysis is by facilitating the workings of society. This was conceived initially in terms of the political system, and took a rather predictable form. The media inform the electorate, provide a forum of public debate and a two-way channel of communication between government and governed; and check the abuse of state power through the disclosure of information (McQuail 1992a; Kelley and Donway 1990). To these three core functions of liberal democratic theory were added others, such as: assisting the aggregation of interests within the political process; providing a channel of communication between elites; facilitating the revision of shared aims and policies; and helping society to identify, and evolve appropriate political responses to, social strains (Rose 1974; Coleman 1973; Alexander 1981; McQuail 1994).

Although this discussion of the media's functioning for the political system goes back to at least the eighteenth century, a 'sociological' counterpart was slow to get off the ground. A pioneer contribution was made in 1948 by Harold Laswell, who argued, in a celebrated essay, that the media have three important social functions: surveillance, correlation and transmission. The media enable people to monitor what is happening in ways that disclose 'threats to the value position of the community and of component parts within it' (Lasswell 1971: 98 [1948]); they facilitate the co-ordination of society by providing channels of communication between different social groups, enabling a concerted response to these threats; and they assist the transmission of values from one generation to the next.

The development of liberal functionalism during the 1950s and 1960s was largely tied to theories of equilibrium or optimality. These are now widely repudiated (save in Germany) and need not detain us.[8] The functionalist tradition was then re-routed in the 1970s and 1980s by the revival of uses and gratifications research. This was inspired by the largely unspoken assumption that, even if the media do not control people's thinking, they occupy a lot of their time. What was needed therefore was a better understanding of what people got out of the media.

Using group discussions and survey research methods, researchers discovered an enormous variety of media functions (i.e. uses), reflecting differences in the goals, psychological needs and social experiences of audience members. These included obtaining a sense of belonging, gaining companionship, facilitating personal interaction, acquiring insight into self and others, forging a desired sense of identity, achieving a feeling of being in control, experiencing emotional release, escaping from unwanted reality, finding a way to relax, to mention only some of the gratifications derived from the media (Blumler and Katz 1974; Rosengren *et al.* 1985; Rubin 1986; Zillman and Bryant 1986). The standard rubric of 'inform, educate and entertain' used to describe the media's functioning does not begin to capture, according to this tradition, the diverse ways in which people obtain pleasure from the media, reflecting their different needs and desires. Indeed, different people derive quite different satisfactions from the *same* television programmes. The media offer not so much a set menu defined by their content as a cafeteria service from which people take what they want (Dayan and Katz 1992).

This research tradition came to be increasingly overshadowed in the 1980s and 1990s by a new version of liberal functionalism, inspired by the resurgence of Durkheimian sociology and social anthropology. Its central theme is that the media are agencies of social integration. In an elegantly written book, James Carey (1992) argues that much mass communication has a ritual meaning which draws people together and affirms the underlying continuity of things. This is similar to Alexander's claim that mass communications help people to visualize society, feel connected to it and make sense of its processes through a shared set of understandings (Alexander 1981). Media representations provide, in his view, a 'functional substitute for concrete group contact, for the now impossible meeting-of-the-whole' of modern differentiated societies. Likewise, Cardiff and Scannell (1987) argue that broadcasting promotes a sense of collective identity and belonging by promoting symbols of the nation, and by presenting a daily, edited version of national, corporate life. The media also foster, according to liberal functionalism, integration into society's normative order of moral values, its sense of what is right and wrong. Thus the media regularly mark out the boundaries of what is acceptable and unacceptable through the expression of 'societal' disapproval for deviants who transgress social norms (Ericson *et al.* 1987), from 'hard' drug users to 'runaway mums' who opt for romance at the expense of caring for their children.

Some of these general arguments were illustrated and developed in a key book by Dayan and Katz (1992), which shows how 'media events' – such as set-piece occasions of state, rites of passage of the great and sporting contests – are given extensive, uncritical coverage on television, and function as unifying, ritual experiences. They provide occasions when the private home is transformed through simultaneous television watching into a shared public space, and individuals are linked to each other, and to society, in a collective celebration of something they hold in common. Typically, these media events affirm a common identity. They can also enable society to see itself in an idealized way, or involve the celebration of a shared value, memory or experience.

Dayan and Katz give as an example the televised wedding of Prince Charles and Lady Diana Spencer, which was watched by millions in Britain in 1981 after an advance fanfare of mounting anticipation and excitement. The broadcast event celebrated the universal experience of love, courtship and betrothal, and ritually affirmed a consensual commitment to the institution of marriage, in an occasion of national rejoicing that induced a liminal sense of togetherness, an 'overflowing of communitas'. While Dayan and Katz tease out other meanings from the event as well, it is the collective and socially integrative aspects of the royal wedding that, as liberal functionalists, they focus attention on (Dayan and Katz 1987 and 1992).

In short, it is not necessary to think of the media as powerful agencies of persuasion in order to recognize that they play a central role in society. That role, according to liberal functionalists, is to assist the collective self-realization, co-ordination, democratic management, social integration and adaptation of society.

RADICAL CRITICISM

The liberal tradition thus developed over half a century a coherent view of the organization, influence and place of the media in modern society. This account contains of course an element of simplification. Some liberal media academics dissent from parts of this analysis, and would not recognise themselves as being part of the same tradition as others who have been cited. Yet, this said, a 'liberal' way of thinking about the media did in fact take shape. It broadly hangs together as a set of ideas. It comes largely, though not exclusively, from the same intellectual universe.

The evolution of this liberal view generated growing rumblings of criticism and dissent from radical critics. The elaboration of a Durkheimian perspective of the media as 'ritual' agencies of social integration provoked, for example, the objection that it misleadingly implies that there is an underlying unity of interest in society (Chaney 1986). Strengthening the bonds of society through the integrative functioning of the media is assumed therefore to be in everyone's interests. However, in reality, winners and losers do not have the same investment in the social order. The media's projection of an idealized social cohesion may serve to conceal fundamental differences of interest. Its effect can be to repress latent conflict, and weaken support for progressive change.

Radical critics also complain that the 'ritual' view of the media usually assumes mistakenly that the media are able to act for society because they are neutral and autonomous institutions. However, this ignores the informal ties that can exist between the media and centres of power in society. It also overlooks the unequal division of resources in society, which can result in the media being co-opted to serve the interests of powerful groups and the agencies they control. The civic rituals mediated by press and television are, according to Philip Elliott (1980), 'performative rites' whose real purpose is to legitimate institutions of authority.

This general perspective is perhaps best illustrated by a counter-interpretation of the 1981 royal wedding. This acknowledges that, at one level, it drew people together in a ritual affirmation of the 'universal' experience of love and marriage. Yet, its more important function, according to Nairn (1988), was to popularize the monarchy, and entrench an institution which sustains Britain's class system, and supports a 'culture of backwardness'.

These critiques of liberal functionalism came out of an alternative radical tradition. In the 1970s, this tradition came to coalesce (though with some notable dissenters) around a radical functionalist view of the media, which irreverently turned upside down almost every aspect of liberal thinking about the media.

RADICAL FUNCTIONALISM

Indeed, radical functionalism is perhaps best viewed as the mirror-opposite of liberal functionalism. Thus, while liberal analysis emphasizes the autonomy of the media, radical functionalism stresses the media's subjugation to authority. According to Ralph Miliband, for example, the British media are shaped by 'a number of influences – and they all work in the same conservative direction'. These influences range from capitalist media ownership and the 'official climate' in which public service broadcasting is 'steeped', through to advertising censorship and the consensual values of media staffs. These merge together, rendering media 'weapons in the arsenal of class domination' (Miliband 1973: 203–13).

Herman and Chomsky offer a radical American counterpart to this analysis. While it is not anchored to a Marxist, class-based view of society like Miliband's account, it is similar in that it assumes that controls within media organizations mesh with wider controls in society to render American media 'effective and powerful ideological institutions that carry out a system-supportive propaganda function' (Herman and Chomsky 1988: 306). It also identifies many of the same conservative influences on the media as those cited in the British study. These influences are portrayed with metaphoric eloquence as 'filters' that interact and reinforce each other:

> The raw material of the news must pass through successive filters, leaving only the cleansed residue fit to print. They fix the premises of discourse and interpretation, and the definition of what is newsworthy in the first place . . . The elite domination of the media and marginalization of dissent . . . results from the operation of these filters.
>
> (Herman and Chomsky 1988: 2; cf. Chomsky 1989; Herman 1999)

The second way in which the radical functionalist approach challenges liberal argument is to maintain that the media actively *produce* – rather than passively reflect – the consensus of society. The media are also held to play a central role in engineering consent for the social order by misrepresenting the true nature and dynamics of power. Thus, the media's focus on the domestic political process and national government tends to conceal, it is argued, the way in which political choices are structured by global capitalism. The media routinely report the news as discrete events, abstracted from their wider contexts. This promotes, according to Golding and Elliott (1979), a tacit view of the social order as natural, inevitable, outside of time – 'the way things are'. More generally, media fiction and its near cousin, human interest stories, promote a view of 'reality' as being influenced primarily by individual actors rather than social and economic structures, and foster the belief that solutions are best sought through individual moral improvement rather than changes in the organization of society (Curran, Douglas and Whannel 1980). More generally, social conflict is routinely concealed, according to Hall (1977), through the media's 'dissolution' of social classes, which are then re-presented as non-antagonistic entities (the 'public' or 'nation'), brought together around an imaginary point of unity (the 'public' or 'national' interest).

The media also support the power structure, it is argued, by unifying dominant forces and dividing their opponents. Dissent is stigmatized as extreme and threatening through a focus on acts of protest rather than the reasons for the protest (Gitlin 1980). Strikes are presented as irrational and harmful as a consequence of a selective news spotlight on their consequences rather than their causes (Glasgow University Media Group 1976). While the media allow some degree of debate, this is allegedly within defined bounds that stop short of challenging the social order (Downing 1980).

The mystifying role of capitalist media was largely conceived, during the hightide of radical functionalism, in terms of supporting class or elite hegemony. However, a feminist functionalist perspective also developed which argued that the media support patriarchy. According to Gaye Tuchman (1978b), the media sustain male domination through 'the symbolic annihilation' and 'trivialization' of women as sex objects and domestic consumers, and by teaching women to direct their hearts towards hearth and home (cf. Sharpe 1976). Another version of radical functionalism maintains that class, gender and ethnicity are merely different aspects of the same structure of control upheld by the media (Parenti 1993; Downing 1980). Although these accounts argue different things, they all assume that the media are both an expression of domination and a key means of reinforcing it.

The third way radical functionalism confronts the liberal tradition is by insisting that the media are powerful. Effects research is fatally flawed, in this view, by its methodological individualism and behavioural orientation (Hall 1982). Media power is best conceived not in the form of separate and discontinuous effects but in terms of ideological influence. The media not only help us to know about the world but also to make sense of it. They structure our understanding by 'actively ruling in and ruling out certain realities, offering the maps and codes which mark out territories and assign problematic events and relations to explanatory contexts' (Hall 1977: 341). Indeed, in a strong version of this argument, the dominant system of ideas and representations relayed by the media provides the means by which people ordinarily 'live' (i.e. selectively experience) an imaginary relationship to their real conditions of existence (Althusser 1984).

Fourth, radical functionalism rejects the underlying conceptions of society which underpin liberal accounts. Whereas liberal functionalism assumes that power is widely diffused, radical functionalism assumes that it is highly concentrated. Indeed, one reason why the media are 'powerful', in this view, is because they operate in a dominated society where other socializing agencies like the family, educational system and churches buttress media propaganda.

> The objection that we overrate the indoctrinating power of the 'media' . . . misses the point. The preconditioning does not start with the mass production of radio and television and the centralisation of their control. The people entered this stage as preconditioned receptacles of long standing.
>
> (Marcuse 1972: 21)

DECLINE OF DOMINATION THEORIES

The radical tradition thus developed a coherent view of the media in direct opposition to the liberal tradition. For a time, the radical functionalist paradigm made major inroads, and became almost an alternative orthodoxy, most notably in France and Britain. Then misgivings surfaced, not in response to liberal criticism but as a reaction to revisionist argument within the radical tradition. The citadel of radical functionalism was surrendered not because liberal assailants overran it, but because most of its defenders spiked their guns and slipped away into the night. While this saga has been alluded to in general terms in the last chapter, some aspects of it need to be clarified.

The first gun, so to speak, to fall silent was a domination perspective of society. In Britain, insightful studies of youth cultures conducted in Birmingham University during the 1970s challenged the simplistic notion that people are indoctrinated 'receptacles' of long standing. These studies portrayed a variety of subcultures – from 'skinheads' who accentuated the core values and style of 'lumpen' working-class life, through to Rastas who rejected their parents' desire for respectability in a celebration of blackness – as the expressions of a submerged form of dissent (Cohen 1972; Clarke 1976; Willis 1977; Hebdige 1979). These sub-cultures were revealed to be highly complex and sometimes contradictory responses to the experience of social disadvantage. Yet, despite the fact that they offered no programme for effective change, they were hailed enthusiastically by Birmingham researchers as a form of resistance in which youth groups 'won space' and kept in play 'contrary cultural definitions' to those that were dominant (Clarke *et al.* 1976). These studies were criticized subsequently for their focus on young men to the exclusion of women (McRobbie 1981), their selective concentration on non-conformist culture (Clarke 1990) and their romantic overstatement of the implications of what remained basically apolitical protests (Gitlin 1991; Skeggs 1992). Yet, despite their limitations, these studies represented at the time an historic breakthrough because they demonstrated very effectively the inadequacy of the conception of an ideologically dominated society.[9]

A similar reassessment also occurred within the feminist tradition. The view that women are socialized into acceptance of a subordinate position through the media and other socializing agencies in a capitalist, patriarchal society was challenged on several counts. It was argued that women do not have an inherent nature, rooted in their gender, which is repressed and denied through patriarchal control. Instead, revisionists stressed that women have different personalities and identities, and that these differences are the outcomes of complex processes of social construction in which women play a part (Zoonen 1991 and 1994). Women, in other words, are partly self-determining rather than controlled. In this reappraisal, the traditional radical argument that capitalism and patriarchy are two facets of the same system of control (eg Women's Studies Group 1978) largely dropped out of sight. Instead, attention was drawn to the gradual advances of women in response to organized feminism and wider economic change.

The once fashionable concept of a 'dominant ideology', relayed by the media, was also attacked on several grounds (Abercrombie *et al.* 1984; Hall 1985). The notion implies, it was argued, a degree of cultural domination that rarely exists. It ignores the relative autonomy of ideas and social identities through its economic reductionism. Above all, it overstates the intellectual coherence of 'ruling' ideologies by ignoring the contradictory ideas they contain. These caveats are all sensible qualifications exposing the limitations of a simplistic concept. However, this criticism was sometimes inflated into an idealist repudiation of the notion that there is *any* connexion between ideas and the play of economic power and self-interest.

The final solvent of domination theory was the revival of pluralism in a new form. Foucauldian and postmodernist analysis emphasized multiple forms of power, the disjunction between economic, political and cultural realms, the contradictory and multi-centred character of state institutions, the lack of coherence of globalised capitalist postmodernity, the cultural self-determination of 'subordinate' groups and the playful movement of subjectivity in an era of relativism and change, mobility and reflexivity (McRobbie 1992; Ang and Hermes 1991; Fiske 1989b, 1989c; Lyotard 1984; Foucault 1980, 1982). This reappraisal began by criticizing the frailties of 1970s theories of 'monopoly capitalism', with its over-simple view of the fusion and concentration of power, and ended up with increasingly opaque accounts of the world which replaced radical simplicity with deradicalized bafflement. Typical of this last is a postmodern lament about the difficulty of making critical sense of society 'when no one is dominating, nothing is being dominated and no ground exists for a principle of liberation from domination' (Poster 1988: 6).

GRAMSCIAN REARGUARD ACTION

In the face of this self-immolation of the radical tradition, an attempt was made to 'hold the line' during the 1980s by adopting and developing the ideas of the Italian Marxist, Antonio Gramsci (1985, 1981 and 1971). Control is normally achieved, according to Gramsci, more through consent than coercion. Yet consent for the prevailing disposition of rewards is conditional and revocable. It depends, in economically advanced societies, upon the continued ascendancy of the dominant social coalition (usually with organized business at its core). However, because this coalition is broad-based, it tends to be weakened by internal division. This coalition also needs to dominate public thought in the face of potentially effective opposition in order to maintain its hegemony. Even when a ruling coalition appears to be firmly in control, its ascendancy is rarely complete in practice and always needs to be renewed. In this wider context – conceived in terms of social conflict rather than static ascendancy – the media are best understood as a 'contested space'.

This position makes a number of intelligent revisions. It emphasizes the existence of dissent which is played down in radical functionalist analysis. It conceives conflict in broad, inclusive terms as being rooted not only in the social relations of production but also in multiple forms of disadvantage – including those linked to gender and ethnicity – which can give rise to broad-based movements of opposition to the status quo (Simon 1982; Mouffe 1981). It brings 'culture' more fully into the frame so that not only the political and economic realms but also the 'politics of everyday life' – for example, the symbolic meaning of clothes and music – can be viewed as inextricably linked 'sites' of contest. And it provides a flexible framework of analysis in which the relationship between ideas and material interests is viewed as linked but not pre-determined.

However, the sandbags of this defence began to leak. The notion of class conflict which was in fact central to Gramsci's own analysis came to be de-emphasized in favour of other axes of conflict. Cultural dissent was increasingly analysed in discrete terms without reference to how it related, concretely, to organized struggle. A qualified notion of economic determinacy became still more attenuated. Indeed, the rise of Gramscianism can be seen retrospectively as being part of a process of reappraisal that helped to discredit radical functionalism without establishing a new radical paradigm in its place.

This was partly beause the Gramscian tradition became something of a blank cheque. Its themes were repressed through extremely partial incorporation by some traditional Marxists (Parenti 1993), stretched by others to fit 'the feminist ticket' (Holub 1992) and absorbed still more selectively into radical postmodern-ism (Hebdige 1988). In effect, it came to mean very different things to different people.

Some media academics also flaunted a Gramscian badge in the 1980s, only to quietly discard it when the intellectual fashion moved on. Rallying behind 'liberal' Marxism, and redefining its meaning, was their way of managing an exit out of Marxism. The short-lived rise of Gramscian theory marked the occasion of a general intellectual diaspora.[10]

SOURCE CONFLICT

If broad reconceptualizations of society undermined radical functionalism, another linked development was a debate about news sources. In his neo-functionalist phase, Hall argued that the suppliers of news played a key role in the maintenance of ideological ascendancy. News media, according to Hall and associates (1978; cf. Hall 1986a), accord accredited status to the 'powerful,' as news sources, and allow them to dictate the 'primary' interpretation of an event or topic. This then ' "commands the field" and sets the terms of reference within which all further coverage of debate takes place' (Hall et al. 1978: 58). Subordin-ate groups are forced to situate themselves within this interpretive framework in order to obtain a media hearing. In this way, the dominant field of discourses tends to be reproduced 'spontaneously' by journalists, without any element of compulsion.

This analysis, though initially influential, was attacked because it did not seem to respond to the new stress on conflict and fragmentation in society.[11] It was challenged by the argument that leading news sources should be conceived not as one bloc ('the powerful') who advance a single definition of events, but rather as rivals, with different degress of access to the media, commanding different degrees of credibility and pursuing different agendas. For example, Schlesinger and Tumber (1994) revealed that opposition political parties and accredited pressure groups in the crime and criminal justice field had less access to the media than state agencies, yet were able to gain space, especially in elite media, for arguments which accused the police of illegitimate violence, racial discrimination and involvement in miscarriages of justice, and which advocated prison reform and a significant rethinking of penal policy. A broadly similar argument was advanced by Daniel Hallin, though it was not related specifically to this debate. He maintained that tensions between the military and the government, and growing disagreements within the political class, changed the way in which the Vietnam War was reported (Hallin 1989 and 1994; cf. Williams 1993). Similarly Lang and Lang (1983) argued that it was divisions within the American political establishment (and consequently in the sourcing of the news) that provided the main driving force behind media exposure of the Watergate scandal and the forced resignation of President Nixon.

While the general theme of this literature is that source disagreement fosters media diversity, there is a subtle difference of emphasis in the presentation of this argument. American studies tend to portray interaction between elites as the key source influence on American news media, in a context where non-elite voices are marginalized (Sigal 1987; Lang and Lang 1983; Hess 1984; Nacos 1990; Hallin 1989, 1994). However, some British case studies argue that non-elite groups – for example, Protestant workers in Ulster mounting a political strike or protesters against the poll tax (among others) – can in certain circumstances gain the upper hand in shaping definitions of the news (Miller 1993; Deacon and Golding 1994). A further complication is added by studies that draw attention to the politics of news-gathering organizations. Which sources are used, and how they are used, is influenced sometimes by the partisan editorial policies of the news media that journalists work for (Nacos 1990; Curran 1987).

Yet despite these differences, one thing was forcefully asserted in this debate. 'Primary' news sources do not underwrite necessarily 'the hegemony of the powerful' (Hall 1982: 86) because 'the powerful' are not always of one mind, and the rest are not always excluded.

REINTERPRETING MEDIA CONTENT

The next domino to fall was 'media ideology'. Where radical functionalists discerned only media mystification, revisionists found mystery. The recurrent refrain of revisionists was that media 'texts' contain contradictions, dislocations and tensions that render them accessible to divergent and non-conformist interpretation. This ambiguity arises, it was suggested, from the market need to accommodate the divergent views of heterogeneous audiences, at a time of social transition.

A celebrated example of this general approach is Tania Modleski's (1982) beguiling claim that American soap operas do not support patriarchy in the simple way that is generally supposed. She argues that the archetypal villainess, who transforms traditional feminine weakness into a source of strength, can be an object of ambivalent or subversive identification among women viewers. This study was followed by numerous others, also exposing the polysemic nature of media content. For example, Claire Johnston (1998) argues that the classic Hollywood films, directed by Dorothy Arzner mostly in the 1930s, employed a strategy of 'dislocation, subversion and contradiction' to undermine the patriarchal themes they ostensibly upheld. Johnston narrates how the central female character in *Dance, Girl, Dance* yearns for self-expression and a career only to surrender these things in favour of the patriarchal man in the film ('silly child, you've had your own way long enough'). But as she is enveloped in his arms, in the final frame, she exclaims, half crying, 'when I think how simple things could have been, I just have to laugh'. The implication of this ironic acceptance of defeat, according to Johnston, is a wish, implicitly shared with women film-goers, that gender relations could be ordered differently.

Analysing the same film, another critic points to the way Arzner subversively denaturalizes the gender order by rendering it both strange and comical. This is exemplified by a scene in which a wind machine seems to be tugging at the clothes of a burlesque dancer. She seeks shelter behind a tree on the stage. Clothes fly in all directions, to the hoots and cat-calls of excited men in the audience. Then the camera angle switches, revealing the woman behind the tree, tossing clothes from a hidden pile beside her (Cook 1998).

The implicit theme of these studies is that the media have fractured meanings, which facilitate progressive audience responses. These revelations of 'textual redemption' were followed by still more upbeat studies in the 1990s. Patriarchy was not merely being subverted through stealth, it was argued, but actively challenged. For example, Angela McRobbie (1996) shows that a new generation of women's and and girls' magazines in Britain offer a more ironic, knowing, plural and ultimately liberated understanding of what it is to be a woman, by comparison with their predecessors. This is, she suggests, a consequence of competitive market pressures, feminist influence and cultural change.

Similarly, Julie D'Acci (1994) argues that the long-running American television series, *Cagney and Lacey*, represented a breakthrough of a sort. It featured in the lead roles two female detectives who are 'in control', good at their jobs, personally sympathetic, with a warm, supportive friendship that helps them to withstand discrimination at work. Although the feminist radicalism of its early episodes became muted due principally to network pressure, it still continued to draw upon the ideas and humour of the American feminist movement. Something of its flavour comes through in this exchange:

Lieutenant Samuels (male boss):   Cagney, will you get on with your job and let me talk to my men?
(Cagney elaborately turns to Lacey and with great interest begins a new tack.)
Cagney: That certainly was a delicious stew you made

last night, Mary Beth. Could you give me the recipe?

Lacey: Well, first you buy a pig.

(Samuels glares at them.)

Cagney: Buy a pig? I didn't know that you could buy a pig in this town.

Lacey: Oh, you can buy a pig almost anyplace in this town. You don't want an old pig, or a fat pig. You just want a nice succulent . . .

(cited in D'Acci 1994: 149)

This revisionist feminist theme of qualified progress finds an echo in the concerned liberal literature about media and race. Traditionally, this literature has argued that ethnic minorities tend to be presented by the media as a problem or threat by being regularly associated with crime and conflict. This negative impression is reinforced by the way in which news reports tend to be decontextualized, so that the implication that ethnic minorites are inherently prone to criminality and cause trouble goes unchallenged. However, some accounts argue that media representations are slowly changing. African Americans are more visible in American media (Martindale 1986), more often portrayed in high-status roles in American television fiction (Jhally and Lewis 1992), and are projected as less threatening in the US media by comparison with the past (Wilson and Gutierrez 1985), though there seems to be greater continuity in representations of ethnicity in the British press (Van Dijk 1991; Troyna 1981; Hartmann and Husband 1974).[12]

REINTERPRETING THE AUDIENCE

The debunking of 'media ideology' was sealed by the rediscovery of audience power in revisionist reception studies. Old and new audience research had different intellectual roots. Effects research drew upon the discovery of the primary group in 1930s and 1940s industrial and urban sociology (Lowery and De Fleur 1983), and the development of cognitive dissonance theory in 1950s social psychology (Sears and Freedman 1971). By contrast, reception studies were inspired by the semiological insight that meaning is mobile rather than fixed, and by a new alertness to the importance of socially situated meaning systems, arising from 1970s social theory and research into radical subcultures.

But although the origins of old and new audience research were different, their paths began to converge. The core insight of effects research – that people respond in selective and divergent ways to communications, as a consequence of their socially embedded differences – was repeated again and again in reception studies. For example, Brown and Schultze (1990) found that black and white university students in the United States tended to make different sense of two

Madonna videos because they brought to their viewing different cultural references and frameworks of understanding. Corner *et al.* (1990) revealed that Conservative and Labour activists, Friends of the Earth campaigners and nuclear industry workers, the unemployed and Rotarians (local business people) responded differently to programmes about nuclear energy. Similarly, John Fiske (1991) described how homeless native Americans in Madison watched enthusiastically the early parts of classic westerns in which their fictional fore-bears took a homestead or wagon, only to turn off the film in order to avoid watching the white settlers' triumphant retribution. His account has almost an allegoric quality in the way in which it celebrates the power and autonomy of the audience.

LIBERAL INCORPORATION

Thus, there was a cumulative implosion within the radical tradition. The view that power is concentrated in society was challenged by the claim that it is fragmented. The portrayal of the media's full integration into the power system was attacked by an alternative account of the media as a 'contested space'. Analysis of media mystification gave way to textual studies of media ambiguity. The traditional radical view of the audience as conditioned and controlled was 'superseded' by another stressing audience autonomy and power.

This revisionist onslaught was not informed by a homogeneous perspective. Indeed, a powerful argument can be made that the strand represented by post-modern pluralism was really a liberal affirmation of popular power in a new guise. However, the more important point for an account of the development of media studies is that revisionist argument was strangely one-sided. Its firepower was directed mainly at the fundamentalist left positions of an older generation of radical academics, and was rarely aimed at the liberal pluralist tradition which this generation sought to overthrow. Partly as a consequence, the liberal tradition grew in influence almost unchallenged. It was also strengthened by the resur-gence of Durkheimian sociology in the 1990s, and in some cases by the skilful incorporation of revisionist argument. This last point is exemplified by a clever but perplexing essay about the democratic role of popular fiction.

Newcomb and Hirsch (1984) argue that just in the way that traditional soci-eties examine themselves through the experience of ritual, so contemporary societies do the same through art, most notably television art.[13] Television presents:

> a multiplicity of meanings rather than a monolithic point of view. It often focuses on our most prevalent concerns, our deepest dilemmas. Our most traditional views, those that are repressive and reactionary, as well as those that are subversive and emancipatory, are upheld, examined, maintained, and transformed. The emphasis is on process rather than product, on discussion

rather than indoctrination, on contradiction and confusion rather than coherence.

(Newcomb and Hirsch 1984: 62)

The fictional world of television enables us to explore our understanding of who we are, our relation to others, and how society can be improved. The world of television fiction offers 'the dramatic logic of public thought' (ibid: 63).

Newcomb and Hirsch take as an example a seemingly unpromising episode in a socially conservative, early 1960s American television series, *Father Knows Best*, in which the eldest daughter of the household aspires to be an engineer. She becomes an intern, but walks out on the first day when she is taunted by a young male apprentice. However, the episode ends on a happy upbeat note when the apprentice comes to her house to apologise and the two strike up a flirtatious relationship. The programme could be analysed, Newcomb and Hirsch suggest, as an example of the way in which television symbolically contains and displaces conflict. But this would miss, they argue, the essential point: namely, that our emotional sympathy is all the time with the daughter. At no time is the viewer encouraged to think that her ambition to be an engineer is unnatural. The episode, thus, poses a question about appropriate sex roles which it does not seek to answer. It offers a commentary rather than a conclusion. In this respect, it is exemplary since 'conflicting viewpoints of social issues are, in fact, the elements that structure most television programmes' (ibid: 65).

This celebration of textual ambiguity provides the prelude to a paean of praise for the diversity of American television 'While each of these [programme] units can and does present its audience with incredibly mixed ideas, it is television as a whole system that presents a mass audience with the range of ideas and ideologies inherent in American culture' (ibid: 64). This wide range of 'interpretive variance' is further expanded by the diversity of audience responses, shaped by divergent interpretive frameworks. In this way, we are told, a pluralist society communes with itself.

This essay has something interesting to say about the role of television drama in public debate. However its unwillingness to acknowledge that some perspectives are privileged while others are excluded, and more generally its exaggeration of the ideological diversity of American television, return us to the innocent days before radical criticism made an impact. In effect, Newcomb and Hirsch offer a restatement of a liberal functionalist view of the media as an open forum of debate, undisturbed by critical thought.

At this point, it is worth pausing and taking stock. A defiant case needs to be made that there are central insights in the *traditional* radical position which are being smothered by revisionist argument. What is needed is a reformulation, which both salvages these insights and also takes account of criticism. As a preliminary contribution to this reformulation, the remainder of this chapter will look again at two key questions: what influences the media, and what influence do the media have on audiences?

INFLUENCES ON MEDIA ORGANIZATIONS

The radical tradition is right to draw attention to the many influences, pressures and constraints that encourage the media to gravitate towards the central orbit of power. A failure adequately to acknowledge these influences is the central weakness of liberal functionalism, and gives rise to its mistaken belief that the media function neutrally on behalf of society.

However, a comparable error is made by radical analysts like Herman and Chomsky, Miliband and others in the radical functionalist tradition, in assuming that all *important* influences to which the media are exposed flow in one direction – in support of the *status quo*. In fact, many media organizations, in liberal democracies, are subject to countervailing influences that pull against the magnetic field of power. This can result in some media adopting a critical, or even radical, stance.

Of course, the influences to which the media are exposed vary significantly in relation to both time and place. But it is worth setting out in a theoretical way the formative influences that *in general* shape the media. First, we will enumerate the eleven main factors that encourage the media to support dominant power interests:

1 State censorship

The state has at its disposal a wide range of coercive, regulatory and patronage powers that potentially enable it to gag and control the media. These include repressive legal limitations on freedom of media expression, backed by tough punishments; the licensing of newspapers; control over entry into the journalism profession; partisan allocation of commercial television and radio franchises; packing public broadcasting and media regulatory authorities with government supporters; the lifting of monopoly restraints and provision of financial aid to assist *only* pro-government media. All these measures have been deployed in actual practice to encourage the media to support dominant government and private interests, especially in authoritarian societies.[14]

2 High entry costs

The principal instrument of market censorship is the large investment needed to establish new media enterprises in the mass market. High entry costs prevent non-elite groups from owning popular media. This, in turn, limits media diversity, and curtails consumer choice.

3 Media concentration

There has been a large increase of multimedia concentration, and also of partnership arrangements between leading media companies, in the context of an expanding media system. This has taken the form of a growing alliance between the providers of media content and controllers of distribution channels, and between companies in the old and new media sectors, both nationally and globally.[15] Producer power has been extended at the expense of consumer influence. Corporate media expansion has also resulted in some media controllers developing relations of compromising intimacy with national governments in order to secure regulatory favours.[16]

4 Corporate ownership

The media are increasingly big businesses. They have a material interest in promoting market-friendly policies. Their principal shareholders and top executives are wealthy people, with a stake in the *status quo*. They influence the ethos, direction and goals of these organizations through the setting of policy, the hiring and firing of key staff, and the allocation of rewards.

This said, their exercise of power within media organizations is constrained in a number of ways, and their political orientations are also not uniform. But numerous examples can be cited of right-wing media moguls promoting their political views and economic interests through the media under their control.[17]

5 Mass market pressures

Economies of scale are especially high in the media industries, with the result that unit costs fall sharply as production (or ratings) increases. This generates a very strong incentive to maximize audiences. Entertainment media in the mass market tend therefore to converge towards the consensual and conventional, advance universal themes with a wide appeal, follow tried and tested formulae and seek to avoid giving offence to significant segments of their audience. This is one of the key factors inhibiting the development of radical network television drama, especially in the United States.[18]

6 Consumer inequalities

Much media provision for niche markets (such as specialist women's magazines) is skewed towards the interests and needs of the affluent because their high disposable incomes make them a prime market.

7 Advertising influence

Consumer inequalities also distort the distribution of media advertising expenditure. Elites around the world are served by advertising-rich minority papers – the 'prestige press' – which give them an influential voice not available to other small minority groups. Media systems tend also to be oriented more towards the wealthy than the poor because the former bring higher advertising rewards.

Advertisers can also exert a direct influence by supporting media which offer a conducive environment for their products or politics, and withholding support from those who do not conform. This last influence tends to be overstated in critical commentary, not least because of the rise of professional advertising media planning, staff resistance and the decline of television advertising sponsorship. In general specialist and local media, dependent on a small pool of advertisers, are more vulnerable to blackmailing advertising influence than mass media.[19]

8 Rise of public relations

There has been an enormous increase in expenditure on public relations by both government and business corporations during the last thirty years. In effect, these powerful institutions subsidise the cost of gathering and processing the news in order to influence positively the way they are reported.[20]

9 News routines and values

News organizations are subject to the pressures of limited time and finite budgets. They assign therefore specialist staff to cover prestige institutions (such as branches of the state) as an economical and effective way of gathering the news. However, this encourages the media to give disproportionate attention to the activities and concerns of these institutions.

By contrast, the weak and unorganized tend not to be included on regular news beats. They also have low credibility which makes checking stories originated by them costly and time-consuming, and therefore unappealing.

10 Unequal resources

The media are shaped by the values, images, explanatory frameworks and premises that are widely shared in society. These tend to be internalized involuntarily by media staff.[21]

The discourses circulating in society are influenced in turn by the unequal resources commanded by different groups. Some have at their disposal greater cultural capital (authority, expertise, communication skills), social capital (prestige and social connexions), or economic capital (economic power and material resources) than others. They can exploit these assets to gain control of leading institutions, which influence public attitudes and behaviour. Thus, the culture of society absorbed by the media often bears the imprint of multiple forms of inequality.

11 Dominant discourses

A key theme of twentieth-century Western ideology was anti-communism. It was deployed again and again against the non-communist left, and was theorized into a bi-polar view of the entire world. Its place was taken in the post-communist era by the war against Islamic terrorism and worship of the market. Both themes were negotiated or contested, though so far with limited success.

COUNTERVAILING INFLUENCES

All these pressures tend, all other things being equal, to propel the media towards conservative positions. However, the media are also subject to countervailing pressures which can pull potentially in the other direction. There are seven principal ways in which popular forces can influence the media in liberal democracies. Some of these are contentious (within the radical tradition), and need to be presented therefore at slightly greater length.

1 Cultural power

Non-elite groups can develop alternative understandings of society, engender a strong sense of collective identity, and transmit collective allegiances and radical commitments from one generation to the next, through personal interaction, social rituals and the institutions under their control or influence. Through collective action in the workplace and civil society, and through participation in the collective dialogue of society, they can seek to change prevailing attitudes. Above all, their numerical strength means that potentially they can secure, through the electoral process, political influence over the state and use its power to modify the organization and culture of society (see below).

Recent trends have weakened the working class, the core group of the progressive alliance, in most Western industrial societies. The working class has become smaller; its economic power has diminished; and its internal cohesion and sense of identity has weakened. Yet, against this background of shrinking strength, there is still a significant variation in the achieved position of the organized working class and its allies. In Scandinavia, workers are still organized into strong trade unions, sustain effective political parties, and their representatives share influence over the state through liberal corporatist arrangements. Collectivist and egalitarian values penetrate deep into Nordic culture, and profoundly influence the Scandinavian media system. In stark contrast, the United States has no popular working-class party; its trade unions are weak and sometimes reactionary; and the country's culture is individualistic and conservative. Its media system is shaped, in other words, by the weakness of countervailing cultural power.

2 State empowerment

The state often features in Marxist, radical libertarian and also neo-liberal accounts as an agency of repression. It is identified respectively with control by capitalist, illiberal or bureaucratic interests exercised at the expense of popular freedom.[22]

In opposition to this strange alliance of opinion, the contrary case needs to be made that the democratic state is the principal means by which people can change society. Through the state, resources can be transferred from the rich to the poor, the healthy to the sick, the employed to the unemployed, in ways that can become part of the popular, media-supported consensus. Through the symbolic power of the state – through new official initiatives, the commissioning of new information, the foregrounding of new concerns, the forging of new state-sponsored alliances – elected governments can potentially change the political 'weather' in which the media operate.

Of course, the power of the state can be directed towards reactionary as well as progressive ends, and is subject to the play of elite influence. However, the practice of democracy – the free election of representatives to public office – changes the ground rules of public life. It means that what people think has to be taken into account by those in authority because people are endowed by democracy with political power. The democratic values of society can also penetrate the news values of the media.

3 Media regulation

Through the state, the public can influence who controls the media, how it is run and for what purpose. While this statist approach can be abused, experiments in contemporary western Europe and elsewhere conclusively demonstrate that it need not lead to government control.[23]

Democratic media regulation takes five main forms. First, public service broadcasting – that is the public ownership or regulation of radio and television channels – seeks to ensure that the public is adequately informed, reporting is fair, plural perspectives are represented, and programme quality and diversity are sustained. Second, social market policies – such as legal limits on media concentration and selective funding for minority media – aim to promote media pluralism. Third, the social responsibility approach seeks to restrain market excess through self-regulation and the professional education of journalists in public institutions. Fourth (and, relatively underdeveloped), the economic democracy approach aims to improve the media by enabling media staff to participate in decision-making. Fifth, a more general approach seeks to secure an equitable balance between the media's freedom of expression and the protection of human rights (such as that to a fair trial). All five approaches attempt to ensure that the media serve the needs of society rather than simply the private interests of shareholders.

4 Source power

A further way in which non-elite groups can influence the media is by establishing organizations which are used as sources of news and comment by the media.

While non-elite groups have in general restricted access to the media, this can be modified through improvements in organization. In Britain, organized labour and numerous public interest groups improved their public relations in the 1980s and 1990s in order to gain a better media hearing, with a significant measure of success (Davis 2002). PR is in fact a relatively low-cost activity which can be utilized potentially by organized groups with limited funds.

Wider changes in society can also influence the structure and hierarchy of the news sources routinely used by the media. For example, greater concern for environmental issues, echoed by the government, led in the 1980s to greater use being made by journalists of environmental pressure groups as news sources (Anderson 1991; Hansen 1991). During the same period, trade unions were demoted as news sources because they were perceived to have lost influence. Though still outside the pale of established politics, Sinn Fein's status as a news source rose sharply in the 1980s in the estimations of British journalists when the party demonstrated that it had a popular base by winning elections in Northern Ireland (Miller 1994). In other words, the marginality or otherwise of non-elite groups is not fixed and immutable. Their status as news sources – whether they are used, and the credibility they command – depends, in part, on how much public backing they receive, the topical resonance of their concerns, their perceived importance and their proven reliability.

5 Consumer power

People can influence the media by their allocation of time and money. This said, the degree of consumer influence that is exercised depends upon the extent of real choice in the market (which tends to be constrained, as we have seen, by a number of factors). There is also no direct correspondence between the ideological or political character of the mass media and the outlook of the public partly because most consumers select media to be entertained rather than to be represented. This is one of the main reasons for the lack of fit between the electoral preferences of the British press and public during the last half century, documented by Butler and Butler (2000).

Yet, market competition does forge a link between the media and the concerns of the public, even if it is sometimes a complex one. Competition leads to market segmentation and specialization as a way of accommodating to the demands of different audiences. More generally, consumer influence can act as a restraint on shareholder and also dominant cultural power. Mass media must seek to offer pleasurable experiences to large numbers of people, whose social position and experience can make them resistant to the cherished beliefs of media controllers, or indeed the prevailing views of the time. This can give rise to media content which pragmatically champions audience perspectives or, more often, which is sufficiently open-ended to allow differing consumer responses and satisfactions.

6 Producer power

Subordinate groups can gain a media voice through owning their own media enterprises. They have met with greatest success in specialist markets where entry costs are low, and also in the past when media costs were sometimes less than they are now.

Thus, organized labour owned a flourishing, popular press in a number of countries during the first half of the twentieth century. This press mostly died save in those countries where minority publications are supported by public finance in the interest of sustaining pluralism. For a time, radical music labels made a considerable impact before being rolled back or incorporated into tie-in arrangements by music majors (Burnett 1990; Hesmondhaulgh 1997). While many countries boast alternative media, their influence has tended to be short-lived. Most of the radical radio stations that were launched in the 1970s in France and Italy subsequently closed down (Lewis and Booth 1989), while alternative film, newspaper, magazine, book and cable television/video companies have had notably chequered histories (Downing 2001). Even the remarkable Radio Pacifica network in the United States, once lauded for its staying power and enduring influence (Barlow 1993), fell on hard times in the late 1990s (Downing 2001).

Many of these alternative ventures were vulnerable because they were undercapitalized, experienced difficulty in securing distribution and lacked relevant business knowledge and management experience. They were also often poorly adapted to the market system because making money was not their main objective.

This record of under-achievement may be modified by the internet. Sceptics point out that access to the internet is restricted by global and class-based inequalities of computer ownership. The internet is also dominated by business use, and its internal signposting systems can sideline alternative communications (Patelis 2000). The unequal distribution of resources in the real world inevitably penetrates the functioning of cyberspace. 'Without promotion', commented one senior internet executive, 'you're just a lemonade stand on the highway' (cited in Herman and McChesney 1997: 124). This said, the arrival of the internet has demonstrably facilitated radical communication (Ford and Gil 2001). This is partly because it provides a means of communication which is cheap, global, interactive and relatively free from official regulation (though this last is becoming less true).

7 Staff power

The peripheral public can also be 'represented' by media staff whose professional self-esteem rests on the claim that they serve society. However, this argument needs to be viewed critically.

The first issue of contention is the degree to which journalists' claims to autonomy, recorded in academic surveys (eg Weaver and Wilhoit 1991), are true. To some degree, journalists' sense of independence may stem from their internalization of the norms of their employing organizations. They can feel autonomous because they do what is expected of them without being told what to do.

The second issue is the extent to which journalists are really independent of the hierarchy of power in society as a consequence of their commitment to professional values. A powerful assault on the professionalisation of journalism has been mounted by critics who argue that it is based on a stunted version of objectivity as a 'strategic ritual' whose real purpose is to obviate the need to evaluate what is true, avoid causing offence to the powerful and facilitate the meeting of deadlines (Tuchman 1978a); that it legitimates reliance on a narrow oligarchy of sources (Sigal 1987); and results in pro-establishment and trivializing forms of journalism (Gitlin 1990).

However, these criticisms arise out of studies conducted in one country (the United States). They do not have a universal application (even though American precepts of journalism have been globally influential). Instead, attention needs to be given to different conceptions of journalism pursued in different contexts. One definition of journalism, strongly entrenched in American television, sees the role of the journalist as representing a unified public (and tends to reproduce 'mainstream' views). Another tradition, more entrenched in western European television, puts greater stress on the role of the journalist in facilitating a public debate (and tends to privilege spokespersons from leading organized groups). Among other significant traditions, there is also a romantic radical strand which holds that the journalist should, in the words of Malcolm Maclean Jnr, 'communicate what it means to be poor among the rich, to be hungry among the well-fed, to be sick among the healthy ... to be unheard, unheard, unheard ... in a society noisy with messages' (cited in Manca 1989: 170). Implicit in these different definitions are divergent understandings of how the public should be served, and how journalism should be practised.

After all necessary qualifications have been made, the claim that media professionals *can* represent the public is not entirely mythical. Indeed, even the 'strategic ritual' of objectivity pursued by journalists can act as a restraint on the partisan commitments of media controllers. The practice of securing balanced quotes from opposed spokespersons is, for example, one of the principal limitations on the right-wing bias of the British popular press. If journalists generally defer to managerial authority, there are also rare examples – recounted in Chapter 8 – when they heroically defy their employers in defence of a professional conception of journalism. If journalists often fail to scrutinize adequately corporate power, yet their record in monitoring the government and official abuses of power is far better.

MEDIA IN LIBERAL DEMOCRACIES

In brief, media organizations are potentially subject to formative influences which can propel them towards the dominant sphere of power. Yet, non-elite groups are seldom without resources. They, too, can influence the media through counter-vailing political, cultural, source, producer and consumer power, and even be represented – at best – as a consequence of the public interest culture of media staff.

This general approach offers a way of breaking free from the rigidities of both liberal and functionalist analysis. It avoids *assuming* that the media have evolved into autonomous institutions, or that they are subject to elite domination. Instead, this approach is alert both to the unequal distribution of power in society which undermines media autonomy, and also to conflict and dissent which weaken elite control.

But if this approach offers advantages, it also has limitations. For the sake of brevity, it tends to refer to the media as if they are a single, uniform entity (a common simplification in media theory), whereas in most societies the media are organized into highly differentiated systems. Indeed, inequalities within society reinforce this differentiation. In most liberal democracies, one part of the media system serves elites, while another caters for the wider public (and subgroups within it).

This model also has the weaknesses (as well as strengths) of ideal-typification. It has been formulated in a deliberately general way so that it broadly applies to any society where there is a conflict between winners and losers (however defined) played out in public debate, sustained by opposed groups and organizations in civil society. This embraces both a wide spectrum of societies and also of interpretive paradigms.

However, this model does not fit some contexts. It does not apply to societies where elite domination is securely achieved, and where radical functionalist arguments consequently have some validity. It does not correspond, for example, to Singapore's authoritarian 'liberal democracy' in the 1980s and early 1990s where the local media were seemingly compliant agencies supporting the ascendancy of a cohesive elite in an economically successful city state (Kuo *et al.* 1993; Hachten 1989; Ramaprasad and Ong 1990). It also fits rather uneasily with liberal corporatist societies where the media are exposed to a consensus predetermined by corporatist networks. For example, the media in Norway appear to have been, in the 1980s, agencies upholding a consensus based on an agreed social settlement between organized labour, corporate business and other social interests mediated through the state (Syvertsen 1992 and 1994; Høst 1990).

In short, the media in liberal democracies are often exposed to pressures from above and below. But how these pressures are manifested – and even whether countervailing influences are present in a significant form – depends upon the specific context in which the media operate.

MEDIA POWER

As we have seen, there are two contrasting views of media power. In one, the media dominate the audience, while in the other the relationship is reversed. However, both views are problematic, not least because they are based on flawed methodologies.

The most obviously defective are studies purporting to show that the media are powerful ideological agencies. Typically, they involve no audience research at all, and are based on inferences derived from media content.[24]

Empirically grounded audience research, stressing audience power, also raises difficulties. Much of this work is directed towards the measurement of short-term media influence, even though the media's influence is primarily long-term and cumulative. A comparision can be drawn with studies of cigarette smoking. Any investigation which sought to measure the impact of smoking on the basis of a single cigarette, or even smoking for a month, would be judged inconclusive if it found no evidence of a carcinogenic effect. The time span would be thought too short to yield meaningful results. Yet, reception studies are generally based on the analysis of viewers' encounters with a *single* television programme. While these studies are clearly not designed to measure influence, this does not prevent sweeping generalizations being derived from them about the determining power of the 'recalcitrant' audience. Effects studies generally cover a slightly longer period of audience exposure – typically three or four weeks, for example, in the case of studies into the effect of the media during election campaigns. Yet this is manifestly too short a period in which to assess media influence (not least because most national election campaigns are 'won' before the first day of the campaign).

A minority of effects studies have sought to measure long-term media influence, using panel studies or longtitudinal survey data. However, these have come up against the central problem of effects research – how to differentiate between media and non-media influence. The longer the time span, the more non-media influences are likely to have influenced the topic under investigation, whether this be, for example, juvenile crime or 'trust in authority'. While various sampling and statistical procedures have been developed to get round this problem, none has been entirely successful.

The only truly effective way of isolating media influence is through experimental methods. For example, the effect of different modes of news presentation can be gauged by exposing comparable groups to compilations of the news edited in different ways. But while experimental methods enable media influence to be controlled and scientifically assessed, they solve one problem only to create other ones. Experimental research is generally limited to measuring short-term media influence. It also entails the viewing of television in untypical situations, and sometimes relies on small samples from which it is difficult to derive general inferences about the population as a whole – something, incidently, that it has in common with reception studies.

Another recurrent difficulty raised by audience research is that it imposes (for understandable reasons) an arbitrary cut-off point. Typically, it monitors the flow of information and meaning between media and audience. The media are analysed, if at all, through their content. The wider contours of society are usually perceived through the prism of the audience and its social characteristics or discourse positions. This narrow framing is distorting in two ways.

It provides a foreshortened view of the media which excludes their wider links to society. For example, audience research into agenda-setting typically examines whether the media set the public agenda but fails to consider how the media's agenda was formed in the first place. In this way, the media are pre-defined as a *source* of potential influence ('agenda-setting'), regardless of whether they are in fact a *vehicle* of influence, relaying an agenda set by a powerful institution or group.

The narrow framing of research also offers a truncated perspective of the audience. How many audience members are able to make oppositional readings of the media depends crucially upon their access to oppositional discourses. This depends in turn upon the extent to which the circulation of oppositional discourses are supported by influential organizations and social networks, and sustained by well-timed ideological interventions. Yet, these wider dynamics contextualising audience responses tend to fall outside the terms of reference of audience research.

This is not to join in fashionable denigration of audience research. It offers illuminating and sometimes counter-intuitive insights, and compels a reassessment of conventional notions of media power. However, its conclusions do need to be viewed critically. What, then, does audience research – sceptically reviewed – tell us?

CONTROL FALLACY

The conviction, central to the radical approach, that the media are important agencies of influence is broadly correct. However, the ways in which the media exert influence are complex and contingent. They do not correspond to the simplistic notion of media indoctrination to be found for example in the work of Marcuse (1972) or early Habermas (1989 [1962]).

A key starting point is to recognize that audience 'activity' should not be equated with control. This is well illustrated by a reception study of the *Cosby Show*, a long-running, American television comedy series featuring a well-to-do black doctor and his family (Jhally and Lewis 1992). The study reveals that black and white American viewers identified with the Cosby family, and related to the series, in different ways. One of the *Cosby Show*'s attractions for African American viewers was that it provided a positive portrayal of a successful black family at a time when this was rare on American television. However, black viewers had mixed responses about what the series revealed about real life in America. For most white viewers, by contrast, the *Cosby Show* symbolized the true realization of the American dream. It also conveyed reassurance that racism had become a thing of the past.

This study is thus entirely conventional in showing that a programme series meant different things to different groups of people. But what it also showed was that selective audience responses were strongly influenced by prevailing beliefs in American society. Many white viewers saw in the series confirmation that a talented family, whatever their colour, was able to prosper in a land of freedom and opportunity. But they were simultaneously aware that, in actual reality, many African Americans were poor. The series supported what Jhally and Lewis call 'enlightened racism': a positive view of black people in principle, combined with cultural contempt for their lack of success. The different responses of black viewers stemmed in part from their more critical relationship to the myth of meritocracy (though, significantly, some black believers in the myth displayed contempt for 'unsuccessful' blacks in ways that almost echoed the opinions of racist white viewers).

In actual fact, vertical social mobility in the United States is rather limited. The social location of large numbers of black people is probably as much due to their inherited class position as their colour. But in revealing that a pervasive myth of social mobility shaped audience responses, this thought-provoking study showed that audiences were manipulated as well as manipulating.

MEDIA REINFORCEMENT

The second key point to register is that the media are powerful agencies of reinforcement. The effects tradition documents this extensively, yet makes little of it. This is because the absence of persuasion or change has been traditionally viewed in this tradition as evidence of limited influence. Thus, when Lazarsfeld and his associates (1944) found that the main effect of the media in the 1940 American presidential election was to activate people to vote in the way in which they intended, they concluded that the media's influence had been minimal. The media's role was likened by them to providing signposts guiding people to pre-determined destinations. This denial of reinforcement as a significant influence has persisted, despite some dissent, throughout the history of effects research. For example, Perloff (1993) classifies any media effect that does not involve change consciously sought as a non-effect.

Lazarsfeld and associates' central finding of media reinforcement in election campaigns has been regularly replicated, though with some modifications due to increased voter volatility. Summarizing a large body of research into the influence of the media in election campaigns, the following conclusions emerge: the media can cause a small number of people to change their voting intentions, or abstain; they can influence a larger number of people to revise their perceptions of key issues, leaders and party performance; but their main impact is to galvanize people to vote in ways which are consistent with their 'predispositional characteristics'

(Norris 2000; Iyengar and Reeves 1997; Iyengar 1991; Iyengar and Kinder 1987; Miller 1991; Harrop 1987; Blumler and Gurevitch 1982; Blumler and McQuail 1968).

This recurring theme of media reinforcement is generally conceived in the effects tradition within a transportation model of influence in which the media are the starting point and the audience is the terminus. However, the same theme takes on a very different meaning when the media are viewed as agencies of the prevailing stucture of power, and the media's primary function is conceived as legitimating the social order. What is viewed in one tradition as a 'weak' influence because it involves little change is viewed in another as a 'strong' influence because it discourages change.

SELECTIVE REINFORCEMENT

This conception of media influence as being primarily one of reinforcement is illuminating. But it also needs to be viewed critically. Strands within both radical functionalism and effects research point towards a sterile circularity in which the media (or elements of mediated communication) and audiences are locked into a perpetual cycle of reinforcement, the outcome of which is merely the fortification of existing beliefs and patterns of behaviour.

Against this, it is important to stress that the media can also induce change through selective reinforcement. This is often how effective propaganda works. The common feature of successful information campaigns on public health and other issues is that they make a personal connection with audiences by linking up to their beliefs or needs (Perloff 1993; Harris 1989).

One classic strategy of persuasion is to activate latent beliefs that have lain dormant. A second is to effect a change in one attitude by reinforcing an opposed view held simultaneously by the same person. A third is to re-route – 'canalize' – the direction of pre-existing attitudes. For example, a Buckingham Palace-inspired programme, *Royal Family*, shown on both the BBC and ITV in 1969, broke new ground by portraying the Windsors as a happy middle-class family, rather than as regal and remote. A BBC 'before and after' study found that it led to significant increases in the perception that the Queen was 'in touch', 'relaxed' and 'modern' among people already strongly predisposed to be in favour of the monarchy (British Broadcasting Corporation 1969).

Change through *selective reinforcement* is also the central theme of moral panic studies. The best of these maintain that that the media are able to mobilize a moral panic around a particular issue, perceived to be symptomatic of a wider malaise in society, because they draw selectively upon widely held values, and provide a focus for current fears and discontents. Thus, Stuart Hall and his colleagues (1978) argue that the press successfully generated growing public indignation against muggers because it drew upon well-established images of deviance, hostility towards black immigrants, fears and resentments arising from social change and a set of well-embedded social values. Similarly, Golding and Middleton (1982) argue that a tabloid offensive against welfare cheats succeeded in mobilizing public anger partly because it drew upon deeply entrenched animosity towards the 'undeserving poor' going back over four centuries, and also because it fanned the resentments of those in work who were suffering a fall in living standards during a recession. Simon Watney (1987) argues that the press was able to generate intense hostility towards gays during the initial outbreak of AIDS because it tapped into homophobic attitudes, supported both by the law and Christian theology.

The second, important aspect of these studies is that they argue that moral panics are generated through *selective* media representations of reality. The moral panic about mugging, argue Hall *et al.* (1978), was based on the misleading media claim that there was an unprecedented increase in a new strain of crime ('mugging'), when the crime was not new and its increase was not unprecedented. The tabloid press's focus on welfare payments to the poor, Golding and Middleton (1982) point out, chose to concentrate on their abuse by the 'work-shy' rather than the fact that large numbers of poor people were not claiming the welfare payments to which they were entitled. Similarly, Watney (1987) and Kitzinger (1993) point out that the initial British press spotlight on AIDS stoked popular fear by greatly overstating the risk of casual contagion through non-sexual means. Tabloids also heightened public indignation by identifying the carriers of the 'killer plague' as deviants – gays, prostitutes and drug users – whose sinful ways endangered the 'innocent' community.

The third, though sometimes implicit, theme of moral panic studies is that media constructions selectively orchestrate elements within popular consciousness. They activate and strengthen some concerns, while ignoring others. Thus, the mugging moral panic bypassed critical attitudes towards the police to mobilize public indignation against 'black' criminals. The 'scrounger' campaign circumvented sympathy for the poor by targeting welfare cheats. The AIDS panic stoked fear among the straight community, rather than eliciting a human response to those dying in distress.

This process of selective reinforcement did have significant consequences in the three cases that we have considered. The moral panic about muggers led more people to demand tougher punishments, and seemingly fuelled support for a time for the creation of a more authoritarian state (Hall *et al.* 1978). The moral panic about 'scroungers' resulted in increased public criticism of welfare payments, and weakened welfarist attitudes (Golding and Middleton 1982).[25] And the panic about AIDS gave rise to unrealistic fears about the number of people who would die from it in Britain, and increased the number of people openly hostile to gay men.[26]

PLURAL PERSPECTIVES

A substantial body of research thus makes the point that public opinion can be modified through selective reinforcement and deinforcement of pre-existing 'dispositions' or elements within popular culture. In this account, influence works not through the simple imposition of opinion on audiences, but through the manipulation of their feelings, concerns, fears and attitudes. Persuasion is always an interactive rather than one-way process.

This general argument needs to be placed in a wider context. Most developed societies have discursive fields of competing, opposed and incommensurate themes. This discursive diversity is the product of history. For example Britain, despite its appearance of unity and continuity, has been profoundly marked by centuries of social struggle. Aristocratic values of ascribed social position, inherited leadership and voluntaristic paternalism (still values with a strong residual presence in some contemporary rural areas) were challenged in the nineteenth century by a middle-class stress on the work ethic, individual self-reliance, competition and reward determined by merit. This in turn was challenged by a working-class ideology of collectivism, solidarity and equality supported by an interventionist state. Similarly, the age-old belief that men and women are inherently different, and destined by nature to occupy different social spheres, was challenged by the modern idea that men and women are fundamentally the same and should have equal and interchangeable roles. To these can be added many other cultural wars and skirmishes. As a consequence, British culture is a complex panoply of different and conflicting traditions. This is even more true of European countries, like Italy, France and Spain, with more conflictual and turbulent pasts than Britain.

This cultural diversity creates the conditions in which the media can enlist selectively elements of popular culture in ways which support either the left or right. For example, the sale of public utilities in 1980s Britain was hailed in the popular press as a major social advance in which millions of people acquired shares for the first time, and gained a personal stake in the investment market. This feting of popular capitalism, with its celebration of resourceful people getting ahead, drew upon well-embedded conservative values stressing the virtues of enterprise and self-reliance. However, it was challenged in the 1990s by a union-inspired campaign which drew attention to the very large bonuses, share options and incentive schemes that the managers of public utilities were awarding themselves. Denunciations of 'fat cats' struck a popular chord, and gained extensive media publicity, because they connected to an egalitarian nerve-end within British popular culture.

This said, the culture of most economically advanced liberal democracies is not made up of a single repertoire of meanings shared and accessible to all. There is of course some interpenetration of opposed cultural traditions, which is why left-wing and right-wing politicians can potentially intervene in public debates in ways that resonate with their supporters and opponents alike. But the concept of a national 'common culture' forged through the rise of the mass media – to be found in the work of some conservative historians (e.g. LeMahieu 1988) – is a myth that fails to take adequate account of cultural differentiation linked to class, gender, ethnicity and geographical location.

In Britain, for example, different social classes were drawn towards different value systems and political loyalties, supported by the uneven circulation of rival discourses within different sections of society. Mass audiences were never part of a 'mass', save in an abstract sense. Rather, members of mass audiences were integrated into class-based networks whose social dynamics and milieux strongly influenced responses to the media.

Class-based societies thus developed social mechanisms which provided high factor protection against the rays of media influence. However, there are indications that this particular form of protection is weakening. De-industrialization, the decline of the factory system, the rise of consumption and the decline of work as sources of social identity, the continued growth of individualism, increasing globalization and greater female participation in the paid workforce, are just some of the changes that have given rise to less socially and culturally segregated societies. People are now more accessible to media influence than their forebears because they are less insulated by coherent class cultures.[27]

DEFINITIONAL POWER

What then are the principal mechanisms of media influence? Much of the relevent literature is concerned with propaganda, persuasion and in effect the workings of rhetoric. However, the media also exert influence in a more oblique and often less consciously sought way than this propaganda-oriented literature suggests.

The media define the world through news, commentary and also fiction. Their mediations determine what gains prominence and what recedes into the background, what is included and what is excluded. In addition to providing 'windows on the world' offering selective perspectives, the media also signify and interpret. They provide explicit frameworks of explanation, as well as tacit understandings based on associations of ideas, evocative images, 'natural' chains of thought. They also furnish codes that label and classify, by, for example, distinguishing between the normal and deviant, natural and unnatural. The media both map the social world and explain its workings.

This account straddles two traditions: a radical perspective of the media's ideological influence and the cognitive psychological tradition of effects research. The latter advances concrete evidence, which we will examine through a notable investigation into the 'framing' effects of American television news.

Shanto Iyengar (1991) argues that there are two main ways of reporting the news: episodic treatments (much the most common mode on American network television) in which the news is presented as discrete and disconnected, and thematic treatments in which the news is contextualized and explained. Using ingenious experimental methods, Iyengar found that episodic reporting encouraged viewers to attribute responsibility to the individuals involved, and to look for solutions in terms of regulating the individual (greater use of the death penalty, longer jail sentences, cutting welfare programmes, military strikes against foreign terrorists). In contrast, thematic news reporting encouraged greater attribution to social causation, and a greater stress on solutions achieved through effecting changes in society.

This pattern of response was not uniform across news topics and categories of viewer. News framing had a strong influence on perceptions of terrorism, a significant influence on perceptions of crime, but only limited influence on understandings of poverty (which were strongly affected by prior attitudes towards race). There were also differences of response between viewers, most notably between committed Republicans and Democrats. However, Iyengar found that 'framing effects do occur regularly in the face of long-term personal predispositions. . . . Exposure to thematic framing can and does override these predispositions.' In other words, the media modify some people's understanding of the world.

Iyengar is advancing a relatively strong paradigm of media power based on the claim that the media can impose, in some instances, a framework of understanding in ways that overcome initial preconceptions (a position supported by other researchers, such as Philo (1990) using a different experimental method). However, media influence is also exerted in a less fundamental but still formative way through changes of media focus. Here, the argument is that the media can modify people's thinking by changing their perspective of what is important. This is a theme which is usually explored in a narrow way by research which shows that the relative salience given to different issues in the media can influence public perceptions of their order of importance.[28] What also needs to be stressed is that a shift in media agenda and public perception can alter the course of a political battle, and lead to a realignment of public opinion. In other words, media agenda-setting matters. This will be illustrated briefly by a British case study of a failed moral panic (Curran 1987 and 1990b; Waller 1988).

In 1981–3, the popular press (including Labour papers) ran a campaign against 'Red Ken' Livingstone and the 'loons' in charge of the Greater London Council (GLC). This centred on the public money that the GLC was spending on 'out groups' – gays, lesbians, feminists and immigrants. The campaign generated public animosity against the GLC (reflected in successive opinion polls), and contributed to the Thatcher government's decision to close down the GLC as an unnecessary expense.

This decision, announced in 1983 but only enacted after much difficulty in 1986, enabled the GLC to regain the political initiative. With the help of radio and television, a major advertising campaign and well-funded, local community protests, the GLC shifted the focus of media debate from 'political extremism' to the 'attack on democracy', represented by the government's plan to abolish it. This enabled the GLC to win support from a wider public by appealing to democratic values, London patriotism and suspicion of central government. In the event, a pariah authority eventually secured the backing of at least two-thirds of Londoners in its battle against abolition.[29] This demonstrated that a popular consensus existed in favour of a London-wide council, and paved the way for the establishment of the Greater London Authority in 2000, once again led by 'Red Ken'.

In brief, the media are not simply palimpsests, bearing the diverse imprints of resourceful, playful audiences. The media can persuade, change and mobilize. However, the principal way in which the media influence the public is not through campaigning and overt persuasion but through routine representations of reality. This power of definition influences public understanding of the world, and in indirect and contingent ways, public attitudes and behaviour.

The power of media

CONCLUSION

In this chapter, we have described the lop-sided development of media studies. The radical tradition was weakened by self-referential revisionist argument, while the liberal tradition expanded relatively unchecked by criticism. Yet, the traditional radical perspective offers important insights that need to be retained. Indeed, once it is weaned from a mechanical form of radical functionalism to which it fell prey particularly in the 1970s and 1980s, and responds to well-targeted criticism, this tradition still offers the most persuasive general account of the media.

Radical analysts are entirely right to insist that the media are, in general, subject to strong elite pressures which propel the media towards the sphere of established power. However, the media can also be exposed to countervailing popular influences.

The radical tradition is also correct to argue that the media are powerful ideological agencies, though not in the simplistic form of brainwashing proposed by members of the Frankfurt school. In sum, a reconstituted radical perspective needs to be championed against the advancing tide of revisionist argument, which overstates popular influence on the media and understates the media's influence on the public.[30]

Chapter 6

Globalization theory: the absent debate[1]

Books about globalization are pouring off the press.[2] This would seem to represent a positive new departure in which media and cultural studies, and the social sciences more generally, are connecting to the central dynamic that is transforming the world.

This 'new' focus on globalization would also appear to represent a welcome reaction against the self-absorbtion and parochialism of much western media theory. It has become routine for universalistic observations about the media to be advanced in English-language books on the basis of evidence derived from a handful of countries. These are nearly always rich states in the West and the occasional honorary 'western' country like Australia. For many media theorists, this tiny, unrepresentative sample constitutes 'society' or 'liberal democracy' about which they feel able to generalise.

Yet, there are indications that some American and European media academics are beginning to feel deeply embarrassed about viewing the rest of the world as forgotten understudies. The unhappy caveat that Michael Schudson inserted towards the end of an influential essay is a straw in the wind. 'All three approaches reviewed here', he laments, 'tend to be indifferent to comparative . . . studies', weakening 'their longer-term value as social science' (Schudson 1996: 156). Similarly, John Downing pours scorn on attempts to universalize the experience of Britain and the United States, as if these affluent, stable democracies with their Protestant histories and imperial entanglements are representative of the world. Like Sparks (1998), he calls for 'communication theorising to develop itself comparatively' (Downing 1996: xi).

But while the attention given to globalization is welcome, it is not quite the unqualified intellectual advance that it appears to be. For a start, it has done little to broaden 'media theory' (as distinct from cultural theory). For the most part, the literature on globalization offers an aerial perspective of the world, and pays little detailed attention to the media of specific countries.

The academic globalization boom is not even breaking new ground in the sense of identifying a new area of research. Indeed, within media and cultural studies, it is merely a continuation of a tradition that has been in existence for at least fifty years. What can be learnt from the history of this tradition, and how does 'cultural globalization theory' – the main focus of this chapter – fit within it?

GEO-POLITICAL PERSPECTIVE

In the 1950s, an enormously influential geo-political view of the world's media system was advanced in a book called *Four Theories of the Press* (Siebert, Peterson and Schramm 1956). This 'four theories' account divided the world into three camps: the free world of liberal democracy (with competing libertarian and social responsibility models of the media); the 'soviet-totalitarian' sphere; and authoritarian societies (a rag-bag category that included most of the developing world, the fascist experience and the West in its pre-democratic phase).

Perhaps the most striking feature of this book, in retrospect, is how little its talented authors felt they needed to know about the things they wrote about. They displayed some knowledge of the American and Russian media, and the history of the American colonial and early English press, but little about any other media system. They got round their evident lack of comparative expertise by advancing a convenient, idealist argument. Media systems, they claim, reflect the prevailing political philosophy of the society in which they operate. To understand the international media system, it is necessary merely to identify 'the philosophical and political rationales or theories which lie behind the different kinds of press we have in the world today' (Siebert *et al.* 1956: 2). In their account, these rationales were written almost entirely by western theorists. By implication, the world's communication system could be laid bare by studying Western thought.

This analysis was viewed as a landmark study for the next forty years. It was summarized, and gravely discussed, in key international textbooks (e.g. Wright 1959 and 1975; McQuail 1983, 1987 and 1994). Why this book was taken quite so seriously seems now something of a mystery. The explanation is probably that its Cold War perspective reflected the ruling orthodoxy of the period, and was thought therefore to be authoritative. Whatever the reason for its success, it established a convention that has stayed with us: lack of knowledge about other countries need not get in the way of confident global generalization.

MODERNIZATION PERSPECTIVE

If the 1950s 'Four Theories' perspective saw the universe only through western eyes, it was followed in the 1960s by 'modernization' theory which called upon the developing world to learn from, and imitate, the West. The media-oriented version of this theory argued that good communication was the key to 'the most challenging social problem of our time – the modernizing of most of the world' (Lerner 1963: 350). Good communication was viewed as the crux of almost everything, from persuading Peruvian peasants to boil their water (Rogers and

Shoemaker 1971) to encouraging fatalistic Turks and Iranians to be more ambitious (McClelland 1961), through to building a nation with a sense of cohesion and social purpose, willing to make collective sacrifices for the sake of progress (Schramm 1963). But if these and other goals were to be achieved, the West had to invest in setting up modern communication systems in the developing world (Pool 1963).

Daniel Lerner offered the most coherent view of how a modern communication system supposedly contributes to the transition from 'tradition' to modernity. He argued that exposure to modern media extends people's horizons and encourages them to want more out of life. 'The diffusion of new ideas and information', wrote Lerner (1963: 348), ' . . . stimulates the peasant to want to be a freeholding farmer, the farmer's son to want to learn reading so that he can work in the town, the farmer's wife to want to stop bearing children, the farmer's daughter to wear a dress and to do her hair.' Modern media also inform people of things outside their village, encourage them to have opinions about public affairs, and foster participation in the democratic process. Consequently, 'the connection between mass media and political democracy is especially close' (Lerner 1963: 342).

In the event, the media in many independent developing nations supported the maintenance of authoritarian regimes rather than 'educated for democracy'. Indeed, modernization theory was sometimes invoked – perversely – to justify repressive media controls in the interests of nation-building.

One reason why modernization theory was so easy to suborn was that it was vague or even ambivalent about what it set out to do. It paid little attention to how media pluralism could be defended in transitional societies. Indeed, 'tradition' often featured in modernization theory as something to be defeated, not as an element of society that could be legitimately valued and defended. Good communication was viewed as a trust-building exercise between leaders and led, rather than an open-ended, collective dialogue. Wilbur Schramm, a leading exponent of modernization theory, made what seems in retrospect to have been an especially revealing comment. 'It is probably wrong for us', he wrote, 'to expect a country which is trying to gather together its resources and mobilize its population for a greater transitional effort to permit the same kind of free, competitive, and sometimes confusing communication to which we have become accustomed in this country [the United States]' (Schramm 1963: 55). He was not alone in thinking that it was sometimes right to curtail 'confusing' communication. Another modernization luminary, Ithiel de Sola Pool, wrote rather chillingly, 'no nation will indefinitely tolerate a freedom of the press that serves to divide the country and to open the floodgate of criticism against the freely chosen government that leads it' (Pool 1973 cited in McQuail 1994: 129).

Lack of local knowledge was another reason why modernization theory was subverted. The expertise of people like Schramm and Pool was in communications rather than 'area studies'. Their lack of real understanding of developing societies, and their immersion in Cold War politics, led them to adopt an uncritical view of westernizing elites.

CULTURAL IMPERIALISM

From the late 1960s onwards, there was a determined and largely successful attempt to dethrone modernization theory led, in media studies, by Herbert Schiller (1969, 1976, 1981 and 1998). He argued that American aid programmes to developing countries, and the 'free flow of information' policies promoted by the American state, powerfully assisted the American media industry in its drive to achieve international dominion. Far from promoting self-sufficiency, the 'modernization' of third world countries encouraged their dependency within an exploitative system of global economic relations. Even more crucially, the expansion of western media and business corporations promoted capitalist and consumerist values, and eroded local cultures. It also weakened resistance to contemporary imperialism based on economic and cultural conquest. 'By their information, selection and control', wrote Herbert Schiller (1981: 2), 'the Western media, wherever they operate or penetrate, assist in providing the transnational corporate business system with diverted and disoriented domestic publics'. Undaunted by mounting criticism, Schiller insisted that the American ascendancy was greatly strengthened by the end of the Cold War. 'Today, the United States exercises mastery of global communications and culture', Schiller (1998: 17) wrote defiantly in almost his last essay.

Like modernization theory, this general critique was invoked to support authoritarian controls in the developing world. The threat posed by western cultural imperialism to 'Asian values', Chinese essentialism and Islamic tradition were pretexts used respectively by conservative, communist and theocratic regimes to justify repressive media censorship (Ma 2000; Nain 2000; Mowlana 1996). Critics of cultural imperialism, argues Hallin (1998), made this distortion easier by failing to give detailed attention to questions of media access and pluralism in the new world information order which they advocated. Rønning and Kupe (2000) also point to tensions between democratic and authoritarian tendencies within national liberation movements, to which critics of media imperialism tended to turn a blind eye.

In the 1980s and 1990s, the media imperialism thesis in turn came under sustained attack. The notion of a one-way flow of communication and influence from the West was challenged by the counter-argument that global flows are 'multi-directional'. Sreberny-Mohammadi (1996) points out that the simple image of western dominion obscures the complex and reciprocal nature of interaction over centuries between different and increasingly hybridized western and eastern cultures. Similarly Giddens (1999a), among others, points to 'reverse colonization', exemplified by the export of Brazilian television programmes to Portugal and the hispanicization of southern California. More generally, it is argued, global media enterprises have been forced to adapt to local cultures, and link up with local partners, in order to sustain their expansion (Croteau and Hoynes 1997). But perhaps the most telling exposition of this 'multi-directionality' argument comes from Sinclair, Jacka and Cunningham (1996)

who show that it is simplistic to imagine that there is a single global television programme market dominated by the United States. Rather, there are multiple global and expanding regional markets organized primarily around different language-based publics. These are served by growing centres of television production in Mexico, Brazil, India, Egypt, Taiwan and Hong Kong.

The second main line of attack on the media imperialism thesis focused on another weak link in its argument, its underestimation of critical responses to American domination. Analysts point out that there is consumer resistance to American television programmes, with comparative research showing a preference for locally made programmes (Silj 1988). There is also political resistance, with a number of states supporting national media production through subsidies, investment quotas, import and ownership restrictions (Humphreys 1996; Mowlana 1996; Curran and Park 2000). Above all, there is cultural resistance, rooted in local tradition and social networks. Thus, *Dallas* may have been transmitted around the world, but it meant different things to viewers from different national or ethnic backgrounds, because they drew upon different belief systems and cultural references to make sense of it (Liebes and Katz 1990).

This last argument – based on revisionist audience research primarily in Israel – was expanded into a frontal attack on the notion that western culture is *imposed* on developing nations. In fact non-western countries are both active and selective in the ways in which they assimilate western influences. Western cultural imports – whether they be television programmes, consumer products, or ideas – are appropriated in ways that modify, hybridize, indigenize or transform their meaning (Tomlinson 1991 and 1999: Martin-Barbero 1993; Lull 1995; Morley 2000). John Tomlinson (1999: 84) gives as an example research which shows that different magical properties are attributed to Coca-Cola in different cultures: smoothing wrinkles (Russia), reviving the dead (Haiti), turning copper into silver (Barbados). Coca-Cola is also indigenized by being mixed with local drinks (*aguadiente* in Bolivia, rum in the Caribbean). In some places, it is even thought to be a local product. In short, the claim that the transnational business system is establishing a capitalist mono-culture around the globe fails, in this view, to take account of the diversity and complexity of local cultural appropriations.

Critics also point to a certain fuzziness in the way in which three different categories – American, western and capitalist – are used almost interchangeably in presentations of the cultural imperialism thesis. To this and other complaints, defenders respond by saying in effect that complexity is being invoked to obfuscate the continuing reality of western cultural preponderance. Media activity, in this view, may be multi-directional but it is still very unequal. Thus, Boyd-Barrett (1998) argues that American or western enterprises are dominant in certain key sectors, most notably film, news wholesaling and computer operating systems. Similarly, Herman and McChesney (1997) and McChesney (1998) show that a relatively small number of transnational media corporations, mostly based in the United States, have a leading position in the evolving global media market.

It is also claimed that, while there is global cultural diversity, it is structured by an underlying hegemonic dynamic. The dominant strain of global popular culture, according to Stuart Hall 'remains centred in the West . . . and it always speaks English'. While adapting to cultural differences, 'it is wanting to recognize and absorb those differences within the larger, overarching framework of what is essentially an American conception of the world' (Hall 1997: 33).

NEW ORTHODOXY

However, these counter-arguments fell on stony ground. A revisionist orthodoxy emerged in the 1990s, in tune with the neo-liberal climate of the time. This new orthodoxy in effect synthesized critiques of media imperialism, and re-presented them as a coherent alternative perspective.

Its first central theme is that, in the words of Anthony Giddens:

> Globalization today is only partly westernisation. . . . Globalization is becoming increasingly decentred – not under the control of any group of nations, still less of the large corporations. Its effects are felt as much in western countries as elsewhere.
>
> (Giddens 1999a)

This argument changes the terms of reference of the globalization debate. Before, this centred on what rich countries were doing to the rest of the world – whether giving them a helping hand (modernization) or controlling and exploiting them (cultural imperialism). Recast in this new form, globalization is about a 'decentred' and 'disorganized' process engulfing all of humankind, and transforming developed and developing countries alike.

The second key claim of this orthodoxy is that globalization is bringing into being a more interconnected and cosmopolitan world. One version of this argument centres on communications technology. During the last 150 years, new methods of communications were introduced that spanned national boundaries: the telegraph, telephone, telex, satellite and the internet. These fostered, it is argued, an increased awareness of other countries and peoples, and a greater openness towards them. According to Marshall McLuhan, the key breakthrough came when the international coverage of television overcame obstacles of space and time to shrink the world into a global village (McLuhan 1964; McLuhan and Fiore 1967). Technological proximity engendered a new sense of global identity.

The internet is now supposedly strengthening global integration. 'The opening up of cyberspace', enthuses Jon Stratton, 'begins a new movement of hyper-deterritorialization' in which people are breaking free from the prejudices of national cultures (Stratton 1996: 257). Through the internet, argues Howard Rheingold, a global 'virtual community' is being brought into being. The internet is 'a citizen-designed, citizen-controlled worldwide communication network' with the 'capacity to challenge the existing political hierarchy's monopoly on powerful communication' (Rheingold 2000: xxix–xxx). Indeed, in some versions of this argument, the internet is a 'postmodern technology' which offers people the opportunity to remake the world by forging a new kind of politics that is global rather than national, through a medium which is decentralized rather than state-controlled, and which enables discourse to transcend the constraints of social inequality. This last benefit, according to Mark Poster (1996: 211), is because, on the internet, 'acts of discourse are not limited to one-way address and are not constrained by the gender and ethnic traces inscribed in face-to-face communication'.

However, most cultural globalization theorists are critical of this technophilia. In this more sceptical view, the internet may unite the globe, but it does so through English – the overwhelmingly dominant language of cyberspace – in a world where only a minority can read English. The internet does not transcend social inequality. On the contrary, inequality is reproduced as a structure of access to the internet. Those excluded from its 'virtual community' include, as John Barlow puts it, 'old people, poor people, the blind ... the illiterate and the continent of Africa' (cited in Morley 2000: 186). New communications technology does not eliminate conflict, but merely alters the terms on which this conflict is conducted (Tomlinson 1999). More generally, it is argued, the effects attributed to new media should be better understood as being the product of multiple causes.

But if the majority revisionist view is critical of technocentrism, it still subscribes to the argument that globalization is promoting a more cosmopolitan world. There is increasing traffic between cultures through increased migration, overseas tourism and the 'indirect travel' experienced through watching television. People's lives are becoming more penetrated by influences which have their origins far away, from the clothes people wear to the international chain stores they visit and the films they see. More generally, the trend is towards more mixed, hybridized cultures. All these changes, it is argued, are contributing to a process of 'disembedding' (the lifting out of social relations from local contexts) and of 'deterritorialization' (the weakening of the link between identity and place). Imaginative and real geographies are beginning to demerge.

The third key argument of this revisionist orthodoxy is that globalization is releasing new cultural and political energy by creating new spaces for bonding and solidarity, enabling new voices and marginal groups to be heard, and fostering multiple identities and greater social diversity.

Globalization is said to be promoting ethnic, cultural, religious and linguistic diversity within nation states (Robins, Cornford and Aksoy 1997). Thus, Korean-Americans can watch Korean television programmes in Los Angeles, just as Indian-British viewers can watch Indian films on cable television in Southall. The identity of diasporic communities can now be sustained not only through treasured postcards and the fading memories of grandparents but through daily media feeds that sustain imperilled ethnic minority identities (Dayan 1998). More generally, globalization is encouraging sub-national identities and movements – such

as Welsh and Scottish nationalism, Basque separatism and the Lombard League –
by weakening the cultural spell of nationalism. The global is promoting the local
by eroding the national.

What Robions, Cornford and Aksoy (1997: 16) call 'peripheral visions' are
being transmitted across boundaries to a wider audience through modern communications. For example, the audio casette recording of speeches made by
Islamic fundamentalists in Paris, and relayed by loudspeaker in mosques in Iran,
played a significant part in the successful revolt against the Shah in 1979
(Sreberny-Mohammadi and Mohammadi 1994). Greenpeace transmitted dramatic video footage by satellite to media around the world as a way of fanning
international protest against French nuclear testing in the Pacific, and Shell's
proposed dumping of the Brent Spar oil rig in the sea, during the mid-1990s
(Manning 2001). Zapatista rebels in Mexico, and their supporters, used cyberspace to win international sympathy for their cause (Castells 1997; Cleaver 1998).
An especially well-documented example of this general argument is provided by
Sonia Serra, who shows that a campaign against the killing of street children in
Brazil had initially very little effect. It was only when campaigners enlisted the
help of international agencies like Amnesty International, and won a sympathetic
hearing from media in the United States, Japan and Europe, that they secured
extensive media and political attention in Brazil, and eventual legal reform (Serra
1996 and 2000).

The interconnectedness of a globalized world is, according to revisionist analysis, producing a new kind of politics played out in international fora, and increasingly directed towards global solutions. Environmentalists have alerted world
opinion to the dangers of ozone depletion and global warming; peace campaigners have drawn public attention to the threat posed by proliferation of
nuclear weapons; the women's movement has developed into a loose-knit network with informal links around the world (Sreberny 1998); a global coalition has
campaigned with growing effectiveness for the relief of world poverty; and a new
alliance has taken to the streets to protest against the self-serving actions of the
G8 countries, the World Trade Organization and International Monetary Fund.
If old social movements transformed the politics of the nation state, new social
movements in this view are transforming the politics of the planet.

Globalization is also said to be giving rise to a more diverse communications
system (a claim that directly confronts the argument that the rise of giant, international media corporations is producing greater uniformity). Some cultural theorists claim that 'globalization . . . pluralises the world by recognizing the value of
cultural niches' (Waters 1995: 136). Minorities too small to be catered for in
national contexts become viable markets in a global context, sustaining minority
media such as 'art house' films. The global system also recognizes local ability,
and secures for it a world audience. In the music business, according to Simon
Frith (1996: 172), 'globally successful sounds may now come from anywhere'.
Kevin Robins also argues that the fission created through mixing elements of the
national and international is generating diversity and innovation. This is a

continuing process since 'audio-visual geographies are thus becoming detached from the symbolic spaces of national culture, and realigned on the basis of the more "universal" principles of international consumer culture' (Robins 1995: 250).

These arguments command the terms of media and cultural studies debate. Textbooks now narrate a linear account of intellectual progress in which those mired in the error of cultural imperialism dogma have been corrected by the sages of cultural globalization theory. One book (Tomlinson 1999) that follows this formula stands out, however, above the rest. It offers an especially clear and seductive synthesis. Indeed, it defines and codifies this second phase of revisionism, in much the way that John Fiske (1987) did for its first phase.

John Tomlinson does not offer an uncritical account of globalization theory. For example, he breaks ranks by conceding that there is a small element of truth in the cultural imperialism thesis. Globalization, acknowledges Tomlinson, is leading to an increased 'commodification' of cultural life – that is, its organization into something bought and sold – in a way that is narrowing. However, he hastens to add that cultural commodification can be enriched by consumer reception. Tomlinson also concedes that globalization has losers as well as winners (though he is vague about who these losers are). But for the most part, his account of globalization is profoundly reassuring. Both its guarded optimism and breadth of vision are conveyed by this account of the transformation of localities into 'glocalities':

> Changes in our actual physical environments, the routine factoring-in of distant political-economic processes into life-plans, the penetration of our homes by media and communications technology, multiculturalism as increasingly the norm, increased mobility and foreign travel, even the effects of the 'cosmopolitanizing' of food culture – all these transformations hold the promise of vital aspects of the cosmopolitan disposition: the awareness of the wider world as significant for us in our locality, the sense of connection with other cultures and even, perhaps, an increasing openness to cultural differences.
>
> (Tomlinson 1999: 199–200)

Decentred global capitalism, Tomlinson tells us, has no necessary affinity with the interests of the West. Indeed, in his view, globalization should be recognized as an emancipatory experience. It is leading to greater awareness of the international community, and increased freedom from the constraints and prejudices of home cultures. New voices are now being heard centre stage; new solidarities are being forged; and a new, progressive, global politics is coming into being.

Yet, there is a strange omission in this wide-ranging and erudite account. It fails to analyse, and discuss, the multiple ways in which globalization is causing power to be redistributed in contemporary society. This omission reflects a blind spot in the revisionist tradition which John Tomlinson comes out of – its reluctance to engage critically with economic power. This reluctance is usually presented as a virtue, born out of a sophisticated rejection of 'reductionism' – that is, the reduction of complex phenomena to simplifying economic explanation. True to this tradition, John Tomlinson is grandly dismissive of the only work of political economy (Hirst and Thompson 1996) outside media studies that he features with any prominence. It is found wanting because of its descent into 'reductionism in which the economy drives all before it' (Tomlinson 1999: 16). This is contrasted with the author's own rounded perspective of 'the complexly related multi-dimensionality of globalization' (Tomlinson 1999: 17). But while the economic and political do indeed feature in Tomlinson's account, they appear only in a fragmented form that obscures a central feature of the globalizing experience. To discover more, it is necessary to leave behind the Panglossian tradition of cultural globalization theory, and turn instead to radical history, economics and political studies.

GLOBAL CAPITALISM RESTORED

What is exciting and pregnant with liberating possibilities, according to cultural globalization theory, is a major reverse for humanity in the view of most radical political economists. They argue that the latest phase of globalization has led to a reassertion of the power of global capital at the expense of organised labour and the democratic state. Workers are now more vulnerable than before, and the political power of people to curb the excesses of big business has been greatly diminished. Key presentations of this general argument are provided by Panitch and Leys (1999) and Leys (2001).

The decisive time when economic globalization remade the world was in the nineteenth and early twentieth centuries (Hobsbawm 1989 and 1975). Indeed, there is a heated debate among political economists about whether economic globalization is more advanced now than it was early in the twentieth century, and whether the world economy is not, even now, better understood as being more regional and national than global (Radice 1999; Weiss 1998; Hirst and Thompson 1996). In fact, the proportion of total output traded internationally was not much higher in the early 1990s than it was shortly before the First World War (Hirst and Thompson 1996).

But this appearance of historical continuity conceals important changes. The most important shift is in the relationship between democracy and the capitalist system. During the high tide of social liberalism (roughly from the 1870s to 1914), the business sector in most developed economies became more regulated, publicly accountable and sensitive to public opinion. This was partly the consequence of the rise of electoral democracy and growing public criticism of 'irresponsible' capitalism. Increased state oversight of business was also enabled by the nature of the contemporary economic system. Industrial production was subject to the effective jurisdiction of territorial states because it could not easily relocate from one country to another. While the mobility of capital was largely unhindered during this period, its domestic impact was limited by trade protection and imperial preference policies.

The second determined attempt to civilize capitalism occurred in the heyday of social democracy (roughly from the 1940s to the early 1970s). This more ambitious project sought to insulate people from insecurity, 'from the cradle to the grave', through comprehensive welfare services and full employment. It also tried to support the values of social mutuality through policies designed to promote equality and inclusion, in opposition to the individualizing, fragmenting, inegalitarian and morally callousing effects of the market system. This social democratic tradition drew heavily upon support from the industrial working class, and the fears engendered by the 1930s world slump. It was opposed, in Europe, by a Christian Democratic tradition that shared many of the same social values. Crucially, it was also enabled by a global regulatory system which made national governments effective agencies of economic management.

The Bretton Woods system was inaugurated in 1944–6. It took the form of controls on cross-border movements of capital; the organization of the international financial system primarily through governments; exchange rates fixed in relation to the dollar; progressive tariff reduction; and the international provision of credit to countries in economic difficulties, designed to prevent competitive devaluation and global recession. This system enabled the governments of developed economies to give precedence to employment and social welfare over those of global financial interests. When an adjustment was necessary in order to boost national competitiveness, it was generally achieved incrementally over time without abandoning a commitment to social objectives.

This system of global governance was gradually undermined from the late 1960s onwards (Helleiner 1994; Strange 1996; Germain 1997; Held *et al.* 1999; Leys 2001). The development of the 1960s Eurocurrency market, outside national controls, initiated a process of financial deregulation. The fixed exchange rate system came to an end in 1971–3. OECD countries abandoned capital controls in the 1980s and 1990s. The regulatory bodies set up under the Bretton Woods system – originally the product of a political settlement between market liberals and social democrats – came to be dominated increasingly by a neo-liberal agenda.

The dissolution of the Bretton Woods system took place within a transformed global economy. During the 1980s and 1990s, there was a spectacular growth of private banking, and currency and derivatives trading. This was driven by market pressures, facilitated by new technology and allowed to continue unchecked by governments. Its effect was to produce an unregulated ebb and flow of capital between countries on a scale (in terms of both velocity and volume) never experienced before.

Multinational corporations also expanded rapidly, especially from 1970 onwards. They grew as a consequence of economies of scale and scope, their lead in technological innovation, and latterly through the organization of flexible business networks. By the late 1990s, multinationals accounted for around two-thirds of world trade (Held *et al.* 1999: 236). They became so central to production in the modern economy that governments were forced to compete for their patronage – and consequent inward investment, wealth–creation and jobs. The leverage available to multinationals was further enhanced by their growing freedom, within a liberalized global economy, to invest, produce, sell and remit profit wherever they wanted. The introduction of more flexible systems of production also made multinational corporations more 'mobile'. They could relocate their operations with increased facility, although they were still constrained to some degree by their need for an appropiate skills and infrastructure base. They remained multinational, rather than 'stateless' transnational, corporations.

The conjunction of these three trends – the collapse of the Bretton Woods system, the rise of private global finance and the growth of multinational corporations – contributed to a cumulative erosion of national democracy. In particular, volatile movements of capital became highly sensitive to the effect of national government policy on short-term profitability. Adverse market judgements led to rapid capital outflows, and this in turn threatened to generate a chain reaction of currency depreciation, increased interest rates, higher mortgage rates and falling demand. A growing number of governments in the 1980s and 1990s – some with different ideologies and bases of support – responded to this pressure by adopting market-friendly policies. These generally took the form of separating the national central bank from government; adopting tight monetary policies, with low public deficits and spending, directed towards price stability; and shifting towards low direct taxation, privatization and deregulation. While global financial pressures did not preclude job-oriented, economic expansion and strong welfare programmes, these policies were made more difficult than before because they carried a higher risk in terms of increased borrowing costs and a reduced exchange rate. Policies judged to be fundamentally imprudent by the financial markets carried a severe penalty – currency collapse. At best, this led to emergency credit from the International Monetary Fund, and a 'structural adjustment' programme, a euphemism for externally imposed economic policies which sometimes produced dire social consequences (Bernard 1999; Boron 1999). Largely unregulated global financial markets thus encouraged conservative or risk-free management of the economy (Webb 1995; Strange 1996; Leys 2001).

Multinational corporations also exerted pressure for pro-market policies (Picciotto 1992; Mahnkopf 1999; Held *et al.* 1999). This was a key factor in the trend towards convergent and lower rates of corporate tax. More generally, the ability of corporate power to locate production transnationally greatly weakened the position of organized labour, not least by eroding the effectiveness of strikes and exposing workers to increased labour competition. The increasing enmeshment of national economies in the global system also made competitiveness in the global market a more central objective of national policy. Finally, the 'Keynsian capacity' of government – its range of instruments for regulating the economy – was also eroded by globalization and deregulation, leading to increased reliance on interest rates (over which a growing number of governments relinquished formal control). In short, the autonomy and effectiveness of governments as agencies of economic management were cumulatively undermined by globalization.

TRIAL SYNTHESIS

We are thus being invited to choose between two sharply contrasting views. Cultural theorists write with enthusiasm about globalization as a process that is promoting planetary consciousness, increasing international dialogue, empowering minorities, creating new alliances and solidarities, and giving rise to a new, progressive politics. Many radical political economists, on the other hand, view the latest phase of globalization as a capitalist victory that is dispossessing democracy, imposing pro-market policies, weakening organized labour and undermining the left.

Informing this clash are often unstated (and therefore undebated) differences of perspective. In the cultural globalization literature, the nation and the territorial state tend to be associated with invented tradition, manipulative ideology, hierarchical control, intolerance, conformism and nationalism. Indeed, globalization is viewed as positive partly *because* it is thought to be weakening the nation and national prejudice. By contrast, the political economy literature has a less schooled approach, with one strand attacking the corrupting legacy of nationalism as the worm inside the apple of social democracy, and deriding idealized notions of state neutrality. But this tradition, in all its diversity, still tends to see the democratic state as an agency that is central to the realization of progressive social and economic objectives. It also views the nation as the place where democracy is primarily practised, and concludes therefore that the weakening of national government is undermining democratic self-determination and popular power.

These two traditions are like ships passing in the night. The relationship between political institutions and economic power scarcely registers on the cultural theory radar screen, save as reductionist static. Similarly, political economists generally pay scant attention to cultural globalization theory, to their loss. Yet, there is clearly an important element of truth in both traditions which calls for some form of critical synthesis. Academics based at the London School of Economics – notably, Anthony Giddens (1999a), Leslie Sklair (2000) and David Held and associates (1999) (each of whom adopts a different position) – have made a start in attempting this.

One general theme of an embryonic synthesis is that economic globalization has created greater prosperity, though in an uneven way. The worldwide diffusion of new technology, increased specialization within the global workforce, improved access to globally organized credit, and the reduction of national tariffs, all contributed to a sustained expansion of the global economy. In the last twenty years, a major beneficiary was East Asia and a major casualty was Sub-Saharan Africa. However, the most consistent winners were the OECD countries. Between 1989 and 1998, the share of the richest fifth of the world increased, while that of the poorest fifth decreased (Giddens 1999a: 15–16). This reflected the skewed structure of the global capitalist system and its international regulation.

A second, more questionable theme, advanced by David Held and his co-authors (1999) in a book of central importance, is that public power has not been eroded but has been reconstituted and 'rearticulated'. While it is true that national governments have lost authority, there has been a rapid growth of inter-national regulation through the General Agreement on Tariffs and Trade (GATT), the World Trade Organization, the United Nations system and other international agencies, combined with the growth of regional government (most notably, the European Union). Nation states are now merely one unit within a system of 'multilayered governance'. This does not prefigure the end of politics, but its rebirth through 'an extraordinary growth of institutionalized arenas and networks of political mobilization, surveillance, decision-making and regulatory activity across borders' answerable to 'transnational civil society' (Held et al. 1999: 444 and 452). This rebuttal of political economy pessimism is combined with a fulsome endorsement of the cultural globalization thesis. Globalization, according to Held and associates, is promoting a more open orientation to the world; greater interchanges between people not merely at an elite but also at a popular level; and diversity sustained through local cultural transformations. Thus, Held and his co-authors seek to reconcile two opposed interpretations in an affirmative account of global transformations.[3]

CALL FOR RETRIAL

However, their attempt to defuse the radical political economy thesis is ultimately unconvincing. One problem with their account is that they offer a simplifying description of communications globalization (Held et al. 1999: 341–75) which, they claim, is supporting the development of global civil society. 'The revolutions in communications and information technology . . . have increased massively the stretch and intensity of all manner of socio-political networks within and across the borders of states' (Held et al. 1999: 445).

But what Held and his colleagues fail to point out is that the globalization of communications is transforming media fiction and music rather than news and current affairs. The overwhelming majority of news outlets – whether they be television, radio or the press – are still national or local. While there are a number of global news media (the best known being perhaps the CNN television news channel and the BBC world radio service) they reach relatively small audiences by comparison with the hundreds of millions exposed daily to the news on national and local media. These last dwarf also the internet, which remains an insignificant source of news for most people.

The domination of national and local news media continues to stunt the development of global politics, and promotes a nationalist and localist perspective of human affairs. Even news organizations, with enormous news-gathering resources and international prestige, contribute to this process. Thus, an estimated 75 per cent of news broadcast by the American television network, CBS, in 2001 ignored the world outside the United States (Milbury 2001). Another study found that 80 per cent of news stories on BBC1, and 84 per cent on ITV, in 1996–7, were about Britain (McLachlan 1998). The insularity of British television news extended also to documentaries and news magazine journalism. Only 19 per cent of British current affairs programmes in 1997–8 looked at issues outside Britain (and most of these appeared on the minority channel, BBC 2) (Barnett and Seymour 1999).

The argument could be made that at least the international news which appears on television draws heavily upon foreign or international agency sources, and represents therefore a deepening of the shared global experience. This claim is misleading for two reasons. First, much of the international news featured on national television is selected only because it has a national dimension. Second, international news tends to be interpreted in terms of national frameworks. This is brought home by Lee *et al.*'s (2000) comparative study of the reporting of the handover of Hong Kong to China in 1997. The transfer was portrayed in Chinese media as a defeat for western imperialism, and a moment of joy in which Chinese communities all round the world celebrated the reunification of the 'Chinese family-nation'. By contrast, the transfer was reported with imperial nostalgia by British media as marking the end of a benign era in which Britain had bequeathed prosperity, liberty and good government to its former colony. In American media, reporting centred on whether human rights and the fragile democracy in Hong Kong would survive the transfer of sovereignty. In Japanese media, by contrast, the main focus was not human rights but whether Hong Kong's prosperity would be maintained under its new rulers. The media in Canada, Australia and Taiwan framed the event in still other ways. In other words, reporting of the Hong Kong handover was consistently structured by the geo-political interests, political cultures and collective memories of different nations.

Thus, news production is organized around the nation state and locality, and provides a restricted prism for viewing the world (from formal politics to tomorrow's weather report). While the increasing globalization of entertainment is promoting greater global awareness, the tenacious traditionalism of news-making is doing little to bring into being a global public sphere.

The second weakness of the 'Held thesis' is that it fails to recognize that there is a growing democratic gap in the new system of 'multilayered governance' that is developing. The Bretton Woods system empowered national governments subject to democratic election, party opposition, media oversight and the influence

of national civil society and public opinion. The dismantling of this system transferred power partly to market institutions that are less subject to democratic audit
and control. It also led to regulatory power being transferred upwards to global
agencies. These are not elected; they are not monitored adequately by the media;
and they are not held to proper account by 'global public opinion' and global civil
society, since both are under-developed. This upper tier of regulation is accountable to national governments in the context of market-driven politics. While the
view that 'globalizing bureaucrats are the main representatives of the state in the
interests of capital' (Slair 1999: 334) is too simple, global regulation is
heavily insulated from public influence. This was partly what drove people to
demonstrate on the streets of Seattle, Genoa, Prague and elsewhere in
1999–2002.

RADICAL RESPONSES

The weakening of democratic power poses a problem for all democratic traditions, whether of the left and the right. However, it is a particularly acute problem
for social democracy because it is a state-centric tradition. It believes in 'big
government' unlike the neo-liberal right and the libertarian left.

Social democracy has responded to this crisis in four different (though not
necessarily mutually exclusive) ways (Mahnkopf 1999; Weiss 1998; Hutton 1997;
Leys 2001). The first strategy, represented by Blairism/Clintonism, favours
pragmatic adaptation. It broadly internalizes market pressures in managing the
national economy, but helps individuals to compete in the global market by, for
example, putting more resources into education and vocational training. The
second strategy, represented by mainstream European social democracy (e.g.
Nordic, Rhineland and Jospin models), opts for market negotiation. It pursues
with increasing difficulty egalitarian and social inclusion policies, while seeking
pro-actively to sustain the competitiveness of the national economy within the
global market. The third strategy seeks to rebuild democratic power through the
creation of effective, transnational government on a regional basis. In Europe,
this approach takes the form of radical federalism – the rapid expansion of the
European Union, increased pooling of sovereignty and new initiatives, such as
the European Monetary Union, designed to lessen market control over the economy. The fourth strategy seeks the reform of global governance, and in particular
the re-regulation of global financial markets. This approach is now symbolized by
the proposed Tobin tax on foreign currency transactions, designed to reduce
currency speculation and generate additional aid for the developing world. The
fact that this proposal was first advanced by an American economist over twenty
years ago, and has only now come to be widely debated as a consequence of its
championship by the French socialist government, is an indication of how far
there is to go in developing what is arguably the most important of the four
strategies.

National politics also needs to adapt to globalization. More attention should be given to global regulation in national political debates. The media need to update their surveillance role by scrutinizing global and regional – and not just national – governance. In Europe, regional government needs to be democratized through the strengthening of the European Parliament, the key to developing a new kind of participatory Euro-politics. There also needs to be a long-term realignment of political forces. Old social forces (from organized labour to the churches) are still stronger, more embedded and better resourced than new social forces (from environmentalists to feminists). But the former operate primarily in the context of declining institutions: the political party and the nation state. They need to forge a closer connexion – certainly on the left – with new social forces oriented towards global politics.

To sum up, cultural globalization theory tends to advance an affirmative, 'everything is for the best' view of globalization. This stems from the way in which it largely evolved – at least in cultural studies – out of a rebuttal of the 'everything is for the worse' perspective of cultural imperialism. This encasement within a narrow debate caused it to lose sight of a central concern in radical history, economics and political studies: the way in which power is increasingly shifting from national electorates, and organized labour, to global capital as a consequence of the way in which the global economy has developed. This creeping dispossession calls for a critical response. It has not been forthcoming from cultural globalization theory which proclaims the coming of a better world in an ever more repetitive and self-referencing way.

EPILOGUE

Without wishing to develop and elaborate a new theme, perhaps one additional argument can be briefly aired. Most contributors to the globalization debate, regardless of which tradition or discipline they come from, are agreed that globalization is eclipsing the nation. Thus, the Marxist historian, Eric Hobsbawm, argues that 'for some purposes . . . the globe is now the primary operational unit and older units such as the "national economies", defined by the politics of territorial states, are reduced to complications of transnational activities' (Hobsbawm 1994: 15). Similarly the social democratic sociologist, Anthony Giddens, argues that the nation has become a 'shell institution' (Giddens 1999a: 19), adding that the 'era of the nation state is over' (Giddens 1999b: 31). For many radical libertarians in the cultural studies tradition, the nation is an imagined community losing its grip on the imagination (Morley and Robins 1995).

When people as divergent as these all agree, a new conventional wisdom has been born – and mental alarm bells should start ringing. The literature on globalization, regardless of its disagreements, has a shared bias. It examines the multiple ways in which globalization is transforming the world. This focus on change causes it to understate – despite the occasional caveat – the extent of continuity with the past.

In fact, national governments are still key sites of power. While authority is draining away from their management of the economy, they are still centrally important, for example, in determining the organization of welfare services, education, moral regulation (or the lack of it), penal policy and acts of war. They also continue to be dominant in an area of particular concern to media studies – communications policy. National governments license the right to broadcast within their jurisdiction. They define a framework of media law that regulates media content. National governments are still free to subsidize media, and impose investment and other quotas on film and television production (because American attempts to outlaw this in the Uruguay round of the GATT negotiations failed). Admittedly, there are a number of ways in which national control over communications policy is weakening. Yet, notwithstanding this, there is an enormous diversity in the communications policies that are being pursued by different countries around the world (Curran and Park 2000).

One reason for this is that the nation is still a very important marker of difference. Nations have different languages, political systems, power structures, cultural traditions, economies, international links and histories. These find continuing expression in the media of different nation states. Indeed, as we shall discover in the next chapter, the nation is still the starting point for making sense of the politics of the media.

Part III

Media politics

Chapter 7

Globalization, social change and television reform

In 1996, Elihu Katz advanced a commanding thesis: changes in the communications order are weakening the foundations of liberal democracy. His argument is built on three apparently solid pillars. The first is that people are no longer connected to each other through the central meeting-ground of mass television, watching the same programmes and participating in the same dialogue about the public direction of society. Instead, the public is being dispersed and fragmented by the multiplication of channels. 'Television', according to Katz, 'has all but ceased to function as a shared public space. Except for occasional media events, the nation no longer gathers together' (Katz 1996: 22).

Second, the decline of public service broadcasting is rendering people less informed.

> No less than in the United States, the governments of Europe – once proud of their public broadcasting systems – are bowing to the combined constraints of the new media technology, the new liberal mood, the economic and political burden of public broadcasting, and the seductions of multinational corporations.
>
> (Katz 1996: 22)

Consequently coverage of public affairs on television 'is being minimised and ghettoised and overwhelmed by entertainment' (Katz 1996: 24).

Katz's third claim is more complex. In essence, it is that liberal democracy takes place in nation states, and depends upon national identification to sustain popular involvement in the democratic process. However, national identities are being weakened by a growing separation between the television system and the nation state. Viewers are increasingly making an individual selection of programmes supplied by the global economy through mutliple channels, instead of watching as before the same national schedule of home-produced television programmes.

The logic of this position, as Katz (1996: 23) explicitly acknowledges, is to regret the passing of monopoly based on 'only one channel of public television commanding attention from all and offering the gamut of views'. This proposition is illustrated by a history of Israeli television in which Katz mourns the dethronement of a once invincible 9 p.m. newsmagazine programme. When it was in its prime in the golden era before competition, to caricature his argument only a little, Israeli society had the same heartbeat and participated every evening in a virtual town meeting.

Katz's general thesis carries conviction because it draws on assumptions that are widely supported. That the expansion of television is causing the mass public to fragment is part of the current received wisdom, prompting one sage analyst to conclude that the public sphere is imploding into 'sphericules' (Gitlin 1998). Equally mainstream is the view that public service broadcasting is everywhere in trouble, causing one leading expert to describe its recent history as one of remorseless 'decline and fall' (Tracey 1998). Equally uncontentious is the view that globalization is weakening national identities (Waters 1995). Katz is seemingly advancing a synoptic account based on the latest, most authoritative scholarship.

BRITISH EXCEPTION

Yet, none of the fashionable assumptions on which Katz draws is seemingly borne out by the experience of the United Kingdom. In the first place, the mass audience has not been 'fragmented' by the multiplication of television channels. British cable television was introduced in a commercial form in 1984, followed by UK satellite television in 1989 and digital television in 1998. Over a hundred new channels became available in the United Kingdom over a period of fourteen years. Yet, by 2000, these accounted for only 11 per cent of prime-time viewing (see Table 7.1).[1]

British people now spend eight-tenths of their television viewing time looking at just four television channels. Two of these, BBC1 and ITV, occupy 67 per cent of their peak-time viewing. A large part of the British nation still quarrels, agrees and laughs together primarily through two channels which have been in existence for over forty years (see Table 7.1).

Second, public service broadcasting has not been eclipsed in Britain. The BBC remains intact as the largest broadcasting organization in the world, with some

Table 7.1 Share of television viewing in United Kingdom, 2000

	BBC1	BBC2	ITV	CH4	CH5	Cable/ satellite	Public service channels
All hours (%)	27	11	30	11	6	16	85
Prime time (%)	28	10	37	8	6	11	89

Source: BARB/Eurodata–TV, derived from European Audiovisual Monitor (2001). The figures relate to viewers, aged four years and above, during January–June, 2000. Prime time is defined as 7–10.30p.m. All figures have been rounded to the nearest whole number.

20,000 employees. Its main television channels (BBC1 and 2) are supplemented by a public service channel controlled by a public trust (Channel 4) and two commercial public service television channels (ITV and Channel 5), all three of which are required, as a condition of obtaining and retaining their licences, to conform to public service requirements. This core system of five major, free-to-air public service channels accounted for 89 per cent of peak-time viewing in 2000. Nor has public information programming been 'minimized'. In 1997, British public broadcasters allocated an estimated 30 per cent of their programmes to 'information' (as distinct from entertainment, arts and sport) (Brants and Bens 2000: 19, table 1.3).[2]

Contrary to Katz's general argument, British television also continues to be a national medium. The Independent Television Commission requires the main commercial television channel (ITV) to 'originate' 65 per cent of its programmes in the European Union (with slightly lower quotas for Channels 4 and 5). This is a national quota in all but name since very few programmes shown in Britain are made in other European countries. The BBC also makes or commissions most of its programmes in the United Kingdom. While cable, satellite and licensed digital multiplex television are not subject to strict origination rules, they account for only a small minority share of total viewing. Thus, British television is shielded from globalization through discreet protectionism and the continuing popularity of its major, programme-originating channels.

In short, almost everything that Katz says has happened in general has not happened in Britain. The trends he discerns certainly exist, but in Britain at least they are gradual and inconstant. Years after the arrival of multiple-channel choice, the major channels are still overwhelmingly dominant. Broadcast information has not been marginalized, and still accounts for a significant part of television's total prime-time output.[3] Programme imports have risen, but only in relation to the insular restrictions that prevailed in the 1980s (when imported programmes were limited to 14 per cent of ITV's and Channel 4's output). Despite this shift, there is a long way to go before British television is fully globalized. The life-support machine supposedly supporting national democracy is not about to be switched off.

MYTH OF FRAGMENTATION

Of course, Britain could merely be behind the times. Indeed, common sense suggests that the more channels there are, the more dispersed audiences will become. It also seems inconceivable that numerous accounts of 'audience frag-mentation', as a consequence of the growth of multi-channel, multi-set television households, advances in programme recording from the video to TiVo,[4] and the growing individualisation of taste, are not securely anchored in reality.

But this is indeed the case, at least to judge from western Europe. In 2000, just three channels accounted for over 60 per cent of prime-time viewing in thirteen out of fifteen major European countries. These channels are the principal meeting places where people in the nations of western Europe still gather together, not for special events but routinely, night after night. Even the two exceptions (Netherlands and Germany) are only partial exceptions: their five main channels accounted for 67 and 70 per cent respectively of peak viewing (see Table 7.2.)

The continuing domination of the main television channels is partly a consequence of consumer resistance to paying for television. Many people became accustomed to having advertising-funded television 'free', after contributing their obligatory television licence fee. Some were reluctant to suscribe to more channels – some of indifferent quality – when they were relatively happy with what they had already. However, this reluctance will decrease over time, aided by the attractions of current subscription packages (in particular, sports, film and music channels and, in the case of cable, cheap telephony) and the allure of new channels that will be launched on digital television.

But while consumer resistance to pay-TV will doubtless diminish, there would appear to be a more fundamental and enduring reason for the continuing ascendancy of a small number of generalist television channels. They have much larger revenues and economies of scale than their small channel rivals. This enables them to spend very much more on making new programmes, and on buying rights to expensive, popular ones. Even in the United States, where there is a mature multi-channel television system serving a highly pluralistic, diverse and localist society, its 'three-and-half' national channels accounted in 1996–7 for 62 per cent of

Table 7.2 Share of prime-time viewing in western European countries, 2000

Main channels	Top Two	Top Three	Top Four	Top Five
As %				
Austria	61	66	70	74
Belgium (French)	49	61	68	74
Belgium (Flemish)	59	68	75	82
Germany	31	46	60	70
Denmark	73	81	84	87
Spain	47	68	86	93
Finland	64	86	97	NA
France	56	74	87	92
United Kingdom	65	75	83	89
Greece	46	62	76	83
Ireland	51	62	70	78
Italy	48	63	75	83
Netherlands	34	47	58	67
Norway	75	83	90	93
Portugal	79	91	96	NA
Sweden	58	79	88	93

Source: Derived from European Audiovisual Monitor (2001). All figures refer to the period January–June and are rounded to the nearest whole number. The definition of prime time varies between some European countries, reflecting differences of national viewing habits and research conventions.

prime-time television viewing (Anon 1997). Although this was lower than in Europe, it scarcely seems to justify the alarmist commentary about new communications technology and the 'disappearing public sphere' that came out of the American academy in the late 1990s.

PUBLIC SERVICE CRISIS

Elihu Katz would seem, superficially, to be on stronger ground when he points to the crisis of public service broadcasting and the decline of current affairs programmes. Throughout much of the world, public service broadcasting has been subject to a combined commercial, political and ideological assault. New private channels have come into being; new deregulatory regimes have been introduced; and new, hostile lobbies have been formed. In general public service broadcasting has suffered, according to numerous accounts, from a loss of legitimacy, underfunding, declining audiences and a less clear sense of purpose (Murdock 2000a; McQuail and Siune 1998; Tracey 1998; Ostergaard 1997; Raboy 1996; Humphreys 1996; Sinha 1996; Achille and Miege 1994; Aldridge and Hewitt 1994; Avery 1993).

But in fact the position of public service broadcasting is more varied than Katz's requiem would suggest. In some countries where public broadcasting is identified closely with the state, as in France, Turkey and India, it has been destabilized (Page and Crawley 2001; Catalbas 1996; Palmer and Sorbets 1997; Kuhn 1995; Vedel and Bourdon 1993); in others, where it operates without significant political support as in the United States, it has been marginalized (Hoynes 1994; Rowland 1993); and in others where it bored people, as in the Netherlands, it ran into deep trouble (McQuail 1992b; Ang 1991). Yet, in many European countries (as well as elsewhere, for example Japan and Korea) public service broadcasting is still well entrenched.

One source of confusion stems from the way in which public service broadcasting is often equated with public broadcasters (publicly owned broadcasting organizations). This equation is misguided because, in many European countries, the main commercial broadcasters are subject to effective regulation, and pursue public objectives, not just private profit. Commercial organizations such as Sweden's TV4 or Finland's MTV are prominent public service broadcasters (Brants and Bens 2000).

This reformulation casts the development of public service broadcasting in a new light. The long-term reduction of audiences for public broadcasters is widely viewed as evidence that *public service broadcasting* is in decline (Picard 2001; Achille and Miege 1994, among others). But in some cases, the very opposite is true. The old monopoly public broadcasters were often highly paternalistic. The transition from a public broadcasting monopoly to a regulated mixed economy improved the broadcasting system in a number of countries, including Britain, Sweden, Norway, Finland and Denmark. It made public service broadcasting more responsive to the public without detracting from its fundamental purpose (Curran and Seaton 1997; Petersen and Siune 1997; Syvertsen 1996; Gustafsson and Hulten 1997; Sepstrup 1993). In other words, the decline of audience share experienced by public broadcasters was sometimes a symptom of renewal rather than 'crisis'. However, this renewal has since been weakened in a number of European countries by increased deregulation of private broadcasters, and cumulative pressures that are leading to the marketization of the entire broadcasting system (Murdock 2000a; Leys 2001).

But because the public service tradition remains the dominant force shaping broadcast output in western Europe, television still keeps its citizens informed. Information programmes accounted for 32 per cent of mean programme output on Nordic television channels between 1988 and 1995 (Hujanen 2000: 79, table 4.1). Outside this Nordic circle of civic virtue, information levels are lower. But public broadcasters still seek to inform their publics, to judge from two recent studies (with discrepant results) (Bens and Smaele 2001; Brants and Bens 2000). The key weakness that has developed is the very low level of information offered by the under-regulated private broadcasting sector in *some* countries, most notably Germany.

Commercial pressures may be encouraging the marginalization and tabloidization of information programmes. However, the proportion of programme content devoted to information still rises in prime time, compared with total output, in most western European public television channels, as well as in effectively regulated commercial ones (Bens and Smaele 2001: 55, table 1). In short, the exclusion of news and political comment from prime-time television – and consequent disenfranchisement of the public – is still primarily an American network rather than European phenomenon.

GLOBALIZATION MYTHS

Katz is also mistaken in thinking that television is being transformed from a national to a global medium. Preben Sepstrup (1990) points out that statistics about international programme 'flows', seemingly documenting American global hegemony, are deeply misleading because they exclude the majority of television programmes which are not traded on the international market. Detailed analysis of actual European television transmissions reveals a picture very different and more complex than one of simple American domination. Hollywood produces most of the films shown on European channels, and is a major supplier of television drama series. It has made major inroads into weak television economies like Ireland, and tends to dominate unregulated commercial television channels. The absolute volume of American imports is also rising, owing to longer transmission hours and the increase in the number of channels. Nevertheless, many leading television channels in Europe import less than a third of their programmes from *any* country, including the United States

(Bens and Smaele 2001; Humphreys 1996; Bens, Kelly and Bakke 1992; Hirsch and Petersen 1992).

There are three main reasons for the continuing national character of European television. The first is that many people like the programmes produced in their own country more than imported ones. Thus, a study of television audience ratings in six European countries found that national television fiction normally came top (Silj 1988). A later study of six European countries found that 'American series cannot touch the popularity of domestic series, which oust the American series in prime-time on both public and commercial channels' (Bens and Smaele 2001: 51). The most popular programmes in most European countries are home-made (Schulz 2000). These national preferences, rooted in the linguistic and cultural divisions of Europe, insulated national television industries from effective attack by transnational television enterprises, whether relying on European or American programmes (Collins 1992). Even, the initially successful transnational music channel, MTV-Europe, aimed at a European youth audience, was forced to abandon its one 'one planet one music' strategy when national music channels were launched successfully against it. MTV-Europe subdivided into four main regional units designed to represent better the different national languages and music cultures of Europe (Roe and Meyer 2000).

Second, national consumer preferences are supported by political power. European national governments sustain national television systems with public finance (usually derived from an annual television licence fee). The European Commission also introduced in 1989 a Directive calling upon national governments to enforce 'where possible' a quota requiring over half of television transmissions (with some exempt categories) to originate from the European Union. An internal audit concluded in 1996 and again in 1998 that European quotas on imported programmes were mostly being adhered to.

The third reason has to do with economics. Much of the staple of national television output – such as the news, chat shows, game shows and sport – is relatively cheap to produce.

Elihu Katz thus greatly simplifies when he suggests that the 'tendency is towards globalization, such that everybody, everywhere, will be viewing *Dallas* or *Dynasty* or the Olympics at the same time' (Katz 1996: 26). This image of globalization fails to note the subdivision of the global market into language-based sectors, mentioned earlier.[5] It also ignores the differentiated nature of the evolving television system, at any rate in western Europe. Public broadcasters make most of their own programmes; deregulated pay-TV import much of theirs; and regulated commercial broadcasters fall between these two polarities. Thus, a study of five European countries in 1997 found that public broadcasters imported only 20 per cent of programmes, whereas 'commercial' (a category that conflates regulated and deregulated) broadcasters imported 52 per cent (Bens and Smaele 2001: 50–52).

Katz's view of globalization is also based on a questionable understanding of media history. He sees this as a serial process in which the newspaper was the 'first medium of national integration', until its integrative function was taken over by radio and then by television. But now that television is going global, 'there is nothing in sight to replace' it (Katz 1996: 33). This is the basis of his fear that national cohesion and political participation is 'in jeopardy'.

In fact, the historical relationship between nation, globalization and communications is vastly more complicated than this. The key shift towards media globalization occurred between 1914 and 1939, with the emergence of American film hegemony, the global advance of 'American' music and its dissemination through the new media of records and radio. The subsequent period exhibited some globalizing tendencies in terms of media ownership, trade and consumption. But in historical terms, television's defeat of the cinema represented a dramatic shift towards the restabilization of national media systems. Even now, most popular television, radio and press media in western European countries still originate most of their content and are owned by national rather than global organizations.

During the twentieth century, the globalization of the economy was incomplete, uneven and discontinuous (Hirst and Thompson 1996). This was even more true of the globalization of media production.

READING THE RUNES?

Perhaps the best way to defend Elihu Katz's analysis is to argue that he has correctly read the runes, and discerned the future. If he is not right now, it can be claimed that he soon will be.

Certainly, there are strong forces that are propelling television towards the direction that Katz outlines. The logic of the market favours globalization: it is generally cheaper to import than to make programmes. Powerful political and economic pressures now support deregulation, the destruction of public television broadcasting and the refocusing of television on entertainment. Above all new technology will transform the media landscape. Digitalization is already multiplying the number of television channels. The convergence of telephone, television, computer and print systems will create new household devices with multimedia functions. In this new environment public service regimes will, it is claimed, contract or disappear.

However, these arguments can each be challenged. Thus, the record of forecasting the future technological development of communications has been abysmal, partly because there is a romantic strain in the world of letters that yearns for technological solutions to intractable problems, and also because the communications industry often has a vested interest in talking up new media. In 1982 Kenneth Baker, then minister for information and technology, predicted that 'by the end of the decade multi-channel cable television will be commonplace countrywide . . . television will be used for armchair shopping, banking, calling emergency services and many other services' (cited in Goldberg, Prosser and

Verhulst 1998: 10). In fact, cable television reached only 1 per cent of house-holds, and armchair shopping in Britain was still a dream, at the end of the 1980s. However, Goldberg *et al.*, who scoffingly cite this erroneous forecast, are them-selves guilty of enormously overestimating the impact of 'off-line services', in particular CD-ROMs, mistakenly thought at the time when they were writing to be about to revolutionize communications. It is not only British ministers and academics who make mistakes in this treacherous area. An entire committee, on the basis of expert advice from Britain and overseas, framed a policy for the future of broadcasting on the basis of a completely misconceived forecast of the take-up of cable or satellite television (Peacock 1986). Similarly, seemingly authoritative assessments of the nature and impact of the internet, made by American academ-ics in the mid-1990s, now seem perversely misjudged (Patelis 2000). Given this record of fallibility, it seems prudent to view all visions of *imminent* communications transformation with caution.

Although there are strong pressures favouring globalization, deregulation and the eclipse of public service television, there are also counter pressures. Indeed, perhaps the principal reservation that needs to be aired in relation to Katz's eloquent thesis is the way in which it tends to portray general trends as inevitable and immutable. The remainder of this chapter will focus on the crisis of public service broadcasting, and emphasize its unresolved ambiguity, its potential to develop in different directions, and the possibility of acting upon events in a positive way (including breaking from a 'national' vision of television). This will be attempted by examining one particular broadcasting system in transition, and the wider context in which it operates. While this case study is nationally specific, some of its conclusions will have, it is hoped, a more general relevance.

DECLINE OF AN IDEA

At first sight, Katz's view of the *underlying* fragility of public service broadcasting is borne out by the British experience. Public service broadcasting appears vulner-able because some of the beliefs that sustained it for two generations have come to be questioned or rejected outright. This erosion of its core justification will be illustrated by a brief look at the reports of successive British public enquiries into broadcasting.

One key justification for public service broadcasting, expressed in every major public report into broadcasting between 1923 and 1986, was that airwave fre-quencies were a scarce national asset that needed to be managed in the public interest. This argument was finally laid to rest in a 1992 government white paper. 'The original justification', it declared, 'for public service broadcasting – that a small number of services should be used for the benefit of the public as a whole – no longer exists' due to the emergence of cable and satellite television technology (National Heritage 1992: 15).

This traditional justification was always an ideological judgement masquerading as a technical argument. It presupposed that, in the context of spectrum scarcity, the public interest was best served by state regulation. Early broadcasting reports assumed that public service broadcasting worked for the general good because the BBC had been established by the state for this purpose. The corporation, they pointed out, was in the care of public trustees, representing the nation, and was directed towards the welfare of society rather than private profit. The BBC was bracketed with the civil service (Ullswater 1936: 18), and likened to universities (Beveridge 1951: 217). It was a branch of the public services.

However, belief in the neutrality and efficacy of public institutions weakened. By the 1970s, misgivings about broadcasting's connexion to the state were only stilled by making a dubious distinction between parliament (good) to which broadcasting should be accountable, and government (potentially bad) from which it should be protected (Annan 1977: 38). The distinction was dubious because the governing party in Britain usually controls both government and parliament. This casuistry gave way in the Thatcherite 1980s to liberal anti-statism. In the key broadcasting report of that period, broadcasting regulation was tacitly equated with 'censorship', and setting broadcasting free from regulation was established as the long term objective of public policy (Peacock 1986: 126 and 132). The state was no longer viewed as a source of legitimation but as a threat from which broadcasting had to be rescued.

The third and more elusive development weakening public service broadcasting was a gradual erosion of the social and cultural values sustaining the public service ideal. This ideal found its most eloquent expression in the Pilkington report (1962). The subsequent discarding of the assumptions of that report reveals the way in which change weakened the ideological foundations of public service broadcasting.

The Pilkington report was produced at the tail end of the 'one nation' Conservative government headed by Harold Macmillan. The report hailed television as a great agency of moral and cultural improvement, a means by which people could gain knowledge of others, develop active leisure interests, extend their intellectual horizons, and grow and develop as human beings. Good broadcasting, in its view, connected to 'the whole range of worthwhile, significant activity and experience' (Pilkington 1962: 9), not simply high culture. Implicitly informing this approach was a moral-cultural aesthetic in which good programmes were thought to be ones that engaged viewers' and listeners' imagination, extended their understanding and strengthened their moral sensibility. To achieve this, broadcasting had to be staffed by people of talent and integrity, who respected rather than patronized their audience, and who worked in a creative environment that supported good broadcasting rather than merely what was most profitable.

The Annan report, published in 1977, was a transitional document. Its most significant feature was to define and defend public service broadcasting as a negotiated settlement between elite and popular cultural values. It saw public service broadcasting as a system that delivered good programmes for the cultivated few, and popular programmes for the masses, in a form that maximized choice.

Some programmes should be made for the most exacting intellectual and aesthetic mountaineers who have scaled the cultural heights. . . . But the bulk of programmes should be provided for the majority of people who will never reach these pinnacles. As a group they have paid most towards the broadcasting services.

(Annan 1977: 331)

Public service broadcasting was not so much about quality as diversity: catering for both cultural mountaineers and couch potatoes.

It reached this position by being paradoxically both more culturally elitist and relativistic than its predecessor. The Annan report viewed cultural value as a single scale or continuum, topped by high culture, in contrast to the multi-centred regime of moral-cultural value advanced by the Pilkington committee. Annan also acknowledged, in contrast to the evangelism of its predecessor, that there no longer existed a consensus about what constituted programme quality. 'The ideals of middle class culture, so felicitously expressed by Matthew Arnold a century ago, which had created a continuum of taste and opinion' had not, the report noted regretfully, weathered the 1960s (Annan 1977: 14). The Annan Committee felt itself to be championing traditional cultural values that had been widely repudiated.

Informing the shift represented by the Annan report was also a different mind-set. It tacitly viewed its precursor's belief in progress as faintly ridiculous (Annan 1977: 30). Where the 1962 committee saw public service broadcasting as a way of making society better, its successor conceived of broadcasting primarily in terms of service delivery. Although the two reports were separated only by fifteen years, they belonged in some respects to different eras. One harked back to the great social movements that had created the free education, library and health systems; the other looked forward to the performance indicators and bland mission statements of 1980s managerialism.

The ideologues of the right marched through the pass opened up by the Annan report. As soon as the notion of programme quality was relativized, it invited an alternative system of valuation based on market preference. The next major report, published in 1986, argued that broadcasting should 'maximise consumer appreciation' in a market system where 'viewers and listeners are . . . the best judges of their own interest' (Peacock 1986: 149 and 128). Viewers should get what they want, as registered in what they choose to watch and pay for. Consequently, the market system should be phased in, and the public service system should be reduced over time to a supplementary role.

The claim that public service broadcasting is an essential guarantee of diversity also came under attack in the Peacock report. The justification was accepted only in the short term on the neo-liberal grounds that the broadcasting market was underdeveloped. But in the long term, it was argued, investment in new technology and the development of a direct consumer payment system would deliver far greater diversity than exists now. Certain sorts of demanding but unpopular programmes might not get made in the market system, but these could be funded by the broadcasting equivalent of the Arts Council. Quality was thus viewed primarily as high culture, which could be delivered through targeted grants, not as a defining characteristic of the broadcasting system.

This right-wing report argued, in effect, that the market empowers the consumer in a more effective way than public bureaucracy. It was a forceful and intelligent presentation of the neo-liberal case. What gave it added force was the way in which the case for public service broadcasting had been eviscerated. This had been reduced to an argument for planned diversity rather than the superior quality of its output. It had also been redefined as service delivery to the consumer rather than serving the needs of society. The Peacock report won the intellectual contest – even in the eyes of critics (Collins 1993) – because the public service side played such low-scoring cards.

The passage of time also revealed another weak joist supporting the intellectual case for public service broadcasting. A view of American television as being crassly uniform was mobilized in successive public reports as a justification for the British public service system. But the ritualized assertion of this view failed to take note of the way in which cable television had greatly expanded programme diversity in the United States. Routine denunciations of 'wall-to-wall *Dallas*' have as much connection with the contemporary American television system as the cartoon cliché of the cigar-puffing, top-hatted capitalist has with capitalism in the era of pension funds and unit trusts. Anachronistic illusion has a way of breeding disillusion.

In short, some of the central ideas on which public service broadcasting is based in Britain – spectrum scarcity, the benign state, social improvement, cultural quality, the uniformity of American television – lost some of their persuasive force.

MARKET LIBERALISM

Public service broadcasting is in trouble not simply because its intellectual rationale is under attack. Its problems are likely to worsen, it can be argued, because they are rooted in fundamental changes in British society.

In the first place, British politics moved to the right. Right-wing Conservative administrations monopolized power throughout the period 1979–97. New Labour, elected in 1997 and again in 2001, continued in a modified form their legacy of market liberalism.

The central tenets of this legacy are implicitly opposed to the public service tradition. Private agencies are more efficient, more responsive and less costly, in the neo-liberal view, than public bureaucracies. The market system is also morally preferable because it fosters freedom and self-reliance. In line with these precepts, a wide range of public services were privatized, marketized or deregulated after 1979 (Jenkins 1996; Riddell 1991; Kavanagh 1987). In these circumstances, it was inevitable that public service broadcasting should also find itself under attack.

A subsidary theme of new right thinking is that liberal corporatism (that is, a system of governance based on consultation and conciliation between government and large corporate groups) enfeebled Britain. It allegedly entrenched producer interests at the expense of the public, and gave rise to shabby compromise in place of the principled politics necessary for national regeneration. Public service broadcasting was indicted by the right on both counts. It was criticised as a producer-dominated institution that presented its vested interest as the public interest (Thatcher 1995). It was also associated with the old liberal consensus that had failed Britain (Tebbit 1989). The thinking that underlay these attacks to some extent persisted: liberal corporatism was not revived by New Labour.

A third theme of neo-liberalism is that high levels of tax are throttling individual initiative and enterprise, and leading to an excessive level of public spending that is crowding out private investment. This is a potentially devastating line of argument since it could lead very easily to the conversion of the licence fee into a voluntary subscription to the BBC (a backdoor form of privatization), and the sale of Channel 4 – both proposals espoused by leading figures on the right.

Yet while the rise of neo-liberalism is clearly a threat to public service broadcasting, there is still considerable disagreement among contemporary historians about the causes and extent of the right-wing shift in Britain. One interpretation argues that the triumph of Thatcherism was based on a successful ideological mobilization that drew, among other things, on popular resentment of welfarist bureaucracy, and on the widespread desire for increased freedom and choice expressed through private consumption. This was in tune with a new era characterized by growing cultural pluralism and the rise of individual subjectivity (Hall 1988b; Hall and Jacques 1989; McRobbie 1994). By implication, a television system inherited from an era of rationing and paternalism was less in keeping with 'new times' than one that favoured an expanded television system based on market freedom and consumer choice.[6]

Another interpretation explains the rise of the right primarily in terms of structural changes in the economy that caused, among other things, a contraction of the working class and weakening of trade unions (Jessop *et al.* 1988; Hobsbawm 1981). This threatened in turn, it is argued, the welfarist social settlement that was forged on the basis of relative parity between organized business and labour. This alternative explanation actually offers even less comfort for public service broadcasting. The implication is that public service broadcasting is the product of a social contract which has been destabilised by a fundamental shift of power in British society.

A third interpretation attributes the rise of the right mainly to the internal divisions and failures of the centre-left (Gamble 1990 and 1988; Curran 1990a; Heath, Jowell and Curtice 1987). It argues that the right-wing shift of British politics did not reflect a fundamental shift of British public attitudes, but rather a shift within Britain's political elite. However, this is of little solace to the BBC, which is the model and inspiration of the 'Morrisonian' approach to public ownership. This approach is now as much anathema to New Labour as it is to the Conservative Party.

SOCIAL CHANGE

Public service broadcasting was also weakened by cumulative social changes that transformed Britain. When the Pilkington committee met in the early 1960s, it was urged to raise programme standards by numerous educational bodies in a display of social consequence and cultural evangelism that has since largely disappeared. Similar pressure also came from established institutions like the Arts Council and the churches, and informally from a new breed of newspaper television critics. The veteran television critic of the Conservative *Daily Mail*, Peter Black, for instance, was openly contemptuous of ITV's early give-away shows, in which a housewife could earn a pound by correctly distinguishing her right foot from her left one or win a refrigerator by whitewashing her husband in thirty seconds starting from *now* (Black 1972: 111).

By contrast, the critical evidence received by the Annan committee in the 1970s was directed against the 'elitism' of the 'broadcasting duopoly'. In the 1980s, the Peacock committee received confident and well-presented submissions arguing that programmes should be determined largely by what people liked.

This cumulative shift partly reflected a breakdown of agreement over judgements of cultural value. Inter-generational conflicts intensified in the 1960s, and were expressed in contrasting definitions of good music, with, as Chapman (1992) argues, the BBC making the strategic mistake of championing the musical tastes of the middle-aged and elderly against the young. The development of a youth culture spawned numerous sub-cultures with different tastes (Thornton and Gelder 1996; Hebdige 1979). The rise of feminism and expansion of ethnic communities established new axes of cultural value, which asserted the worth of certain forms of low-status popular culture (Brunsdon 1997; McRobbie 1994). The continued growth of the market for cultural goods provided also a means of expressing divergent individual preferences (Hewison 1997). Underlying the growing pluralization of British society was the decline of the homogenizing influences of nation, neighbourhood and class.

The power dynamics underpinning cultural judgements also changed. The 1960s and 1980s were both periods of cultural revolt (though expressed through different politics) in which working-class deference declined markedly. The liberal professions – once key arbiters in the determination of cultural value – declined in status and influence. Above all, the middle class expanded, lost social cohesion and ceased to have a shared understanding of cultural value.

The rise of cultural studies during the 1980s was symptomatic of this change. Cultural studies was based primarily in polytechnics, now the new universities, at the margins of class privilege. It developed a perspective that was defiantly opposed to the literary norms of traditional university English departments. The new discipline taught almost as an orthodoxy that cultural judgements are not transcendant evaluations that exist outside of time, but forms of self-definition and social legitimation, a way of expressing group membership and exclusion (Frow 1995; Thornton and Gelder 1996; Bourdieu 1986a). This led to a stream of publications perceiving in popular television programmes valid pleasures, progressive protest, or the expression of social experience and cultural tradition that needed to be championed against social condescension (Geraghty 1991; Ang 1985; Hobson 1982).

Cultural judgements that had once seemed axiomatic were now questioned. 'The word "quality"', writes John Keane (1991: 120), 'has no objective basis, only a plurality of ultimately clashing, contradictory meanings amenable to public manipulation.' Cultural value dissensus became fertile ground for accusations of elitism. As one leading media historian proclaimed:

> The history of its [broadcasting] development in Britain has undoubtedly been coloured by the patrician values of a middle-class intelligentsia, and a defence of public service broadcasting in terms of quality and standards tied to prescriptive and elitist conceptions of education and culture is no longer feasible.
>
> (Scannell 1990: 260)

The institutional politics of the media also changed. A key factor in the original establishment of the BBC was the absence of an economic lobby pressing, as in the United States, for the development of commercial radio (Scannell and Cardiff 1991). During the conservative 1950s, the commercial lobby was reformist, pressing for commercial television in a public service mould (Sendall 1982; Lambert 1982) But in the last two decades, there emerged a formidable lobby fundamentally opposed to public service broadcasting. Its leading figure is Rupert Murdoch who controls a third of the British national press (Goodwin 1998; O'Malley 1994).

In addition, public service broadcasting was exposed to a new challenge. Cable and satellite television, under minimal regulation, threatened to gnaw into its audience, and further weaken its legitimacy and revenue base. The writing is on the wall, and it spells out – in the view of some – the slow death of the public service approach.

COUNTERVAILING TRENDS

The trouble with this contingent reasoning, entirely in keeping with the hand-wringing tradition of the 'crisis of public communication' literature, is that it stumbles into one awkward obstruction: the fact that British public service broadcasting, so seemingly beset by crisis, has remained resilient for so long. Why, if the political and social trends of society are so inimical to public service broadcasting, is it still standing bruised but intact?

One reason is that public service television is popular. Its channels are the ones which most people prefer to watch most of the time. Britain was the first major European country to introduce regulated commercial television. The resulting mixed economy system was well adapted to fend off the challenge of largely deregulated, subscription television channels.

The second reason is that the collectivist arrangements which lie at the heart of public service broadcasting (and which endow it with enormous resources) are supported by British political culture. Even during the heyday of Thatcherite dominance in the 1980s, there continued to be mass support for collectivist policies across a wide area of activity, from medical care to social welfare (Crewe 1988; Jowell, Witherspoon and Brook 1987; Jowell and Airey 1984). A comparative study found that in the mid-1980s British society was markedly more state-oriented and less individualistic than America (Davis 1986). While the new right made ideological inroads, it failed to transform public attitudes. Its cultural ascendancy was exaggerated by Britain's first past-the-post electoral system, which converted a minority of votes into a majority of parliamentary seats.

Third, public service broadcasting in Britain has a reputation for being independent of government. While broadcasting authorities were partly packed by government during the 1980s, rank-and-file broadcasters fought a determined rearguard action to defend their autonomy (including an unprecedented strike at the BBC in protest against government censorship). Successive surveys show that public service television is thought to provide a more trustworthy and credible source of news than the market-based press (Negrine 1989; Curran and Seaton 1997).

Fourth, public service broadcasting is valued on the grounds that it provides quality. Crucially, Britain's political elite continued to adhere to traditional cultural values at a time when these were increasingly repudiated in university cultural studies departments, and in social constituencies to which these departments were connected. Leading Conservative MPs, during the period of Conservative hegemony, perceived regulation and public funding to be necessary to prevent the reduction of programmes to the lowest common denominator. As William Whitelaw, Thatcher's deputy prime minister, wrote in his memoirs: 'I am always disturbed by talk of achieving higher standards in programmes at the same time as proposals are introduced leading to deregulation and financial competition because I do not believe that they are basically compatible' (Whitelaw 1989: 285). The same thinking informed the unanimous report of the all-party, Commons Home Affairs Committee that considered broadcasting legislation in the late 1980s. Its starting point was that 'the principles of public service broadcasting should be an integral part of the new broadcasting environment' in order to maintain 'high quality programmes', a commitment it believed to be incompatible with market freedom (House of Commons 1988: x–xi). This view was later championed by Virginia Bottomley, the Conservative cabinet minister responsible for broadcasting in the mid 1990s. The BBC, in her view, is 'our most successful . . . cultural institution' (Bottomley 2000: 143).

The BBC defused right-wing criticism by performing an organizational cart-wheel in the 1980s and 1990s. It introduced an internal market for its services, outsourced some programme production and made staff redundant. This gener-ated a wave of union protest which government ministers found reassuring. The right eventually split between gradualists and fundamentalists over the pace of broadcasting 'reform', with in the end the fundamentalists being isolated within the government as well as in the country (Barnett and Curry 1994; Goodwin 1998).

The institutions of public service broadcasting in Britain all survived. How-ever, the managerialist regime introduced in the BBC to placate right-wing critics left the corporation more centralized, less creative and less public service oriented (Curran and Seaton 1997). Commercial public service television was even more gravely undermined. It had been based on a compact, refined in the 1960s, in which ITV was given a television advertising monopoly in return for public service virtue, enforced by an active regulator. The public service ele-ment of this system began to weaken when ITV was forced to compete for advertising against new television channels in the 1980s and 1990s. Just when regulatory reinforcement was needed, the government deregulated. The Broadcasting Acts of 1990 and 1996 introduced a 'light touch' regulatory authority; a public auction of television franchises (though with quality safeguards); and lighter monopoly controls that led to a wave of mergers. Commercial public service television became as a consequence much more market-oriented, and performed less well. Yet, the incoming New Labour administration did not reverse this inheritance. Indeed, it seems likely that Labour ministers will extend deregulation of television after protracted consultation (HMSO 1998 and 2000).

In short, a price was paid when public service broadcasting survived. It deteriorated at a time when political and social change was moving against it. However, what is now needed is not further academic speculation about whether public service broadcasting will be swept away by the tidal wave of history, but constructive thought about how it can be strengthened in the future. This should begin with rethinking its justification.

NEED FOR RENOVATION

'Public broadcasters have failed', according to Rowland and Tracey (1990: 20), 'to articulate an intellectual argument for the continuing validity of public service values.' Another American scholar, Craig Calhoun, loftily concurs: 'The standard defences of public service broadcasting are weak' (Calhoun 1996: 224).

In fact, the standard case for public service broadcasting (Broadcasting Research Unit 1988; Blumler 1992) is not quite as deficient as these, and other commentators, suggest. It has also been strengthened in recent years. This said, it is still in need of major renovation.[7]

This can only be achieved successfully if public service theorists step outside the framework of market thinking. In the nature of things, the market is an aggregation of individual decisions, and does not have a conception of the needs of society. What a revised rationale for public service broadcasting should attempt to do is to identify these wider needs, and explain why they are best fulfilled through public service arrangements. As we still see, this reappraisal should lead, in turn, to rethinking the objectives and organization of public service broadcasting.

WELFARE ECONOMICS

However, radical market theory has provided the most notable advances in public service theory during the last decade. Its central argument is that 'broadcasting as a medium suffers from "market failure"' (Graham 2001: 1), and needs as a consequence to be publicly owned or regulated.

This is not a fundamentally new argument, since it has long been claimed that advertising distorts television. In this view, advertisers are interested in how *many* viewers see their commercials, not in how *much* viewers enjoy programmes. This generates pressure on mass commercial broadcasters to supply programmes with a wide appeal to different kinds of viewers rather than ones that generate intense interest among minorities. Public regulation is needed, therefore, to offset advertising distortion by extending consumer choice.

This argument had to be modified when channel expansion made possible niche provision for minorities. It was also challenged directly by neo-liberals who argued that the drawbacks of funding television by advertising – its bias against diversity and its lack of responsiveness to intensity of demand – do not apply to subscription services (Brittan 1989).[8] This led some neo-liberals to argue that television should be switched to a pay-TV system, now that new technology offered an almost infinite technical capacity for channel expansion.

Neo-Keynesian economists countered by arguing that public service broadcasting is not a transitional arrangement made unnecessary by cable and satellite television. On the contrary new technology strengthens the need for public control because it reinforces the factors that limit competition. Already, television has high fixed and low marginal costs, which generate enormous economies of scale and therefore competitive advantage to leading operators. The digital revolution is now encouraging the coming together of previously separate industries, and giving rise to economies of scope (the decrease of costs or increase of revenues through joint activity). 'Thus, while one source of monopoly, spectrum scarcity, has gone, it has been replaced by another – the natural monopoly of economies of scale and scope . . . ' (Graham and Davies 1997: 1). More channels and outlets are being created, but they are being controlled by fewer, merged companies. Indeed, as Graham (1999) points out, this trend is already under way, and cannot be dismissed as mere theory. In addition, control over new 'gateway' technologies (such as electronic programme guides) also has the potential to be abused through excluding or placing competitors at a disadvantage.

Public regulation and ownership is needed, therefore, more than ever to sustain real consumer choice. Regulation alone, it is argued, is not sufficient because regulators tend to be influenced unduly by the industries they oversee. A public organisation like the BBC is needed because it offers 'merit goods' that set standards, and influence both the wider broadcasting industry and the market.

Welfare economists also justify public service broadcasting in terms of the 'public good' properties of television. 'If one person eats a loaf of bread', explain Koboldt *et al.* (1999: 8), 'it is not available to someone else to eat, but one person watching a television programme still leaves that programme available for others to watch', at almost zero cost. Public television exploits these natural advantages for the public by funding the fixed cost of production through the licence fee, enabling viewers to benefit from the cheap supply of programmes. It offers, in other words, a good package deal for the consumer. By contrast, pay-TV operators alone profit from the public good properties of television, while excluding by price people who could be reached with minimal extra cost.

DEMOCRATIC SYSTEM

The democratic case for public service broadcasting is another area where new arguments have supplemented old ones. Its starting point is that people are not only consumers in the market economy: they are also citizens within the democratic system (Murdock 1992). Citizens have rights, including the right to be adequately informed about matters relating to the public good. The basis of this right is that the people are sovereign in liberal democracies. If they are to be effective and responsible, they need to be adequately informed.

This entitlement to information is best secured through public service broadcasting because it gives due attention to public affairs, and is less dominated than market-based systems by entertainment. While the market can generate dedicated news or information channels, these tend to attract elite audiences and to reinforce therefore the knowledge gap between elites and the general public. By contrast, public service broadcasting raises general levels of political awareness by including news and current affairs programmes in prime time on popular, generalist channels. One system takes into account the informational needs of democracy: the other does not and tends to disempower large sections of the electorate through lack of information.

Second, public service broadcasting produces, it is argued, a more rational democracy (Scannell 1992; Garnham 2000 and 1986). It encourages the transfer of relevant specialist knowledge to the political domain, and promotes balanced, evidence-based and reciprocal debate directed towards the public good. This contrasts with the market-based system in the United States, where the drive to sustain ratings has encouraged the tabloidization of news coverage, the blurring of information and entertainment, and the increasing domination of political analysis by brief, and rapidly shrinking, soundbites that make few demands on the audience (Hallin 1996 and 1994).

Third, public service arrangements contribute to a fairer, more equitable democracy. Unlike the United States, Britain bans political advertising on television. This public service approach limits the cost of campaigning, and curtails therefore the influence of money on politics. The requirement of 'due impartiality' in British broadcasting ensures that opposed sides are represented. The prominence given to politics allows for sustained oversight of government, and promotes greater public involvement and participation in the political process (Blumler and Gurevitch 1995). Public service broadcasting also underpins the democratic system by supporting a national public culture of shared knowledge, values and points of reference (Dahlgren 2000).

SOCIAL SYSTEM

The argument that public service broadcasting fosters an informed, rational and fair democratic system is currently its single most important justification (though one that is being weakened by increased commercialization). An equivalent intellectual case needs to be developed in relation to the social needs of society.

Here, the problem is that there is no consensus in favour of a particular form of social organisation of society in the way that there is for its political organisation. The democratic case for public service broadcasting is easy to make because it draws upon a shared understanding that electoral democracy is desirable and has certain requirements that need to be met if it is to function well. The same set of understandings do not exist in relation to the 'social system'.

This said, there is not a total absence of agreement, certainly in western Europe. There is a dawning realization that the neo-liberal programme, if pursued without qualification, will produce ultimately a society composed of an aggregation of individuals, driven by self-interest, bound together by the cash nexus of market relations, constrained merely by the law of the land. Opposed to this is another conception of society as a social system in which social relations are underpinned by a sense of community and concern for others, a set of ethical norms that influence social behaviour, and open dialogue that enables different groups to participate in the shaping and revision of shared values. This latter view still has a broad measure of support even in the era of market liberalism.

This understanding of a civilized society is best served by public service broadcasting. This organizes television in a way that promotes a strong sense of community. Sparsely populated, mountainous and outlying areas are enabled to view free-to-air television because an 'uneconomic' investment has been made in installing transmission facilities that can reach them. Public service regulation in Britain prevents licensed cable operators from excluding – as happens in the

United States – low-income areas within their franchise. More generally, public service television does not exclude by price any section of the population in contrast to subscription services. Key sporting contests, and national events that commemorate the shared life of the nation, are 'reserved' for general transmission, and cannot be bought for exclusive use by a commercial company. In short, one cardinal principle of the public service approach is that everyone is included, catered for and brought together within the compass of a universal service.

The symbolic community projected by public service television also supports a sense of social cohesion and belonging. The groups most prone to social exclusion are old people, single parents, the unemployed and some ethnic minorities (Corfield 1999). They are all part of the social world reproduced in the two leading soap operas of British public service television, *Eastenders* and *Coronation Street*. More generally, public service broadcasting has nurtured a progressive social realist tradition which gives prominence to the working class (McKnight 1997; Brandt 1993 and 1981), in contrast to the glamourised, 'upscale' settings that dominate much of American domestic TV drama.

Public service broadcasting's cultivation of social unity has negative aspects. But its positive virtue is that it fosters a feeling of mutual identification that breeds concern for others. This is reinforced and extended by the way in which public service broadcasting promotes sympathetic understanding of 'the other'. At best, its programmes empathise rather than demonise; offer explanatory contexts rather than identikits of good and evil; render explicable the alien and unfamiliar; and find room for complexity rather than stereotypical simplification. This is because its programmes are not wholly subordinated to market dictates. The need for 'simple, and simply motivated, stories full of conflict, endings resolved, uplift apparent, and each act . . . ends[ing] on a note of suspense sufficient to carry the viewer through the commercial break' that Gitlin (1994: 165–6) argues characterizes US network made-for-television films reflects the cultural straitjacket imposed by a different political economy.

More generally, public service broacasting facilitates debate about common social processes. Control over broadcasting resides not with one sectional interest, corporate business, as in the market system but with representatives of the public. This should promote, in principle at least, an open and reciprocal dialogue between different sections of the community. By supporting original production, public service broadcasting also creates a space in which programme-makers can engage with the specific concerns and social experiences of their audience. This can result in illuminating dramas that cast a shaft of light and understanding on the way society is developing, exemplified by the BBC's outstanding series, *Our Friends from the North*.

CULTURAL SYSTEM

New thought also needs to be given to the cultural justification of public service broadcasting because traditional claims seem increasingly unconvincing. One standard argument is that public service broadcasting delivers demanding pro- grammes of high quality, usually associated with high culture. Another is that the system delivers a planned diversity of programmes catering for the different minorities that make up the majority. To this, the neo-liberal retort is now simple. High culture programming can be supplied by a publicly funded, elite channel (as in the United States), and does not justify an entire broadcasting system. Second, a mature broadcasting market generates specialist and niche channels catering for minority demand, like those that are mushrooming on cable and satellite television.

A better case has to be made for interpreting and justifying the cultural role of public service broadcasting. One way to attempt this is to conceive of a 'cultural system' in a way that is analogous to the democratic system, with requirements that need to be met if it is to function properly. These requirements are perhaps conservation, innovation, reproduction, diversity and social access. They are better served by a public service than a market system of broadcasting.

Thus, public service broadcasting helps to conserve the cultural system by transmitting works of literature, music and art, judged to be of outstanding value by past generations, to the next generation. It renews the part of the cultural system constituted by broadcasting by supporting innovation through the alloca- tion of resources to original and experimental work. It fosters the diversity of the cultural system through internal cross-subsidies within public service organisa- tions designed to sustain production for minorities (including, crucially, ones that are not viable in the marketplace). It helps the cultural system to reproduce itself by sustaining concentrations of craft skill, experience and talent, and by support- ing creativity through the ceding of a high degree of autonomy to production teams. And it facilitates social access to the cultural system through low, collect- ively subscribed costs of admission, and through mixed programmes schedules that encourage viewers to try new experiences.

Thinking in these abstract terms runs counter both to the empirical temper of British intellectual life,[9] and to relativistic thinking in cultural studies. But the fact that there is no longer a cultural-value consensus does not mean that we should refrain from making cultural judgements about the sort of programmes that ought to be made. Not making a judgement does not mean in reality avoiding one. It merely delegates this to others: in a market system to accountants, advertisers, commissioning editors and other decision makers.

'NATIONAL' DISTORTION

The case for public service broadcasting thus needs to be revised. The 'quality' that it embodies cannot be reduced to a specific aspect of programme making (for example, craft professionalism) or a specific category of programme (such as 'high culture'). Rather, it refers to the way in which public service forms of organisation provide a programme service that serves the political, social and cultural needs of society.

This exposition is partly normative: it relates to how things ought to be as well as how they are. In actual practice, public service broadcasting has a number of defects that cause it to deviate from its idealized justification. This stems partly from the way in which public service broadcasting is the product of the nation state, and has been highjacked by the national project. It is now time to rethink this legacy as a first step to renewing the public service tradition.

However, this is not intended to suggest that public service broadcasting should be detached altogether from the nation. After all, the nation is still important to the organization of democratic life. It is therefore appropiate that the national state should be subject to critical oversight; that national debates and elections should be foregrounded; and that the concerns of groups within the national electorate should be thoroughly aired. Connecting to the nation also makes sense as a strategy for promoting the values of social mutuality since the nation is a major focus of identity and sense of belonging. But the nation-centredness of public service broadcasting poses a number of problems that now need to be addressed.

First, British television is failing to adjust adequately to shifts in the system of power. As noted in the last chapter, the power of the nation state has been partly ceded to continental-regional and global governmental agencies, and to global financial markets and business corporations. Yet, the critical scrutiny of British television is still firmly fixed on the national state. Its reporting of European institutions and politics remains sparse and erratic; its reporting of global regulation is sketchy; and its reporting of the global financial markets and business sector lacks insight into their political influence.

Underlying all these failures is an inherited reflex from the past. The BBC's conception of its mission 'beyond 2000' is especially revealing:

> The BBC's core purpose[s] remain constant . . . to enable all sides to join the debate on issues of *national, regional and local significance.*
>
> (BBC 1998: 1, emphasis added)

This is the only part of the corporation's mission statement that is concerned explicitly with politics, and makes clear where its vision of political debate begins and ends – the nation state. This makes for an imperfect oversight of the new 'multi-layered' system of governance. It also tends to preclude coverage of political debates, promoted by new social movements, in the arena of global politics.

Second, the national definition of public service broadcasting distorts Britain's relationship to the wider world. The lack of programme imports from mainland Europe contributes to the continuing underdevelopment of a European identity among British people.[10] This in turn undermines participation in European elections and political debate. Television's national focus also weakens a sense of connection with 'foreigners', and leaves British viewers relatively uninformed about whole areas of the globe, stretching from the Islamic Middle East through to Asia and, now very little reported, South America.

The third problem has to do with who gets to speak for the 'nation', and define the national interest. A recurrent refrain of much academic research is that British television news and current affairs programmes are often defined by elite assumptions and sources (Philo and Miller 2001; Eldridge 1995; Philo 1995; McNair 1995 and 1988). This is partly a consequence of the way in which the terms of the debate in Westminister – its agenda, premises and preferred solutions – tend to be adopted as a template for defining the 'national' debate on television.

This approach always under-presented the diversity of views and perspectives in the country. It is made still more problematic now by the decline of political parties. They have lost much of their active, mass memberships. They have ceased to command the loyalty, and exert the sort of influence, that they once did. They are no longer representative of coherent social constituencies in the way they were even thirty years ago. Yet, their dominance over news and current affairs programmes has, if anything, increased due to the increasing professionalism of their public relations (Barnett and Gaber 2001).

The fourth, related problem has to do with who gets invited to participate in the mediated conversations of the nation. In general, the holders of power and accredited knowledge, and spokespersons of the legitimated democratic order, tend to monopolize television debates. However, the rise of talk shows gave a new forum in which the unorganized took part. These allowed ordinary people to become the principal protagonists of debate, and made television more responsive to wider social concerns, in particular neglected women's issues (Morley 2000). However, the opening represented by these talk shows tends to be quarantined within particular categories of programme.

The fifth issue is concerned with who is included and excluded in symbolic representations of the nation. One of the few positive aspects of the Birt era in the BBC (1992–2000) is that significantly more black and Asian people came to be television presenters, reporters, actors and producers (but more rarely senior managers), and more resources were put into ethnic minority programmes. However, increased awareness of the need to connect to ethnic minorities brought a rude awakening. Research commissioned by the BBC revealed that:

A significant part of the disillusion Blacks and Asians feel with the BBC stems not merely from our programmes but also from the perception that the

Corporation is an integral part of the white establishment which does not have their interests at heart.

(BBC 1995b: 168)

The BBC's research also found that Afro-Carribean viewers tended to prefer American sitcoms that featured black people as central and rounded characters in programmes directed at a general audience rather than the BBC's programmes targeted at ethnic minorities. Subsequent research showed that black and Asian viewers continued to feel that they were not effectively addressed by public service broadcasting, and to be more inclined than the average to subscribe to cable and satellite television (Morley 2000).

The sixth issue is whether the enormous attention given to 'British' culture is misplaced. Why foreground, for example, British classical music when the classical music of other countries is so much better?

Public service broadcasting was forged in the crucible of a conservative (with a small c), one-nation, imperial tradition. Although it has since changed, it still bears traces of its origins. Indeed, public service broadcasting's continued emphasis on its national mission prevents it from adjusting more fully to the more pluralistic, globalizing environment in which it now operates.

SELF-REGENERATION

However, the public service tradition is potentially able to regenerate itself through internal reform. It has a vigorous professional culture of critical self-reflection that is noticeably absent in the more commercialised British press industry (Curran 2000a).

This professional culture has generated a long running debate about how to cover politics. The traditionalist view holds that the role of the broadcast journalist is analogous to that of a civil servant. The broadcaster briefs the people about current developments and presents coherent political options to choose between. This mandarin tradition abhors emotionality and spectacle, and has ill-concealed disdain for 'uninformed' opinion. Thus, Lord Reith, the founder of the BBC, told the American journalist Edward Murrow that his 'man-on-the-street' reporting 'will drag radio down to the level of Hyde Park Speaker's Corner' (Persico 1988: 112). The same image of demotic speech was invoked with patrician disdain by the Annan report when it attacked the conception of broadcasting as 'a mass conversation' or 'dialogue'. This misguided idea, it warned, would reduce broadcasting to the level of 'an aerial Hyde Park Corner' (Annan 1977: 24).

The opposing view argues that, whatever the intention, broadcasting does inevitably reproduce a form of public dialogue. An excessive stress on legitimated forms of public knowledge and accredited speakers unduly restricts participation in this dialogue. This counter-argument galvanized a reform movement among broadcasters intent upon extending social access, and expanding the range of voices and views on air. This was manifested in new phone-in programmes, audience-participant formats and access slots (Livingstone and Lunt 1994). It even penetrated some of the citadels of establishment journalism. 'Involve a wider range of experts and members of the public, get away from white men in grey suits, get away from the M25 [the ring road around London]', commanded one internal memorandum in *Newsnight*, BBC2's prestige daily news magazine programme (BBC 1995a). This injunction led to a number of outstanding programmes that enabled marginalized groups to occupy the central ground of debate (Curran 2000b). Above all, the movement in favour of greater pluralism resulted in Channel 4 developing in ways that were not fully anticipated. Norman Tebbit, then a senior cabinet minister, told its first chief executive, Jeremy Isaacs, that 'Parliament never meant' there to be 'these programmes for homosexuals and such', but instead had expected the channel to cater for minority 'hobbies' like golf, sailing and fishing (Isaacs 1989: 65). The channel's legislative remit was in fact ambiguous, merely calling for innovation and minority programmes (HMSO 1981 and 1990). This was interpreted by the channel's pioneer senior executives like Liz Forgan to mean that the new venture should open up the airwaves to minority views and concerns that were marginalized by other channels.

The rise of Channel 4 was part of a general a shift of orientation. During the 1990s, senior executives in the BBC stressed the need to reflect the diversity of a multicultural, multi-ethnic society in the full range of the corporation's output (BBC 1992, 1995b and 1998).

PLURALISM AND GLOBALISM

However, this reformist movement inside the broadcasting community received little official support. Parliamentary statutes, government green and white papers, and official broadcasting reports published since 1982 consistently downplay representative pluralism as an objective of broadcasting policy.[11] Within this official canon, 'access' tends to be understood as access to the best of British culture and entertainment, or the access of people living in remote places to public service broadcasting. In other words, it is about the right to listen, rather than to be heard. Similarly, the concept of 'diversity' is advanced primarily in terms of catering for different tastes rather than giving expression to different perspectives and cultures.

Pluralism should now be added to the objectives of the broadcasting system. Public service broadcasting organizations should be required to give adequate expression to the diversity of opinions, perspectives and values in society. This should be incorporated into the BBC's Charter, the next Broadcasting Act and be one of the official aims of the proposed new regulator of commercial broadcasting, the Office of Communications.

Public service broadcasting also needs to renegotiate its relationship to

Britain's national heritage. The official understanding that it supports a national culture and identity needs to be extended to other cultures and peoples. The public service commitment to inform should include major events, developments and trends outside Britain.

It is still important that public service broadcasting enables the national community to come together and debate through generalist channels. But the public service tradition cannot afford to be boxed into a one-nation tradition, allowing its market rivals to present themselves as the principal agents of globalism and pluralism. The advent of digital television provides a golden opportunity for public service broadcasting to redefine itself. By launching new channels, it should be able to connect more effectively to minority audiences, and promote a stronger sense of connection to the outside world. These new channels can be targeted towards different age groups, ethnic groups, music and cultural taste audiences, and perhaps include a European channel (drawing on films and programmes made in other European countries) and a global film channel (taking advantage of the availability of fine films almost unwatched in Britain).[12] In addition, the internet provides an opportunity – to which the BBC is already responding – to supplement programmes with information of greater depth and detail, and provide new forms of audience access and interaction.

INSTITUTIONAL REPAIRS

Of all the institutional repairs that are needed, two ought to be singled out. The public service element in commercial television should be strengthened through more effective regulation. Even more important, the political independence of the broadcasting system needs to be reinforced.

The system of government appointments to broadcasting authorities in Britain has become corrupted and debased. All those appointed to chair the BBC, for example, during the Conservative ascendancy were known Conservative supporters. Indeed, Marmaduke Hussey, a longstanding chairman of the BBC (1986–96), was a brother-in-law of a cabinet minister; Stuart Young, his predecessor (1983–6), was a brother of one.

Broadcasting appointments should be removed from direct, unmediated patronage. The New Labour administration tacitly acknowledged this when, in 2001, it set up for the first time a panel to interview candidates for chairmanship of the BBC, and make a public recommendation to the government. The reform did not go far enough. The small panel consisted of mostly leftish members of the establishment: their choice was a New Labour insider, Gavyn Davies. The result was that a crony of the governing party (albeit an impressive one) was once again appointed to chair the BBC Board of Governors.

An independent appointments committee, made up of nominees from representative organizations in the country and from the broadcasting industry, should publicly recommend all appointees to the BBC Board of Governors and the public board of the future Office of Communications. Their brief should be to select people of talent who are drawn from a cross-section of society to represent the public. They should guard against not only government but also establishment 'packing'.

The BBC should also be protected from financial intimidation. When its income automatically increased, due to the growth of radio, television and then colour television licenses, it was financially independent. When this natural growth dried up, the BBC became economically vulnerable to pressure from government which alone has the power to authorize licence fee increases. In order to restore the BBC's economic independence and sustain its development in the digital age, the licence fee should rise automatically in relation to the increase in the wealth of the country (as defined by the gross domestic product).

The other cudgel used to intimidate the BBC is the periodic renewal of its royal charter. The lead-up to renewal has often been the time when the BBC has been most sensitive to government and elite opinion (Briggs 1985). The BBC should be established by act of parliament. After eighty years distinguished service, it should no longer be considered a probationer on a temporary contract.

REINVENTING TRADITION

Channel 4 was established in 1982, and was an imaginative way of reinterpreting the public service tradition. But there have been no public service experiments since then. Channel 5, established in 1997, is merely a low-budget equivalent of ITV.

The key moment for major innovation is when the conversion is made from analogue to digital transmission. This will release additional spectrum that can be sold, and produce a large dowry for a new type of public service organization, Free TV. The central idea informing this proposal is that Free TV would provide an environment in which broadcasting staff would be free to explore the potential of television as a creative medium. The new organization would be insulated from market pressure through public funding. However, it would also be shielded from state pressure since it would be subject to no obligation or regulation other than the law of the land.

The traditional strength of British public service television between approximately 1960 and 1985 was that it allowed greater autonomy to its staff, at the level of producer, than either the market-driven model of the United States or the representative-ridden models of continental European broadcasting. Admittedly, this much vaunted autonomy contained strongly mythical elements particularly in the areas of news and current affairs, though less so in drama (Schlesinger 1978; Burns 1977; Kumar 1975). Admittedly also, relative staff autonomy made the broadcasting system rather unrepresentative and unaccountable (which is why it does not constitute a model to be elevated now for the entire broadcasting system). But at its best the freedom given to broadcasters produced imaginative programmes. However, this freedom was eroded by increased centralization within the BBC, and by increased commercialization in ITV and Channel 4. As a consequence, the inventive quality of programmes – and in particular of single 'plays', comedy, documentaries and satire – tended to decline.

A new institution is needed which will recapture the elan of the declining British model: a broadcasting system that is neither politicized nor subject to ratings rule. Centred in Glasgow and Liverpool, it would be exposed to a significantly different social and political culture to that of other major television channels, and would hopefully give airtime to perspectives and experiences that are different from the mainstream of broadcasting. Above all, it would break new ground through, paradoxically, the attempt to reinvent tradition. The new organization would be less subject to market and state constraint than any other broadcaster in the world.

CONCLUSION

If this chapter questions Elihu Katz's general analysis, it does so with admiration and respect. Katz is one of the founding fathers of media studies[13] and an inspirational figure in the field. He is also a doer as well as a sage, who has the distinction of founding a new public service television system.[14]

But this does not mean that his account of the crisis of communication should go unchallenged. Certainly as far as western Europe is concerned, his suggestion that liberal democracy is now being undermined by audience fragmentation, the eclipse of public information and globalization is not justified by the evidence.

More generally, Katz's analysis can be seen as an inversion of a standard argument. It is fashionable to assume that a *market-based* technological transformation of communications is both inevitable and desirable. Katz differs in seeing this neo-liberal utopia as a dystopia, but does not dissent from the technological determinism that underlies it. However, the British case study presented here argues that there is nothing inexorable or irreversible about the decline of the public service experiment. On the contrary, the potential exists for it to be renewed through internal and external reform in the context of continuing public support.

Katz invokes an appealing image of the past, as a way of dramatizing what has been lost. But his nostalgic vision of an entire nation coming together through monopoly television to debate current developments omits one thing, at least in a British context. Elites largely controlled the agendas of these virtual meetings, and did most of the talking. Indeed, the limitations of the past distort even now who defines on British television the national interest, and who is included in symbolic representations of the British nation. The past also bequeaths inadequate reflexes in overseeing a changed system of power, and curtails people's connection to 'foreign' others. In short, rose-tinted evocations of the past – in

Israel or elsewhere – provide an uncertain guide for the future. The national definition of public service broadcasting always was problematic and remains so. It is a legacy that needs to be renegotiated if public service broadcasting is to survive the transition to a more pluralistic and globalized world.

Chapter 8

Media and democracy: the third way

Many of the received ideas about the democratic role of the media derive from a frockcoated world where the 'media' consisted principally of small-circulation, political publications and the state was still dominated by a landed elite. The result is a legacy of old saws, which bear very little relationship to contemporary reality. They need to be reassessed.[1]

Discussion of the media's democratic role is intimately bound up with a debate about the media's organization and regulation. Indeed, the classic liberal theory of a free press on which we still rely was refined and elaborated in the nineteenth century as part of a political campaign for press deregulation (Curran 1978b). Rethinking classic liberal theory necessarily implies a rethinking of media policy.[2]

This chapter will attempt therefore both to re-evaluate traditional conceptions of the democratic role of the media, and outline the form which an ideal democratic media system should take. This reappraisal may be rejected in favour of a better considered alternative. But whatever conclusion is reached, one thing is clear. The literature on media and democracy is in need of a removal van to carry away lumber accumulated over two centuries. What should be discarded, what should be kept and how the intellectual furniture should be rearranged is something that needs to be thought about in a new way.

FREE MARKET WATCHDOG

The principal democratic role of the media, according to traditional liberal theory, is to act as a check on the state. The media should monitor the full range of state activity, and fearlessly expose abuses of official authority. 滥用职权

This watchdog role is said in traditional liberal theory to override in importance all other functions of the media. It dictates the form in which the media system should be organized. Only by anchoring the media to the free market, in this view, is it possible to ensure the media's complete independence from government. Once the media becomes subject to state regulation, they may lose their bite as watchdogs. Worse still, they may be transformed into snarling Rottweillers in the service of the state.

This orthodox view is especially well entrenched in the United States. For instance, Kelley and Donway, two American political scientists of conservative sympathies, argue that any reform of the media, however desirable, is unacceptable if it is 'at the cost of the watchdog function. And this is the inevitable cost. A press that is licensed, franchised or regulated is subject to political pressures when it deals with issues affecting the interests of those in power' (Kelley and Donway 1990: 97). This reservation is restated by the centrist political theorist, Stephen Holmes, as a rhetorical question: 'Doesn't every regulation converting the media into a "neutral forum" lessen its capacity to act as a partisan gadfly, investigating and criticising government in an aggressive way?' (Holmes 1990: 51). Even many American analysts with strongly reformist views share the same fear. 'I cannot envision any kind of content regulation, however indirect', writes the media critic, Carl Stepp, 'that wouldn't project government into the position of favouring or disfavouring some views and information over others. Even so-called structural steps aimed at opening channels for freer expression would post government in the intolerable role of super-gatekeeper' (Stepp 1990: 194).

This free market argument was deployed with great effect in the United States during the 1980s to justify broadcasting deregulation. Television channels were 'freed' from the fairness doctrine which required them to present alternative views on controversial issues of importance (Baker 1998). Rules restricting media concentration were also relaxed (Croteau and Hoynes 1997; Tunstall and Machin 1999).

A parallel campaign was mounted in Britain. As the media magnate, Rupert Murdoch (1989: 9), succinctly put it, 'public service broadcasters in this country [Britain] have paid a price for their state-sponsored privileges. That price has been their freedom' (Murdoch 1989: 9; cf. Adam Smith Institute 1984; Veljanovski 1989). Although this rhetoric encountered more opposition in Britain than in the United States, it influenced the government of the day. Regulation of commercial broadcasting content was reduced, and anti-monopoly restraints were eased during the 1990s (Goodwin 1998).

The liberal watchdog argument was effective partly because it invoked a premise which was widely accepted in relation to the press.[3] Regulation of the press, other than through the 'ordinary' law of the land, was vehemently opposed in both the United States and Britain on the grounds that it would stifle free expression, and curtail critical scrutiny of power. Thus, the American Supreme Court struck down in 1974 a press right of reply law in Florida on the grounds that it would 'chill' critical debate (Barron 1975). Similarly, the last Royal Commission on the Press in Britain opposed in 1977 any form of selective newspaper subsidy because 'it would involve in an obvious way the dangers of government interference in the press' (Royal Commission on the Press 1977: 126).

Market liberals had only accepted more extensive regulation of broadcasting on the grounds that the limited number of airwave frequencies made it a 'natural monopoly' (Royal Commission on the Press 1977: 9; cf. Horwitz 1991). When the number of television channels multiplied with the introduction of advanced cable and satellite, this 'special case' argument was undermined. What was right in principle for the press was now applicable, it was argued, to broadcasting. Television should be set free.

Attention has focused for convenience on Britain and the United States. However, a very similar sequence of argument and pressure occurred in many other countries. The same freedom rhetoric was invoked; the same opportunities beckoned with the development of new television channels; and a shift towards broadcasting deregulation followed (Avery 1993; Aldridge and Hewitt 1994; Raboy 1996; Weymouth and Lamizet 1996; Humphreys 1996; Herman and McChesney 1997; Ostergaard 1997; Robins 1997; Tracey 1998; Catalbas 2000; Curran and Park 2000).

Limits of the 'watchdog' perspective

The traditional public watchdog definition of the media thus legitimates the case for broadcasting reform, and strengthens the defence of a free market press. At first glance, this approach appears to have much to commend it. After all, critical surveillance of the state is clearly an important aspect of the democratic functioning of the media. Exposure of the Watergate scandal during the Nixon presidency or lesser known exploits (outside their country) such as press disclosure of the 'Narcogate' scandal in 1991 when senior officials in the Argentine government were revealed to be involved in drug-money laundering operations or Caco Barcello's revelations of the cold-blooded murder of black and mestizo suspects in the 1990s by Sao Paulo's military police (Waisbord 2000a: 34–5 and 41), are all heroic examples of the way in which the media served society by investigating the abuse of authority by public officials.

However this argument is not as clear-cut as it seems. While the watchdog role of the media is enormously important, it is perhaps quixotic to argue that it should be paramount and determine media policy. This conventional view derives from the eighteenth century when the principal 'media' were public affairs-oriented newspapers. By contrast, media systems in the early twenty-first century are given over largely to entertainment. Even many so-called 'news media' allocate only a small part of their content to public affairs[4] – and a tiny amount to disclosure of official wrongdoing. In effect, the liberal orthodoxy defines the main democratic purpose and organizational principle of the media in terms of what they do *not* do most of the time.

The watchdog argument also appears timeworn in another way. Traditionally, liberal theory holds that government is the sole object of press vigilance. This derives from a period when government was commonly thought to be the 'seat' of power. However, this traditional view fails to take account of the exercise of economic power by shareholders and managers. A revised conception is needed in which the media are conceived as being a check on *both* public and private authority.

This modification diminishes the case for 'market freedom' since it can no longer be equated with independence from all forms of power. A growing section of the world's media has been taken over by major industrial and commercial concerns such as General Electric, Westinghouse, Toshiba, Fiat, Bouyges and Santo Domingo groups, in a development that extends from the United States and Japan to Hungary and Colombia (Bagdikian 1997; Herman and McChesney 1997; Ostergaard 1997; Tunstall and Machin 1999; Curran and Park 2000). A number of media organizations has also grown into huge leisure conglomerates that are among the largest corporations in the world. The issue is no longer simply that the media are compromised by their links to big business: the media *are* big business.

The conglomeration of news media mostly took place during the last three decades. It gave rise sometimes to no-go areas where journalists were reluctant to tread for fear of stepping on the corporate toes of a parent or sister company (Hollingsworth 1986; Bagdikian 1997; Curran and Seaton 1997). It is also claimed plausibly that the media are in general less vigilant in relation to corporate than public bureaucracy abuse because they are part of the corporate business sector (McChesney 1997).

Market corruption

The classic liberal response to these criticisms is that the state should be the main target of media scrutiny because the state has a monopoly of legitimated violence, and is therefore the institution to be feared most. For this reason, it is especially important to establish a critical distance between the media and the governmental system through private media ownership.

This seemingly persuasive argument ignores the way in which the world has changed since the early eighteenth century when 'Cato' (1983 [1720]) set out with such powerful eloquence the press watchdog thesis. Media organizations have become more profit oriented. The sphere of government has been greatly enlarged, with the result that political decisions more often affect their profitability. Yet, governments need the media more than ever, because they now have to retain mass electoral support to stay in office.

These cumulative changes have given rise to a relationship that is increasingly prone to corruption. This is highlighted by Chadwick's (1989) pioneering research which shows that a number of media entrepreneurs formed a tactical alliance with the Labour government in Australia in the late 1980s as a way of securing official permission to consolidate their control over Australia's commercial television and press. This resulted in an unprecedented number of editorial endorsements for the Labour Party in the 1987 election, as well as opportunistic fence-sitting by some traditionally anti-Labour papers. Similarly Rupert Murdoch removed the critically independent BBC World News service from his Asian Star satellite system in 1994, and vetoed HarperCollins's publication of ex-Hong Kong governor Chris Patten's memoirs in 1998, because he wanted to curry favour with the Chinese government in order to obtain permission to expand his operations in China. In much the same way the Argentine media tycoon, Eduardo Eurnekian, axed a critical television report on the building of an expensive airstrip on President Menem's private property. At the time, Eurnekian was bidding for (and duly obtained) a major stake in Argentina's privatized airports (Waisbord 2000b).

Indeed, the potential for media corruption was enormously increased by the deregulatory policies that were pursued in the 1980s and 1990s. Lucrative broadcasting and telecommunications franchises were disposed off; new arrangements were made for their operation, which affected their costs and profitability; and the rules governing media acquisitions and cross-media ownership were changed. Whether leading media corporations became much bigger, more dominant and more profitable depended, in part, on political and bureaucratic decisions. This encouraged a number of non-aggression pacts typified by the tacit understanding that was reached between Tony Blair, as leader of the Labour opposition in Britain, and Rupert Murdoch in the mid-1990s. Tabloid hounds pursuing Labour were called to heel in return for very strong signals that a New Labour government would not attack Murdoch's monopolist empire (Curran and Leys 2000).

In other words, the market can give rise not to independent watchdogs serving the public interest but to corporate mercenaries which adjust their critical scrutiny to suit their private purpose.

Market suppression

Still more serious is the way in which the market can silence media watchdogs altogether. Many privately owned media organizations supported right-wing military coups in Latin American countries (Fox 1988; Waisbord 2000b). This collusion was typified by *El Mercurio*, which backed the military coup in Chile, loyally supported the Pinochet dictatorship and largely overlooked its violation of human rights. Similarly, the Globo television network gave unconditional support to the military regime in Brazil, while most of Argentina's privately owned media failed to investigate state-sponsored 'disappearances' during the period of military rule. Less dramatically, private media in Taiwan 'not only accepted authoritarian rule', according to Lee (2000: 125), 'but also helped to rationalize it' during the period before 1987. In each case, these media collaborations with authoritarian states arose because media owners were part of the system of power.

Even in societies where market-based media have a more independent and adversarial relationship to government, appearances can still be deceptive. Media attacks on official wrongdoing can follow private agendas. 'Fearless' feats of investigative journalism, in these circumstances, are not necessarily the disinterested acts undertaken on behalf of the public that they appear to be. For example, a seven-person team from Northwestern University examined six investigative stories exposing official fraud, failure or injustice that appeared in the American media in the period 1981–8 (Protess *et al.* 1991). All these stories, it turned out, were initiated and sourced by well-positioned power holders. In most cases, media tip-offs were part of a conscious agenda-building strategy by 'policy elites' who were preparing the ground for a policy change or were engaged in boosting their personal reputations. Media disclosure can be best understood, according to this debunking account, as an integral part of elite media management in which the public are regularly sidelined.[5]

Even the Watergate investigation (exposing high-level Republican involvement in the 1972 break-in into the Democrat headquarters and President Nixon's subsequent cover-up, leading to his forced resignation), cited earlier as an example of heroic media vigilance, is not immune from this demythologizing approach. It has gone down in legend as an example of intrepid journalists doggedly tracking down the truth, and changing the course of history. In fact, most of the press's independent investigation took the form of receiving pre-culled information from state officials. Furthermore 'the moving force', according to Gladys and Kurt Lang (1983: 301), 'behind the effort to get to the bottom of Watergate came neither from the media nor public opinion but from political insiders' who maintained pressure for the story to be pursued, and to be recognized as important. This elite guidance, the Langs suggest, was a mixed blessing. It resulted in Watergate being defined narrowly by the news media as a legal-juridical issue, which limited unduly the reform of the political system that followed after Nixon's resignation.

What all these examples point to is the inadequacy of the liberal model which explains the media solely in terms of market theory. The media are assumed to be independent, and to owe allegiance only to the public, if they are funded by the public and organized through a competitive market. This theory ignores the many other influences which can shape the media, including the political commitments and private interests of media shareholders, the influence exerted through news management and the ideological power of leading groups in society. In short, this extremely simplistic theory fails to take into account the wider relations of power in which the media are situated. This is a key point to which we shall return when we consider other aspects of the media's democratic role.

State control

If private media are subject to compromising constraint, so too of course are public media. There is no lack of examples where public broadcasters have acted as little more than mouthpieces of government (Downing 1996; Sparks 1998; Curran and Park 2000; Waisbord 2000a). These cautionary experiences reveal the variety of levers that governments can pull to get the broadcasting they want. Public broadcasters have been subject to direct censorship through restrictive laws and regulations; licences to broadcast have been allocated to government supporters; broadcasters have been encouraged to censor themselves in response to a variety of pressures (public criticism, private intimacy, information management, refusals to increase public funding, the threat of privatization or the loss of a television franchise); and journalists who cannot be intimidated have been summarily sacked, jailed or even killed.

However, a qualifying note needs to be introduced at this point. The radical media literature is bedevilled by a simplifying 'system logic' which assumes that state-controlled media serve the state, and business-controlled media serve business. This ignores or downplays countervailing influences. Privately owned media need to maintain audience interest in order to be profitable; they have to sustain public legitimacy in order to avoid societal retribution; and they can be influenced by the professional concerns of their staff. All these factors potentially work against the subordination of private media to the political commitments and economic interests of their shareholders. Likewise, the long-term interest of public broadcasters is best served by developing a reputation for independence that wins public trust, and sustains political support beyond the duration of the current administration. In many liberal democracies, the ideal of broadcasting independence is not only pursued by broadcasting staff for professional reasons, but is supported also by the political elite partly out of self-interest. Senior politicians of all major parties know they they will need access to broadcasting when they are voted out of office.

The autonomy of publicly regulated broadcasting is also supported by a system of checks and balances. While this varies from country to country, it usually includes in western Europe a number of the following features: the constitutional guarantee of freedom of expression; formal rules requiring broadcasting impartiality, enshrined in law; civic society or all-party representation on broadcasting authorities; funding by licence fee rather than direct government grant; competition between broadcasters for audiences; diversity of broadcasting organizational structures; and the devolution of authority within them (Ostergaard 1997; Humphreys 1996; Raboy 1996). The ultimate safeguard of broadcasting independence is that it has generally the support of the public.

Since these qualifying arguments run counter to the tenor of conventional radical accounts (such as those provided by Herman and Chomsky 1998 and Herman 1998), perhaps they should be exemplified by two miniaturized case studies. The first concerns journalistic resistance to corporate control. In April 1984, the chief executive of Lonrho, Tiny Rowland, intervened to protect the corporation's profitable investments in Zimbabwe. One of Lonrho's many newspapers, the London-based *Observer*, was about to report that the Zimbabwe army had massacred civilians in the country's dissident Matabele province. Lonrho's relations with the Zimbabwe government were already strained since Lonrho had backed the losing party in the recent election. The corporation had also been widely attacked in Zimbabwe as a relic of colonial power. Anxious to avoid further trouble, Rowland told his editor, Donald Trelford, not to run the story. Trelford refused and was backed by the paper's staff and independent directors. The dispute at the paper was leaked, and Rowland was widely criticized. He hastily backed down to avoid further public censure (Curran and Seaton 1997).

The second example illustrates journalistic resistance to state control. In 1988,

Thames Television, part of the British publicly regulated ITV network, made a programme, *Death on the Rock*, which reported in effect that a British army Special Air Service (SAS) unit had unlawfully killed unarmed members of an Irish Republican Army (IRA) active-service unit in Gibraltar. The programme also claimed that the official version of this event was misleading. The Foreign Secretary, Sir Geoffrey Howe, asked the commercial television regulatory authority, the Independent Broadcasting Authority (IBA), to veto the programme on the technical grounds that it would prejudice the official inquest that was due to take place. The IBA refused, and the programme was transmitted on 28 April 1988.

This was not the end of the saga. The government made known its anger at the decision. Its displeasure was echoed by much of the press, which lambasted the programme as bad and irresponsible journalism. 'TV slur on the SAS' was the *Daily Star*'s headline (29 April 1988). 'Fury over SAS "trial by TV"', reported the *Daily Mail* (29 April), which also published a television review calling the programme 'a woefully one-sided look at the killings'. The *Sunday Times* ran several articles which impugned the reliability of the programme's main witness, and cast doubt on the programme's claims.

This public flak failed to intimidate. Thames Television ordered an internal enquiry which hailed the programme as 'trenchant' and its makers as 'painstaking and persistent' (Windlesham and Rampton 1989: 143). The programme was given subsequently the top annual (BAFTA) award of the television industry in a symbolic act which deliberately snubbed both the government and the Conservative press. Thames Television then rubbed salt in political wounds by repeating the programme in May 1991, as an example of outstanding journalism.

But if these two examples illustrate professional aspirations for independence in both the public and private sectors, it should be remembered that these aspirations are not equally supported. The political culture of liberal democracies is very alert to the threat posed by governments to the freedom of public media, but is much less concerned about the threat posed by shareholders to the freedom of private media. Government ministers are attacked if they seek to dictate the contents of public television, yet proprietors are not exposed to equivalent criticism if they seek to determine the editorial line of their media properties. Elaborate checks and balances have been established in old liberal democracies to shield public media from the state. Yet, equivalent checks have not yet been developed to shield private media from their corporate owners.[6]

In sum, an unthinking, catechistic subscription to the free market is not the best way to secure fearless media watchdogs that serve democracy. Instead, practical steps should be taken to shield the media from the corruptions generated by *both* the political and economic systems.

Settling of accounts

Since the discussion so far has followed a number of twists and turns, it may be helpful to reiterate here our central claim. The conception of the media as a democratic watchdog is important but it does not legitimate, as neo-liberals claim, a free market system. This is for a number of reasons. Market pressures can lead to the downgrading of investigative journalism in favour of entertainment, while corporate ties can subdue critical surveillance of corporate power. More importantly, controllers of market-based media are not necessarily independent. They can muzzle media surveillance of government because they are government supporters or because they want to secure a regulatory favour. The market, in short, does not guarantee critical scrutiny of either public or private power.

Pressures can also be brought to bear to silence media watchdogs with links to the state. However, elaborate defences have been developed to prevent ministers from intimidating public broadcasters in contrast to the much weaker protections that have been constructed against shareholder abuse.

INFORMATION AND DEBATE

The watchdog perspective of the media is defensive. It is about protecting the public by preventing those with power from overstepping the mark. However, the media can also be viewed in a more expansive way, in liberal theory, as an agency of information and debate which facilitate the functioning of democracy.

In this view, free media brief the electorate, and assist voters to make an informed choice at election time. Independent media also provide a channel of communication between government and governed. Above all, the media provide a forum of debate in which people can identify problems, propose solutions, reach agreement and guide the public direction of society.

All this can best be achieved in the liberal view through the free market. The freedom of the market allows any one to publish an opinion. This extends participation in public debate, and ensures that all significant points of view are aired. It also means that people are exposed through market competition to contrary views and sources of information. This makes for good judgement and wise government. As the American jurist, Oliver Holmes, declared in a much quoted statement, 'the best test of truth is the power of the thought to get itself accepted in the competition of the market . . .' (cited in Barron 1975: 320).

As with the watchdog perspective, there is much to commend this approach. It assumes that democracies need informed and participant citizens to manage their common affairs. It also believes that public debate is more likely to produce rational and just outcomes if it takes account of different views and interests. At the heart of this approach – what is called in the United States the republican tradition – is an admirable stress on the need for civic information, public participation, robust debate and active self-determination.

There is, however, one flaw at its centre: its wide-eyed belief in the free market. Its espousal of neo-liberalism undermines what it sets out to achieve in four different ways.

First, the high costs of market entry curtail the freedom to publish. When liberal press theory was first framed, it really was the case that groups of ordinary people could set up their trestle-table, so to speak, in the main market-place of ideas because it was relatively cheap to publish. As noted in Chapter 3, great national newspapers were launched in 1830s Britain with minimal outlays. Now at least £20 million is needed to establish a new national broadsheet, and more than this to establish a new popular cable television channel in Britain.[7] While there are still some media sectors where costs are low, these tend to be marginalized or have low audiences. A lone website on the internet is virtually free but it does not have the same communicative power as a mass television channel or newspaper. The town square of the public sphere has been rendered inaccessible, in short, by the rise in the investment and operating costs of the mass media.

Second, the free market undermines the provision of information. The dynamics of this process are explored by Curran, Douglas and Whannel (1980) in relation to the British press. Pioneer market research undertaken for publishers over a forty-year period showed that human-interest stories consistently obtained the highest readership scores because they appealed to all categories of reader, whereas public affairs had only a minority following concentrated among certain social groups. Competitive market pressure to maximize sales resulted in public affairs coverage giving way to more universally popular human interest content. Indeed, by the late 1970s, public affairs accounted for less than 20 per cent of the editorial content of the national popular press. A comparable process is now developing in mass television. In Britain, for example, news was shunted in 1999 to 6.30p.m. and 11p.m. slots on the main commercial channel, ITV, to give a clear run for top-rated programmes. It required countervailing pressure from the regulator (Independent Television Commission) for the news to be returned in 2000 to its prime slot, on some days.

Third, the free market restricts participation in public debate. It generates information-rich media for elites, and information-poor media for the general public. The result, in many countries, is a polarization between prestige and mass newspapers. Something rather similar is now developing in the public space being constructed around the emergent Euro-polity. Only the European elite is being specifically catered for by high-information newspapers, magazines and television channels (Schlesinger 1999). While this recurring pattern reflects social inequalities, the market confirms rather than challenges these.

Fourth, the market undermines intelligent and rational debate. Market-oriented media tend to generate information that is simplified, personalized, decontextualized, with a stress on action rather than process, visualisation rather than abstraction, stereotypicality rather than human complexity (Epstein 1973; Inglis 1990; Iyengar 1991; Gitlin 1994; Hallin 1994; Liebes 1998). This is a by-product of processing information as a commodity. The first inkling of this came as a terrible shock to liberals like Matthew Arnold (1970) who reacted with horrified amazement to the market-oriented 'new journalism' of the 1880s. More than a century later, we have rather less reason to be surprised.

Ironically, successful public service broadcasting systems come closest to embodying the liberal ideal of informed, rational and inclusive public debate.⟩ They give priority to public affairs programmes, reasoned discussion and (in some systems) pluralistic representation. This is because they put the needs of democracy before those of profit, and are supported in this by public law and regulation. However, this approach implies an intellectual adjustment. It means abandoning seventeenth-century fears of the leviathan state (when absolutist, arbitary authority was viewed with good reason as an ever-present threat) and recognizing that the democratic state, elected by the people, can extend the sphere of information and debate in the interests of democratic self-rule.

VOICE OF THE PEOPLE

Representing people to authority is, in liberal theory, the third key democratic function of the media. In one version, this is the culmination of the media's mission. After having briefed the people and staged a debate, the media relay the public consensus that results from this debate to government. In this way, the government is supervised by the people between elections. As Thomas Carlyle (1907: 164) famously proclaimed, the press is 'a power, a branch of government with an inalienable weight in law-making', derived from the will of the people.

The introduction of opinion polls took some of the wind out of this 'fourth estate' argument. More often now, the claim is made simply that the media speak for the people, and represent their views and interests in the public domain. The assumption is that 'the broad shape and nature of the press is ultimately determined by no one but its readers' (Whale 1977: 85) because the press must respond in a competitive market-place to what people want, and express their views and interests. As a consequence the privately owned press – and, by extension, the privately owned broadcasting system – speak up for the people.

This argument is advanced so frequently that it is necessary to explain in some detail why it is fundamentally flawed.

Market failures

The influence of the consumer is reactive rather than proactive. It is exerted through choosing between what is available in the market-place. The extent of real market choice is consequently central to how much power the consumer has. If choice is curtailed, then consumer influence is correspondingly diminished.

Up until the early 1980s, consumer choice was strongly constrained by media oligopoly. Indeed, the press in many countries degenerated into networks of local monopolies controlled by expanding chains (Høyer, Hadenius and Weibull 1975; Commission of the European Communities 1992; Sanchez-Tabernero et al. 1993; Bagdikian 1997). Radio and television offered only a few competing channels. The media sectors that first became globalized – news agencies, film and music – were dominated by a relatively small number of companies (Herman and McChesney 1997).

This stable, controlled media landscape was transformed in the 1980s and 1990s by the diffusion of new communications technologies. Fibre-optic cable, high-powered satellite, digitalization, personal computers and the internet offered new communications 'pipelines' into the home. Some also crossed national frontiers. This expanded the range of media products, established new niche markets and introduced new sources of competition. For a time it seemed as if oligopolistic market control would be ended, and the consumer would be greatly empowered.

The response of leading media producers to this threat was a well-judged combination of political lobbying and market adaptation. They pressed for a relaxation of anti-monopoly controls by arguing initially that the increase in the number of media outlets diminished the need for regulation, and subsequently that concentration was necessary in order to compete effectively in the global market. The success that rewarded their efforts in many countries (including, crucially, the United States) enabled them to embark on an extended acquisition spree supported by generous bank credit. Out of market fragmentation there developed a new pattern of multimedia concentration.

In the United States, film and television companies merged to establish a new axis for large media corporations, around which other media interests were grouped. The key landmarks in this change were the pioneer coupling of the film major Twentieth Century Fox and Metromedia (television) under Rupert Murdoch in the mid-1980s, followed by Viacom's acquisition of Paramount and Blockbuster in 1994, Disney's purchase of the ABC television network in 1995, and the merger of Time Warner (itself the result of a 1989 merger) with Turner Broadcasting in 1996, among other marriages of convenience (Herman and McChesney 1997; Tunstall and Machin 1999). Almost certainly a new portent of things to come was the merger of the telecommunications giant, AT&T, with the cable television giant, TCI, in 1998, and that of Time Warner with America OnLine (AOL) in 2000. This presaged the arrival of telecommunications and net companies as two further players in the cumulative process that is reshaping the Amercian media system.

The number of corporations dominating the United States media shrank from an estimated fifty in 1983 to ten in 1997, with another twelve having major positions in particular media markets (Bagdikian 1983 and 1997). These megacorporations typically control film and television production companies, a 'bouquet' of television channels delivered through different systems, and a portfolio of media and leisure interests (such as books, newspapers, magazines, cinemas, music labels, sports teams and even theme parks). In addition, these corporations tend to be bankers and distributors for so-called 'independent' media companies, and are involved in multiple joint ventures in e-commerce, digital services and other new communications applications. Their activities now conform to a classic oligopolistic pattern. They compete against each other; sell to each other; and have co-ownership, revenue-sharing, co-production and co-purchasing deals with each other. This enables them to increase profitability through economies of scale and scope, share the cost of risk-taking and above all limit competition. While this is good for large media companies, it limits the effective power of consumers through an informal system of market regulation (Tunstall and Machin 1999).

What happened in the United States was duplicated, with national variations, in numerous other countries. In Britain, where there is almost no film industry left, the main new axis for media concentration is a partnership between press and television, around which other media interests are grouped. Once again, Murdoch led the way by ducking and weaving through anti-monopoly controls. He acquired rival titles to become the biggest press publisher in Britain, and to this he added a pioneer satellite television system (which became a British monopoly through the BSkyB merger in 1990), and the leading digital television service, SkyDigital, launched in 1998. During the 1990s, major independent television companies (some with press interests) merged to become three, owning all but five of the UK's sixteen regional licences, as well as cable television and ITV digital channels. Although the trend towards media concentration has been rapid in Britain, it is still well behind that in Germany where the merging of press and television businesses, among others, began earlier (Herman and McChesney 1997).

If one defensive response to market fragmentation was corporate concentration, another was attempted global conquest. The introduction of new ways of delivering television programmes provided an opportunity to break into formerly protected national markets, while privatisation policies led to the sale of state media assets. However, this global expansionist strategy ran into mounting resistance. New centres of media production, from Taiwan to Brazil, developed to challenge the might of the transational 'majors', mostly with headquarters in the United States (Sinclair *et al.* 1996). In many countries, television audiences showed a strong preference for their national product. The adaptive response of transnational media corporations to these setbacks was, increasingly, to 'think global but act local'. They formed alliances with leading national media corporations, in this way strengthening the forces of national oligopoly. They brought to these alliances formidable weapons: additional financial resources, cross-media promotion, popular production formulae, accumulations of stock and often a global distribution network.

The first key factor limiting consumer influence is, thus, an increase in the concentration of media ownership, and of the resources that giant media corporations are able to bring to bear in limiting competition and managing demand. The second factor, already referred to, is high market entry costs. This is interpreted in traditional liberal analysis in a restricted way as tending to exclude insights that might enhance public enlightenment. This overlooks its key significance as an invisible form of censorship which excludes social groups with limited financial resources from competing. The result is a market system which is not genuinely open to all, and which tends to be controlled by right-wing leadership. A long list of right-wing media tycoons – for example, the Australian/ American Rupert Murdoch, the Canadian Conrad Black, the German Leo Kirch, or the Italian Silvio Berlusconi – is matched, at best, only by pro-market social democrats.

Right-wing media controllers are subject to a number of constraints. This is illustrated by the career of Rupert Murdoch. He has always been willing to rein in his ideological commitments in order to gain regulatory favours from politicians, to conform to state-imposed impartiality rules, or even to woo audiences with subversive material (such as the television series, *The Simpsons*), if the situation required it. But informing his last thirty years, and indeed giving to it a principled continuity, has been a steadfast determination to promote, *wherever possible*, right-wing values (Munster 1985; Leapman 1983; Shawcross 1993; Chenoweth 2001). As one of his closest lieutenants, Andrew Neil, records: 'Rupert expects his papers to stand broadly for what he believes: a combination of right-wing repub-licanism from America mixed with undiluted Thatcherism from Britain. . . . ' (Neil 1996: 164), a view echoed by other senior Murdoch employees (Evans 1983; Giles 1986). What has assisted Murdoch, and fellow ideologues, is that the link between media and public opinion that used to exist has been weakened by the media's increasing orientation towards entertainment. Increasingly, also, audiences seek from the media enjoyment rather representation. This has increased the relative freedom of media controllers to pursue their private agendas as long as these do not alienate audiences.

The third limitation on consumer influence derives from the operation of the market. High sales or ratings produce not only large receipts but also major economies of scale (that is, the lowering of unit costs by spreading the initial outlay on the 'first copy'). This tends to privilege provision for the majority at the expense of minorities. While niche provision has increased during the last two decades, this has tended to be geared more towards affluent than low-income groups because the former have more money to spend. This distortion is further accentuated by advertising funding of terrestial television, magazines and news-papers, which exerts a gravitational pull towards upscale, profitable audiences (Curran 1986; Baker 1994; D'Acci 1994). In short, market democracy is a universe where individuals do not have equal votes.

The claim that market expansion has led to more consumer choice thus needs to be viewed critically. More media outlets does not necessarily mean 'more of the same', as some left-wing critics maintain. But what it does mean is that the expan-sion of choice is always *pre-structured* by the conditions of competition. In a contemporary context, this means provision for unequal consumers, in oligopolistic markets where entry is restricted. The constraints this imposes are well illustrated by the development of American television and the British press.

American television is the most mature, multi-channel market system in the world. Instead of being dominated, as in the 1970s, by three organisations, it is now dominated by six. Whereas before it offered mainly formulaic network programmes for mass audiences, now it offers an enormous range of specialist programmes, including stand-up alternative comedy, Christian fundamentalism, interactive shopping, Hollywood classics, sitcom classics, twenty-four hour news, differentiated sports coverage, new American films, children's cartoons, history programmes, natural science programmes, classical opera, Korean soap opera and much else besides. But while there has been a spectacular increase in the genre variety of American television, there has not been a corresponding increase in its *ideological* range (Entman 1989; Kellner 1990; Croteau and Hoynes 1997; McChesney 1999).

The British press gives the appearance of being one of the most competitive in the world. In contrast to the monopolistic local structure of most press systems, it has a dominant national press boasting no less than twenty (general) daily and Sunday titles.[8] This number was significantly boosted by the adoption of 'new' printing technology in the mid-1980s. However, appearances can be deceptive. Just five groups controlled over four-fifths of national newspaper circulation in 2000. No new national newspaper launched in the last eighty years has been able to stay independent. Moreover, the ideological range of this press has contracted over the last thirty years, while remaining generally more right-wing than its public. During the 1980s and early 1990s, the Conservative press's share of national daily circulation was some 50 per cent more than that of the Conservative party in general elections (Seymour-Ure 1996: 217–18). The national press has reproduced a remarkably narrow arc of opinion, indeed sometimes only one opinion, in its editorials on a range of issues (Curran and Seaton 1997).

Comparative perspective

If privately owned media are not automatically the voice of the people, who then do they represent? The answer to this question depends partly upon the configuration of power to which the media are linked.

In authoritarian corporatist societies, political power tends to be monopolized by the ruling party, and maintained through a clientelist system of patronage that binds together different social groups within the structure of the party and the state. The 'will of the people' represented by the media tends to be defined by the ruling party. This broadly corresponds to the situation in contemporary Malaysia (Main 2000) and the one that prevailed until recently in Korea (Park *et al.* 2000), Taiwan (Lee 2000) and Mexico (Hallin 2000). In these societies, the media can be influenced politically more by the interaction of factions within the dominant party than by consumers. According to Hallin, the liberalizing changes that occurred in late 1980s Mexican television, for example, were due to pressure not so much from the general public as from a determined reformist faction within the ruling party which pushed the old guard controlling commercial television 'kicking and screaming' into a more pluralistic mould (Hallin 2000: 103).

In liberal corporatist societies, a consensus is formed through consultation between government and organized interests. The system is 'liberal' in the sense that political parties tend to alternate, the armed forces are firmly under the

control of civil authority and freedoms are not undermined by coercive measures. But within this system, the consensus of society tends to be defined by the
major players; to prevail whichever party is in power; and to be echoed by the
media. Essentially, this defines the system of power that operates in most northern European countries, although as Dahlgren (2000) notes in an acute analysis
of Sweden, the balance of advantage within this corporatist system is shifting in
favour of economic power.

In still other societies, power is organized in a more fluid and less stable way. To
take a maverick example, in post-communist Russia an oligarchy established a
leading position in the economy, a stranglehold over national media and a strong
presence within the state (McNair 2000). This power group directed the main
commercial television channels, under its control, to join public broadcasting in
providing partisan support for its chosen candidate, Boris Yeltsin, and helped to
secure his re-election despite his obvious frailty. However, the oligarchy was challenged by Yeltsin's successor, President Putin, and despite being reconstituted no
longer holds the sway that it once did.

Thus, one key variable influencing media representations is the way in which
power is organized within the political system. Another significant influence is the
degree to which the prevailing power network coheres. If disagreements develop
within it, these are generally reproduced in the media. In such situations, the
media can operate in a way that seems to exemplify liberal theory. Tip-offs from
rival, elite groups can trigger investigative journalism; their conflicts can generate
media debate; and the consensus arising from this debate can be relayed to government. But in these situations, the initiative for change usually comes from
within the structure of power rather than from the people.

However, another important contextual influence is the extent to which the
central network of power is able to maintain control over mediated debate. To
pick up on arguments developed in Chapter five, an energized civil society, well-
developed alternative networks of communication, professionally oriented or radically oriented media staffs, and consumer pressure can combine to detach part of
the media from the prevailing system of power. In this situation (in important
respects resembling that in early nineteenth-century Britain),[9] part of the media
can indeed represent critical public opinion and became an emancipatory force.

This is a necessarily condensed alternative view to that of private media as
tribunes of the public. What it stresses is the need to take account of the full range
of influences shaping the media, in social contexts that are different and cannot be
reduced to a single, liberal economistic interpretation of the media as the voice of
the consumer.

Democratic agency

So far we have provided a critical exposition of liberal theories of media and
democracy, and argued both that they are conceptually flawed and that their
objectives cannot be realised through a free market programme. Two other

aspects of the liberal tradition need to be reviewed: its tacit understanding of the democratic system and its idealist legacy.

Liberal thought about the democratic role of the media has been rejuvenated by the German political theorist, Jürgen Habermas. From his early work (Habermas 1989 [1962]) has been extrapolated a normative model of the media and the public sphere (Scannell 1989; Hallin 1994; Corner 1995; Dahlgren 1995, among others). This conceives the public sphere as a 'space' where access to information affecting the public good is widely available, where discussion is free of domination and where all those participating in public debate do so on an equal basis. Within this public sphere, people collectively determine through rational argument the way in which they wish to see society develop, and this shapes in turn government policy. The media facilitate this process by providing an arena of public debate, and by reconstituting private citizens as a public body in the form of public opinion.

One difficulty with this seemingly engaging argument is that it clings generally to an archaic understanding of polity developed in the late eighteenth century. What it fails to recognize is that in the twenty-first century people are represented primarily through political parties, interest groups and the myriad structures of civil society. These (rather than individual citzens represented by the media) are the principal building blocks of contemporary liberal democracy. A view of the democratic role of the media needs to be related, in other words, to the collective and institutional forms of the modern political system.

Another limitation of the traditional Habermasian conception of the public sphere is that it is viewed as a single entity which is assumed to be co-extensive with the nation state. This ignores the reality of multiple public spheres – what John Keane (1996) calls micro-public spheres, meso-public spheres and macro-public spheres – which are both smaller and larger than the nation state (cf. Morley 2000). A further, much reiterated line of criticism is that Habermas's conception of rationality fails to engage adequately with issues of exclusion and control (Calhoun 1992; Neght and Kluge 1993; Thompson 1995; Garnham 2000; and Morley 2000, among others).

Much of the media studies debate triggered by Habermas surprisingly goes no further than his first work which was published in German in 1962, but was not translated into English until 1989. This early work contrasted a period of rational public life in the eighteenth and early nineteenth centuries (the inspiration of neo-Habermasian models of the media) with its debasement in the subsequent period.[10] Habermas now offers a more developed model of the media within the contemporary democratic media system (Habermas 1996 [1992]), as a considered response to criticism of his early work.[11]

In place of his early, broad brush-stroked account of twentieth-century 'refeudalization', Habermas presents a very different version of the workings of the contemporary political system. At the core of liberal democracy, argues Habermas, are government, the civil service, judiciary, parliament, political parties, elections and party competition. This centre has, on its inner perimeter, a number of bodies, such as regulatory agencies, with powers delegated by parliament or government. Outside this core system (corresponding to conventional definitions of the state) is the outer periphery of society made up of two sorts of organization that can be broadly categorized as 'customers' (business associations, labour unions and private organizations) and 'suppliers' (voluntary associations, churches, new social movements and public interest groups). According to Habermas, a healthy democratic system is one in which concerns are transmitted from the civil-social periphery to the political centre for deliberative debate and appropiate action.

Habermas has also changed his understanding of the public sphere. Instead of viewing it as an aggregation of individuals gathered together as a single public, he now views it as 'a network for communicating information and points of view' which connects the private world of everyday experience to the political system (Habermas 1996: 360). This network is multiple rather unitary. It 'branches out into a multitude of overlapping international, national, regional, local, and subcultural arenas' (Habermas 1996: 379).

What is also new in Habermas's reformulation is the pivotal importance that he attaches to an *organized* form of civil society. The groupings of civil society, in his normative account, should prevent the public sphere from being subverted by power. They also draw attention to and interpret social problems, propose solutions and organize in a way that ensures that they get listened to. They are assisted, in this model, by the media which should transmit concerns from the periphery, generate a public debate coalescing into 'topically specified *public opinions*' (Habermas 1996: 360, original emphasis), and mount sustained pressure for a considered response from the political system. However what actually happens in practice depends crucially, according to Habermas, on the level of activity of civil society. When civil society is 'at rest', influence tends to flow from administrative and social power at the core of the political system to the periphery. But when civil society is energized, 'the balance of power between society and the political system then shifts' (Habermas 1996: 379).

Habermas's reformulation (which is part of a larger work on a 'proceduralist' theory of law and democracy) deserves to be widely debated. Yet despite its manifest improvements, this version still offers a largely nation-centred understanding of democracy which ignores the impact of globalization. In reality, the deliberative responses of the parliamentary complex to the impulse-generating periphery – to use Habermas's terminology – are constrained by the responses of global financial markets and the conditions set by global regulation.[12] While Habermas makes a hopeful reference to an 'emerging global public sphere' (Habermas 1992: 444), it is not something that he develops. In other words, he does not explain how global forces impinge on his understanding of the national democratic process.

How then should we attempt to make sense, in a preliminary way, of the links between global civil society, global regulation, national government and the mass media? Organizations like the World Trade Organization, World Bank,

International Monetary Fund and the United Nations constitute an emergent tier of international regulation. It is accountable, in a very imperfect way, to national governments and national publics. In addition, it is also subject to the scrutiny and influence of public interest groups operating on an transnational basis that have made a growing impact through appeals to the international community in a number of areas: (most notably human rights, environmental protection, relief of world poverty, world peace and global market regulation.) In principle, the communication system should enable international, national and other publics to exert increased pressure on the tier of global governance to operate in the general global interest (rather than privileging the interests of OECD countries and multinational business).

However, one enduring problem is that an underdeveloped global communication system is failing to provide an adequate conduit of communication between relevant publics and global governance. The internet is now an important international channel of communication for activists, and played a significant part for example in the mobilization of 'anti-globalization' protests in 1999–2001. But there are very few international media linking civil society organizations to a general international public. For this reason, Amnesty International relies mainly on national media to reach an international public, and communicates its concerns through press releases and other material produced in numerous languages. A number of international aid agencies distribute video news releases to television organizations in the West, in the hope that moving pictures (in both senses of the word) transcend national barriers. Greenpeace in the mid-1990s communicated via satellite unedited footage of its protests to television organizations around the globe (Manning 2001: 196). However, these adaptive strategies have not overcome the obstacle to effective global communication presented by the national partitioning of the global media system. The introversion of national media makes it difficult to gain attention for international debates, while the national cultures in which national media are steeped (Lee *et al.* 2000) makes shared perspectives and common positions more difficult to achieve within international civil society.

A second key problem relates to the way in which the global inequality of power distorts international debate. A ground-breaking study looked at television coverage, in three countries, of the historic Reagan–Gorbachev summits in 1985–8, towards the end of the Cold War (Hallin 1994). It found that reporting was defined by national interests and perspectives, and failed to forge a common and reciprocal dialogue within an international public sphere. It also discovered that peace campaigners and other representatives of global civil society were generally excluded, while the reactions of other nations to these summits tended to be ignored. The leaders of the then two super-powers, and their entourages, tended to monopolize television coverage and discussion.

Similarly, the way in which British television reported in 2001 the building of the international coalition against terrorism, and the war in Afghanistan, was very strongly influenced by state office holders in two countries, Britain and the United States. This may well be part of a wider pattern, to be found elsewhere. In short, the mediation of international public life raises the same problems of restricted access and definition as the mediation of national public life.

Idealist legacy

A critical re-evaluation of liberal theory needs also to rethink its idealist assumptions. Some of these need to be jettisoned, while others ought to be defended in a revised form.

The traditional justification for media pluralism – that truth will automatically confound error in open debate – now seems implausible. As Chafee (1983: 294) wryly puts it, 'I can no longer think of open discussion as operating like an electric mixer. . . . Run it a little while and truth will rise to the top with the dregs of error going down to the bottom.' His reservations were based on distortions in the distribution of information and the subjective element in making judgements. This last point has been highlighted by research emphasizing the highly selective ways in which people assimilate information and form opinions (Graber 1988; Corner et al. 1990; Neuman et al. 1992). To these misgivings should be added a further reservation: the 'best' argument in the sense of the one best supported by evidence and logic does not necessarily prevail against arguments that have more publicity and are more congenial to those in power. Yet, the liberal idea that media should offer a plurality of opposed opinion still seems essential, and defensible, for other reasons. It promotes not 'truth' but more equitable outcomes informed by awareness of opposed positions and interests. It also fosters a tradition of civic independence that comes from robust public debate, and embodies the democratic tradition of freedom and choice.

This raises the question of how media plurality should be conceptualized. The traditional liberal approach, still dominant in American jurisprudence, is to equate it with the free trade of ideas. This has given rise to the yardstick which measures media pluralism in terms of the number of competing media outlets or distribution of market shares. The assumption is that if there is a significant level of competition, there is no lack of pluralism. This is a view regularly endorsed in American legal judgements (Horwitz 1991; Baker 1997a), and in the early 1990s by the European Commission (CEC) (1992 and 1994a).

This ignores *where* opinions come from. Indeed, usually absent from this market competition approach is a recognition that ideas and systems of representation are part of the discursive arsenal which competing groups use to advance their interests. This argument can be pitched in a simple and rudimentary way in terms of party agendas. Political parties on the right tend to emphasize tax, law and order, and defence, while those on the left tend to stress welfare provision and employment, because these are areas where they are traditionally perceived to be strong by voters. Rival political parties consequently vie with each other at election time to get television to make their 'issues' the dominant ones of election coverage.

A comparable but more complex process of contestation takes place between rival social groups at the level of ideology. Different ways of making sense of society, different codes and explanatory contexts, different premises and chains of association privilege some social interests as against others. The media's role is never solely confined to imparting information: it always involves arbitrating between the discursive frameworks of rival groups. Which frameworks are included or excluded matter because over time it can affect collective opinion and, indirectly, the distribution of resources and life chances in society.

For this reason, media pluralism cannot be equated just with competition. It should be conceived as a contest that is *open* to different social groups to enter. One implication of this is that media pluralism has sometimes to be defended through structural reform that widens social access to public debate. Anti-monopoly controls that prevent market domination by one company is not enough if the market as a whole is rigged by high entry costs in favour of one class or sectional interest.

Another implication is that conflict and difference need to be embraced as integral elements of pluralist democracy. In idealist liberal argument, conflicts are resolved through good communication and good will. The assumption is that people have an underlying harmony of interest, and should be able therefore to identify the common good through the application of reason. From this is derived the argument that media debate should culminate in agreement that is relayed to authority. However, this approach ignores the existence of conflicts of interest between social groups that cannot be dissolved magically through discussion. It also pays too little attention to the ways in which material interests can be cloaked in altruism. Indeed, the reasonableness that this liberalism extols can be used to exclude the 'irrational' (for example, 'emotional' women or the 'loony left'), producing a 'reason-based' debate that reaches conclusions that are conveniently congenial to 'civilized' people. This idealist tradition is in fact nothing like as benign as it appears to be. However, it is necessary to retain a commitment in principle to truth, 'rightness' and sincerity of intention in order to engage in a meaningful and reciprocal debate, and to cling to some notion of a general interest as a shared aspiration.[13]

Another issue raised by the liberal inheritance is the democratic status of media entertainment. The conventional liberal approach excludes this from its understanding of the media's democratic functioning on the grounds that entertainment is not part of rational exchange, and is not concerned with public issues debated in a political arena. Both objections seem increasingly threadbare.

Collective self-management does not only take place in the bounded world of politics. It also takes the form of social regulation achieved through shared understandings of what is acceptable and unacceptable in social behaviour, registered in social interactions expressing approval or disapproval. These understanding are debated, affirmed and revised through collective dialogue conducted partly through media entertainment. For example, much human interest news is about deviancy, about where boundaries are or should be drawn, and about what happens to those who flout society's moral rules (Ericson *et al.* 1987). It has the same normative and regulatory dimension within a complex, differentiated society as gossip in traditional village communities.

The exclusion of entertainment as being outside the political domain also seems wrong on several counts. First, media fiction offers cognitive maps of reality, and furnishes social understandings which have political implications. For example, whether crime is regularly portrayed in television drama, as arising primarily from innate evil or from a social context has a bearing potentially on attitudes towards law and order. Second, media entertainment is bound up with discussion of social values and identities (McGuigan 1996), which strongly influence political positions and allegiances. Third, media entertainment is an important forum of discussion about race and gender relations, single parenthood and sexual minorities, all areas which are subject to public legislation or regulation (Geraghty 1995; Goldsmiths Media Group 2000). Fourth, entertainment (and in particular popular music) is an important way in which disempowered groups are able to register their opposition to dominant structures and ideologies (Hebdige 1979; Gelder and Thornton 1996). Rap music, in the words of Chuck D (formerly of the group Public Enemy), is 'the CNN black people never had' (cited in Cross 1993: 108).

The debate about the political status of entertainment has found a focus in evaluations of television talk shows (Livingstone and Lunt 1994; Dahlgren 1995; Shattuc 1997; Morley 2000; Murdock 2000b, among others). In one corner, defenders argue that they promote empathy and understanding; enable ordinary people (and in particular working-class women) to define public discourse; and introduce important but previously neglected issues, like child abuse and wife-battering, for public debate. In the other corner, critics argue that talk shows elevate irrationality; turn ordinary people into performers in freak shows; and imply that politics is only personal. These arguments need to be related to specific talk shows since they differ. But in general, champions of the genre have so far made the stronger case.

But if entertainment should be recognized as a positive part of the media's contribution to the democratic process, traditionalist concerns are not all misplaced. Soap opera can extend democratic insight and understanding, but it is not an ideal way of debating the relative merits of alternative policy options. An entertainment-only diet displacing public information and political debate is a recipe for mass passivity and elite control, something that is welcomed by a particular style of paternalistic leadership. As Emilio Azcarraga, head of Mexico's main commercial television network, memorably observed in 1991: 'Mexico is a country of a modest, very fucked class, which will never stop being fucked. Television has an obligation to bring diversion to these people . . .' (cited in McChesney 1998: 17). People who are informed and active participants in civil society are a much more formidable and less biddable force than those who are only 'active' at the level of consumption. The disadvantaged who 'fight back' through cultural subversion of popular entertainment are, in the absence of concerted action in the political domain, engaged in seeking an essentially 'magical' solution to their social situation. At some level, public information and political involvement are the prerequisites of exerting collective influence for change. In the succinct words of the American political theorist, Alexander Meiklejohn (1983: 276): 'self-government is a nonsense unless the "self" which governs is able and determined to make its will effective'.

Prioritizing new objectives

If the conventional liberal approach has a number of flaws, how might it be replaced with something better?[14] In addition to retaining traditional liberal objectives – watchdog oversight, information, debate and representation – we should also foreground two objectives that tend not to be featured in traditional liberal analysis. The first is to facilitate the expression of conflict and difference; the second is to assist social conciliation.

A democratic media system should both enable opposed or separate groups to express themselves effectively,[15] and aid a process of communal understanding and equitable compromise. Elites tend to manage society in a way that serves their interests, and to present this as being in everyone's interest. It is desirable therefore that groups outside the structure of privilege should have the media resources to question prevailing ideological representation, explore where their own group interest lies, and be able to present alternative perspectives. However, it is also important that conflicts of identity and interest do not become embedded in endemic social hatred, and that the pursuit of group interest is tempered by concern for the general interest and the claims of others. Mutualism should coexist with freedom and equality as general societal objectives.

Underlying this twin-track approach is a hope but not a prescription. The hope is that tolerance of deep inequality, based on habituation, will be replaced by a more egalitarian society founded on consent; that a managed society will be replaced by a republic of unbiddable citizens; and that democratic political control will be restored over increasingly unaccountable economic power. But there is no way of knowing how a better media-resourced pluralism might develop within the context of representative democracy. Different hopes can be nurtured and pursued within the same electoral rules.

The implications of this approach can be outlined first in general terms. Its starting point is that the media are not a single institution with a common democratic purpose. Rather, different media should be viewed as having different functions within the democratic system, calling for different kinds of structure and styles of journalism.

One part of the media system should assist social groups to constitute themselves and clarify their objectives (Baker 1998). How their interest as a social group is best served is not something that springs pre-formed into people's consciousness as a consequence of their social circumstances. It needs to be explored through internal group processes of debate.

A democratic media system needs therefore a well-developed, specialist sector, enabling different social groups to debate within their terms of reference issues of social identity, group interest, political strategy and social–moral values. Part of this sector should also aid social groups to organize effectively. There should be activist minority media which assist collective organizations to recruit support; provide an internal channel of communication for their members; and transmit their concerns and policy proposals to a wider public. In other words, the representative role of the media includes helping civil society to be effective.

Above this specialist sector should be a general media sector, which enables different groups in society to come together in a common debate. This should be staged in a form that promotes mutual understanding, and furthers a shared search for solutions. In addition, this general media sector should facilitate democratic procedures for defining agreed aims and regulating conflict. In a national context, this includes informing the electorate about the political choices involved in elections in a way that helps to constitute these as defining moments for collective decision. General media need also to be responsive to public interest group initiatives, and maintain pressure for adequate responses to them from the governmental system.

The pluralistic design of this media system will almost certainly make the attainment of collective agreement more difficult. In most societies, the media are linked to the hierarchy of power, and tend to promote social integration on its terms. An approach that seeks, by contrast, to destabilize this link, and allocate effective communications resources to subordinate and minority groups is liable to promote fissiparous tendencies at a time when general societal ties appear to be weakening. However, general media remain a source of social cohesion, in this model. They will tend to draw people together through the sharing of the same cultural experiences, and reproduce ritualized events that affirm common identities, values and memories (Peters 1989; Dayan and Katz 1992; Liebes and Curran 1998).

What might this media system look like in terms of structure and organization? What kinds of journalism would it foster? What follows is only concerned with the democratic role of the media. It does not consider the generation of pleasure and rewarding cultural experience, which lies outside the terms of references of this analysis. It is therefore only a partial imput to a larger debate about the role and design of the media. But with this qualification in mind, let us consider what concrete form a democratic media system might take.

Towards a working model

The outline that follows may seem to American eyes detached from political reality. But although it does not exist in any country as a single functioning model, it draws upon and composites features derived from the practice of different European countries. Indeed, it is proposed in this form precisely because it works with the grain of what is attainable.

The model can be viewed at a glance in Figure 8.1. It has a core sector, constituted by general interest television channels which reach a mass audience. This is

Figure 8.1 Working model of a democratic media system.

where different individuals and groups come together to engage in a reciprocal debate about the management of society.

This core sector is fed by peripheral media sectors, three of which are intended to facilitate the expression of dissenting and minority views. The *civic* media sector consists of channels of communication linked to organized groups and social networks. The *professional* media sector occupies a space in which professional communicators relate to the public on their own terms, with the minimum of constraint. The *social market* sector subsidises minority media as a way of promoting market diversity and consumer choice. To this is added a conventional *private* sector which relates to the public as consumers, and whose central rationale within the media system is to act as a restraint on the over-entrenchment of minority concerns to the exclusion of majority pleasures.

This media system is organised in different ways, and connects to different segments of society, in order to enhance its diversity. Publicly accountable in multiple ways, it is intended to be broadly representative of society. Above all, its architecture is designed to create spaces for the incubation and communication of opposed viewpoints, and a common space for their mediation. Both the detail and thinking behind this outline are explored further below.

Civic media sector

The civic media sector supports the activist organizations of civil society. These are defined to include political parties as well as new social movements, interest groups and sub-cultural networks. Political parties have a particularly strategic role in liberal democracies as organizations that aggregate interests, distribute

costs, define electoral choices and offer avenues for influencing society as a whole as distinct from promoting single issues. They are badly in need of rejuvenation and, often, democratization. Their decline makes it still more imperative that the other organizations of civil society are effective in voicing the concerns of citizens.

The civic media sector can be viewed analytically as having three main tiers (although these sometimes overlap in practice). The first consists of media, such as party-controlled newspapers or social movement websites, which provide a link between civil society organizations and the wider public. They are generally propagandist, and seek to build support for a partisan perspective and set of objectives. The second tier consists of sub-cultural media, such as gay or lesbian magazines, which relate to a social constituency rather than an organized group. These can have an important 'constitutive' function that facilitates organizational effectiveness: in particular, they can promote a sense of social cohesion and common identity, and clarify values and goals through internal processes of discussion (Gross 1998). The third tier consists of intra-organizational media, such as trade union journals, whose main purpose is in principle to reinforce collective identity, hold leaderships to account to rank-and-file members, assist in the sharing of relevent information and experience, and provide a context for developing new ideas and initiatives.

The civic media sector is in trouble. Party-controlled newspapers have been in decline throughout the western world for a very long time. Many politically aligned magazines have an uncertain future. The intra-organizational media of the civic sector are dwarfed by the products of corporate public relations such as company videos and magazines. Only sub-cultural media, in some areas, are flourishing.

There are two ways in which the civic media sector can be reinvigorated. One strategy is to award grants to the media of civil society organizations, from websites to membership journals, to enhance their communication effectiveness. For example, in Norway the weekly journals of the political parties, immigrant groups and other organizations receive financial support, amounting in 1995 to £2.6 million (Murschetz 1998: 297). The case for doing this is the same as for the public funding of political parties. It is a way of facilitating the working of democracy, and supporting collective organizations as a public interest counterweight to private corporate interests.

The alternative, more ambitious strategy is to assign spectrum, technical facilities and some public funding to civil society organizations linked to the size of their memberships. This would enable civil society to control, through lease and time-share arrangements, radio or television channels, or other technologies of communication. This approach is derived from the Dutch public service broadcasting system which assigns three national public television channels to seven main organizations, and a considerable number of smaller bodies, that are judged to be representative of Dutch society. These are largely ideological, religious or social organizations. Their share of airtime, technical facilities and public funding is determined by membership levels (registered through payment of a fixed membership due or subscription to an organization's television programme guide) (Brants and McQuail 1997; Niewenhuis 1993). While this approach has proved to be unsuccessful as a way of organizing general public service television channels (Curran 2001), it has perhaps more merit as a way of allocating *minority* public communication facilities.

Social market sector

The social market sector consists of minority media, operating within the market, which are supported by the state. Its purpose is to promote media pluralism and diversity of ownership.

One aim of social market policy is to enhance producer access to the market. Thus, all European countries have some form of anti-monopoly media legislation, one aim of which is to prevent market domination from excluding new market entrants (Commission of the European Communities [CEC] 1992). Broadcasting organizations within countries of the European Union are required to commission a set quota of programmes from independent production companies. In addition, newspaper publishers in France have the legal right to be distributed, subject to an administration charge for returns. Norwegian film makers, an endangered species, are able to get their films exhibited in Norway as a consequence of the country's municipal ownership of cinemas (Solum 1994).[16]

A second aim of the social market approach is to facilitate the establishment of new media by providing seed finance. In Austria, preferential loans are available to consortia seeking to acquire premises and plant to launch a newspaper. The level of production support for new films in France makes it the leading film-making country in Europe. In Britain, valuable frequency was allocated to a national public television channel (Channel 4) which commissions rather than makes programmes specifically for minorities. This gave minority programme makers (and subsequently art house film-makers) two vital things: money to make programmes, and a means of reaching a significant audience. The channel is funded by advertising, and proved so successful in reaching a young, lucrative audience that it was able to dispense with an initial cross-subsidy arrangement.

A third aim is to sustain minority media through a drip-feed of selective subsidy. This is typified by the press subsidy schemes developed in Nordic countries, with variants in Austria and the Netherlands (Murschetz 1998; Skogerbo 1997). Thus in Sweden, grants encourage cost-cutting co-operation between rivals, particularly in the area of distribution, as a way of helping vulnerable papers. A graduated production subsidy also goes to non-market leaders, calculated neutrally in relation to circulation and volume of newsprint without reference to editorial politics. It is administered by a public body, with all-party representation. Its effect has been to keep alive a local political press, and sustain a greater degree of editorial diversity than would otherwise exist (Gustafsson and Hulten 1997). Its further unplanned consequence has been to promote internal debate within the party-aligned press since public subsidies loosened dependence on party (Weibull 1995). However, the support system sustains relatively mainstream newspapers. An equivalent scheme in Norway preserves more diverse publications, including a remarkable cultural Marxist daily, *Klasskampen.*

There are cautionary lessons to be learnt from the social market approach. The traditional neo-Keynesian justification for selective subsidy is that 'secondary' producers (such as minority papers or European film-makers) have lower scale economies than their larger rivals, and need compensatory support if they are to survive. However, this has resulted in public money being spent on some films that have never gained a commercial release, and have as a consequence been virtually unseen (CEC 1994b). Even the Swedish press subsidies scheme is now running into difficulties because rising levels of public funding are needed for it to continue to be effective. Rather than seek to remodel markets according to neo-Keynesian precepts, it is probably better to set up a public trust, with all party representation, with a brief to promote media pluralism as effectively as possible within a defined budget. This will almost certainly result in money being diverted from the high-cost sectors of film and newspapers where the social market sector is most developed, in favour of low-cost sectors where limited money will go further in terms of fostering media diversity.

There is also a case for funnelling support towards certain project categories: minority media that the market will not support (for example political weeklies, a class of publication which fails to deliver a coherent consumer market that advertisers want, and consequently relies unhealthily on handouts from millionaire 'sugar daddies'); distribution agencies, the weak link of the minority media sector most notably in the music industry; innovatory forms of media organisation; and ventures that exploit the potential of new technology (such as the much needed development of global journalism that takes advantage of the internet's capacity to lower costs, forge an international audience and allow new forms of participation and interaction).

Professional media sector

The professional media sector should be composed of media which are under the control of professional communicators, or which are organized in a form that gives staff maximum creative freedom. This is the only part of the proposed media plan that does not already exist in prototype, and for this reason may seem especially fanciful. Precedents could be cited in the form of individual media organizations that operate as public trusts, co-operatives or public interest ventures (Dowmunt 1993; Downing 2001). However, the 'professional sector' concept really derives from the de-politicized, British model of public service broadcasting, during its hey-day.[17]

The professional media sector could consist of one minority television and radio channel. It should be publicly funded in order to be insulated from market pressure. Yet, it should be free from public regulation. Its staff would be in the enormously privileged position of being more independent than any of their peers.

This should assist their fearless oversight of the state and other centres of power. It should also help to forge a distinctive form of journalism. Journalists working for market media are increasingly entertainers; those working for civic media are advocates; while those in public service broadcasting are constrained by an obligation to mediate a 'balanced' perspective. By contrast, journalists in the professional sector should be guided by truth-seeking.

Hopefully, the professional sector will also promote a renaissance of socially relevent television drama. Just as novelists in the second half of the nineteenth century expanded the boundaries of conscience and understanding, and offered arresting interpetations of social change that galvanised public debate in Russia, France, Britain and elsewhere, so television dramatists should occupy a similar place in the imaginative landscape of contemporary society, and generate comparable public reflection about the direction in which society is moving.

Private sector

A private enterprise media sector should also be part of this blueprint. It will make the media system as a whole more responsive to popular pleasures. It will also tend to privilege right-wing perspectives. This is a positive feature of the plan, enhancing its pluralism.

In principle, the private sector should be subject to minimal regulation other than public law. However, the private television sector will need to be subject to a public service regime to prevent it from subverting the core public service system. Monopoly controls ought to be retained. There is also a strong case for supporting the independence of staff in large multimedia corporations as a way of resisting pressures for uniformity arising from media concentration, and as a way of restraining corrupt forms of cross-media promotion. This could be achieved by legally underwriting the freedom of editors and their equivalents, and introducing new procedures for staff participation in senior appointments (Curran 1995). Another approach, adopted in the Austrian press, is for the editorial independence of journalists to be protected in legally binding contracts.

Public service core

The core media sector is where people come together to engage in a reciprocal debate about the management of society. This core sector is best organized in the form of competing public service organizations because the public service approach is socially inclusive, and does not exclude viewers through price. It gives prominence to public affairs. It reports the news with due impartiality, and gives space to different views. The version of the public service approach adopted here – the liberal corporatist model – has the additional advantage of seeking to reflect the diversity of society.

This model is exemplified by German television (with liberal corporatist variants in Sweden, Norway, Denmark and elsewhere). German public service television is a devolved, federal system subject to regional administration. It is controlled by representative broadcasting councils which lay down broad strategy and appoint the chief executive. These councils have democratic representatives appointed on the basis of one of three methods, depending upon the region. In some states, representatives are nominated by organizations representing business, labour, politics, consumers, pensioners, women, tenants, education and other leading institutions or groups. In other states, council members are appointed by the local state assembly and government, usually in proportion to the current party balance. In still other states, the method of securing council members is a mix of these civil society and parliamentary models (Kleinwachter 1998; Sandford 1997; Hickethier 1996; Humphreys 1994).

This stress on representative pluralism is reinforced by the German constitution ('basic law') which lays down that 'everybody has the right to free expression and publication of his opinion in word, writing and picture and the right to obtain information without hindrance from sources generally accessible' (cited in Kleinsteuber and Wilke 1992: 79). This is interpreted by the Constitutional Court to mean that significant groups in society must be given the opportunity to air their viewpoints within the overall programme schedule of television, including entertainment as well as information programmes. What makes this different from the more limited American First Amendment is that it underwrites not only freedom of expression but also the audience's right of access to diverse opinion.

The representative pluralism of German television is further strengthened by its independence from the central state. This independence is secured as a consequence, paradoxically, of television's politicization. This is perhaps best exemplified by the Arbeitsgemeinschaft der Rundfunkanstalten Deutschlands (ARD), which is made up of local organizations formed into a national network. ARD organizations in left-wing regions tend to have radical broadcasting councils and a radical tradition of programme making, while the opposite is the case in right-wing regions. Their combined output is fed into a nationally networked schedule, producing a mix of radical and conservative elements. In effect, opposed political tendencies are embedded in the decentralized management structure of ARD in a way that prevents federal government control.

This pluralistic approach to organising a general television system can have shortcomings in practice. The German version, for example, over-presents political parties, and under-represents other important groups, most notably immigrants, in the management of television. But the liberal corporatist model of television, when implemented successfully, is a good way of enabling society to commune with itself.

CONCLUSION

Implicit in this outline is a complex set of requirements for a democratic media system. It should empower people by enabling them to explore where their interest lies; it should support sectional group identities and assist the functioning of organizations necessary for the effective representation of group interests; it should sustain vigilant scrutiny of government and centres of power; it should provide a source of protection and redress for weak and unorganized interests; and it should create the conditions for real societal agreement or compromise based on an open discussion of differences rather than a contrived consensus based on elite dominance. This can be best realized through the establishment of a core public service broadcasting system, encircled by a private, social market, professional and civic media sectors. These latter will strengthen the functioning of public service broadcasting as an open system of dialogue, and give added impetus to the collective, self-organized tradition of civil society.

The media plan which attempts to fulfil these different requirements has been derived from different aspects of already existing media policy. Its principal feature is that it seeks to create a media system which is controlled neither by the market nor the state.

It is the product of a distinctive 'third way' tradition which has taken root in western Europe. This tradition both comes out of capitalism, and is a democratic response to the limitations of capitalism. It has given rise to eighty years of experimentation in the organisation of radio and film, and subsequently of television and the press. From this rich legacy, it is possible to pick successes and avoid failures to produce an optimal media system.

Notes

Introduction

1 The books and journal where these essays were first published are listed on page xi.
2 I hope that this will be followed by a second volume of my selected essays. These will be case studies in media political economy, with a general introduction.

I Rival narratives of media history

1 In a detailed survey of this sort, the Harvard bibliographical system interrupts the flow of argument, and makes summarizing paragraphs read like a sequence of annotated notes. To be consistent with the rest of the book, this system has been retained. But where appropiate, I have tucked away multiple citations as notes. In this context, the pioneering histories of the press, and founding texts of media studies, in Britain are Hunt (1850), Andrews (1859), Grant (1871–2) and Fox Bourne (1887).
2 The relationship of media and society in a contemporary context is debated in Chapter 5.
3 Useful comparative reflections are provided by Briggs (1960), Stevens and Garcia (1980), Ward (1989), Schudson (1991b), Dahl (1994), Garnham (2000) and, above all, Briggs and Burke (2002).
4 This account is presented in summary form since it is covered more fully in Chapter three. Key liberal studies documenting the 'winning of press freedom' include Wickwar (1928) (still worth reading), Siebert (1952), Cranfield (1962 and 1978), Christie (1970), Aspinall (1973), Koss (1981 and 1984), Sutherland (1986), Harris (1987), Harris (1993) and Somerville (1996).
5 Pronay (1981 and 1982); Pronay and Croft (1983), Robertson (1985), Mathews (1994) and Richards (1997a).
6 Briggs (1961; 1965; 1970; 1979a; 1979c; 1985; 1995), Burns (1977), Wyndham Goldie (1977), Cardiff and Scannell (1981), Sendall (1982 and 1983); Cathcart (1984), Potter (1989 and 1990), McDowell (1992) and Crisell (1997).
7 Christie (1970), Aspinall (1973), Boston (1988), among others.
8 This is presented by Koss (1981 and 1984), largely in response to criticisms from within the liberal tradition, such as those by Seymour-Ure (1977) and Boyce (1978). Seymour-Ure (2000) offers an updated account of press, party and public that tacitly repudiates Koss's tendentious history.
9 See for example Read (1961), Brewer (1976), Briggs (1979b) and Brett (1997).

An important study by Barker (2000) offers in effect a synthesis of the first and second interpretations of liberal press history.

10 Gash (1979), Clark (1985), Reid (1992), Rubinstein (1998), among many others.

11 Harrison (1982), Feuchtwanger (1985), Jones (1988, 1990, 1996) and Newsome (1998). The most notable exponent of this gradualist view, in a form that demotes the role of the press, is Black (2001).

12 Ensor (1936), Lee (1976) and Engel (1996), among others.

13 Wyndham Goldie (1977), Briggs (1985), Scannell (1992) and Negrine (1989).

14 Dugaw (1989), Todd (1989) and Wiltenburg (1992).

15 Social histories of gender tend to overstate the modernity of 'two spheres' ideology. This ideology was already well developed in the Middle Ages, as exemplified by the *Romances* of Chrétien of Troyes, written in the third quarter of the twelfth century.

16 For differing interpretations, see Bourke (1994), Rowbotham (1997), McKibbin (1998) and Kent (1999).

17 This is a condensed account that leaves unresolved a key dispute. Cultural studies feminism often narrates the recent development of feminist thought as a story of progress in which feminist essentialism was followed by feminist pluralism (e.g. Kember 1996). Another view argues that this is a foreshortened perspective which ignores pre-1980s activist and socialist feminism (Segal 1997). For an informative general history of British feminism which stops frustratingly at 1980, see Caine (1997).

18 For example, Millum (1975), Sharpe (1978), Women's Study Group (1978), Baehr (1980), McRobbie (1982).

19 Desjardins (1993), Geraghty (1991), King (1996), Rowbotham (1997), among others.

20 This cries out to be researched. The relevent newspapers are readily accessible in Colindale Library, and most of the journalists involved are still alive.

21 A critical exposition and review of this tradition is provided by McGuigan (1992). For an example of cultural studies populism that has clear parallels with the populist historical narrative, see Willis (1990). Among other things, he argues that 'the market offers a contradictory empowerment which has not been offered elsewhere', and that 'the coming together of coherence and identity' occurs 'in lesiure not work, through commodities not political parties, privately not collectively' (Willis 1990: 159).

22 Walvin (1978), McKendrick, Brewer and Plumb (1983), Brewer and Porter (1993), Bermingham and Brewer (1995), Brewer (1997) and J. Black (2000), among others.

23 See, for example, Plumb (1983b), Perkin (1989), Cannadine (1992 and 1998), Hewison (1997) and McKibbin (1998).

24 Kelly (1977), Snape (1995) and A. Black (2000).

25 Murphy (1992 and 1997), Aldgate and Richards (1994), Street (1997), among others.

26 Smith (1975), Engel (1996) and Bromley (1999).

27 Hind and Mosco (1985) and Chapman (1992).

28 Corrigan (1983), Morley (1986), Moores (1988), Richards (1989), Scannell and Cardiff (1991), O'Sullivan (1991).

29 Good or typical examples of a very extensive literature are Chambers (1986), Buckingham (1987), Hebdige (1988) and Willis (1990).

30 An exception is Tracey and Morrison (1979).

31 For example, Barker and Petley (1997), Murdock (1997) and Petley (1997).

32 Hall *et al.* (1978) and Hall (1988b).

33 Watney (1987), Kitzinger (1993) and Miller *et al.* (1998).
34 Pronay (1981), Kuhn (1988), Mathews (1994), Aldgate (1995), Robertson (1985 and 1989), Richards (1997), Robertson and Nichol (1992) and Barendt and Hitchens (2000).
35 Colley (1992) and O'Gorman (1997).
36 Capp (1979), Colley (1992) and Guy (1990), among others.
37 London Press Exchange (1934), Incorporated Society of British Advertisers (1936) and Incorporated Institute of the Practitioners in Advertising (1939).
38 Ibid.
39 London Press Exchange (1934), White (1970) and McAleer (1992).
40 Political and Economic Planning (1952), Spraos (1962) and Street (1997).
41 Richards (1984 and 1997b), Dodd and Dodd (1996) and Higson (1997).
42 Murphy (1992), Aldgate and Richards (1994), Richards (1997) and Geraghty (2000).
43 Laing (1986), Cardiff and Scannell (1987), Dayan and Katz (1987), Buckingham (1987), Brandt (1993), among others.
44 Cardiff and Scannell (1987) and Scannell and Cardiff (1991).
45 Royal Commission on the Press (1949: 253, table 9).
46 Hill (1986 and 1997), Geraghty (1997) and Higson (1997).
47 Information derived from the Independent Television Commission. The traditional restriction on imported programmes was in effect replaced in 1993 (and amended in 1998) by a requirement that a set proportion of programmes, transmitted on British television, should originate in a European country. This origination quota was an import restriction in all but name. It is more restrictive and also effective than the Television Without Frontiers Directive (1989) which requires that, 'where possible', the majority of television programmes shown on any channel in the EU should be made in EU countries.
48 Dodd and Dodd (1992), Pines (1997) and Street (1997).
49 The rise of minority media was due primarily to the expansion of the media system. However, mass television channels continued to be dominant – see Chapter 7.
50 The classic book in this tradition is Foster (1989).
51 This is described with engaging openness by Williams (1979) under fearsome interrogation by editors of *New Left Review*. His intellectual re-orientation was followed by a nervous breakdown described by Inglis (1995).
52 Hall's illuminating historical reflections, like his initial work as a 'literary' critic of popular culture, are largely ignored in two volumes devoted to a critical appreciation of his work and influence – Morley and Chen (1996) and Gilroy, Grossberg and McRobbie (2000). The latter volume also virtually ignores Hall's finest book (Hall *et al.* 1978).
53 For example, Clarke *et al.* (1976), Hall and Jefferson (1976), Hall (1986c).
54 This is unfolded in a series of instalments in Hall (1977), (1978), (1982) and (1985, reprinted in Curran, Morley and Walkerdine (1996)), and is developed in a concrete way in Hall (1988b).
55 Aspects of this general argument are developed further in Curran (1978b, 1986 and 1980), Curran, Douglas and Whannel (1980) and Curran and Seaton (1997).
56 See, in particular, Williams (1970), Berridge (1978), Chalaby (1998) and Conboy (2002).
57 Lee (1976) and Brown (1987).
58 Tulloch (1993), Scammell (1995), Miller and Dinan (2000) and Davis (2002).
59 For other studies advancing a similar argument, see Glasgow University Media Group (1976 and 1982), Connell (1980) and Morley (1991).

60 This was not only the consequence of a neo-liberal ascendancy. The notion of a 'power structure' also became so complexified by Foucaldian and postmodernist analysis that for some people it became impossible to pin down in any coherent form.

61 Significant exceptions are Thane (1991) and Skeggs (1997).

62 Garnham (1986 and 2000), Skogerbo (1990), Calhoun (1992), Neght and Kluge (1993), Dahlgren (1995), Corner (1995), Thompson (1995), McGuigan (1996), among many others.

63 What Habermas (1989) calls his 'stylized' historical analysis presents the history of the early press in normative mode; his critique of twentieth-century media in desciptive mode; and, to confuse things further, this critique then refers back to the history of the early press as something approximating to descriptive reality.

64 See, in particular, Cranfield (1962), Werkmeister (1963), Wiles (1965), Smith (1978a), Black (1987) and Harris (1987).

65 In particular, Thompson (1963), Wiener (1969b), Hollis (1970), Harrison (1974) and Thompson (1984).

66 Habermas (1989: xviii) acknowledges in a defensive preface the existence of a 'plebeian public sphere', but does not take into account the implications of this alternative public sphere when presenting a normative view of the bourgeois public sphere and early press. See the perceptive comments of Eley (1992).

67 See Chapter 4.

68 This is acknowledged in effect by Habermas (1992) in a gracious response to criticism. He also changed his mind about mass audience susceptibility to media indoctrination (see Habermas 1996).

69 Schlesinger (1978); Schlesinger et al. (1983); Cathcart (1984); Curtis (1984); Bromley (1991); Butler (1991a and b and 1995); Miller (1994); Rolston (1991); Miller and McLaughlin (1996); Rolston and Miller (1996).

70 Schlesinger (1978), Hall et al. (1978), Connell (1980), among others.

71 Much the best general account of this period is O'Gorman (1997).

72 This attempt to develop a new synthesis has taken the route of developing a contextualized national history of the media. The alternative route is to develop systematically a comparative history of the media. For pioneer studies, see Smith (1978b), Ward (1989), Smith and Patterson (1998), Crook (1998) and Briggs and Burke (2002).

73 The key studies making this claim are Innis (1950 and 1951), McLuhan (1962 and 1967), Eisenstein (1979), Ong (1982), Anderson (1983) and James Carey (1992).

74 Rheingold (1994) and Negroponte (1995).

75 The Zapatistas are not, as Castells claims, the 'first informational guerilla movement', but merely one of a succession of such movements. A PhD student of mine, Maurice Walsh, will reveal for example how Sinn Fein was a successful informational guerrilla movement in the Irish War of Independence (1919–21).

2 New media and power

1 I would like to express my thanks to the late Walter Ullmann for his very detailed and helpful comments on the section of this essay dealing with the medieval papacy.

2 By the central Middle Ages, the Catholic church was established in a monopoly position throughout most of Europe, extending from Estonia to northern Spain on an east–west axis, and from Iceland to Sicily on a north–south axis. Regular church attendance was maintained not only through the pull of religious belief, but also sometimes by penalties imposed for non-attendance. For evidence about

the level of newspaper readership in different European countries, see JICNARS (1979), Hoyer, Hadenius and Weibull (1975) and Smith (1977).

3 General questions about the cultural impact of new media have been largely ignored. For an admirable examination of the cultural impact of print see, in particular, Eisenstein (1968, 1969 and 1979), whose analysis is very much more interesting than the better known commentary of McLuhan (1962).

4 For a particularly illuminating interpretation of the rise of the papacy, upon which this essay draws heavily, see Ullmann (1969, 1970, 1975, 1977 and 1978).

5 For instance, Pope Innocent I claimed in the early fifth century that St Peter or his pupils were the founders of all the bishoprics in Italy, Spain, Gaul, Africa and Sicily. This was deeply misleading.

6 Much of the following information is derived from Thomas (1973), whose research, although mainly concerned with the early modern period, also sheds light on popular religious devotion in the Middle Ages.

7 This is discussed further in Curran (1977).

8 Calculated from the Royal Commission on the Press (1949) appendices 3 and 4, and readership per copy estimates derived from the Institute of Incorporated Practitioners in Advertising (1939).

9 This process of political disaffiliation resulted in half the national daily press in the October 1974 general election being opposed to the election of a government constituted by a single party (Seymour-Ure, 1977). However, press partisanship was reactivated during the Thatcherite 1980s before it declined again in the 1990s.

10 A number of political and social changes, usefully reviewed in Butler and Stokes (1976), also contributed to the decline of partisan allegiance in Britain.

11 There are also numerous modern examples of 'new media' displacement. For example, the rise of the mass media under secular control almost certainly contributed to the decline of religion in Britain. The transmission of views opposed to those of the official teaching of the Catholic church on divorce, abortion and contraception contributed to internal division over these issues within the Catholic community. The development of mass media hostile to trade unions (Hartmann, 1975/6 and 1979; Morley 1976; Glasgow University Media Group 1976 and 1980; McQuail 1977) cut across the internal communications system of trade unions, and contributed to their cumulative weakening. The rise of the television studio diminished the significance of parliament as a forum of debate. The growth of election campaigning through television, and the rise of opinion polls and focus groups, all weakened the mediational and electoral role of members of political parties. However, probably the most important example of contemporary 'disintermediation' is the challenge posed by new media, under secular control, to Islamic teaching and the legitimacy of theocratic Islamic states. It has set in motion a process of resistance not unlike the Counter-Reformation.

12 An earlier challenge to the social order promoted by print took place in the sixteenth century, in the form of England's only social revolution, and the 'revolution within the revolution' represented by the Levellers' revolt. As Siebert (1952) shows, the censorship system began to collapse in the years leading up to the Revolution. The Revolution itself produced an unprecedented spate of polemical literature. Stone (1972) estimates that 22,000 speeches, pamphlets, sermons and newspaper titles were published between 1640 and 1660. For a scholarly, but not very illuminating, study of the early newspaper press during this period, see Frank (1961).

13 These studies provide a conventional Whig interpretation of the rise of the press as

an independent fourth estate. However, they mostly close their accounts before 1850, and consequently ignore evidence relating to the later period which challenges their thesis. Thus government subsidies continued in the form of government advertising allocated to friendly papers well into the nineteenth century (Hindle 1937); government management of news remained an enduring form of influence (Anon 1935 and 1939); newspaper proprietors and editors long continued to be intimately connected with one political party or other, whether in or out of office (Lee 1976; Boyce 1978); indeed, a number of leading newspapers received political subsidies well into the twentieth century (Seymour-Ure 1975; Inwood 1971; Taylor 1972). The detachment of the press from the political parties, and consequently from government, was a much more gradual and extended process than the accounts cited in the text suggest.

14 For accounts of the rise of the radical press, see, in particular, Glasgow (1954), Thompson (1963), Read (1961), Wiener (1969), Hollis (1970), Harrison (1974), Prothero (1974), Tholfsen (1976), Epstein (1976), Berridge (1978), Curran (1979a) and Curran and Seaton (1981).

3 Capitalism and control of the press

1 My thanks to John Dennington for his assistance.
2 The founding fathers of this narrative are Hunt (1850), Andrews (1859), Grant (1871-2), Fox Bourne (1887). It remains the orthodoxy to this day. See, for example, the following publications, all published since 1945: Aspinall (1973), Siebert (1952), Altick (1957), Frank (1961), Woodward (1962), Roach (1965), Crawley (1965), Williams, R. (1965), Webb (1969), Christie (1970), Asquith (1975).
3 Good accounts in this tradition are Aspinall (1949), Cranfield (1962), Wiles (1965) and Christie (1970).
4 For example, Wiener (1969a: x) writes, 'their [press taxes] removal in 1861 has been correctly regarded as a landmark in the history of journalism, comparable in its effects to the termination of press censorship in 1695 and to the modification of libel laws in 1843'.
5 The examination of the early development of the radical press, in this article, draws very extensively on these studies – notably Thompson (1963), Wiener (1969a), Hollis (1970) and Epstein (1976).
6 Royal Commission on the Press Report (1949: 100–6 et passim) and Royal Commission on the Press Report (1962: 19–20 et passim). This model of the press encourages a limited set of prescriptions – greater efficiency, higher professional standards and ineffectual anti-monopoly measures. (Report 1949, ch. 17 and report 1962: 112–18.)
7 In fact the traditional view of the rise of the press as an autonomous institution standing above party ignores ample evidence that contradicts it. The 1906 parliament contained, for instance, thirty newspaper proprietors (Thomas, 1958). The nature of continuing editorial and proprietorial involvement in partisan politics in the twentieth century is illustrated by numerous biographies, diaries and memoirs (for instance, Spender (1927); Wrench (1955); Wilson (1970); King (1972)). And if the press is to be conceived of as a fourth estate, many papers were clearly rotten boroughs – like the Daily Express, bought by Beaverbrook to facilitate his entry into politics (Taylor 1972).
8 It was supplemented by 'ex officio informations' which were used principally as a method of harassing publishers and journalists and forcing them to incur legal expenses. Ex officio suits had to be prosecuted within twelve months after 1819,

and the number of *ex officio* suits declined in common with seditious libel prosecutions.

9 The estimated combined total circulation of six leading unstamped papers in 1836 was 200,000 (Hollis 1970: 124), which, on the basis of 10 readers per copy, amounts to 2 million readers. The total unstamped press readership was certainly larger, given the number of unstamped publications in 1836 (see Wiener 1969b).

10 The rise of the radical press was boosted by, but not based on, the favourable price differential which it enjoyed when it evaded payment of the stamp duty. This is borne out by the fact that it flourished both before and after this non-payment phase. Furthermore, radical unstamped papers very successfully competed against moderate unstamped papers *selling at the same price*. The authorites turned a blind eye to these latter publications in the mid 1830s in the vain hope that this would help them to win the circulation battle with the radical unstamped press.

11 Both Wiener (1969: 18) and Hollis (1970: 12) estimate the circulation of the *Weekly Police Gazette* as 40,000. It may have been more, however, since Spring Rice told the Commons that 40,000 copies of an unstamped paper had been seized on a Thursday two days before it was due to be distributed (*Parl. Deb.*, vol. 3, 20 June 1836, col. 627). More copies would probably have been produced in the extra two days.

12 Other estimates of readers per copy of papers in the first half of the nineteenth century are as high as 50–80 (Read 1961: 202; Webb 1955: 31–4).

13 Estimated at a ratio of 20 readers per copy.

14 Cole (1947: 207) estimates 40,000–50,000, although Hollis (1970: 95) estimates 20,000–30,000, probably the more reliable figure.

15 Read's estimate of 50,000 is based on a short-term peak (Read 1961: 101). The annual average circulation of the *Northern Star* in 1839 was fractionally less than three times more than that of *The Times*, then regarded as a leading circulation paper (House of Commons Accounts and Papers 1840).

16 While individual radical papers set new circulation records, the radical newspaper press as a whole probably never attained before 1855 the gross circulation it had attained in 1836. Nor did radical publishers make substantial inroads into family magazine journalism.

17 The trend towards radicalization of the popular press was not continuous and uninterrupted. The decline of the *Northern Star* in the 1840s and the rise of *Lloyd's Weekly*, edited initially by two moral force Chartists, represented a shift away from militancy. But the *Northern Star* was replaced by *Reynolds' News*, which achieved a meteoric rise of circulation in the early 1850s and was then firmly on the left.

18 For an assessment of the class composition of readers of unstamped papers, see Hollis (1970); and of readers of the *Northern Star*, see Epstein (1976). At least two-thirds of the urban working class were literate (though not necessary possessing developed reading skills) during this period. See Webb (1950; 1955) and the more cautious estimates of Stone (1969) and Sanderson (1972).

19 Coltham (1960) suggests, however, that a different approach might have secured more trade-union funds for the *Bee-Hive*.

20 *Clarion* had a circulation of 70,000 at its peak in 1906 and *Labour Leader* had a circulation of 40,000–50,000 by 1911 (Holton 1974).

21 This advertising bounty was sometimes conferred on papers with quite small sales, as measured by the stamp duty. For information on stamp and advertisement duty returns, see in particular the appendices of the Select Committee of the House

of Commons on Newspaper Stamps, *Parliamentry Papers*, xvii (1851). See also *House of Commons Accounts and Papers* 1831–2 (xxiv); 1840 (xxix); and 1842 (xxvi).

22 Even in the late eighteenth century the majority of newspapers depended on advertising for their profits. (See Cranfield 1962; Haig 1968; Wiles 1965; Christie 1970; Asquith 1975.) What was new about the post-stamp press was that all national newspapers in the mass market came to depend on advertising.

23 The generally low opinion held of down-market publications as advertising media tended to be corroborated by their poor performance in analyses of coupon returns from keyed advertisements. These provided, however, an inadequate measure of general advertising effectiveness.

24 Its circulation exceeded that of the *Leader, John Bull, Britannia, Empire, Atlas, Illustrated Times* and the *Spectator* among others (*Mitchell's Newspaper Press Directory 1857–8*).

25 No reference has been made to the strategic control that W.H. Smith acquired over the distribution of newspapers in mid-Victorian Britain. The extent of its market ascendancy is indicated by Chilston (1965) and its role in the censorship of books is suggested by Altick (1957) and Mumby and Norrie (1974). Smith's may have performed a similar role in relation to newspapers. This is an aspect of the development of the press which should be investigated and which can be readily researched in view of the very extensive historical archives retained by the company.

26 These estimates are derived from annual editions of *Mitchell's Newspaper Press Directory*. The figures for regional dailies relate to Britain, while those for other publications relate to the United Kingdom.

27 The national press mostly looked back on the 1926 General Strike as a conflict between the majority and the minority. In this way, the nature of the conflict – essentially between miners and their employers, which escalated into a conflict between organized labour and supporters of the coalmine owners (including the Conservative government) – was resignified in a way that tacitly denied any element of class conflict. For instance the *Observer* (16 May 1926) declared 'trade unionists in this country . . . are and always will be a minority, and if they seriously try to break the majority, they make it quite certain that the majority, if further provoked, will break them'. The minority-majority paradigm contained an implicit explanation of why the conflict had arisen: it was the work of an extremist minority and their defeat was a victory not for the mine owners but for the majority. 'The defeat of the General Strike,' declared the *Daily Mail*, ' . . . would end the danger of communist tyranny in Europe' (*Daily Mail*, 14 May 1926). This victory was hailed as a triumph for the sense of public service and resolution displayed by the people against their potential oppressors. 'Our people have shown during this crisis an immense courage, and undaunted spirit. They have come forward in their hundreds of thousands to resist the attack upon their hard-won freedom' (*Daily Mail*, 14 May 1926). The same majority *versus* malignant minority rhetoric was deployed to delegitimate the National Union of Unemployed Workers during the 1930s and radical protest during the 1960s. For this last, see an insightful study by Hall (1973).

28 Circulation data derived from Belson (1959).

29 Derived from the Audit Bureau of Circulation.

30 'A statistical survey of press advertising during 1936', London Press Exchange archives. It excludes certain forms of classified advertising but this does not affect a comparison between the *Daily Mail* and *Daily Herald*.

31 Despite illusions to the contrary, a wealth of empirical evidence documents the high degree of allegiance to British political institutions and the continuing stability of modern British society. See, for example, Almond and Verba (1963), Butler and Stokes (1969), Blumler *et al.* (1971), Rose (1970 and 1974).

4 New revisionism in media and cultural studies

1 This essay benefited from conversations with Michael Gurevitch when planning a co-edited book (Curran and Gurevitch 1991).
2 Philo (1987) replied to this attack on behalf of the Glasgow University Media Group.
3 Hebdige (1988) argues persuasively that one strand of postmodernist thought rejects the teleological aspirations and rationalism that is a common intellectual heritage of *both* Marxism and liberalism.
4 In fact, Cook and Johnston's admirable essay was first published in 1974 in an obscure film festival publication, and has only became widely available much later. It was ahead of its time.
5 Ironically, Morley (1980) offered a more complex and less misleading historical account of early audience research nine years earlier.
6 This last point is only brought out fully in the analysis of the same data undertaken by Cooper and Jahoda (1947).
7 For further discussion of this, see Tan (1985).
8 For a useful, brief review of the ways in which Katz and Lazarsfeld's two-step flow model of mediation was complexified, see McQuail and Windahl (1981).
9 There is a certain inherent implausibility in the relatively high degree of group consensus that Morley (1980) encountered in his field work. Greater intra-group differences would probably have emerged if he had conducted individual interviews. For an example of research that highlights striking individual differences within groups in the processing of news, see Graber (1988).
10 My comments are based on a lengthy exposition and discussion of this research in English (Fornas 1989).
11 I responded to David Morley's criticisms just once, in Curran (1996). I never replied to Ien Ang's attack (1996) because life is too short. If further evidence is needed of the creative ability of audience members to defy signifying mechanisms in texts, derail their meaning and subvert their intention, Ang's vivacious essay provides it.
12 It was in fact not my account of audience research but of media political economy that most needed amendment, partly in response to useful criticisms from Mosco (1996).
13 This was also partly because many radical researchers argued at the time that liberal audience research was so methodologically and conceptually flawed that it had liitle to offer (e.g. Hall 1982).

5 Renewing the radical tradition

1 The word 'liberal' is again used in its British rather than American sense.
2 For a considered, conservative version of this argument, see Noelle-Neumann (1981).
3 This is outlined more fully in the preceding chapter.
4 A cogent but later study advancing this claim is Graber (1988) (and, from a different tradition, Neuman *et al.* 1992). For a useful general review of the cognitive psychological tradition in communications research, see Harris (1989).

5   McCombs (1994) provides a useful review of agenda-setting research, though he tends to highlight selectively only those studies providing strong support for the media agenda-setting hypothesis.

6   For an exchange which illustrates some of the methodological difficulties involved in distinguishing between media and non-media effects, see the acrimonious debate between Hirsch (1980, 1981a and 1981b) and Gerbner *et al.* (1981).

7   See Schudson (1993) for a useful antidote to the romanticization of rational political discourse in the pre-television era.

8   Part 1 of Schramm and Roberts (1971) provides a guide to how early liberal functionalist theory developed in relation to the media. The classic exposition of the system theory approach is Wright (1975).

9   In retrospect, they can be seen as part of a wider intellectual movement in which radical revisionist historians, using rather similar arguments, also challenged the notion of 'bourgeois domination' in Victorian Britain.

10 Contrary to current fashion, Gramscian analysis still seems to me to offer valuable insights. They are drawn upon in the concluding synthesis of Chapter 1.

11 An influential critique was provided by Schlesinger (1990), and was followed by a number of studies of news sources (usefully reviewed by Manning (2001)). While Schlesinger has telling quotations from Hall's writing on news production which seem to imply an unyielding commitment to a functionalist viewpoint, in fact the trajectory of Hall's more general, evolving framework of argument points by implication towards a more complex, conflictual and historically situated analysis of news sources.

12 A good overview is provided by Ferguson (1998).

13 For an interesting development of this theme, see the lengthy introduction in Mukerji and Schudson (1991).

14 For recent examples, see Curran and Park (2000).

15 See, among others, Croteau and Hoynes (2001), Murdock (2000a), Herman (1999), Herman and McChesney (1997), Curran and Seaton (1997), Sanchez-Tarbernero *et al.* (1993) and European Commission (1992).

16 A good example of this is provided by Rupert Murdoch's long courtship of the Chinese government in order to obtain access to the Chinese broadcasting market. To gain favour with the government, Murdoch's executives dropped the overly critical BBC news from Star TV in 1994. This was followed in 1998 by the cancellation of HarperCollins' publication of the memoirs of the former governor of Hong Kong, Chris Patten, again to win approval.

17 Recent contributions to a large literature include Barnett and Gaber (2001) and Chenoweth (2001).

18 This general argument is powerfully presented by Gitlin (1994) and D'Acci (1994).

19 The best general study is Baker (1994). For a view which stresses the indirect 'structuring' rather than direct influence of advertising, in a British context, see Curran (1978a, 1980 and 1986).

20 For recent accounts of the rise of public relations, see Davis (2002), Miller and Dinan (2000) and Ewen (1996).

21 My own limited experience as an amateur journalist – writing a weekly column for *The Times* – brought home to me the enormous influence exerted by the ideas, images and also shorthand phrases which are carried like pollen in the air we breathe. Although I was completely free to write what I wanted, I found that right-wing phrases and images sprang unsummoned in my head, especially when I was writing fast or trying to inject a little colour. These phrases and images had then to be pulled out systematically like unwanted weeds.

22 Held (1996) provides an introduction to the relevant literature.
23 For useful accounts, see Wieten, Murdock and Dahlgren (2000), Tracey (1998), Raboy (1996), Humphreys (1996), Aldridge and Hewitt (1994) and Avery (1993).
24 A notable exception to this are moral panic studies, some of which are reviewed later.
25 Golding and Middleton show, on the basis of a local survey, the way in which welfarist attitudes were weakened. Further evidence supporting the conclusion that the tabloid campaign against 'scroungers' influenced public attitudes is to be found in Crewe (1988: 34 (table 1)) who reports that the proportion of people who said that welfare benefits available to people had gone 'much too far' rose from 34 to 50 per cent between 1974 and 1979.
26 Watney fails to provide concrete evidence that press reporting did have an influence. However, this is supported by Kitzinger's ethnographic audience study (1993). It is also consistent with survey evidence presented by Brook (1988), who shows that in 1987, no less than 60 per cent thought that AIDS would kill more people than any other disease in the next five years, while those saying that homosexual relations were always or mostly wrong increased from 62 to 74 per cent between 1983 and 1987.
27 For a well-documented account of the closed nature of class cultures, and of gender sub-cultures within these, during 1940s and early 1950s Britain, see McKibbin (1998).
28 An exception is provided by Iyengar and Kinder (1987) who expand the agenda-setting concept to include 'priming', by which they mean the media's influence on criteria of public judgements. They also consider the wider impact of media agenda-setting on American politics.
29 A number of factors contributed to this rehabilitation of the GLC, most notably its popular transport policy. But the key influence was the way in which the ground of debate shifted in the GLC's favour. This enabled a substantial number of people who continued to be critical of the GLC's administration and leader (Waller 1988) to rally to its cause.
30 This view is shared by some radical revisionists, notably Morley (1966).

6 Globalization theory: the absent debate

1 This essay derives from a joint introduction to a book that I wrote with Myung-Jin Park (Curran and Park 2000). It is in this sense jointly authored, though Myung-Jin Park cannot be blamed for the version that appears here.
2 For example, Albrow 1996, Braman and Sreberny-Mohammadi 1996, Castells 1996 and 1997, Golding and Harris 1998, Held et al. 1999, Hoskins et al. 1997, King 1997, Marsden 2000, Mohammadi 1997, Morley 2000, Panitch and Leys 1999, Sreberny-Mohammadi et al. 1997, Strange 1996, Sussman and Lent 1998, Taylor 1997, Thussu 1998 and 2000, Tomlinson 1999, Van Ginnekin 1998. And this is only a small sample of recent globalization books.
3 In fact Held et al. (1999) provide a clear exposition of radical political economy arguments in the main body of their book. It is not until their last unconvincing chapter that they attempt to square the circle, by arguing in effect that market erosion of the democratic process is being rectified, to a large extent, by a new system of governance operating at different levels.

7 Globalization, social change and television reform

1 My thanks to Richard Smith for help in updating data for this chapter.
2 Estimates vary due to differences in the way 'information' is defined. For a lower 1997 estimate, see another survey (Bens and Smaele 2001: 55, table 1).
3 The general trend is sharply fluctuating. In 1997–8, British television peak-time current affairs programme ouput (as a percentage of total peak-time output) was sharply down on ten years before but almost the same as twenty years earlier (Barnett and Seymour 1999: 18, table 1).
4 The TiVo system enables viewers to record their favourite kinds of programme, and download them on to a disc capable of storing up to thirty hours of material.
5 See Chapter 6.
6 This inference is not drawn explicitly by 'new times' theorists.
7 Many of my students are unconvinced by the rationale for public service broadcasting, something that was not true twenty years ago. It is this that convinces me that the case needs to be rethought.
8 This is contested by, among others, Koboldt, Hogg and Robinson (1999).
9 This said, there is a running debate about what criteria should be used in making judgements of popular culture. See, among others, Garnham (2000), Frith (1998), Brunsdon (1997), Frow (1995), Connor (1992) and Mulgan (1990).
10 This is a general problem not confined to Britain and British public service broadcasting. There is very little internal trade of television programmes within Europe, despite the EU's ineffective Media Programme, and this contributes to the under-development of a European identity within the European Union as a whole. Held *et al.* (1999: 375) cite a survey of European countries, published in 1993, in which 5 per cent said that they felt first and foremost Europeans compared with 88 per cent who closely identified with their nation or region. Only 45 per cent felt any European component to their identity.
11 Occasionally, representative pluralism is cited as an aim. The government's white paper (HMSO 2000: 94) contains a single – and, hopefully significant – reference to 'plurality of expression' as a public service objective. A previous government white paper (HMSO 1995: 17) contains what seems in the context to be a disapproving description of current policy: 'programme requirements are focused on securing qualitative objectives or ensuring the accurate and impartial reporting of views and opinions, rather than securing plurality'.
12 In 2001, the BBC sought permission to introduce four new digital channels; for pre-school children, 6–12-year-olds, those aged 16–34 and a culture channel.
13 For admiring assessments of Katz's life work to date, see Simonson (1996), Livingstone (1997) and Curran and Liebes (1998).
14 Elihu Katz was Israel Television's first director. For a positive evaluation of the institution he founded, see Etzioni-Halevey (1987).

8 Media and democracy: the third way

1 My thanks go to staff and students at the Department of Communications, University of California, San Diego for helpful suggestions incorporated into the original essay on which this chapter is based.
2 'Liberal' is a confusing word, meaning different things in Britain and the United States. It is used here in its British historical sense of thought, emphasizing individualism, freedom, tolerance and free trade.
3 In Britain, there is press-specific regulation in only one area – monopoly law.
4 Estimates for the proportion of public affairs content in mass media are provided

by Curran and Seaton (1997), Strid and Weibull (1988), Neumann (1986) and Abramson (1990).

5 In its key last chapter this admirable, thought-provoking book fails to distinguish between progressive and conservative elites. This distinction is one way of reinterpreting the authors' conclusions.

6 In this context it is worth noting that the *Observer*, when it was owned by Lonrho, was different from most privately owned media in having 'independent directors', largely selected by staff, who played a key role in seeking to defend the paper's editorial integrity.

7 These estimates are based on the start-up and run-in costs, respectively, of the *Independent* and *Live TV*, as estimated by senior executives working for these ventures.

8 These figures exclude the *Sport*, *Sunday Sport* and *Sunday Business* on the grounds that they are specialist publications, and the *Morning Star* because it is rarely stocked by newsagents and is therefore not nationally available.

9 See Chapters 1 and 3.

10 This account is summarized and critically assessed in Chapter 1.

11 See Habermas (1992) for a generous, self-critical and reflective response to attacks upon him – exemplifying the 'communicative rationality' he extols.

12 See Chapter 6.

13 For an eloquent defence of universalism, civic virtue and public rationality, see Habermas (1986).

14 Useful starting points for rethinking media and democracy, in addition to Habermas, are Garnham (1986), Keane (1991), Dahlgren (1995), McChesney (1999) and the publications of an American radical lawyer, Edwin Baker (Baker 1989, 1997a and b, and 1998), which deserve a much wider audience than American lawyers and law students. Baker shows how productive it is to synthesize media research with alternative theories of democracy. Those wanting to follow the same route might start with Held (1996), who offers a good overview of models of democracy. Like the literature he reviews, Held barely mentions the mass media.

15 A minor but telling illustration of the way in which different groups can be ignorant of what the other thinks, even though they live cheek by jowl in ostensibly integrated communities, occurred when I conducted jointly two group discussions in an East Anglia village for the Eastern Counties Newspapers Group. The first group of working-class couples said that they were worried about the lack of good job prospects for their children, the lack of leisure facilities for the young and the problem of social discipline among teenagers. The second group of middle-class couples were mainly concerned about conserving the environment, and opposed encroaching urbanization (which was generating a wider range of jobs and more leisure facilities). They were convinced that the first group fully shared their concerns. When informed that this was not the case, they were visibly taken aback, with some arguing rightly that the local paper should have alerted them to what other people in the community were thinking. This may seem to illustrate an aspect of rural, socially stratified England. But other monopoly papers also fail to provide an adequate channel of communication between social classes in their local community. For example the *Los Angeles Times* was remarkably uninformative about Los Angeles' black ghettoes in 1990, giving little indication of smouldering resentments that were to erupt in 1992 in one of the most serious riots in twentieth-century America.

16 This results in Norwegian cinema-goers also being able to see films from all over the world, not just from Hollywood.

17 This was discussed further in Chapter 7.

Bibliography

My thanks to Richard Smith for consolidating this bibliography

Abercrombie, N., Hill, S. and Turner, B. (1984) *The Dominant Ideology Thesis*, London: Allen & Unwin.

Abramson, J. (1990) 'Four criticisms of press ethics' in J. Lichtenberg (ed.) *Mass Media and Democracy*, New York: Cambridge University Press.

Achille, Y. and Miege, B. (1994) 'The limits to the adaptation strategies of European public service television', *Media, Culture and Society*, 16 (10).

Adam Smith Institute (1984) *Omega Report: Communications Policy*, London: Adam Smith Unit.

Advertising Association (1949) Evidence to the Royal Commission on the Press 1947–1949, *Royal Commission on the Press 1947–9*, vol. 5, London: HMSO.

—— (1962) Evidence to the Royal Commission on the Press 1961–2, *Royal Commission on the Press 1961–2*, vol. 3, London: HMSO.

Alberoni, F. (1972) 'The powerless elite: theory and sociological research on the phenomenon of the stars' in McQuail, D. (ed.) *Sociology of Mass Communication*, Harmondsworth: Penguin.

Albrow, M. (1996) *The Global Age*, Cambridge: Polity.

Aldgate, A. (1995) *Censorship and the Permissive Society*, Oxford: Clarendon Press.

Aldgate, A. and Richards, J. (1994) *Britain Can Take It*, Edinburgh: Edinburgh University Press.

Aldridge, A. and Hewitt, R. (eds) (1994) *Controlling Broadcasting*, Manchester: Manchester University Press.

Alexander, J. (1981) 'The mass media in systemic, historical and comparative perspective' in E. Katz and T. Szecsko (eds) *Mass Media and Social Change*, Beverly Hills, Cal.: Sage.

Allen, C. (1993) *Eisenhower and the Mass Media*, Chapel Hill, NC: University of North Carolina Press.

Almond, G. and Verba, S. (1963) *The Civic Culture*, Princeton, NJ: Princeton University Press.

Althusser, L. (1971) *Lenin and Philosophy*, London: New Left Books.

—— (1976) *Essays in Self-Criticism*, London: New Left Books.

—— (1984) *Essays on Ideology*, London: Verso.

Altick, R.D. (1957) *The English Common Reader: A Social History of the Mass Reading Public, 1800–1900*, Chicago: University of Chicago Press.

Anderson, A. (1991) 'Source strategies and the communication of environmental affairs' *Media, Culture and Society*, 13 (4).

Anderson, B. (1983) *Imagined Communities*, London: Verso.

Anderson, P. and Weymouth, A. (1999) *Insulting the Public?*, London: Longman.

Andrews, A. (1859) *History of British Journalism*, 2 vols, London: Bentley.

Ang, I. (1985) *Watching 'Dallas'*, London: Methuen.

—— (1991) *Desperately Seeking the Audience*, London: Routledge.

—— (1996) *Living Room Wars*, London: Routledge.

Ang, I. and Hermes, J. (1991) 'Gender and/in media consumption' in J. Curran and M. Gurevitch (eds) *Mass Media and Democracy*, London: Edward Arnold.

Annan (1977), *Report of the Committee on the Future of Broadcasting*, London: HMSO.

Anon (1851) *Guide to Advertisers*, London: Effingham Wilson.

—— (1935) *History of the Times: 'The Thunderer' in the Making 1785–1841*, vol. 1, London: The Times.

—— (1939) *History of the Times: The Tradition Established*, vol. 2, London: The Times.

—— (1997) 'America's television networks: the dash for the off switch', *Economist*, June 7.

Arnold, M. (1970) *Selected Prose*, Harmondsworth: Penguin.

Aspinall, A.(1950) 'Statistical accounts of London newspapers 1800–1836', *English Historical Review*, LXV.

—— (1973), *Politics and the Press c.1780–1850*, Brighton: Harvester Press.

Aspinall, S. (1983) 'Women, realism and reality in British films, 1943–53' in J. Curran and V. Porter (eds) *British Cinema History*, London: Weidenfeld & Nicolson.

Asquith, I. (1975) 'Advertising and the press in the late eighteenth and early nineteenth centuries: James Perry and the Morning Chronicle, 1790–1821', *Historical Journal*, 17 (4).

—— (1976) 'The Whig Party and the press in the early nineteenth century', *Bulletin of the Institute of Historical Research*, xlix.

—— (1978) 'The structure, ownership and control of the press 1780–1855' in G. Boyce, J. Curran and P. Wingate (eds) *Newspaper History*, London, Constable.

Avery, R. (1993) (ed.) *Public Service Broadcasting in a Multichannel Environment*, White Plains, NY: Longman.

Baehr, H. (1980) (ed.) *Women and the Media*, Oxford: Pergamon.

Bagdikian, B. (1983) *The Media Monopoly*, 1st edn, Boston: Beacon Press.

—— 1997: *The Media Monopoly*, 5th edn, Boston: Beacon Press.

Bailey, P. (1978) *Leisure and Class in Victorian England*, London: Routledge & Kegan Paul.

—— (1986) (ed.) *Music Hall: The Business of Pleasure*, Milton Keynes: Open University Press.

Baistow, T. (1985) *Fourth-Rate Estate*, London: Commedia.

Baker, C. (1989) *Human Liberty and Freedom of Speech*, New York: Oxford University Press.

—— (1994) *Advertising and a Democratic Press*, Princeton, NJ: Princeton University Press.

—— (1997a) 'Giving the audience what it wants', *Ohio State Law Journal*, 58 (2).

—— (1997b) 'Harm, liberty, and free speech', *Southern Law Review*, 70 (4).

Baker, C. (1998) 'The media that citizens need', *University of Pennsylvania Law Review*, 147 (2).

Ballaster, R., Betham, M., Frazer, E. and Hebron, S. (1991) *Women's Worlds*, London: Macmillan.

Barendt, E. and Hitchens, L. (2000) *Media Law*, Harlow: Longman.

Barker, H. (1998) *Newspapers, Politics, and Public Opinion in Late Eighteenth Century England*, Oxford: Oxford University Press.

—— (2000) *Newspapers, Politics and English Society 1695–1855*, Harlow: Longman.

Barker, M. and Petley, J. (1997) 'Introduction' in M. Barker and J. Petley (eds) *Ill Effects*, London: Routledge.

Barlow, W. (1993) 'Democratic praxis and Pacifica Radio' in O. Manaev and Y. Pryliuk (eds) *Media in Transition*, Kyiv: Abris.

Barnett, S. and Curry, A. (1994), *The Battle for the BBC*, London: Aurum.

Barnett, S. and Gaber, I. (2001) *Westminister Tales*, London: Continuum.

Barnett, S. and Seymour, E. (1999) *A Shrinking Iceberg Travelling South*, London: Campaign for Quality Television.

Barron, J. (1973) *Freedom of the Press for Whom?*, Bloomington, Ind.: Indiana University Press.

Barthes, R. (1975) *The Pleasure of the Text*, New York: Hill & Wang.

Baudrillard, J. (1980) 'The implosion of meaning in the media and the implosion of the social in the masses' in K. Woodward (ed.) *The Myths of Information*, London: Routledge & Kegan Paul.

—— (1983) *Simulations*, New York: Semiotexte.

—— (1985) 'The ecstasy of communication' in Hal Foster (ed.) *Postmodern Condition*, London: Pluto.

Beaverbrook, Viscount (1925) *Politicians and the Press*, London: Hutchinson.

Belson, W. (1959) *The British Press*, London: London Press Exchange.

Bennett, H.S. (1952) *English Books and Readers, 1475–1557*, Cambridge: Cambridge University Press.

Bens, E. De and Smaele, H. de (2001) 'The inflow of American television fiction on European broadcasting channels revisited', *European Journal of Communication*, 16 (1).

Bens, E., Kelly, M. and Bakke, M. (1992) 'Television content: Dallasification of culture?' in K. Siune and W. Truetzschler (eds) *Dynamics of Media Politics*, London: Sage.

Bermingham, A. (1995) 'Introduction' in A. Bermingham and J. Brewer (eds) *The Consumption of Culture 1600–1800*, London: Routledge.

Bermingham, A. and Brewer, J. (1995) (eds) *The Consumption of Culture 1600–1800*, London: Routledge.

Bernard, M. (1999) 'East Asia's tumbling dominoes: financial crises and the myth of the regional model' in L. Panitch and C. Leys (eds) *Global Capitalism Versus Democracy*, Rendlesham: Merlin.

Berridge, V. (1975) 'Political attitudes and the popular Sunday press in mid-Victorian England', *Acton Society Paper*.

—— (1978) 'Popular Sunday papers and mid-Victorian society' in G. Boyce, J. Curran and P. Wingate (eds) *Newspaper History*, London: Constable.

Beveridge (1951), *Report of the Broadcasting Committee*, London: HMSO.

Black, A, (1996) *A New History of the English Public Library*, Leicester: Leicester University Library.

—— (2000) *The Public Library in Britain 1914–2000*, London: British Library.

Black, J. (1987) *The English Press in the Eighteenth Century*, London: Croom Helm.

—— (2000) *Modern British History since 1900*, Basingstoke: Macmillan.

—— (2001) *The English Press 1621–1861*, Stroud: Sutton.

Black, P. (1973) *The Mirror in the Corner: People's Television*, London: Hutchinson.

Blackman, L. and Walkerdine, V. (2001) *Mass Hysteria*, Basingstoke: Palgrave.

Bloch, M. (1961) *Feudal Society*, London: Routledge & Kegan Paul.

Blumler, J. (1992) (ed.) *Television and the Public Interest*, London: Sage.

Blumler, J. and Gurevitch, M.(1982) 'The political effects of mass communication' in M. Gurevitch, T. Bennett, J. Curran and J. Woollacott (eds) *Culture, Society and the Media*, London: Methuen.

—— (1986) 'Journalists' orientations to political institutions: the case of parliamentary broadcasting' in P. Golding. G. Murdock and P. Schlesinger (eds) *Communicating Politics*, Leicester: Leicester University Press.

—— (1995) *The Crisis of Public Communication*, London: Routledge.

Blumler, J. and Katz, E. (1974) *The Uses of Mass Communications*, Beverly Hills, Cal.: Sage.

Blumler, J. and McLeod, J. (1983) 'Communication and voter turn-out in Britain' in T. Leggatt (ed.) *Sociological Theory and Survey Research*, Beverly Hills, Cal.: Sage.

Blumler, J. and McQuail, D. (1968) *Television in Politics*, London: Faber & Faber.

Blumler, J.G. (1986) 'Television in the United States: funding sources and programme consequences' in *Research on the Range and Quality of Broadcasting Services* (Report for the Committee on Financing the BBC), London: HMSO.

—— (1989a) 'The modern publicity process' in Ferguson, M. (ed.) *Public Communication*, London: Sage.

—— (1989b) 'Multi-channel television in the United States: policy lessons for Britain', Markle Foundation Report (mimeo).

Blumler, J.G., Brown, J., Ewbank, A. and Nossiter, T. (1971) 'Attitudes to the monarchy', *Political Studies*, xix (2).

Bondebjerg, I. (1989) 'Popular fiction, narrative and the melodramatic epic of American television' in Michael Skovmand (ed.) *Media Fictions*, Aarhus: University of Aarhus Press.

Boron, A. (1999) 'State decay and democratic decadence in Latin America' in L. Panitch and C. Leys (eds) *Global Capitalism Versus Democracy*, Rendlesham: Merlin.

Boston, R. (1988) 'W.T. Stead and democracy by journalism' in J. Wiener (ed.) *Papers for the Millions*, New York: Greenwood Press.

Bottomley, V. (2000) 'Maintaining the gold standard' in S. Barnett *et al., e-Britannia: The Communications Revolution*, Luton: University of Luton Press.

Bourdieu, P. (1986a) 'The aristocracy of culture' in R. Collins, J. Curran, N. Garnham, P. Scannell, P. Schlesinger and C. Sparks (eds) *Media, Culture and Society: A Critical Reader*, London: Sage.

—— (1986b) 'The production of belief: contribution to an economy of symbolic goods' in R. Collins, J. Curran, N. Garnham, P. Scannell, P. Schlesinger and C. Sparks (eds), *Media, Culture and Society: A Critical Reader*, London: Sage.

Bourke, J. (1994) *Working Class Cultures in Britain 1890–1960*, London: Routledge.

Boyce, G. (1978) 'The fourth estate: the reappraisal of a concept' in G. Boyce, J. Curran and P. Wingate (eds) *Newspaper History*, London: Constable.

Boyd-Barrett, O. (1998) 'Media imperialism reformulated' in D. Thussu (ed.) *Electronic Empires*, London: Edward Arnold.

Braman, S. and Sreberny-Mohammadi, A. (1996) (eds) *Globalization, Communication and Transnational Civil Society*, Cresskill, NJ: Hampton Press.

Brandt, G. (1981) (ed.) *Television Drama*, Cambridge: Cambridge University Press.

—— (1993) (ed.) *British Television Drama in the 1980s*, Cambridge: Cambridge University Press.

Brants, K. and Bens, E. de (2000) 'The status of TV broadcasting in Europe' in J. Wieten, G. Murdock and P. Dahlgren (eds) *Television Across Europe*, London: Sage.

Brants, K. and McQuail, D. (1997) 'The Netherlands' in B. Ostergaard (ed.) *The Media in Western Europe*, 2nd edn, London: Sage.

Brett, P. (1997) 'Early nineteenth century reform newspapers in the provinces: the *Newcastle Chronicle* and *Bristol Mercury*' in M. Harris and T. O'Malley (eds) *Newspaper and Periodical History Annual 1995*, Westport, Conn.: Greenwood Press.

Brewer, J. (1976) *Party Ideology and Popular Politics at the Accession of George III*, Cambridge: Cambridge University Press.

—— (1989) *The Sinews of Power*, London: Unwin Hyman.

—— (1997) *The Pleasures of the Imagination*, London: HarperCollins.

Brewer, J. and Porter, R. (1993) 'Introduction' in J. Brewer and R. Porter (eds) *Consumption and the World of Goods*, London: Routledge.

Briggs, A. (1960) *The Rise of Mass Entertainment*, Adelaide: University of Adelaide Press.

—— (1961) *The Birth of Broadcasting* (History of Broadcasting in the United Kingdom, vol. 1), London: Oxford University Press.

—— (1965) *The Golden Age of Wireless* (History of Broadcasting in the United Kingdom, vol. 2), London: Oxford University Press.

—— (1970) *The War of Words* (History of Broadcasting in the United Kingdom, vol. 3), London: Oxford University Press.

—— (1979a) *The Age of Improvement*, 2nd edn, London: Longman.

—— (1979b) *Governing the BBC*, London: BBC.

—— (1979c), *Sound and Vision* (History of Broadcasting in the United Kingdom, vol. 4), Oxford: Oxford University Press.

—— (1985) *The BBC: The First Fifty Years*, Oxford: Oxford University Press.

—— (1995) *Competition 1955–1974* (History of Broadcasting in the United Kingdom, vol. 5), Oxford: Oxford University Press.

Briggs, A. and Burke, P. (2002) *A Social History of the Media*, Cambridge: Polity.

Brigham, J. and Giesbrecht, L. (1976), 'All in the family: racial attitudes', *Journal of Communication*, 26 (3).

British Broadcasting Corporation (BBC) (1969) *Royal Family*, BBC Audience Research Department (unpublished).

—— (1992) *Extending Choice*, London: BBC.

—— (1995a) *Newsnight Objectives 1995/6*, internal office memo, 1995.

—— (1995b) *People and Programmes*, London: BBC.

—— (1996) *Extending Choice in the Digital Age*, London: BBC.

British Broadcasting Corporation (BBC) (1998) *The BBC Beyond 2000*, London: BBC.

Brittan, S. (1989) 'The case for the consumer market' in C. Veljanovski (ed.) *Freedom in Broadcasting*, London: Institute of Economic Affairs.

Broadcasting Research Unit (BRU) (1988) *The Public Service Idea in British Broadcasting*, London: BRU.

Bromley, M. (1991) 'Sex, Sunday papers and the "swinging sixties": cultural consensus in Northern Ireland before the troubles' in Y. Alexander and A. O'Day (eds.) *The Irish Terrorism Experience*, Aldershot: Dartmouth.

—— (1999) 'Was it the *Mirror* wot won it? The development of the tabloid press during the Second World War' in N. Hayes and J. Hill (eds) *Millions Like Us?*, Liverpool: Liverpool University Press.

Brook, L. (1988) 'The public's response to AIDS' in R. Jowell, S. Witherspoon and L. Brook (eds) *British Social Attitudes: The 5th Report*, Aldershot: Gower.

Brooke, C. (1964) *Europe in the Central Middle Ages 962–1154*, London: Longman.

Brown, J. and Schultze, L. (1990) 'The effects of race, gender and fandom on audience interpretations of Madonna's music videos', *Journal of Communication*, 40 (2).

Brown, L. (1987) *Victorian News and Newspapers*, Oxford: Clarendon Press.

—— (1990) 'The growth of a national press' in L. Brake, A. Jones and L. Madden (eds) *Investigating Victorian Journalism*, Basingstoke: Macmillan.

Brunsdon, C. (1981) '*Crossroads*: notes on soap opera', *Screen*, 22.

—— (1997) *Screen Tastes*, London: Routledge.

Buckingham, D. (1987) *Public Secrets*, London: British Film Institute.

Buerkel-Rothfuss, N. with Mayes, S. (1981) 'Soap opera viewing: the cultivation effect', *Journal of Communication*, 31.

Burnett, R., (1990) *Concentration and Diversity in the International Phonogram Industry*, Gothenburg: University of Gothenburg.

Burnham, Lord (1955) *Peterborough Court: The Story of the Daily Telegraph*, London: Cassell.

Burns, T. (1977) *The BBC: Public Institution and Private World*, London: Macmillan.

Butler, D. (1991a) 'Broadcasting in a divided community' in M. McLoone (ed.) *Culture, Identity and Broadcasting in Ireland*, Belfast: Institute of Irish Studies.

—— (1991b) 'Ulster Unionism and British broadcasting journalism' in B. Rolston (ed.) *The Media and Northern Ireland*, London: Macmillan.

—— (1995) *The Trouble with Reporting Northern Ireland*: Aldershot: Avebury.

Butler, D. and Butler, G. (2000) *Twentieth Century British Political Facts 1900–2000*, Basingstoke: Macmillan.

Butler, D. and Stokes, D. (1969) *Political Change in Britain*, London: Macmillan.

—— (1976) *Political Change in Britain*, rev. edn, Harmondsworth: Penguin Books.

Caine, B. (1997) *English Feminism, 1780–1980*, Oxford: Oxford University Press.

Calhoun, C. (1992) (ed.) *Habermas and the Public Sphere*: Cambridge, Mass.: Massachusetts Institute of Technology Press.

—— (1996) 'Comment on John Keane: the death of the public sphere' in M. Andersen (ed.) *Media and Democracy*, Oslo: University of Oslo Press.

Cannadine, D. (1992) *The Decline and Fall of the British Aristocracy*, London: Picador.

—— (1998) *Class In Britain*, New Haven, Conn.: Yale University Press.

Cantor, M. (1971) *The Hollywood TV Producer*, New York: Basic Books.

Cantor, M. and Cantor, J. (1992) *Prime Time Television*, 2nd edn, New York: Basic Books.

Capp, B. (1979) *Astrology and the Popular Press*, London: Faber & Faber.

Cardiff, D. (1980) 'The serious and the popular: aspects of the evolution of style in the radio talk, 1928–1939', *Media, Culture and Society*, 2 (1).

Cardiff, D. and Scannell, P. (1981) 'Radio in World War II', *The Historical Development of Popular Culture*, Milton Keynes: Open University Press.

—— (1986) ' "Good luck war workers!" Class, politics and entertainment in wartime broadcasting' in T. Bennett, C. Mercer and J. Woollacott (eds) *Popular Culture and Social Relations*, Milton Keynes: Open University Press.

—— (1987) 'Broadcasting and national unity' in J. Curran, A. Smith and P. Wingate (eds) *Impacts and Influences*, London: Methuen.

Carey, James (1992) *Communication as Culture*, London: Routledge.

Carey, John (1992) *The Intellectuals and the Masses*, London: Faber & Faber.

Carlyle, T. (1907) *On Heroes, Hero-Worship and the Heroic in History*, London: Chapman & Hall.

Castells, M. (1996) *The Rise of the Network Society*, Oxford: Blackwell.

—— (1997), *The Power of Identity*, Oxford: Blackwell.

Catalbas, D. (1996) *The Crisis of Public Service Broadcasting: Turkish Television in the 1990s*, Goldsmiths College, University of London PhD.

—— (2000) 'Broadcasting deregulation in Turkey: uniformity within diversity' in J. Curran (ed.) *Media Organisations in Society*, London: Edward Arnold.

Cathcart, R. (1984) *The Most Contrary Region*, Belfast: Blackstaff.

Cato (1983/1720) 'Of freedom of speech: that the same is inseparable from publick liberty', *Cato's Letters*, no. 15, 4 February 1720. Reprinted in H. Bosmajian (ed.) *The Principles and Practice of Freedom of Speech*, 2nd edn, Lanham: University Press of America.

Chadwick, P. (1989) *Media Mates*, Melbourne: Macmillan.

Chafee, Z. Jnr (1983) 'Does freedom of speech really tend to produce truth?' in H. Bosmajian (ed.) *The Principles and Practice of Freedom of Speech*, 2nd edn, Lanham, University Press of America.

Chalaby, J. (1998) *The Invention of Journalism*, London: Macmillan.

Chambers, I. (1986) *Popular Culture*, London: Methuen.

Chaney, D. (1972) *Processes of Mass Communication*, London: Macmillan.

—— (1986) 'The symbolic form of ritual in mass communication' in P. Golding, G. Murdock and P. Schlesinger (eds) *Communicating Politics*, Leicester: Leicester University Press.

—— (1987) 'Audience research and the BBC in the 1930s: a mass medium comes into being' in J. Curran, A. Smith and P. Wingate (eds) *Impacts and Influences*, London: Methuen.

Chapman, R. (1992) *Selling the Sixties*, London: Routledge.

Chenoweth, N. (2001) *Virtual Murdoch*, London: Secker & Warburg.

Chibnall, S. (1977) *Law-And-Order-News*, London: Tavistock.

Chilston, Viscount (1965) *W.H. Smith*, London: Routledge & Kegan Paul.

Chomsky, N. (1989) *Necessary Illusions*, Boston, Mass.: South End Press.

Christie, I.R. (1970) *Myth and Reality in Late Eighteenth Century British Politics*, London: Macmillan.

Clark, J.C.D. (1985) *English Society 1688–1832*, Cambridge: Cambridge University Press.

Clarke, G. (1990) 'Defending ski-jumpers: a critique of theories of youth subcultures' in S. Frith and A. Goodwin (eds) *On Record*, London: Routledge.

Clarke. J. (1976) 'The skinheads and the magical recovery of working class community' in S. Hall and T. Jefferson (eds) *Resistance Through Rituals*, London: Hutchinson.

Clarke, J., Hall, S., Jefferson, T. and Roberts, B. (1976) 'Subcultures, cultures and class' in S. Hall and T. Jefferson (eds) *Resistance Through Rituals*, London: Hutchinson.

Cleaver, H. (1998) 'The Zapatistas and the electronic fabric of struggle' in J. Holloway and E. Pelaez (eds) *Zapatista*, London: Pluto.

Cobban, A.B. (1969) 'Episcopal control in the medieval universities of northern Europe' in Cuming, G.J. and Baker, D. (eds) *Studies in Church History*, London: Cambridge University Press.

Cockerell, M. (1988) *Live from Number 10*, London: Faber & Faber.

Cockett, R. (1989) *Twilight of Truth*, London: Weidenfeld & Nicolson.

Cohen, S. (1980) *Folk Devils and Moral Panics*, 2nd edn, Oxford: Martin Robertson.

Cohen, S. and Young, J. (1981) (eds) *Manufacture of News*, 2nd edn, London: Constable.

Cohen. P. (1972) 'Sub-cultural conflict and working class community', *Working Papers in Cultural Studies*, 2.

Cole, G.D.H. (1947) *The Life of William Cobbett*, 3rd edn, London: Home & Van Thal.

Coleman, J.S. (1973) *Power and the Structure of Society*, New York: Norton.

Colley, L. (1992) *Britons*, London: Pimlico.

Collins, R (1989) 'The language of advantage: satellite television in western Europe' *Media, Culture & Society*, 11 (3).

—— (1990) *Television: Policy and Culture*, London: Unwin Hyman.

—— (1992) *Satellite Television in Western Europe*, rev. edn, London: Libbey.

—— (1993) 'Public service versus the market ten years on: reflections on critical theory and the debate about broadcasting policy in the UK', *Screen*, 34 (3).

Coltham, S. (1960) 'The *Bee-Hive* newspaper: its origins and early development' in A. Briggs and J. Saville (eds) *Essays in Labour History*, London: Macmillan.

Commission of the European Communities (1992): *Pluralism and Media Concentration in the Internal Market*, Brussels: CEC.

—— (1994a): *Follow-Up to the Consultative Process Relating to the Green Paper on 'Pluralism and Media Concentration in the Internal Market'*, Brussels: CEC.

—— (1994b) *Report by the Think Tank on the Audiovisial Policy in the European Union* (Vasconcelos Report), Luxembourg: CEC.

Conboy, M. (2002) *The Press and Popular Culture*, London: Sage.

Connell, I. (1980) 'Television news and the social contract' in S. Hall, D. Hobson, A. Lowe and P. Willis (eds), *Culture, Media and Language*, London: Hutchinson.

Connor, S. (1992) *Theory and Cultural Value*, Oxford: Blackwell.

Cook, P. (1998) 'Approaching the work of Dorothy Arzner' in C. Penley (ed.) *Feminism and Film Theory*, New York: Routledge.

Cook, P. and Johnston, C. (1998) 'The place of woman in the cinema of Raoul Walsh' in C. Penley (ed.), *Feminism and Film Theory*, London: Routledge.

Cooper, E. and Jahoda, M. (1947) 'The evasion of propaganda', *Journal of Psychology*, 23.

Corfield, I. (1999) 'Broadcasting and the socially excluded' in A. Graham *et al.*, *Public Purposes in Broadcasting*, Luton: University of Luton Press.

Corner, J. (1995) *Television Form and Public Address*, London: Edward Arnold.

Corner, J., Richardson, K. and Fenton, N. (1990) *Nuclear Reactions*, London: Libbey.

Corrigan, P. (1983) 'Film entertainment as ideology and pleasure: towards a history of audiences' in J. Curran and V. Porter (eds) *British Cinema History*, London: Weidenfeld & Nicolson.

Cranfield, G.A. (1962) *The Development of the English Provincial Newspaper*, Oxford: Clarendon Press.

—— (1978) *The Press and Society*, London: Longman.

Crawley, C.W. (1965) 'Introduction' in C.W. Crawley (ed.) *War and Peace in the Age of Upheaval 1793–1830*, New Cambridge Modern History vol. 9, Cambridge: Cambridge University Press.

—— (ed.) (1965) *War and Peace in an Age of Upheaval 1793–1830*, New Cambridge Modern History vol. 9, Cambridge: Cambridge University Press.

Crewe, I. (1988) 'Has the electorate become Thatcherite?' in R. Skidelsky (ed.) *Thatcherism*, London: Chatto & Windus.

Crisell, A. (1997) *An Introductory History of British Broadcasting*, London: Routledge.

Critchley, R. (1974) *UK Advertising Statistics*, London: Advertising Association.

Crook, T. (1998) *International Radio Journalism*, London: Routledge.

Cross, B. (1993) *It's Not About a Salary*, London: Verso.

Croteau, D. and Hoynes, W. (1997), *Media/Society*, Thousand Oaks, Cal.: Pine Forge Press.

—— (2001) *The Business of Media*, Thousand Oaks, Cal: Pine Forge Press.

Curran, J. (1970) 'The impact of television on the audience for national newspapers 1945–68' in Tunstall, J. (ed.) *Media Sociology*, London: Constable.

—— (1976) 'The impact of advertising on the structure of the modern British press', *Royal Commission on the Press Research Paper*.

—— (1977) 'Mass communication as a social force in history' in *The Media: Contexts of Study* (DE 353–2), Milton Keynes: Open University Press.

—— (1978a) 'Advertising and the press' in Curran, J. (ed.) *The British Press: A Manifesto*, London: Macmillan.

—— (1978b) 'The press as an agency of social control: an historical perspective' in G. Boyce, J. Curran and P. Wingate (eds.) *Newspaper History*, London: Constable.

—— (1979a) 'Capitalism and control of the press, 1800–1975' in Curran, J., Gurevitch, M. and Woollacott, J. (eds) *Mass Communication and Society*, rev. edn, London: Edward Arnold.

—— (1979b) 'Press freedom as private property: the crisis of press legitimacy', *Media, Culture and Society*, 1.

—— (1980) 'Advertising as a patronage system' in H. Christian (ed.) *The Sociology of Journalism and the Press*, Sociological Review Monograph, no. 29, Keele: University of Keele.

—— (1986) 'The impact of advertising on the British mass media' in R. Collins,

J. Curran, N. Garnham, P. Scannell, P. Schlesinger and C. Sparks (eds) *Media, Culture and Society: A Critical Reader*, London: Sage.

Curran, J. (1987) 'The boomerang effect: the press and the battle for London, 1981–6' in J. Curran, A. Smith and P. Wingate (eds) *Impacts and Influences*, London: Methuen.

—— (1990a) 'The crisis of opposition: a reappraisal' in B. Pimlott, A. Wright and T. Fowler (eds) *The Alternative*, London: W.H. Allen.

—— (1990b) 'Culturalist perspectives of news organisations: a reappraisal and case study' in M. Ferguson (ed.) *Public Communication*, London: Sage.

—— (1995) *Policy for the Press*, London: Institute for Public Policy Research.

—— (1996) 'Media dialogue: a reply' in J. Curran, D. Morley and V. Walkerdine (eds) *Cultural Studies and Communications*, London: Edward Arnold.

—— (1998) 'Newspapers and the press' in A. Briggs and P. Cobley (eds) *The Media*, Harlow: Longman.

—— (2000a) 'Press reformism 1918–98: a study of failure' in H. Tumber (ed.) *Media Power, Professionals and Policies*, London: Routledge.

—— (2000b) 'Television journalism: theory and practice, the case of *Newsnight*' in P. Holland, *Television Handbook*, 2nd edn, London: Routledge.

—— (2001) 'Media regulation in the era of market liberalism' in G. Philo and D. Miller (eds) *Market Killing*, Harlow: Pearson Education.

Curran, J., Douglas, A. and Whannel, G. (1980) 'The political economy of the human-interest story' in A. Smith (ed.) *Newspapers and Democracy*, Cambridge, Mass: Massachusetts Institute of Technology.

Curran, J. and Gurevitch, M. (1977) 'The audience', *Mass Communication and Society* Block 3, Milton Keynes: Open University Press.

—— (1991) (eds) *Mass Media and Society*, 1st edn, London: Edward Arnold.

—— (2000) (eds) *Mass Media and Society*, 3rd edn, London: Edward Arnold.

Curran, J., Gurevitch, M. and Woollacott, J. (1977) (eds) *Mass Communication and Society*, London: Edward Arnold.

—— (1982) 'The study of the media' in M. Gurevitch, T. Bennett, J. Curran and J. Woollacott (eds) *Culture, Society and the Media*, London: Methuen.

Curran, J. and Leys, C. (2000) 'Media and the decline of liberal corporatism in Britain' in J. Curran and M.-J. Park (eds) *De-Westernizing Media Studies*, London: Routledge.

Curran, J. and Liebes, T. (1998) 'The intellectual legacy of Elihu Katz' in T. Liebes and J. Curran (eds) *Media, Ritual and Identity*, London: Routledge.

Curran, J., Morley, D. and Walkerdine, V. (1996) (eds) *Cultural Studies and Communications*, London: Edward Arnold.

Curran, J. and Park, M.-J. (2000) (eds) *De-Westernizing Media Studies*, London: Routledge.

Curran, J. and Seaton, J. (1981) *Power Without Responsibility*, 1st edn, London: Fontana.

—— (1997) *Power Without Responsibility: The Press and Broadcasting in Britain*, 5th edn, London: Routledge.

Curtis, L. (1984) *Ireland: The Propaganda War*, London: Pluto.

D'Acci, J. (1994) *Defining Women*, Chapel Hill: University of North Carolina.

Dahl, H.F. (1994) 'The pursuit of history', *Media, Culture and Society*, 16 (4).

Dahlgren, P. (1995) *Television and the Public Sphere*, London: Sage.

—— (2000) 'Media and power transitions in a small country: Sweden' in J. Curran and M.-J. Park (eds) *De-Westernizing Media Studies*, London: Routledge.

Davies, C.S.L. (1976) *Peace, Print and Protestantism, 1450–1558*, London: Hart-Davis, MacGibbon.

Davies, R.H.C. (1957) *A History of Medieval Europe*, London: Longman.

Davis, A. (2001) 'Public relations, news production and changing patterns of source access in the British national media', *Media, Culture and Society*, 22 (1).

—— (2002) *Public Relations Democracy*, Manchester: Manchester University Press.

Davis, J. (1986) 'British and American attitudes: similarities and contrasts' in R. Jowell, S. Witherspoon and L. Brook (eds) *British Social Attitudes: The 1986 Report*, Aldershot: Gower.

Dayan, D. (1998), 'Particularistic media and diasporic communication' in T. Liebes and J. Curran (eds) *Media, Ritual and Identity*, London: Routledge.

Dayan, D. and Katz, E. (1987) 'Performing media events' in J. Curran, A. Smith and P. Wingate (eds) *Impacts and Influences*, London: Methuen.

—— (1992) *Media Events*, Cambridge, Mass: Harvard University Press.

Deacon, D. and Golding, P. (1994) *Taxation and Representation*, London: John Libbey.

DeFleur, M. and Ball-Rokeach, S. (1989) *Theories of Mass Communication*, 5th edn, New York: Longman.

Desjardins, M. (1993) 'Free from the apron strings: representations of mothers in the maternal British state' in L. Friedman (ed.) *British Cinema and Thatcherism*, London: University College London Press.

Dickens, A.G. (1964) *The English Reformation*, London: Batsford.

Dijk, T.A. van (1991) *Racism and the Press*, London: Routledge.

Dimaggio, P. (1986) 'Cultural entrepreneurship in nineteenth century Boston: the creation of an organizational base for high culture in America' in R. Collins, J. Curran, N. Garnham, P. Scannell, P. Schlesinger and C. Sparks (eds), *Media, Culture and Society: A Critical Reader*, London: Sage.

Dodd, K. and Dodd, P. (1992) 'From the East End to *Eastenders*: representations of the working class, 1890–1990' in D. Strinati and S. Wagg (eds) *Come on Down?*, London: Routledge.

—— (1996) 'Engendering the nation: British documentary film, 1930–1939' in A. Higson (ed.) *Dissolving Views*, London: Cassell.

Dowmunt, T. (1993) *Channels of Resistance*, London: British Film Institute.

Downing, J. (1980) *The Media Machine*, London: Pluto.

—— (1996) *Internationalizing Media Theory*, London: Sage.

—— (2001) *Radical Media*, 2nd edn, London: Sage.

Drotner, K. (1989) 'Intensities of feeling: emotion, reception and gender in popular culture' in M. Skovmand (ed.), *Media Fictions*, Aarhus: University of Aarhus Press.

Dugaw, D. (1989) *Warrior Women and Popular Balladry, 1650–1850*, Cambridge: Cambridge University Press.

Dyer, R. (1990) *Now You See It*, London: Routledge.

Eco, Umberto (1972) 'Towards a semiotic enquiry into the TV message', *Working Paper in Cultural Studies* (3), Birmingham: Birmingham Centre for Contemporary Cultural Studies.

Eisenstein, E. (1968) 'Some conjectures about the impact of printing on western society and thought: a preliminary report', *Journal of Modern History*, xl.

Eisenstein, E. (1969) 'The advent of printing and the problem of the Renaissance', *Past and Present*, 45.
—— (1979) *The Printing Press as an Agent of Change*, 2 vols, Cambridge: Cambridge University Press.
Eldridge, J. (1995) (ed.) *Glasgow Media Group Reader*, vol. 1, London: Routledge.
Eley, G. (1992) 'Nations, publics, and political cultures: placing Habermas in the nineteenth century' in C. Calhoun (ed.) *Habermas and the Public Sphere*, Cambridge, Mass: MIT Press.
Elliott, P. (1977) 'Media organisations and occupations: an overview' in J. Curran, M. Gurevitch and J. Woollacott (eds) *Mass Communication and Society*, London: Edward Arnold.
—— (1980) 'Press performance as a political ritual' in H. Christian (ed.) *The Sociology of Journalism and the Press*, Sociological Review Monograph 29, Keele: University of Keele Press.
Elliott, T.S. (1948) *Notes Towards a Definition of Culture*, London: Faber & Faber.
Ellmann, R. (1988) *Oscar Wilde*, London: Penguin.
Elton, G.R. (1975) (ed.) *The Reformation 1520–59*, Cambridge: Cambridge University Press (first published 1958).
Emery, E. (1972) *The Press in America*, 3rd edn, Englewood Cliffs, NJ: Prentice-Hall.
Engel, M. (1996) *Tickle the Public*, London: Gollancz.
Ensor, R.C.K. (1936) *England 1817–1914*, Oxford: Clarendon Press.
Entman, R. (1989) *Democracy Without Citizens*, New York: Oxford University Press.
Epstein, E. (1973) *News from Nowhere*, New York: Random House.
—— (1975) *Between Fact and Fiction*, New York: Vintage.
Epstein, J.A. (1976) 'Feargus O'Connor and the Northern Star', *International Review of Social History*, 22 (1).
Ericson, R., Baranek, P. and Chan, J. (1987) *Visualizing Deviance*, Milton Keynes: Open University Press.
—— (1989) *Negotiating Control*, Milton Keynes: Open University Press.
Ericson, S. (1989) 'Theorizing popular fiction' in M. Skovmand (ed.) *Media Fictions*, Aarhus: Aarhus University Press.
Etzioni-Halevy, E. (1987) *National Broadcasting Under Siege*, London: Macmillan.
European Audiovisual Observatory (2001) *Statistical Yearbook: Film, Television, Video and New Media in Europe*, Strasbourg: Council of Europe.
Evans, H., 1983: *Good Times, Bad Times*, London: Weidenfeld & Nicolson.
Evans, J. (1948) *Art in Medieval France, 978-1498*, Oxford: Oxford University Press.
Ewen, S. (1996) *PR! A Social History of Spin*, New York: Basic Books.
Febvre, L. and Martin, H.J. (1976) *The Coming of the Book*, London: New Left Books.
Ferguson, M. (1983) *Forever Feminine*, London: Heinemann Educational Books.
Ferguson, R. (1998) *Representing 'Race'*, London: Edward Arnold.
Ferris, P. (1971) *The House of Northcliffe*, London, Weidenfeld & Nicolson.
Feuchtwanger, E. (1985) *Democracy and Empire 1865–1914*, London: Edward Arnold.
Fiske, J. (1987) *Television Culture*, London: Methuen.
—— (1989a) 'Moments of television: neither the text nor the audience' in E. Seiter, H. Borchers, G. Kreutzuer and E. M. Warth (eds) *Remote Control*, London: Routledge.

—— (1989b) *Reading the Popular*, Boston, Mass: Unwin Hyman.

—— (1989c) *Understanding Popular Culture*, Boston, Mass: Unwin Hyman.

—— (1991) 'Postmodernism and television' in J. Curran and M. Gurevitch (eds) *Mass Media and Society*, London: Edward Arnold.

Ford, T. and Gil, G. (2001) 'Radical internet use' in J. Downing (with T. Ford, G. Gil and L. Stern) *Radical Media*, 2nd edn, Thousand Oaks, Cal: Sage.

Fornas, J. (1989) 'Papers on pop and youth culture' *University of Stockholm Centre for Mass Communication Research Working Papers*, 1.

Fornas, J., Lindberg, U. and Sernhede, O. (1988) *Under Rocken*, Stockholm: Symposion.

Foster, J. (1974) *Class Struggle and the Industrial Revolution: Early Industrial Capitalism in Three English Towns*, London: Weidenfeld & Nicolson.

Foster, R. (1989) *Modern Ireland 1600–1972*, London: Penguin.

Foucault, M. (1978) *The History of Sexuality*, Harmondsworth: Penguin.

—— (1980) *Power/Knowledge*, Brighton: Harvester.

—— (1982) 'Afterword: the subject and power' in H. Dreyfus and P. Rabinow (eds) *Michel Foucault: Beyond Structuralism and Hermeneutics*, Chicago: University of Chicago Press.

Fox Bourne, H.R. (1887) *English Newspapers: Chapters in the History of the Press*, London: Chatto & Windus.

Fox, E. (1998) (ed.) *Media and Politics in Latin America*, London: Sage.

Frank, J. (1961) *The Beginnings of the English Newspaper 1620–1660*, Cambridge, Mass.: Harvard University Press.

Fraser, N. (1992) 'Rethinking the public sphere: a contribution to the critique of actually existing democracy' in C. Calhoun (ed.) *Habermas and the Public Sphere*, Cambridge, Mass.: Massachusetts Institute of Technology Press.

Frayn, M. (1998) *Copenhagen*, London: Methuen.

Freer, C. (1921) *The Inner Side of Advertising: A Practical Handbook for Advertisers*, London: Library Press.

Frith, S. (1996) 'Entertainment' in J. Curran and M. Gurevitch (eds) *Mass Media and Society*, 2nd edn, London: Edward Arnold.

—— (1998) *Performing Rites*, Oxford: Oxford University Press.

Frow, J. (1995) *Cultural Studies and Cultural Value*, Oxford: Oxford University Press.

Fyffe, G. (1985) 'Art and reproduction: some aspects of the relations between painters and engravers in London 1760–1850', *Media, Culture and Society*, 7 (4).

Gallaher, R. (1989), 'American television: fact and fantasy' in C. Veljanovski (ed.) *Freedom in Broadcasting*, London: Institute of Economic Affairs.

Gamble, A. (1988) *The Free Economy and Strong State*, London: Macmillan.

—— (1990) 'The Thatcher decade in perspective' in P. Dunleavy, A. Gamble and G. Peele (eds) *Developments in British Politics*, vol. 3, London: Macmillan.

Gandy. O. (1982) *Beyond Agenda Setting*, Norwood, NJ: Ablex.

Gans, H. (1974) *Popular Culture and High Culture*, New York: Basic Books.

—— (1980) *Deciding What's News*, London: Constable.

Garnham, N. (1986) 'The media and the public sphere' in P. Golding, G. Murdock and P. Schlesinger (eds) *Communicating Politics*, Leicester: Leicester University Press.

—— (1990) *Capitalism and Communication*, London: Sage.

Garnham, N. (2000) *Emancipation, the Media and Modernity*, Oxford: Oxford University Press.

Gash, N. (1979) *Aristocracy and People*, London: Arnold.

Gelder, K. and Thornton, S. (1996) *The Subcultures Reader*, London: Routledge.

Geraghty, C. (1991) *Women and Soap Opera*, Cambridge: Polity.

—— (1995) 'Social issues and realist soaps: a study of British soaps in the 1989s and 1990s' in R. Allen (ed.) *To Be Continued*, London: Routledge.

—— (1997) 'Women and sixties British cinema: the development of the "Darling" girl' in R. Murphy (ed.) *The British Cinema Book*, London: British Film Institute.

—— (2000) *British Cinema in the Fifties*, London: Routledge.

Gerbner, G., Gross, L., Morgan, M. and Signorielli, N. (1981) 'Final reply to Hirsch', *Communication Research*, 8 (3).

—— (1986) 'Living with television: the dynamics of the cultivation process' in J. Bryant and D. Zillmann (eds) *Perspectives on Media Effects*, Hillsdale, NJ: Lawrence Erlbaum.

—— (1994) 'Growing up with television: the cultivation perspective' in J. Bryant and D. Zillman (eds.) *Media Effects*, Hillsdale, NJ: Lawrence Erlbaum.

Germain, R. (1997) *The International Organisation of Credit*, Cambridge: Cambridge University Press.

Giddens, A. (1999a) 'Comment: the 1999 Reith lecture. New world without end', *Observer* (11 April).

—— (1999b) *Runaway World*, London: Profile Books.

Giles, F., 1986: *Sundry Times*, London: John Murray.

Gilroy, P., Grossberg, L. and McRobbie, A. (2000) (eds.) *Without Guarantees*, London: Verso.

Gitlin, T. (1980) *The Whole World is Watching*, Berkeley, Cal.: University of California.

—— (1986) (ed.) *Watching Television*, New York: Pantheon.

—— (1990) 'Bites and blips: chunk news, savvy talk and the bifurcation of American politics' in P. Dahlgren and C. Sparks (eds) *Communication and Citizenship*, London: Routledge.

—— (1991) 'The politics of communication and the communication of politics' in J. Curran and M. Gurevitch (eds) *Mass Media and Society*, London: Edward Arnold.

—— (1994) *Inside Prime Time*, rev. edn, London: Routledge.

—— (1998) 'Public sphere or spericules?' in T. Liebes and J. Curran (eds) *Media, Ritual and Identity*, London: Routledge.

Glasgow University Media Group (GUMG) (1976) *Bad News*, London: Routledge & Kegan Paul.

—— (1980) *More Bad News*, London: Routledge & Kegan Paul.

—— (1982) *Really Bad News*, London: Writers & Readers.

—— (1985) *War and Peace News*, Milton Keynes: Open University Press.

Glasgow, E. (1954) 'The establishment of the *Northern Star* newspaper', *History*, 39.

Goldberg, D., Prosser, T. and Verhulst, S. (1998) 'Regulating the changing media' in D. Goldberg, T. Prosser and S. Verhulst (eds.) *Regulating the Changing Media*, Oxford: Clarendon Press.

Golding, P. (1981) 'The missing dimensions: news media and the management of social change' in E. Katz and T. Szescho (eds) *Mass Media and Social Change*, Beverly Hills. Cal.: Sage.

Golding, P. and Elliott, P. (1979) *Making the News*, London: Longman.

Golding, P. and Harris, P. (1998) (eds) *Beyond Cultural Imperialism*, London: Sage.

Golding, P. and Middleton, S. (1982) *Images of Welfare*, Oxford: Martin Robertson.

Golding, P. and Murdock, G. (2000) 'Culture, communications, and political economy' in J. Curran and M. Gurevitch (eds) *Mass Media and Society*, London: Edward Arnold.

Goldsmiths Media Group (2000) 'Media organisations in society: central issues' in J. Curran (ed.) *Media Organisations in Society*, London: Edward Arnold.

Goodwin, P. (1998) *Television under the Tories*, London: British Film Institute.

Gorham, D. (1982) *The Victorian Girl and the Feminine Ideal*, London: Croom Helm.

Gorz, A. (1983) *Farewell to the Working Class*, London: Pluto.

Graber, D. (1988) *Processing the News*, 2nd edn, White Plains, NY: Longman.

Graham, A. (1999) 'Broadcasting policy in the multimedia age' in A. Graham *et al.*, *Public Purposes in Broadcasting*, Luton: University of Luton Press.

—— (2001) 'Quality not profit', *openDemocracy*, 1: www.openDemocracy.net.

Graham, A. and Davies, G. (1997) *Broadcasting, Society and Policy in the Multimedia Age*, Luton: John Libbey.

Gramsci, A. (1971) *Selections from Prison Notebooks*, London: Lawrence & Wishart.

—— (1981) 'Gramsci' in T. Bennett, G. Martin, C. Mercer and J. Wollacott (eds) *Culture, Ideology and Social Process*, Milton Keynes: Open University Press.

—— (1985) *Selections from Cultural Writings*, London: Lawrence & Wishart.

Grant, J. (1871–2) *The Newspaper Press*, 3 vols, London: Tinsley Brothers.

Greenfield, J. and Reid, C. (1998) 'Women's magazines and the commercial orchestration of femininity in the 1930s: evidence from *Women's Own*', *Media History*, 4 (2).

Grodal, T. (1989) 'The postmodern melancholia of Miami Vice' in M. Skovmand (ed.) *Media Fictions*, Aarhus: Aarhus University Press.

Gross, L. (1989) 'Out of the mainstream: sexual minorities and the mass media' in E. Seiter, H. Barchers, G. Kreutzner and E.M. Warth (eds) *Remote Control*, London: Routledge.

—— (1998) 'Minorities, majorities and the media' in T. Liebes and J. Curran (eds) *Media, Ritual and Identity*, London: Routledge.

Grossberg, L., Wartella, E. and Whitney, D. (1998) *MediaMaking*, Thousand Oaks, Cal.: Sage.

Gurevitch, M. and Blumler, J. (1977) 'Linkages between the mass media and politics: a model for the analysis of political communications systems' in J. Curran, M. Gurevitch and J. Woollacott (eds) *Mass Communication and Society*, London, Edward Arnold.

Gurevitch, M., Bennett, T., Curran, J. and Woollacott, J. (1982) (eds) *Culture, Society and the Media*, London: Methuen.

Gustafsson, K. and Hulten, O. (1997) 'Sweden' in B. Ostergaard (ed.) *The Media in Western Europe: The Euromedia Handbook*, 2nd edn, London: Sage.

Guy, J. (1990) *Tudor England*, Oxford: Oxford University Press.

Habermas, J. (1986) *The Theory of Communicative Action*, vol. 1, Cambridge: Polity.

—— (1989) *The Structural Transformation of the Public Sphere*, Cambridge: Polity.

Habermas, J. (1992) 'Concluding remarks' in C. Calhoun (ed.) *Habermas and the Public Sphere*, Cambridge, Mass.: Massachusetts Institute of Technology Press.

—— (1992) 'Further reflections on the public sphere' in C. Calhoun (ed.) *Habermas and the Public Sphere*, Cambridge, Mass.: Massachusetts Institute of Technology Press.

—— (1996) *Between Facts and Norms*, Cambridge: Polity.

Hachten, W. (1989) 'Media development without press freedom: Lee Kuan Yew's Singapore', *Journalism Quarterly*, 66.

Haig, R.L (1968) *The Gazetteer 1735–97*, Carbondale, Ill.: South Illinois University Press.

Hall, C. (1992) *White, Male and Middle Class*, Cambridge: Polity.

Hall, S. (1973) 'Encoding and decoding the TV message', Birmingham Centre for Contemporary Cultural Studies Paper (mimeo).

—— (1974) 'Deviancy, politics and the media' in M. McIntosh and P. Rock (eds) *Deviance and Social Control*, London: Tavistock.

—— (1977) 'Culture, the media and the "ideological effect"' in J. Curran, M. Gurevitch and J. Woollacott (eds) *Mass Communication and Society*, London: Edward Arnold.

—— (1978) 'Newspapers, parties and classes' in J. Curran (ed.) *The British Press*, London: Macmillan.

—— (1979) 'Culture, the media and the "ideological effect"' in J. Curran, M. Gurevitch and T. Woollacott (eds) *Mass Communication and Society*, rev. edn, London: Edward Arnold.

—— (1982) 'The rediscovery of ideology: return of the repressed in media studies' in M. Gurevitch, T. Bennett, J. Curran and J. Woollacott (eds) *Culture, Society and the Media*, London: Methuen.

—— (1983) 'The great moving right show' in S. Hall and M. Jacques (eds) *The Politics of Thatcherism*, London: Lawrence & Wishart.

—— (1984) 'The crisis of Labourism' in J. Curran (ed.) *The Future of the Left*, Cambridge: Polity.

—— (1985) 'Signification, representation, ideology: Althusser and the post-structuralist debates', *Critical Studies in Mass Communication*, 2.

—— (1986a) 'Media power and class power' in J. Curran, J. Ecclestone, G. Oakley and R. Richardson (eds) *Bending Reality*, London: Pluto.

—— (1986b) 'Cultural studies: two paradigms' in R. Collins, J. Curran, N. Garnham, P. Scannell, P. Schlesinger and C. Sparks (eds), *Media, Culture and Society: A Critical Reader*, London: Sage.

—— (1986c) 'Popular culture and the state' in T. Bennett, C. Mercer and J. Woollacott (eds) *Popular Culture and Social Relations*, Milton Keynes: Open University Press

—— (1988a) 'Brave New World', *Marxism Today*, October.

—— (1988b) *The Hard Road to Renewal*, London: Verso.

—— (1997) 'The local and the global' in A. King (ed.) *Culture, Globalization and the World System*, London: Macmillan.

Hall, S. and Whannel, P. (1964) *The Popular Arts*, London: Hutchinson Educational.

Hall, S., Connell, I. and Curti, L. (1976) 'The "unity" of current affairs television', *Working Papers in Cultural Studies*, 9.

Hall, S., Critchner, C., Jefferson, T., Clarke, J., and Roberts, B. (1978) *Policing the Crisis*, London: Macmillan.

Hall, S. and Jacques, M. (1989) (eds) *New Times*, London: Lawrence & Wishart.

Hall, S. and Jefferson, T. (1976) (eds) *Resistance Through Rituals*, London: Hutchinson.

Hall, S. and Schwarz, B. (1985) 'State and society, 1880–1930' in M. Langan and B. Schwarz (eds) *Crises in the British State*, London: Hutchinson.

Hall, S. and Whannel, P. (1964) *The Popular Arts*, London: Hutchinson Educational.

Hallin, D. (1989) *The 'Uncensored War'*, Berkeley and Los Angeles, Cal.: University of California Press.

—— (1994) *We Keep America on Top of the World*, London: Routledge.

—— (1996) 'Commercialism and professionalism in the American news media' in J. Curran and M. Gurevitch (eds) *Mass Media and Society*, 1st edn, London: Edward Arnold.

—— (1998) 'Broadcasting in the third world: From national development to civil society' in T. Liebes and J. Curran (eds) *Media, Ritual and Identity*, London, Routledge.

—— (2000) 'Media, political power, and democratization in Mexico' in J. Curran and M-Y. Park (eds) *De-Westernizing Media Studies*, London: Routledge.

Hallin, D., and Mancini, P. (1984) 'Speaking of the president: political structure and representational form in US and Italian television news', *Theory and Society*, 13.

Halloran, J. (1977) 'Mass media effects: a sociological approach', *Mass Communication and Society* Block 3, Milton Keynes: Open University Press.

Halloran, J., Elliott, P. and Murdock, G. (1970) (eds) *Demonstration and Communication*, Harmondsworth: Penguin.

Hamilton, Sir D. (1976) *Who Is to Own the British Press?*, London: Birkbeck College.

Hansen, A. (1991) 'The Media and the social construction of the environment', *Media, Culture and Society*, 13 (4).

Hanson, L. (1936) *Government and the Press, 1695–1763*, Cambridge: Cambridge University Press.

Harper, S. (1996) 'From *Holiday Camp* to high camp: women in British feature films, 1945–1951' in A. Higson (ed.) *Dissolving Voices*, London: Cassell.

Harris, B. (1993) *A Patriot Press*, Oxford: Clarendon Press.

—— (1996) *Politics and the Rise of the Press*, London: Routledge.

Harris, M. (1974) *London Newspaper Press 1700–1750*, unpublished PhD thesis, University of London.

—— (1987) *London Newspapers in the Age of Walpole*, London: Associated University Presses.

Harris, R. (1989) *A Cognitive Psychology of Mass Communication*, Hillsdale, NJ: Lawrence Erlbaum.

Harrison, B. (1982) 'Press and pressure group in modern Britain' in J. Shattock and M. Wolff (eds) *The Victorian Periodical*, Leicester: Leicester University Press.

Harrison, M. (1985) *TV News: Whose Bias?*, London: Policy Journals.

Harrison, S. (1974) *Poor Men's Guardians: Record of the Struggles for a Democratic Newspaper Press 1763–1970*, London: Lawrence & Wishart.

Harrop, M. (1987) 'Voters' in J. Seaton and B. Pimlott (eds) *The Media in British Politics*, Aldershot: Avebury.

Hartmann, P. (1976) 'Industrial relations in the news media', *Industrial Relations Journal*, 6 (4).

—— (1979) 'News and public perceptions of industrial relations', *Media, Culture and Society*, 1 (3).

Hartmann, P. and Husband, C. (1974) *Racism and the Mass Media*, London: DavisPoynter.

Hastorf, A. and Cantril, H. (1954) 'They saw a game: a case study', *Journal of Abnormal and Social Psychology*, 49.

Heath, A., Jowell, R. and Curtice, J. (1987) 'Trendless fluctuation: a reply to Crewe', *Political Studies*, 35.

Heath, P. (1969) *English Parish Clergy on the Eve of the Reformation*, London: Routledge & Kegan Paul.

Heath, S. (1976) 'Narrative space', *Screen*, 17 (3).

—— (1977) 'Notes on suture', *Screen*, 18 (4).

Heath, S. and Skirrow, G. (1977) 'Television: a world in action', *Screen*, 18 (2).

Hebdige, D. (1979) *Subculture*, London: Routledge.

—— (1988) *Hiding in the Light*, London: Routledge.

—— (1981) 'Skinheads and the search for white working class identity', *New Socialist*, 1 (1).

Held, D. (1996) *Models of Democracy*, 2nd edn, Cambridge: Polity.

Held, D. and McGrew, A, Goldblatt, D. and Perraton, J. (1999) *Global Transformations*, Cambridge: Polity.

Helleiner, E. (1994) *States and the Re-emergence of Global Finance*, Ithaca, NY: Cornell University Press.

Herd, Harold (1952) *The March of Journalism*, London: George Allen & Unwin.

Herman, E. (1998) 'The propaganda model revisited' in R. McChesney, E. Wood and J. Foster (eds) *Capitalism and the Information Age*, New York: Monthly Review Press.

—— (1999) *The Myth of Liberal Media*, New York: Lang.

Herman, E. and Chomsky, N. (1988) *Manufacturing Consent*, New York: Pantheon.

Herman, E. and McChesney, R. (1997) *The Global Media*, London: Cassell.

Herzog, H. (1944) 'What do we really know about daytime serial listeners?' in P. Lazarsfeld and F. Stanton (eds) *Radio Research 1942–1943*, New York: Duell, Sloan & Pearce.

Hesmondhaulgh, D. (1997) 'Post-punk's attempt to democratise the music industry: the success and failure of Rough Trade', *Popular Music*, 16 (3).

Hess, S. (1984) *The Government/Press Connection*, Washington, DC: Brookings Institution.

Hetherington, A. (1985) *News, Newspapers and Television*, London: Macmillan.

Hewison, R. (1997) *Culture and Consensus*, rev. edn, London: Methuen.

Hickethier, K. (1996) 'The media in Germany' in T. Weymouth and B. Lamizet (eds) *Markets and Myths*, London: Longman.

Higson, A. (1997) *Waving the Flag*, Oxford: Clarendon Press.

Hill, C. (1974) *The Century of Revolution, 1603–1714*, London: Sphere Books (originally published 1961).

Hill, J. (1986) *Sex, Class and Realism*, London: British Film Institute.

—— (1997) 'British cinema as national cinema: production, audience and representation' in R. Murphy (ed.) *The British Cinema Book*, London: British Film Institute.

Hind, J. and Mosco, S. (1985) *Rebel Radio*, London: Pluto.

Hindle, W. (1937) *The Morning Post, 1772–1937*, London: G. Routledge and Sons.

Hirsch, F. and Gordon, D. (1975) *Newspaper Money: Fleet Street and the Search for the Affluent Reader*, London: Hutchinson.

Hirsch, M. and Petersen, V. (1992) 'Regulation of media at the European level' in K. Siune and W. Truetzschler (eds) *Dynamics of Media Politics*, London: Sage.

Hirsch, P. (1972) 'Processing fads and fashions', *American Journal of Sociology*, 77.

—— (1980) 'The "scary world" of the non-viewer and other anomalies: a reanalysis of Gerbner *et al.*'s findings on cultivation analysis, part 1', *Communication Research*, 7.

—— (1981a) 'On not learning from one's own mistakes: a reanalysis of Gerbner *et al.*'s findings on cultivation analysis, part 2', *Communication Research*, 8.

—— (1981b) 'Distinguishing good speculation from bad theory: rejoinder to Gerbner *et al.*', *Communication Research*, 8.

Hirst, P. and Thompson, G. (1996) *Globalisation in Question*, Cambridge: Polity.

HMSO (1981) *Broadcasting Act*, London: HMSO

—— (1990) *Broadcasting Act*, London: HMSO.

—— (1995) *Media Ownership*, London: HMSO.

—— (1998) *Regulating Communications*, London: HMSO.

—— (2000) *A New Future for Communications*, London: HMSO.

Hobsbawm, E. (1975) *The Age of Capital*, London: Weidenfeld & Nicolson.

—— (1981) 'The forward march of labour halted?' in M. Jacques and F. Mulhern (eds) *The Forward March of Labour Halted?*, London: Verso.

—— (1989) *The Age of Empire*, London: Sphere.

—— (1994) *Age of Extremes*, London: Michael Joseph.

Hobson, D. (1982) *Crossroads*, London: Methuen.

Hollingsworth, M. (1986) *The Press and Political Dissent*, London: Pluto Press.

Hollis, P. (1970) *The Pauper Press: A Study in Working-Class Radicalism of the 1830s*, Oxford: Oxford University Press.

Holmes, S. (1990) 'Liberal constraints on private power?: Reflections on the origins and rationale of access regulation' in J. Lichtenberg (ed.) *Mass Media and Democracy*, New York: Cambridge University Press.

Holton, R.J. (1974) '*Daily Herald* v. *Daily Citizen* 1912–15', *International Review of Social History*, xix.

Holub, R. (1992) *Antonio Gramsci: Beyond Marxism and Postmodernism*, New York: Routledge.

Hood, S. (1980) *On Television*, London: Pluto.

Horwitz, R. (1991) 'The First Amendment meets some new technologies: broadcasting, common carriers, and free speech in the 1990s', *Theory and Society*, 20 (1).

Hoskins, C., McFadyen, S. and Finn, A. (1997) *Global Television and Film*, Oxford: Clarendon Press.

House of Commons (1988) *The Future of Broadcasting*, House of Commons Home Affairs Committee, London: HMSO.

House of Commons Accounts and Papers (1831–2), xxiv; (1840), xxix; (1842), xxvi, London: Hansard.

Hovland, C., Janis, I. and Kelley, H. (1953) *Communication and Persuasion*, New Haven, Conn.: Yale University Press.

Hoynes, W. (1994) *Public Television for Sale*, Boulder, Col.: Westview.

Høst, S. (1990) 'The Norwegian newspaper system: structure and development' in

H. Ronning and K. Lundby (eds) *Media and Communication*, Oslo: Norwegian University Press.

Høyer, S., Hadenius, S. and Weibull, L. (1975) *The Politics and Economics of the Press: A Developmental Perspective*, Beverly Hills, Cal.: Sage.

Hufton, O. (1995), *The Prospect Before Her: A History of Women in Western Europe*, vol. 1, London: HarperCollins.

Hujanen, T. (2000) 'Programming and channel competition in European television' in J. Wieten, G. Murdock and P. Dahlgren (eds) *Television Across Europe*, London: Sage.

Humphreys, P. (1994) *Media and Media Policy in Germany*, Oxford: Berg.

—— (1996) *Mass Media and Media Policy in Western Europe*, Manchester: Manchester University Press.

Hunt, F.K. (1850) *The Fourth Estate: Contributions towards a History of Newspapers and of the Liberty of the Press*, London: David Bogue.

Hunter, N. (1925) *Advertising Through the Press: A Guide to Press Publicity*, London: Pitman.

Hutton, W. (1997) *The State to Come*, London: Vintage.

Hyman, H. and Sheatsley, P. (1947) 'Some reasons why information campaigns fail', *Public Opinion Quarterly*, 9.

Incorporated Society of British Advertisers (ISBA) (1936) *The Readership of Newspapers and Periodicals*, London: ISBA.

Inglis, F. (1990) *Media Theory*, Oxford: Blackwell.

—— (1995), *Raymond Williams*, London: Routledge.

Innis, H. (1950) *Empire and Communication*, Oxford: Clarendon Press.

—— (1951) *The Bias of Communication*, Toronto: Toronto University Press.

Institute of Incorporated Practioners in Advertising (IIPA) (1939) *Survey of Press Readership*, London: IIPA.

Inwood, S. (1971) 'The press in the First World War, 1914–16', unpublished PhD thesis, University of Oxford.

Isaacs, J. (1989) *Storm over 4*, London: Weidenfeld & Nicolson.

Iyengar, S. (1991) *Is Anyone Responsible? How Television Frames Political Issues*, Chicago: University of Chicago Press.

Iyengar, S. and Kinder, D. (1987) *News That Matters: Television and Public Opinion*, Chicago: University of Chicago Press.

Iyengar, S. and Reeves, R. (1997) (eds) *Do the Media Govern?*, London: Sage.

Jenkins, P. (1996) *Accountable to None*, Harmondsworth: Penguin.

Jessop, B., Bonnett, K., Bromley, S. and Ling, T. (1988) *Thatcherism*, Cambridge: Polity.

Jhally, S. and Lewis, J. (1992) *Enlightened Racism*, Boulder, Col.: Westview.

Johnston, C. (1998) 'Dorothy Arzner: critical strategies' in C. Penley (ed.) *Feminism and Film Theory*, New York: Routledge.

Joint Industry Committee for National Readership Surveys (JICNARS) (1979) *National Readership Survey*, London Institute of Practitioners: Advertising.

Jones, A. (1988) 'The new journalism in Wales' in J. Wiener (ed.) *Papers for the Millions*, New York: Greenwood Press.

—— (1990) 'Local journalism in Victorian political culture' in L. Brake, A. Jones and L. Madden (eds) *Investigating Victorian Journalism*, Basingstoke: Macmillan.

—— (1996) *Powers of the Press*, Aldershot: Scolar Press.

Jordan, M. (1983) 'Carry on . . . follow that sterotype' in J. Curran and V. Porter (eds) *British Cinema History*, London: Weidenfeld & Nicolson.

Jowell, R. and Airey, C. (1984) (eds) *British Social Attitudes: The 1984 Report*, Aldershot: Gower.

Jowell, R., Witherspoon, S. and Brook, L. (1987) (eds) *British Social Attitudes: The 1987 Report*, Aldershot: Gower.

Kaldor, N. and Silverman, R. (1948) *A Statistical Analysis of Advertising Expenditure and of the Revenue of the Press*, Cambridge: Cambridge University Press.

Kaniss, P. (1991) *Making the News*, Chicago: Chicago University Press.

Kantorowicz, E.H. (1957) *The King's Two Bodies: A Study in Medieval Political Theology*, Princeton, NJ: Princeton University Press.

Katz, E. (1996) 'And deliver us from segmentation', *Annals of the American Academy of Political and Social Science*, 546.

Katz, E. and Lazarsfeld, P. (1955) *Personal Influence*, New York: Free Press.

Kavanagh, D. (1987) *Thatcherism and British Politics*, Oxford: Oxford University Press.

Kavoori, A. and Gurevitch, M. (1993) 'The purebread and the platypus: disciplinarity and site in mass communication research', *Journal of Communications*, 43 (4).

Keane, J. (1991) *The Media and Democracy*, Cambridge: Polity.

—— (1996) 'Structural transformation of the public sphere' in M. Andersen (ed.) *Media and Democracy*, Oslo: University of Oslo Press.

Kelley, D. and Donway, R. (1990) 'Liberalism and free speech' in J. Lichtenberg (ed.) *Mass Media and Democracy*, New York: Cambridge University Press.

Kellner, D. (1990) *Television and the Crisis of Democracy*, Boulder, Col.: Westview.

Kelly, T. (1977) *A History of Public Libraries in Great Britain 1845–1975*, 2nd edn, London: Library Association.

Kember, S. (1996) 'Feminism, technology and representation' in J. Curran, D. Morley and V. Walkerdine (eds) *Cultural Studies and Communications*, London: Edward Arnold.

Kendall, P. and Wolff, K. (1949) 'The analysis of deviant case studies in communications research' in P. Lazarsfeld and F. Stanton (eds.) *Communications Research, 1948–1949*, New York: Harper.

Kent, S.K. (1999) *Gender and Power in Britain, 1640–1990*, London: Routledge.

King, A. (1997) (ed.) *Culture, Globalisation and the World System*, London: Macmillan.

King, C. (1967) *The Future of the Press*, London: MacGibbon & Kee.

—— (1972) *Diary, 1965–7*, London: Jonathan Cape.

King, J. (1996) 'Crossing thresholds: the contemporary British woman's film' in A. Higson (ed.) *Dissolving Views*, London: Cassell.

Kippax, S. (1988) 'Women as audience: the experience of unwaged women of the performing arts', *Media, Culture and Society*, 10 (1).

Kitzinger, J. (1993) 'Understanding AIDS: researching audience perceptions of acquired immune deficency syndrome' in J. Eldridge (ed.) *Getting the Message*, London: Routledge.

Klapper, J. (1960) *The Effects of Mass Communication*, New York: Free Press.

Klein, L. (1995) 'Politeness for the plebs: consumption and social identity in early eighteenth-century England' in A. Bermingham and J. Brewer (eds) *The Consumption of Culture 1600–1800*, London: Routledge.

Kleinsteuber, H. and Wilke, P. (1992) 'Germany' in B. Ostergaard (ed.) *The Media in Western Europe: The Euromedia Handbook*, 1st edn, London: Sage.

Kleinwachter, W. (1998) 'Germany' in D. Goldberg, T. Prosser and S. Verhulst (eds) *Regulating the Changing Media*, Oxford: Clarendon Press.

Knightley, P. (1975) *The First Casualty: The War Correspondent as Hero, Propagandist and Myth Maker from the Crimea to Vietnam*, London: Andre Deutsch.

Kobolt, C., Hogg, S. and Robinson, B. (1999) 'The implications for funding broadcasting output' in A. Graham *et al.*, *Public Purposes in Broadcasting*, Luton: University of Luton Press.

Kosicki, G. and McLeod, J. (1990) 'Learning from political news: effects of media images and information processing strategies' in S. Kraus (ed.) *Mass Communication and Political Information*, Hillsdale, NJ: Lawrence Erlbaum.

Koss, S. (1981/1984) *The Rise and Fall of the Political Press in Britain*, 2 vols, London: Hamish Hamilton.

Kuhn, A. (1988) *Cinema, Censorship and Sexuality*, London: Routledge.

Kuhn, R. (1995) *The Media in France*, London, Routledge.

Kumar, K. (1975) 'Holding the middle ground: the BBC, the public and the professional broadcaster', *Sociology*, 9 (3).

Kuo, E., Holaday, D. and Peck, E. (1993) *Mirror on the Wall*, Singapore: Asian Mass Communication Research and Information Centre.

Laing, S. (1986) *Representations of Working Class Life 1957–1964*, Basingstoke: Macmillan.

Laistner, M.L.W. (1957) *Thought and Letters in Western Europe, 500–900*, London, Methuen.

Lambert, S. (1982) *Channel Four*, London: British Film Institute.

Landy, M. (1991) *British Genres: Cinema and Society, 1930–1960*, Princeton, NJ: Princeton University Press.

Lang, G. and Lang, K. (1983) *The Battle for Public Opinion*, New York: Columbia University Press.

Lansbury, George (1925) *The Miracle of Fleet Street*, London: Victoria House.

Lasswell, H. (1971) 'The structure and function of communication in society' in W. Schramm and D. Roberts (eds) *The Processes and Effects of Mass Communication*, rev. edn, Urbana, Ill.: University of Illinois Press.

Lazarsfeld, P., Berelson, B. and Gaudet, H. (1944) *The People's Choice*, New York: Columbia University Press.

Leapman, M. (1983) *Barefaced Cheek*, London: Hodder & Stoughton.

Lee, A. (1974) 'The radical press' in Morris, A.J. (ed.) *Edwardian Radicalism 1900–14*, London: Routledge & Kegan Paul.

Lee, A.J. (1976) *The Origins of the Popular Press in England 1855–1914*, London: Croom Helm.

Lee, C.-C. (2000) 'State, capital and media: the case of Taiwan' in J. Curran and M.-J. Park (eds) *De-Westernizing Media Studies*, London: Edward Arnold.

Lee, C.-C., Chan, J., Pan, Z. and So, C. (2000) 'National prisms of a global media event' in J. Curran and M. Gurevitch (eds) *Mass Media and Society*, 3rd edn, London: Edward Arnold.

Leff, G. (1958) *Medieval Thought*, Harmondsworth, Penguin.

LeMahieu, D.L. (1988) *A Culture for Democracy: Mass Communication and the Cultivated Mind in Britain between the Wars*, Oxford: Clarendon Press.

Lerner, D. (1963) 'Toward a communication theory of modernization' in L. Pye (ed.) *Communications and Political Development*, Princeton, NJ: Princeton University Press.

Levine, J. and Murphy, G. (1943) 'The learning and forgetting of controversial material', *Journal of Abnormal and Social Psychology*, 38.

Levy, D. (1999) *Europe's Digital Revolution*, London: Routledge.

Lewis, P. and Booth, J. (1989) *The Invisible Medium*, London: Macmillan.

Leys, C. (2001) *Market-Driven Politics*, London: Verso.

Liebes, T., (1998) 'Television's disaster marathons: a danger for democratic processes?' in T. Liebes and J. Curran (eds) *Media, Ritual and Identity*, London: Routledge.

Liebes, T. and Curran, J. (1998) *Media, Ritual and Identity*, London: Routledge.

Liebes, T. and Katz, E. (1990) *The Export of Meaning*, New York: Oxford University Press.

Light, A. (1991) *Forever England*, London: Routledge.

Livingstone, S. (1997) 'The work of Elihu Katz: conceptualising media effects in context' in J. Corner, P. Schlesinger and R. Silverstone (eds) *The International Handbook of Media Research*, London: Routledge.

Livingstone, S. and Lunt, P. (1994) *Talk on Television*, London: Routledge.

London Press Exchange (LPE) (1934) *A Survey of Reader Interest*, London: LPE.

Lowenthal, L. (1961) *Literature, Popular Culture and Society*, Englewood Cliffs, NJ: Prentice-Hall.

Lowery, S. and DeFleur, M. (1983) *Milestones in Mass Communication Research*, New York: Longman.

Lucas, R. (1910) *Lord Glenesk and the Morning Post*, London: Alston Rivers.

Lull, J. (1995) *Media, Communication, Culture*, Cambridge: Cambridge University Press.

Lyotard, J.-F. (1984) *Postmodern Condition*, Manchester: Manchester University Press.

Ma, E. (2000) 'Rethinking media studies: The case of China' in J. Curran and M.-J. Park (eds) *De-Westernizing Media Studies*, London: Routledge.

McAleer, J. (1992) *Popular Reading and Publishing in Britain 1914–1950*, Oxford: Clarendon Press.

McChesney, R. (1997) *Corporate Media and the Threat to Democracy*, New York: Seven Stories Press.

—— (1998) 'Media convergence and globalisation' in D. Thussu (ed.) *Electronic Empires*, London: Edward Arnold.

—— (1998) 'The political economy of global communication' in R. McChesney, E. Wood and J. Foster (eds) *Capitalism and the Information Age*, New York: Monthly Review Press.

—— (1999) *Rich Media, Poor Democracy*, Urbana: University of Illinois Press.

McClelland, D. (1961) *The Achieving Society*, Princeton, NJ: Van Nostrand.

McCombs, M. (1994) 'News influence on our pictures of the world' in J. Bryant and D. Zillman (eds) *Media Effects*, Hillsdale, NJ: Lawrence Erlbaum.

Macdonald, D. (1957), 'A theory of popular culture' in B. Rosenberg and D. White (eds) *Mass Culture: The Popular Arts in America*, New York: Free Press.

McDowell, W. (1992) *The History of BBC Broadcasting in Scotland 1923–1983*, Edinburgh: Edinburgh University Press.

McGuigan, J. (1992) *Cultural Populism*, London: Routledge.

McGuigan, J. (1996) *Culture and the Public Sphere*, London: Routledge.

McKendrick, N. (1983a) 'Commercialization and the economy' in N. McKendrick, J. Brewer and J.H. Plumb, *The Birth of a Consumer Society*, London: Hutchinson.

—— (1983b) 'Introduction. The birth of a consumer society: the commercialization of eighteenth-century England' in N. McKendrick, J. Brewer and J.H. Plumb, *The Birth of a Consumer Society*, London: Hutchinson.

McKendrick, N., Brewer, J. and Plumb, J.H. (1983) *The Birth of a Consumer Society*, London: Hutchinson.

Mackenzie, J. (1984) *Propaganda and Empire*, Manchester: Manchester University Press.

McKibbin, R. (1998) *Classes and Cultures*, Oxford: Oxford University Press.

McKnight, G. (1997) (ed.) *Agent of Challenge and Defiance*, Trowbridge: Flick Books.

McLachlan, S. (1998) 'Who's afraid of the news bunny?: the changing face of the television evening news broadcast', Department of the Social Sciences, Loughborough University.

McLeod, J. (1988) 'The mass media and citizenship', Stevenson Lecture. Department of Politics, University of Glasgow: mimeo.

McLeod, J., Becker, L. and Byrnes, I. (1974) 'Another look at the agenda-setting function of the press', *Communication Research*, 1.

McLeod, J. and McDonald, D. (1985) 'Beyond simple exposure: media orientations and their impact on political process', *Communication Research*, 12.

McLuhan, M. (1962) *The Gutenberg Galaxy*, Toronto: Toronto University Press.

—— (1964) *Understanding Media*, London: Routledge & Kegan Paul.

McLuhan, M. and Fiore, Q. (1967) *The Medium Is the Message*, Harmondsworth: Penguin.

McManus, J. (1994) *Market-Driven Journalism*, London: Sage.

McNair, B. (1988) *Images of the Enemy*, London: Routledge.

—— (1995) *An Introduction to Political Communication*, London: Routledge.

—— (2000) 'Power, profit, corruption and lies: the Russian media in the 1990s' in J. Curran and M-J. Park (eds) *De-Westernizing Media Studies*, London: Routledge.

McQuail, D. (1969) *Towards a Sociology of Mass Communication*, London: Collier-Macmillan.

—— (1977a) 'Industrial relations content in national daily newspapers 1975' in *Analysis of Newspaper Content*, Royal Commission on the Press Research Series 4, London: HMSO.

—— (1977b) 'The influence and effects of the mass media' in J. Curran, M. Gurevitch and J. Woollacott (eds) *Mass Communication and Society*, London: Edward Arnold.

—— (1983) *Mass Communication Theory*, 1st edn, London: Sage.

—— (1987) *Mass Communication Theory*, 2nd edn, London: Sage.

—— (1992a) *Media Performance*, London: Sage.

—— (1992b) 'The Netherlands: safeguarding freedom and diversity under multi-channel conditions' in J. Blumler (ed.) *Television and the Public Interest*, London: Sage.

—— (1994) *Mass Communication Theory*, 3rd edn, London: Sage.

—— (2000) *McQuail's Mass Communication Theory*, London: Sage.

McQuail and Siune, K. (1998) (eds) *Media Policy*, London: Sage.

McQuail and Windahl, S. (1981) *Communication Models*, New York: Longman.

McQuail, D., Blumler, J.G. and Brown, J.R. (1972) 'The television audience: a revised perspective' in D. McQuail (ed.) *Sociology of Mass Communications*, Harmondsworth: Penguin.

McRobbie, A. (1981) 'Settling accounts with subculture: a feminist critique' in T. Bennett, G. Martin, C. Mercer and J. Woollacott (eds) *Culture, Ideology and Social Process*, Milton Keynes: Open University Press.

—— (1982) 'Jackie: an ideology of adolescent feminity' in B. Waites, T. Bennett and G. Martin (eds) *Popular Culture*, London: Croom Helm.

—— (1992) 'Postmarxism and cultural studies: a post-script' in L. Grossberg, C. Nelson and P. Treichler (eds) *Cultural Studies*, New York: Routledge.

—— (1994) *Postmodernism and Popular Culture*, London: Routledge.

—— (1996) 'More!: new sexualities in girls' and women's magazines' in J. Curran, D. Morley and V. Walkerdine (eds.) *Cultural Studies and Communications*, London: Edward Arnold.

Mahnkopf, B. (1999) 'Between the devil and the deep blue sea: the German model under pressure of globalisation' in L. Panitch and C. Leys (eds) *Global Capitalism Versus Democracy*, Rendlesham: Merlin.

Maisel, R. (1973) 'The decline of mass media', *Public Opinion Quarterly*, 37.

Manca, L. (1989) 'Journalism, advocacy and a communication model for democracy' in M. Raboy and P. Bruck (eds) *Communication For and Against Democracy*, Montreal: Black Rose Books.

Manning, P. (2001) *News and News Sources*, London: Sage.

Marcuse, H. (1972) *One Dimensional Man*, London: Sphere.

Marsden, C. (2000) (ed.) *Regulating the Global Information Society*, London: Routledge.

Marshall, G., Rose, D., Newby, H. and Vogler, C. (1989) *Social Class in Modern Britain*, London: Unwin Hyman.

Martin-Barbero, J. (1993) *Communication, Culture and Hegemony*, London: Sage.

Martindale, C. (1986) *The White Press and Black America*, New York: Greenwood.

Mathews, T.D. (1994) *Censored*, London: Chatto & Windus.

Meiklejohn, A. (1983) 'The rulers and the ruled' in H. Bosmajian (ed.) *The Principles and Practice of Freedom of Speech*, Lanham, Md: University Press of America.

Meyer, Timothy P. (1976) 'The impact of "All in the Family" on children', *Journal of Broadcasting* (winter issue).

Meyrowitz, J. (1985) *No Sense of Place*, New York: Oxford University Press.

Milbury, O. (2001) 'Culture and the evening news', unpublished MA thesis, Goldsmiths College, University of London.

Miliband, R. (1973) *The State in Capitalist Society*, London: Quartet.

Miller, D. (1993) 'Official sources and "primary definition": the case of Northern Ireland', *Media, Culture and Society*, 15 (3).

—— (1994) 'The struggle over and impact of media portrayals of Northern Ireland', PhD thesis, University of Glasgow.

—— (1994) *Don't Mention the War*, London: Pluto.

Miller, D. and Dinan, W. (2000) 'The rise of the PR industry in Britain, 1979–98', *European Journal of Communications*, 15 (1).

Miller, D., Kitzinger, J. Williams, K. and Beharrell, P. (1998) *The Circuit of Mass Communication*, London: Sage.

Miller, D. and McLaughlin, G. (1996) 'Reporting the peace in Northern Ireland' in

B. Rolston and D. Miller (eds) *War and Words*, Belfast: Beyond the Pale Publications.

Miller, W. (1991) *Media and Voters*, Oxford: Clarendon Press.

Millington, B. (1993) 'Boys from the Blackstuff' in G.W. Brandt (ed.) *British Television Drama in the 1980s*, Cambridge: Cambridge University Press.

Millum, T. (1975) *Images of Women*, London: Chatto & Windus.

Mitchell's Newspaper Press Directory, annual series, London: Mitchell.

Modleski, T. (1982) *Loving With a Vengeance*, Hamden, Conn.: Arch Books.

Mohammadi, A. (1997) (ed.) *International Communication and Globalization*, London: Sage.

Moores, S. (1988) ' "The box on the dresser": memories of early radio and everyday life', *Media, Culture and Society*, 15 (4).

—— (1993) *Interpreting Audiences*, London: Sage.

Morgan, K.O. (1999) *The People's Peace*, 2nd edn, Oxford: Oxford University Press.

Morgan, M. (1982) 'Television and adolescents' sex-role stereotypes: a longitudinal study', *Journal of Personality and Social Psychology*, 43.

Morley, D. (1976) 'Industrial conflict and the mass media', *Sociological Review*, 24 (2).

—— (1980) *The 'Nationwide' audience*, London: British Film Institute.

—— (1981) 'Industrial conflict and the mass media', reprinted in S. Cohen and J. Young (eds) *Manufacture of News*, 2nd edn, London: Constable.

—— (1986) *Family Television*, London: Comedia.

—— (1989) 'Changing paradigms in audience studies' in E. Seiter, H. Borchers, G. Kreutseur and E.M. Warth (eds) *Remote Control*, London: Routledge.

—— (1991) 'Industrial conflict and the mass media' in S. Cohen and J. Young (eds) *Manufacture of News*, 2nd edn, London: Constable.

—— (1992a)'Populism, revisionism and the 'new' audience research', *Poetics*, 21 (4).

—— (1992b) *Television, Audiences and Cultural Studies*, London: Routledge.

—— (1993) 'Active audience theory: pendulums and pitfalls', *Journal of Communication*, 43 (4).

—— (1996) 'Media dialogue: reading the reading of the readings . . .' in J. Curran, D. Morley and V. Walkerdine (eds) *Cultural Studies and Communications*, London: Arnold.

—— (1997) 'Theoretical orthodoxies: textualism, constructivism and the "new ethnography" ' in M. Ferguson and P. Golding (eds) *Cultural Studies in Question*, London: Sage.

—— (1999) ' "To boldly go . . .": the third generation of reception studies' in P. Alasuutari (ed.) *Rethinking the Media Audience*, London: Sage.

—— (2000) *Home Territories*, London: Routledge.

Morley, D. and Chen, K.-H. (1996) (eds) *Stuart Hall*, London: Routledge.

Morley, D. and Robins, K. (1995) *Spaces of Identity*, London: Routledge.

Morris, C. (1972) *Medieval Media: Mass Communications in the Making of Europe*, University of Southampton.

Mosco, Vincent (1996) *The Political Economy of Communication*, London: Sage.

Mouffe, C. (1981) 'Hegemony and ideology in Gramsci' in T. Bennett, G. Martin. C. Mercer and J. Woollacott (eds) *Culture, Ideology and Social Process*, Milton Keynes: Open University Press.

Mowlana, H. (1996) *Global Communication in Transition*, Thousand Oaks, Cal.: Sage.

Mukerji, C. and Schudson, M. (1991) (eds) *Rethinking Popular Culture*, Berkeley, Cal.: University of California Press.

Mulgan, G. (1990) 'Television's holy grail: seven types of quality' in G. Mulgan (ed.) *The Question of Quality*, London: British Film Institute.

Mumby, F. and Norrie, L. (1974) *Publishing and Bookselling*, 5th edn, London: Jonathan Cape.

Munster, G. (1985) *Rupert Murdoch*, Ringwood, Australia: Viking.

Murdoch, R., 1989: *Freedom in Broadcasting* (MacTaggart Lecture), London: News International.

Murdock, G. (1973) 'Political deviance: the press presentation of a militant mass demonstration' in Cohen, S. and Young, J. (eds) *The Manufacture of News*, London: Constable.

—— (1982) 'Large corporations and the control of communication industries' in M. Gurevitch, T. Bennett, J. Curran and J. Woollacott (eds) *Culture, Society and the Media*, London: Methuen.

—— (1984) 'Reporting the riots: images and impacts' in J. Benyon (ed.) *Scarman and After*, Oxford: Pergamon.

—— (1992) 'Citizens, consumers, and public culture' in M. Skovmand and K. Schroder (eds) *Media Cultures*, London: Routledge.

—— (1997) 'Reservoirs of dogma: an archaeology of popular anxieties' in M. Barker and J. Petley (eds) *Ill Effects*, London: Routledge.

—— (2000a) 'Digital futures: European television in the age of convergence' in J. Wieten, G. Murdock and P. Dahlgren (eds) *Television Across Europe*, London: Sage.

—— (2000b) 'Talk shows: democratic debates and tabloid tales' in J. Wieten, G. Murdock and P. Dahlgren (eds) *Television Across Europe*, London: Sage.

Murdock, G. and Golding, P. (1974) 'For a political economy of the mass media' in Miliband, R. and Saville, J. (eds) *The Socialist Register 1973*, London: Merlin Press.

—— (1977) 'Capitalism, communication and class relations' in J. Curran, M. Gurevitch and J. Woollacott (eds) *Mass Communication and Society*, London: Edward Arnold.

Murphy, G. (1987) 'Media influence on the socialization of teenage girls' in J. Curran, A. Smith and P. Wingate (eds) *Impacts and Influences*, London: Methuen.

Murphy, R. (1992) *Realism and Tinsel*, London: Routledge.

—— (1997) 'The heart of Britain' in R. Murphy (ed.) *The British Cinema Book*, London: British Film Institute.

Murschetz, P. 1998: 'State support for the daily press in Europe: A critical appraisal', *European Journal of Communication*, 13 (3).

Musson, A.E. (1954) *The Typographical Association: Origins and History up to 1949*, Oxford: Oxford University Press.

Nacos, B. (1990) *The Press, Presidents and Crises*, New York: Columbia University Press.

Nain, Z. (2000) 'Globalized theories and national controls: the state, the market and the Malaysian media' in J. Curran and M-J. Park (eds) *De-Westernizing Media Studies*, London: Routledge.

Nairn, T. (1988) *Enchanted Glass*, London: Century Hutchinson.

National Heritage (1992), *The Future of the BBC*, London: HMSO.

Neght, O. and Kluge, A. (1993) *Public Sphere and Experience*, Minneapolis: University of Minnesota.

Negrine, R. (1989) *Politics and the Mass Media in Britain*, London: Routledge.

—— (1994) *Politics and the Mass Media in Britain*, 2nd edn, London: Routledge.

Negroponte, N. (1995) *Being Digital*, London: Hodder & Stoughton.

Neil, A. (1996) *Full Disclosure*, London: Macmillan.

Neuman, W. (1986) *The Paradox of Politics*, Cambridge, Mass.: Harvard University Press.

Neuman, W., Just, M. and Crigler, A. (1992) *Common Knowledge*, Chicago; University of Chicago Press.

Newcomb, H. and Hirsch, P. (1984) 'Television as a cultural forum: implications for research' in W. Rowland and B. Watkins (eds) *Interpreting Television*, Beverly Hills, Cal.: Sage.

Newman, B. (1994) *The Marketing of the President*, London: Sage.

Newsome, D. (1998) *The Victorian World Picture*, London: Fontana.

Nieuwenhuis, A.J. (1993) 'Media policy in the Netherlands: beyond the market?', *European Journal of Communication*, 7 (2).

Noelle-Neumann, E. (1981) 'Mass media and social change in developed countries' in E. Katz and T. Szecsko (eds) *Mass Media and Social Change*, Beverly Hills, Cal.: Sage.

Norris, P. (2000) *A Virtuous Circle*, New York: Cambridge University Press.

Northcliffe, Viscount (1922) *Newspapers and Their Millionaires*, London: Associated Newspapers.

Nowak, K. (1984) 'Cultural indicators in Swedish advertising 1950–1975' in G. Melischek, K. Rosengren and J. Stappers (eds) *Cultural Indicators: An International Symposium*, Vienna: Verlag der Osterreichischen Akademie der Wissenschaften.

—— (1997) 'Effects no more?' in U. Carlsson (ed.) *Beyond Media Uses and Effects*, Gothenburg: Gothenburg University Press.

O'Gorman, F. (1997) *The Long Eighteenth Century*, London: Edward Arnold.

O'Malley, T. (1994) *Closedown?*, London: Pluto.

O'Neill. O. (1990) 'Practices of toleration' in J. Lichtenberg (ed.) *Democracy and the Mass Media*, Cambridge: Cambridge University Press.

O'Sullivan, T. (1991) 'Television memories and cultures of viewing, 1950–65' in J. Corner (ed.) *Popular Television in Britain*, London: British Film Institute.

Ong, W. (1982) *Orality and Literacy*, London: Methuen.

Ostergaard, B. (1997) (ed.) *The Media in Western Europe: The Euromedia Handbook*, 2nd edn, London: Sage.

Page, D. and Crawley, W. (2001) *Satellites Over South Asia*, New Delhi: Sage.

Palmer, M. and Sorbets, C. (1997) 'France' in B. Ostergaard (ed.) *The Media in Western Europe: The Euromedia Handbook*, 2nd edn, London: Sage.

Panitch, L. and Leys, C. (1999) (eds) *Global Capitalism Versus Democracy* (*Socialist Register* 1999), Rendlesham: Merlin.

Panovsky, E. (1951) *Gothic Architecture and Scholasticism*, Cambridge, Mass., Harvard University Press.

Parenti, M. (1993) *Inventing Reality*, 2nd edn, New York: St Martin's Press.

Park, M.-J., Kim, C.-N. and Sohn, B.-W. (2000) 'Modernization, globalization, and the powerful state: the Korean media' in J. Curran and M.-J. Park (eds) *De-Westernizing Media Studies*, London: Routledge.

Patelis, K. (2000) 'The political economy of the internet' in J. Curran (ed.) *Media Organisations in Society*, London: Sage.

Peacock (1986) *Report of the Committee on Financing the BBC*, London: HMSO.

Pearson, G. (1983) *Hooligan*, London: Macmillan.

Pegg, M. (1983) *Broadcasting and Society 1918–1939*, Beckenham: Croom Helm.

Perkin, H. (1969) *The Origins of Modern English Society, 1780–1880*, London: Routledge & Kegan Paul.

—— (1989) *The Rise of Professional Society*, London: Routledge.

Perloff, R. (1993) *The Dynamics of Persuasion*, Hillsdale, NJ: Lawrence Erlbaum.

Perry, G. (1975) *The Great British Picture Show*, St Albans: Paladin.

Persico, J. (1988) *Edward R. Murrow*, New York: Dell.

Peters, J., 1989: 'Democracy and American mass communication theory: Dewey, Lippmann, Lazardsfeld', *Communication*, 11.

Petersen, V. and Siune, K. (1997) 'Denmark' in B. Ostergaard (ed.) *The Media in Eastern Europe: The Euromedia Handbook*, 2nd edn, London: Sage.

Peterson, T. (1956) 'The social responsibility theory' in F. Siebert, T. Peterson and W. Schramm (eds) *Four Theories of the Press*, Urbana: University of Illinois Press.

Pethick-Lawrence, F.W. (1943) *Fate Has Been Kind*, London: Hutchinson.

Petley, J. (1997) 'Us and them' in M. Barker and J. Petley (eds) *Ill Effects*, London: Routledge.

Philo, G. (1987) 'Whose news?, *Media. Culture and Society*, 9 (4).

—— (1989) 'News content and audience belief: a case study of the 1984–5 miners strike', PhD dissertation, Glasgow: Glasgow University.

—— (1990) *Seeing and Believing*, London: Routledge.

—— (1995) (ed.) *Glasgow Media Group Reader*, vol. 2, *Industry, Economy, War and Politics*, London: Routledge.

Philo, G. and Miller, D. (2001) 'Media/cultural studies and social science' in G. Philo and D. Miller (eds) *Market Killing*, Harlow: Longman.

Picard, R. (2001) *Audience Economics of European Union Public Service Broadcasters*, Turku: Turku School of Economics and Business Administration.

Picciotto, S. (1992) *International Business Taxation*, Oxford: Clarendon Press.

Pilkington (1962) *Report of the Committee on Broadcasting*, London: HMSO.

Pimlott, B. (1998) 'Monarchy and the message' in J. Seaton (ed.) *Politics and the Mass Media*, Oxford: Blackwell.

Pines, J. (1997) 'British cinema and black representation' in R. Murphy (ed.) *The British Cinema Book*, London: British Film Institute.

Plumb, J. (1983a) 'The commercialization of leisure' in N. McKendrick, J. Brewer and J.H. Plumb, *The Birth of a Consumer Society*, London: Hutchinson.

—— (1983b) 'The acceptance of modernity' in N. McKendrick, J. Brewer and J.H. Plumb, *The Birth of a Consumer Society*, London: Hutchinson.

Political and Economic Planning (PEP) (1952) *The British Film Industry*, London: PEP.

Pool, I. de Sola (1963) 'The mass media and politics in the development process' in L. Pye (ed.) *Communications and Political Development*, Princeton, NJ: Princeton University Press.

—— (1973) 'Newsmen and statesmen – adversaries or cronies?' in W. Rivers and

N. Nyhan (eds) *Aspen Papers on Government and Media*, London: Allen & Unwin.

Poster, M. (1988) 'Introduction' in M. Poster (ed.) *Baudrillard: Selected Writings*, Stanford, Cal.: Stanford University Press.

—— (1996) 'Cyberdemocracy: the internet and the public sphere' in D. Porter (ed.) *Internet Culture*, New York: Routledge.

Potter, J. (1989) *Independent Television in Britain: Politics and Control 1968–80*, vol. 3, London: Macmillan.

—— (1990) *Independent Television in Britain: Companies and Programmes 1968–80*, vol 4, London: Macmillan.

Pound, R. and Harmsworth, G. (1959) *Northcliffe*, London: Cassell.

Price, R. (1972) *An Imperial War and the British Working Class: Working Class Attitudes and Reactions to the Boer War 1899–1902*, London: Routledge & Kegan Paul.

Pronay, N. (1981) 'The first reality: film censorship in liberal England' in K. Short (ed.) *Feature Film as History*, London: Croom Helm.

—— (1982) 'The political censorship of films between the wars' in N. Pronay and D. Spring (eds) *Propaganda, Politics and Film 1918–45*, London: Macmillan.

—— (1987) 'Rearmament and the British public: policy and propaganda' in J. Curran, A. Smith and P. Wingate (eds) *Impacts and Influences*, London: Methuen.

Pronay, N. and Croft, J. (1983) 'British film censorship and propaganda policy during the Second World War' in J. Curran and V. Porter (eds) *British Cinema History*, London: Weidenfeld & Nicholson.

Protess, D., Cook, F., Dopelt, J., Ettema, J., Gordon, M., Leff, D. and Miller, P. (1991) *The Journalism of Outrage*, New York: Guilford Press.

Prothero, I. (1974) 'William Benbow and the concept of the "General Strike"', *Past and Present*, 63.

Raboy, M. (1996) *Public Broadcasting for the 21st Century*, Luton: University of Luton Press.

Radice, H. (1999) 'Taking globalisation seriously' in L. Panitch and C. Leys (eds) *Global Capitalism Versus Democracy*, Rendlesham: Merlin.

Radway, J. (1987) *Reading the Romance*, London: Verso.

Ramaprasad, J. and Ong. J. (1990) 'Singapore's guided press policy and its practice on the forum page of the *Straits Times*', *Gazette*, 46 (1).

Ranney, A. (1983) *Channels of Power*, New York: Basic Books.

Read, D. (1961) *Press and People, 1790–1850: Opinion in Three English Cities*, London: Edward Arnold.

Reid, A. (1992) *Social Classes and Social Relations in Britain, 1850–1914*, London: Macmillan.

Reimer, B. and Rosengren, K.E. (1989) 'Cultivated viewers and readers: a life style perspective' in N. Signorelli and M. Morgan (eds) *Advances in Cultivation Analysis*, Beverly Hills, Cal.: Sage.

Rheingold, H. (1994) *The Virtual Community*, London: Secker & Warburg.

—— (2000) *The Virtual Community*, rev. edn, Cambridge, Mass.: Massachusetts Institute of Technology Press.

Richards, J. (1979) *The Popes and the Papacy in the Early Middle Ages*, London, Edward Arnold.

—— (1989) *The Age of the Picture Palace*, London: Routledge & Kegan Paul.

—— (1997a) 'British film censorship' in R. Murphy (ed.) *The British Cinema Book*, London: British Film Institute.

—— (1997b) *Films and British National Identity*, Manchester: Manchester University Press.

Riddell, P. (1991) *The Thatcher Era and Its Legacy*, Oxford: Blackwell.

Roach, J. (1965) 'Education and public opinion' in Crawley, C.W. (ed.) *War and Peace in an Age of Upheaval 1793–1830*, Cambridge: Cambridge University Press.

Robertson, G. and Nicol, A. (1992) *Media Law*, 3rd edn, Harmondsworth: Penguin.

Robertson, J. (1985) *The British Board of Film Censors*, London: Croom Helm.

—— (1989) *The Hidden Cinema*, London: Routledge.

Robins, K. (1995) 'The new spaces of global media' in R.J. Johnston, P. Taylor and M. Watts (eds) *Geographies of Global Change*, Oxford: Blackwell.

—— (1997) (ed.) *Programming for People*, Newcastle: Centre for Urban and Regional Studies, University of Newcastle.

Robins, K., Cornford, J. and Aksoy, A. (1997) 'Overview: from cultural rights to cultural responsibilities' in K. Robins (ed.) *Programming for People*, Newcastle: Centre for Urban and Regional Development Studies, University of Newcastle and European Broadcasting Union.

Roe, K. and Meyer, G. de (2000) 'Music television: MTV-Europe' in J. Wieten, G. Murdock and P. Dahlgren (eds) *Television Across Europe*, London: Sage.

Rogers, E. and Dearing, J. (1988) 'Agenda-setting research: where has it been and where is it going?' in J. Anderson (ed.) *Communication Year Book*, vol. 11.

Rogers, E. and Shoemaker, F. (1971) *Communication of Innovations*, New York: Free Press.

Rogers, P. (1972) *Grub Street: Studies in a Subculture*, London: Methuen.

Rolston, B. (1991) (ed.) *The Media and Northern Ireland*, London: Macmillan.

Rolston, B. and Miller, D. (1996) (eds) *War and Words*, Belfast: Beyond the Pale Publications.

Rønning, H. and Kupe, T. (2000) 'The dual legacy of democracy and authoritarianism: the media and the state in Zimbabwe' in J. Curran and M-Y. Park (eds) *De-Westernizing Media Studies*, London: Routledge.

Rose, R. (1970) *People in Politics: Observations Across the Atlantic*, London: Faber & Faber.

—— (1974) *Politics in England*, London: Faber & Faber.

Rosengren, K. E. (1981) 'Mass media and social change' in E. Katz and T. Szecsko (eds) *Mass Media and Social Change*, Beverly Hills, Cal.: Sage.

—— (1993) 'From field to frog ponds', *Journal of Communication*, 43 (4).

—— (1996) 'Combinations, comparisons, and confrontations: towards a comprehensive theory of audience research' in J. Hay, L. Grossberg and E. Wartella (eds) *The Audience and Its Landscape*, Boulder, Col.: Westview.

Rosengren, K., Wenner, K. and Palmgreen, P. (1985) (eds) *Media Gratifications Research*, Beverly Hills, Cal.: Sage.

Rostenburg, L. (1971) *The Minority Press and the English Crown: A Study in Repression 1558–1625*, Nieuwkoop: De Graaf.

Rowbotham, S. (1997) *A Century of Women*, London: Viking.

Rowland, W. (1993) 'Public service broadcasting in the United States: its mandate, institutions and conflicts' in R. Avery (ed.) *Public Service Broadcasting in a Multichannel Environment*, White Plains, NY: Longman.

Rowland, W. and Tracey, M. (1990), 'Worldwide challenges to public service broadcasting', *Journal of Communication*, 40 (2).

Royal Commission on the Press 1947–9 Report (1949) (Cmd 7700), London: HMSO.

Royal Commission on the Press 1961–2 Report (1962) (Cmnd 1811), London: HMSO.

Royal Commission on the Press 1974–7 Final Report (1977) (Cmnd 6810), London: HMSO.

Rubin. A. (1986) 'Uses, gratifications, and media effects research' in J. Bryant and D. Zillmann (eds) *Perspectives on Media Effects*, Hillsdale, NJ: Lawrence Erlbaum.

Rubinstein, W. (1998) *Britain's Century*, London: Edward Arnold.

Rude, G. (1962) *Wilkes and Liberty*, Oxford: Clarendon Press.

Sanchez-Tabernero, A. with Denton, A., Lochon, P-Y, Mournier, P. and Woldt, R. (1993) *Media Concentration in Europe*, Düsseldorf: European Institute for the Media.

Sanderson, M. (1972) 'Literacy and social mobility in the industrial revolution', *Past and Present*, 56.

Sandford, J., 1997: 'Television in Germany' in J. Coleman and B. Rollet (eds) *Television in Europe*, Exeter: Intellect.

Scammell, M. (1995) *Designer Politics*, London: Macmillan.

Scannell, P. (1980) 'Broadcasting and the politics of unemployment, 1930–1935', *Media, Culture and Society*, 2 (1).

—— (1989) 'Public service broadcasting and modern public life', *Media, Culture and Society*, 11 (2).

—— (1990) 'Public service: the history of a concept' in A. Goodwin and G. Whannel (eds) *Understanding Television*, London: Routledge.

—— (1992) 'Public service broadcasting and modern public life' in P. Scannell, P. Schlesinger and C. Sparks (eds) *Culture and Power*, London: Sage.

Scannell, P. and Cardiff, D. (1982) 'Serving the nation: public service broadcasting before the war' in B. Waites, T. Bennett and G. Martin (eds) *Popular Culture*, London: Croom Helm.

—— (1991) *Serving the Nation, 1922–39*, Oxford: Blackwell.

Schiller, H. (1969) *Mass Communication and American Empire*, New York: Kelly.

—— (1976) *Communication and Cultural Domination*, White Plains, NY: Sharpe.

—— (1981) *Who Knows*, Norwood, NJ: Ablex.

—— (1998) 'Striving for communication dominance' in D. Thussu (ed.) *Electronic Empires*, London: Edward Arnold.

Schlesinger, P. (1978) *Putting 'Reality' Together*, London: Constable.

—— (1987) *Putting 'Reality' Together*, rev. edn, London: Methuen.

—— (1990) 'Rethinking the sociology of journalism: source strategies and the limits of media centrism' in M. Ferguson (ed.) *Public Communication*, London: Sage.

—— (1998) 'Scottish devolution and the media' in J. Seaton (ed.) *Politics and the Media*, Oxford: Blackwell.

—— (1999) 'Changing spaces of political communication: the case of the European Union', *Political Communication*, 16 (3).

Schlesinger, P. and Tumber, H. (1994) *Reporting Crime*, Oxford: Clarendon Press.

Schlesinger, P., Murdock, G. and Elliott, P. (1983) *Televising Terrorism*, London: Comedia.

Schoyen, A. R. (1958) *The Chartist Challenge: A Portrait of George Julian Harney*, London: Heinemann.

Schramm, W. (1963), 'Communication development and the development process' in L. Pye (ed.) *Communications and Political Development*, Princeton, NJ: Princeton University Press.

Schramm, W. and Roberts. D. (1971) (eds) *The Process and Effects of Mass Communication*, rev. edn, Urbana: University of Illinois Press.

Schroder, K. (1989) 'The playful audience: the continuity of the popular cultural tradition in America' in M. Skovmand (ed.) *Media Fictions*, Aarhus: Aarhus University Press.

Schudson, M. (1978) *Discovering the News*, New York: Basic Books.

—— (1982) 'The politics of narrative form: the emergence of news conventions in print and television', *Daedalus*, 111.

—— (1987) 'The new validation of popular culture: sense and sentimentality in Academia', *Critical Studies in Mass Communication*, 4 (1).

—— (1989) 'The sociology of news production', *Media, Culture and Society*, 11 (3).

—— (1991a) 'The sociology of news production revisited' in J. Curran and M. Gurevitch (eds) *Mass Media and Society*, London: Edward Arnold.

—— (1991b) 'Historical approaches to communication studies' in K.B. Jensen and N. Jankowski (eds) *A Handbook of Qualitative Methods for Mass Communication Research*, London: Routledge.

—— (1993) 'Was there ever a public sphere? If so, when? Reflections on the American case' in C. Calhoun (ed.) *Habermas and the Public Sphere*, Cambridge, Mass.: Massachusetts Institute of Technology Press.

—— (1994) 'Question authority: a history of the news interview in American journalism, 1860s–1930s', *Media, Culture and Society*, 16 (4).

—— (1996) 'The sociology of news production revisited' in J. Curran and M. Gurevitch (eds) *Mass Media and Society*, 2nd edn, London: Edward Arnold.

Schulz, W. (2000) 'Television audiences' in J. Wieten, G. Murdock and P. Dahlgren (eds) *Television Across Europe*, London: Sage.

Sears, D. and Freedman, J. (1971) 'Selective exposure to information: a critical review' in W. Schramm and D. Roberts (eds), *The Process and Effects of Mass Communication*, rev. edn, Urbana: University of Illiniois Press.

Segal, L. (1997) 'Generations of feminism', *Radical Philosophy*, 83.

Seiter, E., Borchers, H., Kreutzner, G. and Warth, E.M. (1989) (eds) *Remote Control*, London: Routledge.

Select Committee of the House of Commons on Newspaper Stamps Report (1851) *Parliamentary Papers*, xvii, London: Hansard.

Sendall, B. (1982) *Independent Television in Britain: Origin and Foundation, 1946–62*, vol. 1, London: Macmillan.

—— (1983) *Independent Television in Britain: Expansion and Change, 1958–68*, vol. 2, London: Macmillan.

Sepstrup, P. (1990) *Transnationalization of Television in Western Europe*, London: Libbey.

—— (1993) 'Scandinavian public service broadcasting: the case of Denmark' in R. Avery (ed.) *Public Service Broadcasting in a Multichannel Environment*, White Plains, NY: Longman.

Serra, S. (1996) 'Multinationals of solidarity: international civil society and the killing of street children in Brazil' in S. Braman and A. Sreberny-Mohammadi (eds)

Globalization, Communication and Transational Civil Society, Cresskill, NJ: Hampton Press.

—— (2000) 'The killing of Brazilian street children and the rise of the international public sphere' in J. Curran (ed.) *Media Organisations in Society*, London: Edward Arnold.

Seymour-Ure, C. (1975) 'The press and the party system between the wars' in G. Peele and C. Cook (eds) *The Politics of Reappraisal, 1918–1939*, London: Macmillan.

—— (1977) 'National daily papers and the party system' in *Studies on the Press*, Royal Commission on the Press Working Paper no. 3, London: HMSO.

—— (1989) 'Prime ministers' reactions to television: Britain, Australia and Canada', *Media, Culture and Society*, 11 (3).

—— (1996) *The British Press and Broadcasting Since 1945*, 2nd edn, Oxford: Blackwell.

—— (2000) 'Northcliffe's legacy' in P. Catterall, C. Seymour-Ure and A. Smith (eds) *Northcliffe's Legacy*, Basingstoke: Macmillan.

Sharpe, S. (1976) *Just Like a Girl*, Harmondsworth: Penguin.

Shattuc, J. (1997) *The Talking Cure*, New York: Routledge.

Shaw, B. (1979) cited in *Oxford Dictionary of Quotations*, Oxford: Oxford University Press.

Shawcross, W. (1993) *Murdoch*, London: Pan.

Shevelow, K. (1989) *Women and Print Culture*, London: Routledge.

Shils, Edward (1961) 'Mass society and its culture' in N. Jacobs (ed.), *Culture for the Millions?*, Princeton, NJ: Van Nostrand.

Shoemaker, R. (1998) *Gender in English Society, 1650–1850*, London: Longman.

Siebert, F. (1952) *Freedom of the Press in England, 1476–1776*, Urbana: University of Illinois Press.

Siebert, F., Peterson, T. and Schramm, W. (1956) *Four Theories of the Press*, Urbana: University of Illinois Press.

Sigal, L. (1987) 'Sources make the news' in R. Manoff and M. Schudson (eds) *Reading the News*, New York: Pantheon.

Silj, A. (1988) *East of Dallas*, London: British Film Institute.

Silverstone, Roger (1994) *Television and Everyday Life*, London: Routledge.

Silvey, R. (1974) *Who's Listening?*, London: Allen & Unwin.

Simon, R. (1982) *Gramsci's Political Thought*, London: Lawrence & Wishart.

Simonson, P. (1996) 'Dreams of democratic togetherness: communication hope from Cooley to Katz', *Critical Studies in Mass Communication*, 13 (December).

Sinclair, J., Jacka, E. and Cunningham, S. (1996) (eds) *New Patterns in Global Television: Peripheral Vision*, Oxford: Oxford University Press.

Sinha, N. (1996) 'Liberalisation and the future of public service broadcasting in India', *Javnost*, 3 (2).

Skeggs, B. (1992) 'Paul Willis, *Learning to Labour*' in M. Barker and A. Beezer (eds) *Reading into Cultural Studies*, London: Routledge.

—— (1997) *Formations of Class and Gender*, London: Sage.

Sklair, L. (2000) 'Globalization' in S. Taylor (ed.) *Sociology*, Basingstoke: Palgrave.

Skogerbo, E. (1990) 'The concept of the public sphere in an historical perspective: an anachronism or a relevant political concept', *Nordicom Review*, 2.

—— (1997) 'The press subsidy system in Norway', *European Journal of Communication*, 12 (1).

Smith, A. (1977) *Subsidies and the Press in Europe*, London: Political and Economic Planning (PEP).

—— (1978a) 'The long road to objectivity and back again: the kinds of truth we get in journalism' in G. Boyce, J. Curran and P. Wingate (eds) *Newspaper History*, London: Constable.

—— (1978b) *The Newspaper: An International History*, London: Thames & Hudson.

Smith, A. and Patterson, R. (1998) *Television: An International History*, 2nd edn, Oxford: Oxford University Press.

Smith, A.C.H. (1975) *Paper Voices*, London: Chatto & Windus.

Snape, R. (1995) *Leisure and the Rise of the Public Library*, London: Library Association.

Solum, O., 1994: 'Film production in Norway and the municipal cinema system', unpublished paper, Department of Media and Communications, University of Oslo.

Somerville, C.J. (1996) *The News Revolution in England*, New York: Oxford University Press.

Southern, R.W. (1959) *The Making of the Middle Ages*, London: Grey Arrow.

—— (1970) *Western Society and the Church in the Middle Ages*, London: Penguin.

Sparks, C. (1998) *Communism, Capitalism and the Mass Media*, London: Sage.

—— (2000) 'Media theory after the fall of European communism: why the old models from East and West won't do any more' in J. Curran and M.-J. Park (eds) *De-Westernizing Media Studies*, London: Routledge.

Spender, J.A. (1927) *Life, Journalism and Politics*, 2 vols, London: Cassell.

Spraos, J. (1962) *The Decline of the Cinema*, London: Allen & Unwin.

Sreberny, A. (1998) 'Feminist internationalism: imagining and building global civil society' in D. Thussu (ed.) *Electronic Empires*, London: Edward Arnold.

—— (2000) 'Television, gender, and democratization in the Middle East' in J. Curran and M.-J. Park (eds) *De-Westernizing Media Studies*, London: Routledge.

Sreberny-Mohammadi, A. (1996) 'Globalization, communication and transnational civil society: introduction' in S. Braman and A. Sreberny-Mohammadi (eds) *Globalization, Communication and Transational Civil Society*, Cresskill, NJ: Hampton Press.

Sreberny-Mohammadi, A. and Mohammadi, A. (1994) *Small Media, Big Revolution*, Minneapolis: University of Minnesota Press.

Sreberny-Mohammadi, A., Winseck, D., McKenna, J. and Boyd-Barret, O. (eds) (1997) *Media in Global Context*, London: Edward Arnold.

Stepp, C. (1990) 'Access in a post-social responsibility age' in J. Lichtenberg (ed.) *Democracy and the Mass Media*, Cambridge: Cambridge University Press.

Stevens, J.D. and Garcia, H.D. (1980) *Communication History*, Beverly Hills, Cal.: Sage.

Stone, L. (1969) 'Literacy and education in England 1640–1900', *Past and Present*, 42.

—— (1972) *The Causes of the English Revolution, 1529–1642*, London: Routledge & Kegan Paul.

—— (1990) *The Road to Divorce*, Oxford: Oxford University Press.

Strange, S. (1996) *The Retreat of the State*, Cambridge: Cambridge University Press.

Stratton, J. (1996) 'Cyberspace and the globalization of culture' in D. Porter (ed.) *Internet Culture*, New York: Routledge.

Street, S. (1997) *British National Cinema*, London: Routledge.

Strid, I. and Weibull, L. (1988) *Mediesveridge*, Göteborg: Göteborg University Press.

Stuart, C. (1975) (ed.) *The Reith Diaries*, London: Collins.

Sussman, G. and Lent, J. (1998) *Global Productions*, Cresskill, NJ: Hampton.

Sutherland, J. (1986) *The Restoration Newspaper and its Development*, Cambridge: Cambridge University Press.

Swann, P. (1987) *The Hollywood Feature Film in Postwar Britain*, London: Croom Helm.

Swanson, D. (1996) 'Audience research: antinomies, intersections and the prospect of comprehensive theory' in J. Hay, L. Grossberg and E. Wartella (eds) *The Audience and Its Landscape*, Boulder, Col.: Westview.

Syvertsen, T. (1992) 'Serving the public: public television in Norway in a new media Age', *Media, Culture and Society*, 14 (2).

—— (1994) *Public Television in Transition*, Oslo: Levende Bilder.

—— (1996) *Den Store TV-Krigen, Norsk Allmennfjernsyn 1988–96*, Bergen-Sandviken: Fagboklaget.

Tan, A. (1985) *Mass Communication Theories and Society*, 2nd edn, New York: Wiley.

Taylor, A.J.P. (1972) *Beaverbrook*, London, Hamish Hamilton,

Taylor, P. (1981) *The Projection of Britain*, Cambridge: Cambridge University Press.

—— (1997) *Global Communications, International Affairs and the Media Since 1945*, London: Routledge.

Tebbit, N. (1989) *Upwardly Mobile*, London: Futura.

Thane, P. (1991) 'Towards equal opportunities? Women in Britain since 1945' in T. Gourvash and A. O'Day (eds) *Britain Since 1945*, London: Macmillan.

Thatcher, M. (1995) *The Downing Street Years*, London: HarperCollins.

Tholfsen, T.R. (1976) *Working-Class Radicalism in Mid-Victorian England*, London, Croom Helm.

Thomas, J.A. (1958) *The House of Commons 1906–11*, Cardiff: University of Wales.

Thomas, K. (1973) *Religion and the Decline of Magic*, Harmondsworth: Penguin.

Thompson, D. (1984) *The Chartists*, London: Temple Smith.

Thompson, E. (1963) *The Making of the English Working Class*, London: Gollancz.

Thompson, J. (1995) *The Media and Modernity*, Cambridge: Polity.

Thomson. J. (1965) *The Later Lollards, 1414–1520*, Oxford: Oxford University Press.

Thornton, S. and Gelder, K. (1996) (eds) *The Subcultures Reader*, London: Routledge.

Thumim, J. (1992) *Celuloid Sisters*, New York: St Martin's Press.

Thussu, D. (1998) (ed.) *Electronic Empires*, London: Edward Arnold.

—— (2000) *International Communication*, London: Edward Arnold.

Tiffen, R. (1989) *News and Power*, Sydney: Allen & Unwin.

Todd, J. (1989) *The Sign of Angelica: Women, Writing and Fiction, 1660–1800*, London: Verso.

Tomlinson, J. (1991) *Cultural Imperialism*, London: Pinter.

—— (1999) *Globalization and Culture*, Cambridge: Polity.

Tracey, M. (1998) *The Decline and Fall of Public Service Broadcasting*, Oxford: Oxford University Press.

Tracey, M. and Morrison, D. (1979) *Whitehouse*, London: Macmillan.

Trevor Roper, H. (1983) 'The invention of tradition: the Highland tradition of Scotland' in E. Hobsbawm and T. Ranger (eds.) *The Invention of Tradition*, Cambridge: Cambridge University Press.

Troyna, B. (1981) *Public Awareness and the Media: A Study of Reporting on Race*, London: Commission for Racial Equality.

Tuchman, G. (1972) 'Objectivity as strategic ritual: an examination of newsmen's notions of objectivity', *American Journal of Sociology*, 77.

—— (1978a) *Making News*, New York: Free Press.

—— (1978b) 'Introduction: the symbolic annihilation of women by the mass media' in G. Tuchman, A. Kaplan and J. Benet (eds) *Hearth and Home*, New York: Oxford University Press.

Tulloch, J. (1993) 'Policing the public sphere: the British machinery of news management', *Media, Culture and Society*, 15 (3).

Tunstall, J. (1971) *Journalists at Work*, London: Constable.

—— (1993) *Television Producers*, London: Routledge.

Tunstall, J. and Machin, D. (1999) *The Anglo-American Connection*, Oxford: Oxford University Press.

Tunstall, J. and Palmer, M. (1991) *Media Moguls*, London: Routledge.

Turkle, S. (1995) *Life on the Screen*, London: Weidenfeld & Nicolson.

Turow, J. (1991) 'A mass communication perspective on entertainment industries' in J. Curran and M. Gurevitch (eds) *Mass Media and Society*, London: Edward Arnold.

Ullmann, W.W. (1969) *The Carolingian Renaissance and the Idea of Kingship*, London: Methuen.

—— (1970) *The Growth of Papal Government in the Middle Ages*, 4th edn, London: Methuen.

—— (1975) *Medieval Political Thought*, Harmondsworth: Penguin.

—— (1977) *A Short History of the Papacy in the Middle Ages*, 2nd edn, London: Methuen.

—— (1978) *Principles of Government and Politics in the Middle Ages*, 4th edn, London: Methuen.

Ullswater (1936), *Report of the Broadcasting Committee*, London: HMSO.

Van Ginnekin, J. (1998) *Understanding Global News*, London: Sage.

Vedel, T. and Bourdon, J. (1993) 'French public broadcasting: from monopoly to marginalization' in R. Avery (ed.) *Public Service Broadcasting in a Multichannel Environment*, White Plains, NY: Longman.

Veljanovski, C. (1989) 'Competition in broadcasting' in C. Veljanovski (ed.) *Freedom in Broadcasting*, London: Institute of Economic Affairs.

Vickery, A. (1993) 'Women and the world of goods: a Lancashire consumer and her possessions, 1751–81' in J. Brewer and R. Porter (eds) *Consumption and the World of Goods*, London: Routledge.

Vidmar, N. and Rokeach, M. (1974) 'Archie Bunker's bigotry: a study in selective perception and exposure', *Journal of Communication*, 24 (2).

Vincent, J. (1972) *The Formation of the British Liberal Party 1857–68*, Harmondsworth: Penguin.

Wagg, S. (1992) 'You've never had it so silly: the politics of British satirical comedy from *Beyond the Fringe* to *Spitting Image*' in D. Strinati and S. Wagg (eds) *Come on Down?*, London: Routledge.

Waisbord, S. (2000a) *Watchdog Journalism in South America*, New York: Columbia University Press.
—— (2000b) 'Media in South America: between the rock of the state and the hard place of the market' in J. Curran and M.-J. Park (eds) *De-Westernizing Media Studies*, London: Routledge.
Waller, J. and Vaughan-Rees, M. (1987) *Women in Wartime*, London: Macdonald Optima.
Waller, R. (1988) *Moulding Political Opinion*, Beckenham: Croom Helm.
Walvin, J. (1978) *Leisure and Society 1830–1950*, London: Longman.
Ward, K. (1989) *Mass Communications and the Modern World*, London: Macmillan Education.
Waters, M. (1995) *Globalization*, London: Routledge.
Watney, S. (1987) *Policing Desire*, London: Comedia.
Weaver, D. and Wilhoit, G. (1991) *The American Journalist*, 2nd edn, Bloomington: University of Indiana Press.
Webb, M. (1995) *The Political Economy of Policy Co-ordination*, Ithaca, NY: Cornell University Press.
Webb, R.K. (1950) 'Working class readers in Victorian England', *English Historical Review*, lxv.
—— (1955) *The British Working Class Reader, 1790–1848*, London: Allen & Unwin.
Weeks, J. (1977) *Coming Out*, London: Quartet.
—— (1991) *Against Nature*, London: Rivers Oram Press.
Weibull, L. (1994) 'Media diversity and choice' in K. Gustafsson (ed.) *Media Structure and the State*, Gothenburg: University of Gothenburg Press.
Weiss, L. (1998) *The Myth of the Powerless State*, Cambridge: Polity.
Werkmeister, L. (1963) *The London Daily Press, 1772–1792*, Lincoln: University of Nebraska Press.
Westmacott, C.M. (1836) 'The stamp duties: serious considerations on the proposed alteration of the stamp duty on newspapers', London: *The Age* Office.
Weymouth, T. and Lamizet, B. 1996 (eds) *Markets and Myths*, Harlow: Longman.
Whale, J. (1977) *The Politics of the Media*, London: Fontana.
Whannel, G. (1979) 'Football, crowd behaviour and the press', *Media, Culture and Society*, 1 (4).
White, C. (1970) *Women's Magazines, 1693–1968*, London: Michael Joseph.
Whitelaw, W. (1989) *The Whitelaw Memoirs*, London: Aurum.
Wickwar, W. (1928) *The Struggle for the Freedom of the Press 1819–32*, London: Allen & Unwin.
Wiener, J. (1969a) *A Descriptive Findings List of Unstamped Periodicals:1830–36*, London: Bibliographical Society.
—— (1969b) *The War of the Unstamped: The Movement to Repeal the British Newspaper Tax 1830–36*, Ithaca, NY: Cornell University Press.
—— (1996) 'The Americanization of the British press, 1830–1914' in M. Harris and T. O'Malley (eds) *Studies in Newspapers and Periodical History: 1994 Annual*, Westport, Conn.: Greenwood.
Wieten, J., Murdock, G. and Dahlgren, P. (2000) (eds) *Television Across Europe*, London: Sage.
Wilensky, H.L. (1964) 'Mass society and mass culture', *American Sociological Review* xxix.

Wiles, R.M. (1965) *Freshest Advices: Early Provincial Newspapers in England*, Columbus: Ohio State University Press.

Wilhoit, G.C. and Bock H. de (1976), '*All in the Family* in Holland', *Journal of Communication*, 26 (3).

Wilks, M.J. (1963) *The Problem of Sovereignty in the Later Middle Ages*, London: Cambridge University Press.

Williams, F. (1957) *Dangerous Estate: The Anatomy of Newspapers*, London: Longmans, Green.

Williams, K. (1993) 'The light at the end of the tunnel: the mass media, public opinion and the Vietnam War' in J. Eldridge (ed.) *Getting the Message*, London: Routledge.

—— (1998) *Get Me a Murder a Day!*, London: Arnold.

Williams, R. (1965) *The Long Revolution*, Harmondsworth: Penguin.

—— (1966) *Communications*, rev. edn, London: Chatto & Windus.

—— (1970) 'Radical and/or respectable' in R. Boston (ed.) *The Press We Deserve*, London: Routlege & Kegan Paul.

—— (1973) *The Country and the City*, London: Chatto & Windus.

—— (1974) *Television: Technology and Cultural Form*, London: Collins.

—— (1979) *Politics and Letters*, London: Verso.

—— (1984) 'Socialists and coalitionists' in J. Curran (ed.) *The Future of the Left*, Cambridge: Polity.

Willis, P. (1977) *Learning to Labour*, London: Saxon House.

—— (1990) *Common Culture*, Milton Keynes: Open University Press.

Wilson, C. and Gutierrez, F. (1985) *Minorities and the Media*, Beverly Hills, Cal.: Sage.

Wilson, T. (1970) (ed.) *The Political Diaries of C.P. Scott 1911–28*, London: Collins.

Wiltenburg, J. (1992) *Disorderly Women and Female Power in the Street Literature of Early Modern England and Germany*, Charlottesville: University of Virginia Press.

Windlesham, L. and Rampton, R. (1989) *The Windlesham/Rampton Report on Death on the Rock*, London: Faber & Faber.

Winship, J. (1987) *Inside Women's Magazines*, London: Pandora.

Winston, B. (1998) *Media Technology and Society*, London: Routledge.

Women's Studies Group (Birmingham Centre for Contemporary Cultural Studies) (1978) *Women Take Issue*, London: Hutchinson.

Woodward, L. (1962) *The Age of Reform 1815–70*, rev. edn, Oxford: Oxford University Press.

Woolf, V. (1965) *Jacob's Room*, Harmondsworth: Penguin.

Wrench, J.E. (1955) *Geoffrey Dawson and Our Times*, London: Hutchinson.

Wright, C. (1959) *Mass Communication*, 1st edn, New York: Random House.

—— (1975) *Mass Communication*, 2nd edn, New York: Random House.

Wyndham Goldie, G. (1977) *Facing the Nation*, London: Bodley Head.

Young, J. (1971) *The Drugtakers*, London: Paladin.

—— (1974) 'Mass media: drugs and deviance' in P. Rock and M. McIntosh (eds) *Deviance and Social Control*, London: Tavistock.

Zillmann, D. and Bryant, J. (1986) 'Exploring the entertainment experience' in J. Bryant and D. Zillman (eds) *Perspectives on Media Effects*, Hillsdale, NJ: Lawrence Erlbaum.

Zoonen, L. van (1991) 'Feminist perspectives on the media' in J. Curran and M. Gurevitch (eds) *Mass Media and Society*, London: Edward Arnold.
—— (1994) *Feminist Media Studies*, London: Sage.

Index